Dedicated to all the soldiers who gave their lives for our *freedom* during the course of our history in Laos.

Muab rau txhua tus tub rog uas tau muab lawv txoj sia mus tiv thaiv txoj kev muaj vaj huam sib luag nyob rau ntawm peb keeb kwm lub sib hawm nyob tebchaws Lostsuas.

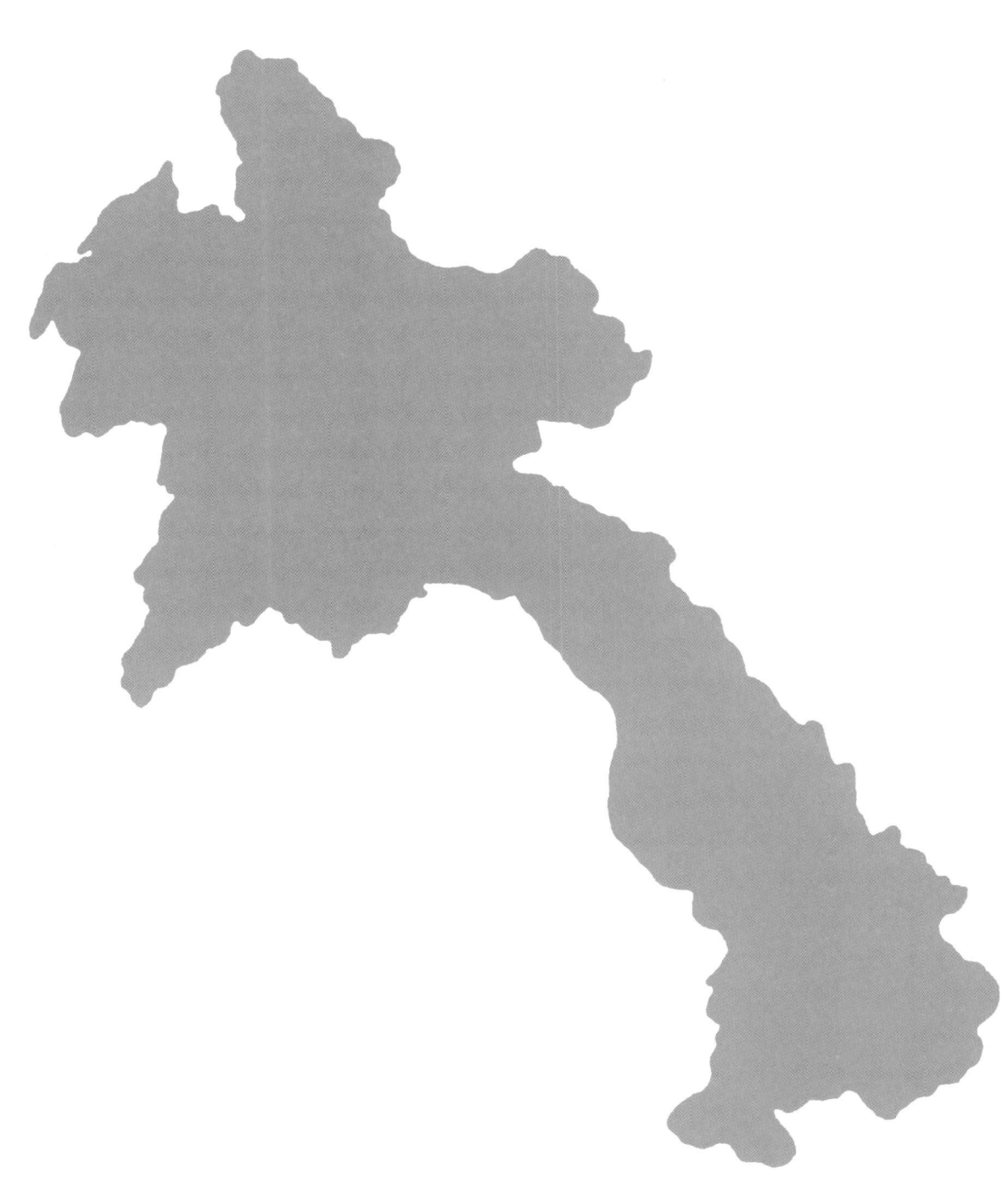

"If I die, don't die with me. Always keep your heads high; always follow your dreams; keep loving the Hmong people. If you keep my dream for the Hmong alive, I will always be with you."

* * *
GENERAL VANG PAO
"FATHER" — A TRIBUTE SONG
RETRIEVED FROM CHA VANG
OPAL STUDIO
JUNE 2011

ຂງຂວນງກນນຍພຶວງປວ

PHAGNA NORAPAMOK
GENERAL VANG PAO

© Copyright 2013.

LIA VANG
NOAH VANG
XANG VANG

All rights reserved.

Second Edition.

2nd Ed. 2011/2012/2013.

Published with the support of the representatives of THE GVP PROJECT 2012 and from the individuals who contributed to the First Edition.

Absolutely no part of this book may be stored or transmitted in any form or by any means, electronic or mechanical, including photocopy, recording, or any storage or retrieval system, without written permission from the author.

For more information about this book, please send an email request to sendhmong@gmail.com.

Proceeds from this manuscript benefit projects and/or initiatives that are related to educating and preserving the late General Vang Pao's life and legacy and contribute to the knowledge and advancement of the Hmong community and society.

Distributed in the United States of America.

Second Edition manufactured in Thailand.

Cataloging-in-Publication Data at the Library of Congress

ISBN: 978-0-615-54661-2

2013 | 1929-12-08 | 1959-12-23 | 1980-11-03

01   02   04   05   06   07   08   09   10

The first exhibition of the majority of the photos in this book was held during General Vang Pao's memorial services in Fresno, California, in February 2011.

PHAGNA NORAPAMOK
GENERAL VANG PAO
An Illustration of His Remarkable Life

Compiled, designed & researched by
NOAH VANG

Chief contributions from
LIA VANG
XANG VANG

Foreword by
B. HUGH TOVAR

With additional supports from
COLONEL GEU VANG
COLONEL TOUFU VANG
KONG XIONG
RICHARD N. VANG
SONG MOUA
THE GENERAL VANG PAO FAMILY

Edited by
DR. JANE HAMILTON-MERRITT
GAYLE L. MORRISON
LEEANN MACHOSKY POMRENKE
LEE PAO XIONG
MARLIN H. HEISE
MAYKAO LYFOUNG VANG
ROGER WARNER
TUA VANG
XIA YANG VANG

Translation done by
CHENG LENG VANG
HOUA VANG
XAO CHOR VANG

MINNESOTA

Foreword
13

Preface
15

Acknowledgements
17

Our Sponsors
19

Table of Contents

An Unsung Hero
21

Military Regions of the Royal Lao Army
24

Peb Txiv Hmoob Vaj Pov Tej Lus Nyiaj Lus Kub
(General Vang Pao's Words of Wisdoms)
29

Brief Introduction
35

Medals
41

Brief Chronology
44

An Illustration of His Remarkable Life
72

In the United States of America
278

A Lifetime Conviction
414

left to right
1. HOWARD BUELL COLLECTION
2. THE GVP FAMILY COLLECTION
3. CHAI VANG COLLECTION
4. THE GVP FAMILY COLLECTION
5. MONG VANG COLLECTION
6. NOAH VANG COLLECTION
7. YE VUE COLLECTION

GENERAL VANG PAO

General Vang Pao was one of the greatest military commanders during the Secret War in Laos, a part of the Vietnam conflict, from 1960 to 1975. He began his military career as an officer in the French army in the early 1940s. Later, as a major general he commanded the Royal Lao Army's Military Region II, which he fought to protect in order to preserve democracy, freedom, and liberty for his country. Furthermore, he assisted the United States in her quest to stop the spread of communism in Southeast Asia during this military conflict. As a leader, he dedicated his lifelong career to seek justice and promote the importance of education, cultural preservation, family unity, and public service to his people worldwide. Today he is revered and will be remembered by many as the *Father of the Hmong People*.

NAI PHOO VAJ POV

Nai Phoo Vaj Pov yog ib tug thawj tub rog tshaj lij heev nyob rau kob tsov rog Secret War nyob hauv lub tebchaws Lostsuas thaum xyoo 1960 txog 1975, uas yog ib feem ntawm kob tsov rog Nyab Laj. Nws tau pib ua hauj lwm tub rog nrog rau tsoom fwv Fabkis thaum 1940 tawm ntawd. Tom qab no uas nws tau txais lub meej mom ua tus tuam thuaj tub rog peb lub hnub qub dawb lawm, nws kuj los tuav tsoom tub rog nyob rau sab ciam teb 2 uas nws tau los tiv thaiv lub tebchaws Lostsuas kom muaj kev ywj pheej, vaj huam sib luag thiab vam meej rau nws lub tebchaws. Nws kuj tau pab lub tebchaws Ameliskas tiv thaib tawm tsav tog Kooj Sam nyob rau hauv Asia sab hnub tuaj qab teb. Los ua ib tug thawj coj, nws tau muab nws lub neej los tho txoj hau kev kom muaj kev ncaj ncees, txhawb nqa kev kawm ntaub kawm ntawv, Hmoob tej kab lis kev cai, kev thooj siab koom ntsws, thiab kev nrhiav noj nrhiav haus rau ntawm nws tsev neeg nyob qhov txhia qhov chaw. Niaj hnub no coob leej ntau tus hawm txog nws yam li ib leej *Txiv ntawm haiv neeg Hmoob.*

(TRANSLATION - LUS TXHAIS)

Foreword

My Central Intelligence Agency's association with General Vang Pao began in early 1961, before the Geneva Agreement on neutralization of Laos in 1962. North Vietnamese intrusions were already causing trouble in the northeastern region of Laos, and had been opposed by Hmong irregular forces led by Vang Pao. The Prime Minister of the Royal Lao Government, Souvanna Phouma, then asked President John Kennedy to provide covert military assistance to those irregular forces. President Kennedy gave his consent, and from a small beginning, the program developed into a major effort of training, equipping and providing air support over the next 10 years. As commander of the Hmong and Lao forces in Military Region 2, General Vang Pao worked closely with James W. Lair and the Agency officers who succeeded him, in holding back the North Vietnamese invaders. That continued unbroken until January 1973, when the cease-fire agreement brought a halt to the war. Laos was thereafter governed by a coalition which included the Communist Pathet Lao, and it was determined that henceforth military assistance would go only to the regular forces of the Royal Lao Government, the *Forces Armee Royale* (FAR). Our covert military support to General Vang Pao's irregulars was halted, and thereafter only limited economic assistance was given to the Hmong.

The cease-fire agreement of 1973 was predicated upon an act of faith on the part of the Royal Lao Government and the US Government. They believed that the cease-fire would be honored by all parties to the agreement. However, the communist side violated the agreement openly in 1974 and 1975. That led to the collapse of the coalition, and to the communist seizure of power, which was followed in turn by the massive exodus of refugees from Laos, most of them being Hmong. Thus the Hmong, having already suffered terribly during the war years, were then obliged to flee from their homeland to escape communist brutality. Eventually, most of them resettled in the United States.

General Vang Pao, having demonstrated his leadership during the years of warfare, shared fully in Hmong tribulation throughout that painful period as the Hmong had to cope with the loss of everything they held dear, including their homeland. We, Americans, who worked with him, had always admired his sterling qualities as a commander of troops in ground combat against the North Vietnamese—first as a brilliant tactician in guerrilla warfare, and later as he directed large forces against a full-scale enemy invasion on a broad front. He was admired and respected by all who knew him and worked with him. He loved his soldiers, and his soldiers loved him. He knew where the enemy was, and he needed no advice on how to hit them. Later, having been obliged to move and take up residence in a new land while still struggling to build a life for themselves and their families, the Hmong people continued to acknowledge and follow General Vang Pao as their guide in civilian life.

For Americans like myself, who had the privilege of working with General Vang Pao during years of warfare, we respected him as a great soldier. We knew and loved him as a friend fighting in a common cause. And then when the era of peace was finally upon us, we saw the General continue to march with his people through the final phase of our alliance, which dated back to 1961 when he and Bill Lair shook hands and went to work to organize and build a unique fighting force.

Today, half a century later, we are proud to share with General Vang Pao and the Hmong people the common badge of American citizenship. The magnificent outpouring of love and friendship which our nation witnessed in celebrating his passing in 2011 left no doubt of his place in our shared history. General Vang Pao was a great and good man!

---- B. HUGH TOVAR
FORMER CIA CHIEF OF STATION
IN LAOS, 1970-1973
NOVEMBER 6, 2012

Preface

After my meeting with General Vang Pao, he attended a dinner with the board members of Lao Family Community of Minnesota and Hmong community leaders at Ho Ho Gourmet Restaurant in St. Paul, Minnesota, on November 26, 2010.

NOAH VANG COLLECTION

From the tattered refugee camps in Thailand to the United States, our Hmong history was rarely a subject of importance. If anything was taught about the Hmong experience to us as grade school students, the written text was merely a page long. How we learned about our place in the human chronology and our leaders were from conversations, not in institutions. When our parents shared oral stories of Hmong heroes and heroines, these characters were from the distant past or in folktales. After 200 years in Laos, our Hmong story began to appear in writing. Our history was possible because of a handful of Hmong leaders who were determined to alter the course of our civil, political, and social involvements in the Lao Government. Most importantly, a few of them, with courage and education, championed hope for our people when all the odds were storming against our backs.

In my earlier years here in the United States, I had an aspiration to search for my identity and to learn more about my history and leaders. I wanted to know who my Hmong leaders were and are: those who had paved the way and given us hope when we were in our darkest moments; those who had unselfishly sacrificed their lives to save the future; and those who had eased the burdens off my people's perilous struggles, and calmed the fears of decades of unprecedented migration from war to freedom.

This was how the story of General

Vang Pao emerged. I was not old enough to witness his leadership skills at the height of his career—especially dealing with calamities that faced our people. Or how he came to the decision to fight against enemy forces that threatened our country's freedom during the Vietnam conflict in Southeast Asia. Yet, through personal stories from common people, I have learned that General Vang Pao was the best leader we had in his generation. Most of them wished we had more extraordinary people like General Vang Pao. But great people are uncommon. I do not know if we will see another Hmong in my generation who will rise to the occasion as General Vang Pao did tirelessly for 67 years of his life. To the Hmong, he was a father and an inspiring, charismatic figure. He was truly a living legend of our time. To me, General Vang Pao was our beacon of hope, a special human being, and a role model who never let his people down—even if it meant risking his life for our safety and well-being.

About this book: When I rigorously began compiling this manuscript in the summer of 2010, I wanted to finish it in time for General Vang Pao. With the help of several other people, we planned to complete it by 2011, hoping he would get to see the final work. We were too late. He passed away in January 2011 while most of his biographical information and photographs were being organized. We were saddened that he did not see the final version of this book that is solely dedicated to him. What he saw was only a rough work-in-progress copy I showed to him at his son Sisouk Vang's home in Blaine, Minnesota on November 26, 2010. When he first saw the unfinished sample, he was surprised and excited. He took an hour to slowly turn each page until he flipped to the back cover of the book. Before he left for an event dinner hosted by members of the Lao Family Community Center of Minnesota, he gave me his blessing to complete this manuscript.

An additional note about this brief chronology is that not all of General Vang Pao's personal history is chronicled. This is a minimal composition of his rich biography told in photographs, quotes, and texts. The quotes were written from the perspective of individuals who had worked with and written about General Vang Pao. Some are from my direct conversations with him. The purpose is to give readers a view of what General Vang Pao did that impacted their lives and the significant role he played in constructing and shaping the Hmong identity and history in Southeast Asia. Also, in this 2nd Edition, at the request of some readers, we have translated certain passages. The translation is focused on the meaning and not word for word. Some are re-edited for clarity.

Unlike our unwritten past, I hope that this work will mark the beginning for our educated generation to start writing about our family histories, role models, leaders, heroes, and best of all, our personal experiences as a people on earth.

— NOAH VANG

Acknowledgements

With all of your support, an idea has been realized. We would like to kindly thank you for helping us complete this book.

When several of us first discussed the groundwork to compiling this manuscript in 2006, it seemed like an impossible journey. There were hurdles. We had only three people who were willing to commit. We did not know where to begin or which direction to take. We had more questions than answers. We lacked a budget. What we had were only hearts and passions. We were convinced that this work was important to preserving General Vang Pao's contribution to our society. At the same time we kept postponing it because it was difficult to collect his history. However, we were determined not to fail. We chanced. We sacrificed personal finances to fund this initial research phase. In 2009, word surfaced that we were composing an illustrated book for him. With gradual family encouragement and community support, we persevered. Today, we are grateful to have many people who devoted their time and resources to making this book possible.

First and foremost, we thank General Vang Pao for giving us the rare opportunity to compose this manuscript on his behalf. In 2008, during our conversations with him in St. Paul, Minnesota, his personal request was for us to disseminate some of his messages, his words of wisdom, and his visions to the public. We have partially done so. Some of the quotes and excerpts contain General Vang Pao's visions that he wanted to share with the people wherever he traveled.

These are some of his convictions that he attempted to achieve during this time. His approval (or written consent) also inspired us to fulfill his wish. Plus, we are blessed to have the best family members in the world. They motivated and pushed us forward to get this done because it was equally meaningful to them as well.

To help us cover the expense for the First Edition of this project, we were fortunate to have 24 business owners and individuals who donated to our cause. Their selfless sponsorships have made a difference in our mission. After the first printing was published, we organized and established THE GVP PROJECT 2012 Committee, which consisted of representatives throughout the United States to assist with the distribution of the book. Without their assiduous effort and willingness, we would not be where we are at this point. Thus, we are appreciative of their devotion.

Moreover, we are indebted to our readers for their generous contributions to our collectible First Edition. Your support served as evidence that we can achieve great things when we walk a common path to advance and better our community. This has given us the confidence to execute our stated objectives. Furthermore, we would like to thank many individuals and organizations that have contributed to this work---especially by providing documents, images, quotes, proofreading, and texts. They are the reason this chapter of the late General Vang Pao's rich story is alive for our memory. Lastly, we apologize if we have omitted anyone in this acknowledgement.

Individuals and organizations that contributed and participated in the First & Second Edition of this book are:

Air America Association
Air Commando Association
Captain Xai Nou Vang
Center for Hmong Studies
Cha Vang
Chai Vang
Chaleunsouk Vang
Chong Jones
Colonel Geu Vang
Colonel James W. Lair
Colonel Ly Teng
Colonel Toufu Vang
Dr. Jane Hamilton-Merritt
Dr. Kou Vang & Family
Eng Yang
Gayle L. Morrison
Hmong Archives
Hmong Cultural Center
Howard Buell
John Willheim
Joua Sue Vang & Mai Nhia Xiong
Kong M. Xiong
Kou Yang
Lang Vang
Lee Pao Xiong
LeeAnn Machosky Pomrenke
Leng Wong Vang
Long Yang
Lt. Colonel Nenglo Yang
Maiker Vang
Major Cher Cha Vang
Major Neng Sho Xiong
Major Ying Vang
Marlin Heise
Mong Vang
Nao Pao Vang & Kaying Lor
Nhia Lue Lee
Nhia Tyler Lee
Page Pajzeb Zuag Lee
Phong Lee
Ravens
Richard N. Vang
Roger Warner
SGU-California Chapter
SGU-Minnesota Chapter
Shia Yang
Shua Sheng Thao
Shua Xiong & Family
Sieng Lee
Sisouk Vang
Song Moua
Song Vang
Sue Vang
Tong Pao Yang & Family
Tua Vang
Txiabneeb Vaj
University of Texas at Dallas
Wa Chong Vang
Xang Vang
Xao Chor Vang
Yang Long
Yenviset Xiong
Yeu Tong Hlao Vu
Zong Lu Vang

OUR SPONSORS

Blia Tou Xiong & Yer V. Xiong
IN HONOR OF CHONG XOU XIONG & MEE VANG
ERIE, COLORADO

Francois C. Vang & Family
WESTMINSTER, CALIFORNIA

Kao Thao
IN HONOR OF MY PARENTS PA XAO THAO &
CHIA VANG
FRESNO, CALIFORNIA

Kong N. Xiong & Family
WESTMINSTER, CALIFORNIA

Long Yang & Family
IN HONOR OF MY PARENTS NYAB LUANG
'CHAO MOUANG' YOUA TONG YANG
FRESNO, CALIFORNIA

Ntsuab Xyooj Vaaj & Dawb Haam
IN HONOR OF TXOOV PAO VAAJ, TW MOUA &
YOUA HAWJ
WESTMINSTER, CALIFORNIA

Ntsuab Xwm Vaj & Maiv Nyiaj Xyooj
OAKDALE, MINNESOTA

Sisouk Vang & Family
BLAINE, MINNESOTA

Sons & Daughters of Lt. Colonel Vang Neng
IN HONOR OF LT. COLONEL VANG NENG
TROY, NORTH CAROLINA

Tou Alan Vang & Family
IN MEMORY OF NAI KONG YOUA TENG VANG
ST. PAUL, MINNESOTA

Wa Chong Vang & Gaohlee Lee
SACRAMENTO, CALIFORNIA

Xaiv Ntaj Vaaj & Ku Thoj Vaaj
IN HONOR OF TXOOJ CHAWV VAAJ & NPAUB
THOJ VANG
MAPLEWOOD, MINNESOTA

Xang Vang & Family
MAPLEWOOD, MINNESOTA

Youa Nou Vang & Mai Thao Vang
DRAPER, UTAH

Lia Vang & Xia Yang Vang
DEDICATED TO MY PARENTS PA VU VANG &
SHOUA THAO
CEDAR HILL, TEXAS

Xiong Yang & Family
MADERA, CALIFORNIA

ASIAN ADULT DAY CARE
Davis Xiong & PaFoua Vang Xiong
1380 ENERGY LANE, STE 113
ST. PAUL, MINNESOTA
651-967-8692

DESTINY CAFE
Chong Soua Vang & Family
995 UNIVERSITY AVENUE WEST
ST. PAUL, MINNESOTA
651-649-0394

GOLDEN HARVEST FOODS, INC.
KHW MOOB
Mr. & Mrs. Shua Xiong
900 EAST MARYLAND AVENUE
ST. PAUL, MINNESOTA 55106
651-772-3200

HERITAGE HOME HEALTH CARE, INC.
Leng & Gloria Wong
635 IVY AVENUE EAST
ST. PAUL, MINNESOTA 55130
651-771-2420

LONG CHENG, INC.
Hmong Livestock & Meat Market
134 HARDMAN AVENUE NORTH
SOUTH ST. PAUL, MINNESOTA 55075
651-450-6868

MIDWEST INTERNATIONAL TRAVEL
Richard N. Vang & Family
302 UNIVERSITY AVENUE WEST
ST. PAUL, MINNESOTA
651-797-3012

WESTERN MOTORS
Kevin Vue & Family
1943 West Broadway Avenue
Minneapolis, MN 554411
612-529-8833

SUSHI TANGO
Cher Pao Thao & Family
8362 TAMARACK VILLAGE, STE #124
WOODBURY, MINNESOTA 55125
WWW.SUSHITANGO.COM
651-578-0064

VANG BAIL BONDS, INC.
Chue Charlles Vang & Family
4903 East King's Canyon Road, Ste. 104
Fresno, California 93272
559-497-8889

THE GVP PROJECT 2012 COMMITTEE

BLIA YANG VANG, CALIFORNIA
BOUA FU HER, MISSOURI
BOUA YA MOUA, ARKANSAS
CAPTAIN XAI NOU VANG, MINNESOTA
CHA VANG, MINNESOTA
CHALEUNSOUK VANG, MINNESOTA
CEEBLEEJ YANG, MINNESOTA
CHER CHENG VANG, CALIFORNIA
CHER PAO VANG, CALIFORNIA
CHONG NENG XIONG, MINNESOTA
CHONG CHENG YANG, TEXAS
CHONG SENG CHA, OKLAHOMA
CHUE CHARLES VANG, CALIFORNIA
DR. NAO CHER VANG, MINNESOTA
DR. STEPHEN VANG, OKLAHOMA
FUYEI XAYKAOTHAO, MINNESOTA
G THAO, WISCONSIN
HOUA VANG, WISCONSIN
HUE YANG, MICHIGAN
JEEMENG VANG, MINNESOTA
JOHN YOUA NOU VANG, UTAH
JOSEPH VANG, MINNESOTA
KAENG YANG, CALIFORNIA
KAZUME XIONG, CALIFORNIA
KER VANG, MINNESOTA
KONG XIONG, CALIFORNIA
KOR XIONG, WISCONSIN
KOU LEE, WISCONSIN
KOU VANG, MINNESOTA
KOU YANG, MINNESOTA
LA PAO VANG, MINNESOTA
LEE PAO XIONG, MINNESOTA
MARK XOUA XIONG, WISCONSIN
MEE VANG, MINNESOTA
MEGAN CHIWU LEE, MINNESOTA
MIKE VANG, CALIFORNIA
NA THAO, CALIFORNIA
NAO SHER VUE, OKLAHOMA

NAO SUE THAO, CALIFORNIA
NAO THAI VANG, CALIFORNIA
NAO TONG VANG, MINNESOTA
NENG VUE, CALIFORNIA
NHIA KAO THAO, CALIFORNIA
DR. NHIA KOUA VANG, WISCONSIN
PA LEE VANG, ARKANSAS
PAGE PAJZEB ZUAG LEE, WISCONSIN
PAO YANG, CALIFORNIA
ROCKY VANG, CALIFORNIA
SAI SHOUA VANG, CALIFORNIA
SAI SHOUA VANG, WISCONSIN
SALINA NOU LEE, MINNESOTA
SHENG LEE, WISCONSIN
SHIA YANG, MINNESOTA
SHONG GER VANG, CALIFORNIA
SHOUA TOUA VANG, CALIFORNIA
SHUA XIONG, MINNESOTA
SIA LO, J.D., MINNESOTA
STEVEN XIONG, WISCONSIN
TONG LENG YANG, CALIFORNIA
TOU ALAN VANG, MINNESOTA
TOU GER YANG, CALIFORNIA
TOU THOMAS VANG, CALIFORNIA
TOUGER VANG, NORTH CAROLINA
THUA VANG, CALIFORNIA
WA CHONG LEE, ARKANSAS
WAMENG XIONG, CALIFORNIA
WANG HER VANG, KANSAS
XAO CHOR VANG, WISCONSIN
XAY DANG VANG, OKLAHOMA
YANG PAO VANG, MINNESOTA
YONG YIA VANG, MINNESOTA
YONG YIA YANG, MINNESOTA
YUPHENG XIONG, MINNESOTA
ZA XIONG MOUA, MINNESOTA
ZE VANG, MINNESOTA
ZONG ZE VUE, OKLAHOMA

An Unsung Hero

General Vang Pao, you and your brave soldiers sacrificed and suffered blood and death defending democracy and freedom in our Kingdom of Laos. Many died defending our country of Laos from communist takeover; many died trying to keep North Vietnamese troops from using the Ho Chi Minh Trail to attack your troops and the U.S. armed forces in South Vietnam; many died from rescuing our fathers and brothers and American downed pilots; and later many died protecting Phou Pha Thi, Lima Site 85, an all-weather radar station that provided your friendly ally, the U.S., accurate bombing missions in North Vietnam.

These brave soldiers are our forgotten heroes: fathers, brothers, and compatriots, who lived alongside us, protected us, our families and friends, and defended our homeland. They were on the frontlines that kept communists out of Laos for 15 years during the course of guerrilla fighting and artillery duels of the Secret War. At times, as many as 100 of your soldiers rescued one downed American pilot whose purpose was the same as ours, to defend freedom's cause.

Let your Military Region II

memories be of pride in your field of actions, of victories and losses, of historical Lima Sites (landing sites), long marches and battles, and rescue missions for us to know our parents' courageous roles in our homeland and in the CIA's Secret War.

This year marks a new era for the Hmong in America since the end of the Secret War, yet the life of 35,000 or more of your servicemen's gallant warfare stories remain untold, unwritten in history texts where they deserve merits of honor and tribute. The time has come for our parents' war-torn experiences to be documented for us, as your children, so that we can know our own history. In this regard, all of your servicemen, servicewomen, your Laotian counterparts, CIA advisors, your everlasting friendship with the Thai PARUs, and your legacy will be remembered in history: in the history of the U.S., in the history of Laos, and wherever the Hmong live.

One day freedom will ring again in our homeland of Laos because of your guidance, because of your leadership, and because of your prominent role as one of Southeast Asia's and the Hmong's greatest military generals.

Military Region Commanders
Of the Royal Lao Army

◆ ◆ ◆ ◆

Commander-in-Chief

General Ouane Rattikone

Deputy Commander-in-Chief

General Kouprasith Abhay

Military Region I	Military Region II	Military Region III	Military Region IV	Military Region V

General Bounchanh Savathphaiphane	*General Vang Pao*	*General Nouphet Daoheuang*	*General Soutchay Vongsavanh*	*General Thonglith Chokbengboune*

Military Regions of the Royal Lao Army

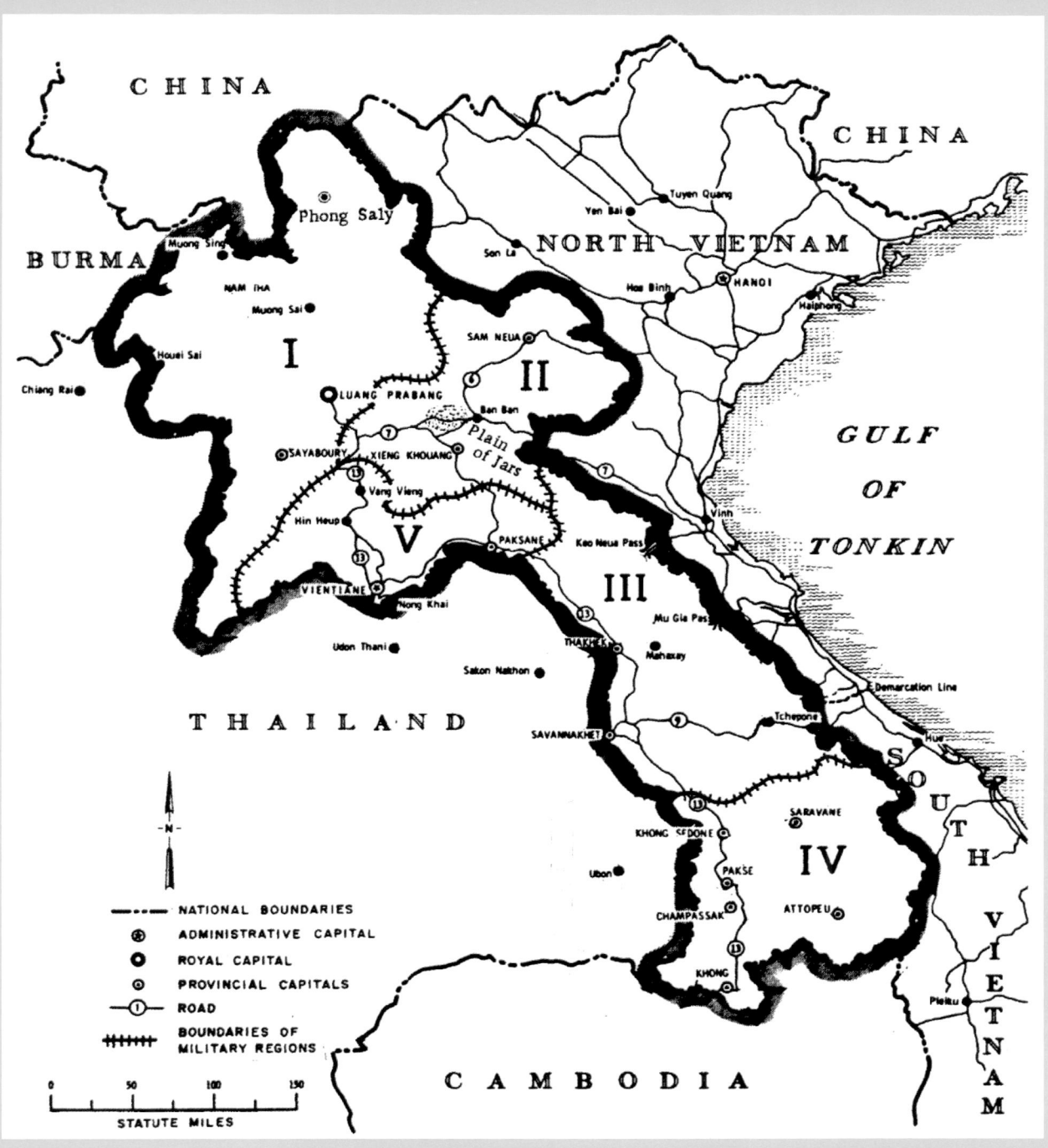

Royal Lao Army's Military Regions & Principal Roads of Laos. Laos is a landlocked country, which is bordered by Myanmar (Burma) and China to the northwest, Vietnam to the east, Cambodia to the south, and Thailand to the west.

SGU—MINNESOTA CHAPTER COLLECTION

Royal Lao Army's Military Region II (MR II)

Military Region II was one of five military regions in Laos and commanded by Major General Vang Pao.

KONG XIONG COLLECTION
LEFT PHOTO FROM CHALEUNSOUK VANG COLLECTION

Peb Txiv Hmoob Vaj Pov Tej Lus Nyiaj Lus Kub

PEB TXIV LUB SIAB SIB

SIB HLUB. (LOVE & CARE)

- Koj yuav tau hlub koj, hlub koj niam thiab txiv nrog rau poj niam tub se, hlub koj tsob neeg, hlub tej nom tswv thiab lub tebchaws uas koj nyob.
- Txoj kev hlub yog txoj kev pub, tsis yog kev taij thov thiab tsib txiaj ntsim.
- Txoj kev hlub yog kev sib nplig, sib to taub, sib zam txim, thiab sib ntseeg siab.
- Koj yuav tau hlub lwm tus tib yam li koj hlub koj, hlub lwm tsev neeg tib yam li koj hlub koj tsev neeg, hlub lwm tsav neeg tib yam li koj hlub koj tsav neeg kom sawv daws ua tau lub neej thaj yeeb nyab xeeb ua ke.
- Yam uas koj yuav tsis taus los luag yeej yuav tsis taus tib yam nkaus.

SIB PAB. (SUPPORT & ENCOURAGEMENT)

- Txhua leej yuav tsum xyaum nquag pab poj niam tub se khwv noj khwv haus kom yus tsev neeg rais ua ib tsev neeg muaj noj muaj haus, muaj hnav muaj siv, muaj zoo vaj zoo tsev nyob, haujlwm ua, zoo lag zoo luam khiav, thiab zoo liaj zoo teb ua noj.
- Sawv daws yuav tau mob siab ntso sib pab khwv thiab sib pab txuag noj txuag siv, khwv tau ntau, siv kom tsawg kom muaj seem coj mus nqis peev rau lub neej.
- Koj yuav tau mob siab ntso muab lub dag zog, tes nyiaj txiag, thiab lub tswv yim mus ua yam zoo thiab muaj nuj nqis pub rau koj lub cuab yig, lub zej zog, haiv neeg, thiab lub tebchaws.
- Tsis txhob xyaum ua neeg khuv xim dag zog, qia dub, thiab qia tswv yim.

SIB NCAJ. (HONOR & JUSTICE)

- Sawv daws yuav tau tsim txoj kev koob pheej ncaj ncees kom zoo tam li lub hnub mus nruab nrab ntug rau txhua leej txhua tus.
- Ua neeg yuav tsum muab lub ntuj daim av los ua pov thawj ntawm koj txoj kev ncaj; tsim txoj kev cai ncaj ncees los siv rau txhua txoj hauj lwm uas sawv daws ua.
- Tsim txoj kev zoo, cai lij choj, thiab kev tswj hwm kom koob pheej ncaj ncees rau txhua leej tib neeg.
- Thaum muaj txoj cai zoo lawm yuav tsis muaj tub sab tub nyiag, tsis muaj neeg deev luag poj tham luag txiv, tsis tsim kev sib ntaus sib tua, tsis sib huab noj huab haus thiab sib quab yuam caij tsuj.

PEB TXIV LUB SIAB SIB

SIB NTSEEG. (INTEGRITY & TRUST)

- Txoj kev sib ntseeg yog txoj kev sib cog phooj ywg, sib koom npoj, sib sau ua pab ua pawg, sib koom tes, sib raug zoo, thiab kev noj sib hlub haus sib ce kom tsis muaj kev sib dag, sib zais, sib cuab, thiab sib ntxub ntxaug.
- Ua neeg muaj li cas hais li ntawd, tsis txhob dag lus, cuab lus, thiab mom lus.
- Yuav tsum hais qhov tseeb thiab ua zaj tseeb xwb.
- Txoj kev phooj ywg, teem caij kom yog caij, teem nyoog kom yog nyoog.
- Txhua yam yuav tsum ua raws caij raws nyoog uas tau teem tseg cia.
- Txoj kev sib ntseeg yuav qhia tau rau lwm tus tias koj hais yam uas koj ua thiab ua yam uas koj tau hais tseg lawm.

SIB PHEEJ. (PEACE & TRANQUILITY)

- Sawv daws yuav tau xyaum tsis txhob ua neeg coj nruj coj tsiv, siv dag siv zog, sib riam siv phom coj los daws teeb meem.
- Yuav tsum siv lub tswv yim, kev pheej xeeb, thaj yeeb, thiab txoj kev cai ncaj ncees coj los sib hais.
- Tseg ncua tsis txhob tsim txoj kev kub ntxhov kom thaum kaw rooj kom yog ib yim zoo neeg, qhib roog kom yog ib lub zoo zos, mus thoob ntuj ces yog ib haiv zoo Hmoob.
- Tus dej nro tsis yeej tus dej ntshiab, txoj kev phem yeej tsis yeej txoj kev zoo.

SIB COB. (LEARNING & TEACHING)

- Txoj kev sib cob qhia yog lub hauv paus ntawm txoj kev kawm txawj kawm ntse uas yuav coj peb haiv neeg Hmoob txhua leej mus rau txoj kev txawj ntse thiab vam meej.
- Mob siab ntso sib cob qhia kom txhua tus Hmoob rais ua tub txawg ntxhais ntse, tub kob xwb ntxhais kws txuj, kws tooj kws hlau thiab tub lag tub luam txhua hom. Tseem ceeb tshaj kom muaj tus mus nrog luag ciaj nom ciaj tswv.
- Thaum pom luag kawm kav tsij mob siab ntso nrog luag kawm, es thaum luag tsaj nrog luag tsaj, luag noj thiaj tsis ua dev nuam yaj.
- Txoj kev sib cob qhia yuav rub peb haiv neeg Hmoob kom txav tawm ntawm lub neej txom nyem tsaus ntuj mus rau txoj kev tshav ntuj kaj nrig; nrug tawm ntawm txoj kev poob qab caum tsis cuag luag mus rau txoj kev vam meej ntsa iab.

Peb Txiv Hmoob Vaj Pov Tej Lus Nyiaj Lus Kub

PEB TXIV LUB SIAB SIB

SIB HWM. (RESPECT & OBEY)

- Koj yuav txawj saib lwm tus rau lub sam xeeb kom tsim nyog nws lub meej mom, tseem ceeb tshaj tus neeg ntawd nyiam li cas koj yuav tau xyaum ua raws li nws lub siab nyiam thiab nws tej lus hais.
- Tej laus hais tias "nyob luag ntuj yoog luag txuj, nyob luag teb yoog luag ze." Koj nyob lub tebchaws twg, lub tebchaws ntawd yog koj lub.
- Koj yuav tau hwm txoj cai kev tswj hwm thiab nom tswv ntawm koj lub teb chaws koj nyob thiab ua ib tug pej xeem zoo rau koj lub tebchaws.
- Peb Hmoob poj yawm hais tau zoo heev tias, "Hwm ntuj tau ntuj ntoo, hwm niam hwm txiv thiaj tau zoo"; "nplij tub nplij roog thiaj tau noj, hwm nom hwm tswv thiaj tau ua tus coj."
- Koj yuav tau paub txog txoj kev hwm thiab nplij lwm leej lwm tus kom meej es koj thiaj li tuaj yeem feeb meej tias koj yog leej twg thiab koj nyob rau lub meej mom twg thaum koj nyob koom npoj nrog luag.
- Ib leeg yuav tsum mloog ib leeg hais, tus yau txawj hwm tus hlob, tus hlob txawj mloog tus yau.
- Kev sib hwm thiab sib mloog yog txoj kev paub tab.
- Hauv koj lub neej muaj 4 tug neeg uas koj yuav tau hwm: 1) nws yog koj niam thiab txiv, 2) koj tus xib, 3) koj tus kws tshuaj, thiab 4) koj tus thawj coj.

SIB TW. (COMPETITION & CREATIVITY)

- Txhua leej Hmoob yuav tau mob siab ntso sib tw ua lub neej kom zoo, sib tw ua qhov tseeb, thiab sib tw coj qhov yog.
- Txoj kev nce qib thiab kev vam meej rau fab kev lag luam, kev txawj ntse, txuj ci technology, kev tswj hwm, kem txhim kho thiab lwm yam kev vam meej ntawd yog tsis nrog luag sib tw ces tsis pom luag qab.
- Kuv cov me nyuam Hmoob txhua leej yuav tau mob siab ntso sib tw mus tshawb nrhiav thiab kawm lub tswv yim tshiab los yog txuj ci zoo ntawm lwm tus thiab lwm tsav neeg uas vam meej dua coj los cob thiab siv rau Hmoob lub neej kom koj ua tau lub neej.

PEB TXIV LUB SIAB SIB

SIB ZAM TXIM. (COMPASSION & TOLERANCE)

- Koj yuav tau ua siab ntev nyiaj ntxeem rau txoj kev txom nyem, kev nyuaj thiab kev khwv ntawm txhua tsav yam hauj lwm uas koj ntsib.
- Tus dej nro tsis yeej tus dej ntshiab, tus neeg ua phem tsis yeej tus coj zoo.
- Txoj kev zam txim rau lawm tus yuav tsis muaj kev puas tsuaj nqaij ntuag ntshav nrog.
- Xyaum ua ib tug neeg txawj uv thiab txawj zam lwm tus, koj zam kuv ib zaug, kuv zam koj kaum zaus.
- Txoj kev sib uv thiab sib zam yog txoj kev thaj yeeb nyab xeeb.
- Koj yuav tau ua lub siab ntev tuav txoj kev zoo kom yeej txoj kev phem; tiv txoj kev khwv kom yeej txoj kev pluag; rau siab ntso rau txoj kev kawm txawj ntse kom yeej txoj kev ruam; tshawb nrhiav lub tswv yim tshiab kom yeej lub qub neej poob qab luag thuam.

SIB TSWJ. (LEADERSHIP & GOVERNANCE)

- Koj pawg neeg lub neej thiab txoj hmoo nyob rau hauv koj lub xib teg, nws zoo nkaus li thooj av thaum koj tso ces yuav tawg ua sab ua sua, thaum koj nyem kom ruaj khov ces yuav ciaj ua pob zeb.
- Koj yuav ua tus qauv zoo rau pej xeem kawm, ua tus thawj coj zoo rau pej xeem poog, ua lub kaus roos tshav rau pej xeem nraim, thiab taw tes tsau kaj rau pej xeem pom kev.
- Koj yuav tau ntaus thawj hlo thaum luag ntshai, muaj cuam sim ntxiag thaum luag nkaum.
- Txoj kev fab koj tho mus kom tshab, tus dej tob koj kwm mus kom dhau, lub txiv ntoo nyob siab koj muab kom tau los rau pej xeem noj.

Peb Txiv Hmoob Vaj Pov Tej Lus Nyiaj Lus Kub

PEB TXIV LUB SIAB SIB

SIB PUAG CAJ DAB. (FRIENDSHIP & UNITY)

- Leej neeg txoj sia muaj ncua, haiv neeg txoj sia tsis muaj ncua.
- Leej neeg teev ntshav cawm haiv yuav zoo tam nkaus li lub hnub ci rau xeeb leej xeeb ntxwv lub siab mus ib txhis.
- Txoj kev ntsim siab yav tag los yuav ua txoj kev ruaj siab thiab ntseeg siab kom sawv daws sib puag caj dab khov khwb kho mus rau lub neej yav pem suab yam muaj cuam sim ntxiag tab txawm yuav ntsib dab ntsib tsov los tsis ntshai.
- Txhua leej hauv kuv haiv Hmoob yuav tau thooj siab koom ntsws, thooj dag koom zog, thooj roj koom ntshav, thooj tswv yim thiab kev txawj ntse ua ke mus tsawb tsa haiv neeg kom muaj vaj huam sib txig, kev ywj siab ywj pheej sib npaug tib yam li lwm haiv neeg hauv lub tebchaws uas koj nyob.
- Ib txhais tes npuaj tsis nrov, ib sab taw sawv tsis ntseg, Ib tug ntiv tes nyom tsis yeej ib sab npab, ib tug rawg tais tsis tau nqaij noj; txoj kev sib tawg npoj yog kev puas tsuaj sawv tsis tsheej haiv.
- Txhua yam yuav tau txo txiaj ntsig ntawm tus kheej kom qis dua es tsa txiaj ntsig ntawm feem koom kom siab tshaj.
- Txhua yam yuav tsum ua raws li suab feem coob txoj kev pom zoo.
- Hu ua Hmoob ces txawm nyob lub tebchaws twg los puav leej yog tib tug; lub xeem cia sib yuav ua tshoob ua kos.
- Txhua leej Hmoob tsis hais tus muaj tus pluag, tus ruam tus ntse, nom tswv los yog pej xeem yuav tsum sib qhau hau ua kev haiv neeg lub neej thiaj caum cuag luag.

SIB PAB TXHIM KHO. (DEVELOPMENT & CHANGE)

- Yuav rhais ib tau roj thiaj txav tau ib kauj ruam, yuav hloov yam qub tawm thiaj muaj yam tshiab los dho.
- Sawv daws yuav txhim kho tej yam uas haiv neeg yeej ib txwm muaj dua lo lawm kom zoo dua qhov qub; hloov yam uas cov nyom thiab ntxhov quav kom yooj yim npliag lias; kho yam uas tsis raug chua kom meej tseeb raug muag; txhim kho haiv neeg tej kab lis kev cai qub qub ntau txhiab xyoo dhau los lawm kom vam meej.
- Muab haiv neeg tej kev coj noj coj ua, kab lis kev cai, kev teev hawm, kev lag luag, kev kawm txawj ntse, thiab kev koom npoj txhim ko kom muaj qab muaj hau kom sawv daws thooj tau ua ib pab, zwm tau ua ib pawg.

Retrieved from Cheng Leng Vang in 2012, who with others, worked closely with the late General Vang Pao to write his words of wisdoms for the people. It took about 12 years (from 1988-2010) to compose these passages.

Left: General Vang Pao greets Hmong women during a village tour.

CHAI VANG COLLECTION

Brief Introduction

"It is my belief that every individual was put on this earth for a purpose. And that purpose is different for everyone, but at the end it is [for us] to make the world a better place for all...."

—General Vang Pao
November 2003

The Hmong migrated from China to North Vietnam and Laos in the beginning of the 1800s; the specific date may have been around 1805 to 1806. The purpose for their migration varies. However, a persistent factor that caused them to migrate south was due to thousands of years of external conflict with the Chinese. In Laos, the Hmong resettled in the remote highlands. In the late 1800s, the Hmong began to feel the nobility and power of taking active administrative roles in the French-controlled Lao Government. At the turn of the 19th century, some Hmong sought public service opportunities. Few had political ambition. Others joined the military. Vang Pao was one of those who enlisted into the army. His generation became exemplary role models who broke through the social, political, and military barriers that had confronted the Hmong for the previous two centuries in Laos.

Vang Pao was born on December 8, 1929, in Phou Kong Khao, Muang Khan Disttrict, in Xieng Khouang Province, Laos. His parents were Phutong Neng Chu Vang and Song Thao. *Phutong* is a local government official. Phutong Neng Chu's father was Dra Mai Vang, but his mother's name was unknown. Phutong Neng Chu had two wives with five sons and 17 daughters. Some of their names were not recorded, have been forgotten, or they died before other children were born. According to Vang Pao, he was the fourth son. Two of his oldest brothers passed away when he was young, and he could only remember his older brothers Doua Vang, Nao Tou Vang, and younger brother Pa Vu Vang.

below left
In March 1960, Major Vang Pao addressed a crowd of Hmong men and boys from a village in MR II to gain their confidence and support to fight against a possible communist invasion in the incoming years.

KONG XIONG COLLECTION

As a child, Vang Pao only received an elementary education. He returned to help his parents farm. This was short lived. He despised the yearly hard labor. Vang Pao asked his father to start a small enterprise by selling livestock. His father agreed. "My older brothers and I would go buy cattle and resell at a higher price in the market," he said. "This was a success and other families picked up the idea, too." What convinced Vang Pao to lead by being an example was that he saw his Hmong people were mistreated by the Laotian people. He saw them struggle under many circumstances. "When the Hmong came from the hills to visit a Laotian town, they had to take off their hats," he stated in a 2005 interview. "If they don't take off their hats, they would be beaten by the Lao people until they could not get up." He also witnessed that the wealthier Hmong disrespected the poorer ones. The main obstacle was that the Hmong were uncivilized. They had limited means to make a living. "They had no salt or oil for cooking," he remembered. "The rich and educated looked down upon us because we were poor."

At the age of 13, Vang Pao worked as a courier for Hmong leader Tasseng Touby Lyfoung, Chao (Prince) Saykham Southakakoumal, who was the Governor of Xieng Khouang Province, and the French. With ambition and vigor, the young and energetic Vang Pao sought opportunities in the French Army. His natural militaristic talent earned him trust and respect among his comrades and superiors. By the late 1940s, he had already established himself as a capable officer. In 1954, he led a battalion from Laos to assist the French at Dien Bien Phu. Vang Pao and his army never saw battle at Dien Bien Phu in Vietnam. They were two weeks late. The North Vietnamese had defeated the French. They returned home. Being optimistic about his future military career, Vang Pao worked his way up the ranks into the Royal Lao Army in the late 1950s.

In 1960, Captain Kong Le, of the Neutralist party, seized Vientiane in a coup d'etat. Kong Le demanded that Vang Pao surrender. He refused. Vang Pao, then a Lt. Colonel, also deflected Neutralist and Communist Pathet Lao troops from the Plain of Jars in Military Region II. This was a critical moment in his history; he had saved his country from Communist takeover for the next 15 years. In January 1961, CIA operative James W. Lair met with Vang Pao, who agreed to join forces with the U.S. to lead and fight the biggest clandestine operation ever conducted by the CIA, known as the Secret War in Laos, from 1961-1975. The U.S. knew the Hmong would fight against the Communists. "When someone tries to change your outcome or to invade your country, it is even necessary to fight to the last man," Vang Pao said in a 1971 interview with anthropologist Dr. Jacques Lemoine. The Hmong and Lao soldiers, who were recruited by the CIA to fight this war against North Vietnamese movements inside Laos, were known as Special Guerrilla Units (SGU). By 1963, Vang Pao was promoted to the rank of Brigadier General by H.R.H. King Sisavang

Brief Introduction

"General Vang Pao was a visionary. He not only provided goods and services, he also contributed his knowledge to help his Hmong people advance."

— Major Cher Cha Vang
General Vang Pao's personal guard

Vatthana. Two years later, he was named the commander of the Royal Lao Army's Military Region II.

By the end of 1961, Vang Pao's first unit of 52 military personnel were trained in Hua Hin, Thailand. For the next 14 years of conventional fighting that literally turned the country into a land of bomb-craters, the Hmong, Lao, and other Laotian ethnic groups held off a Communist takeover of Laos. This distinguished General Vang Pao as an elite commander and one of the greatest military generals in Southeast Asia.

Throughout General Vang Pao's military career, he also had accomplishments beyond the war zones. He lived up to his personal conviction by helping those who were in need. "Vang Pao gave money to the poor, to those in desperate situations, including widows, orphans, and elderly," said Va Vang, a former personal staff to the General. "He cared about the people who had been torn by the war. He made sure civilians were rescued and rice and essential supplies were dropped to them."

General Vang Pao used the U.S. military funds to build schools in places where children had not had access to schools previously. In 1971, many Hmong families were displaced from their towns and villages due to the war. General Vang Pao converted his farmland in Hong Seng at the nation's administrative capital, Vientiane, by constructing temporary shelters and schools for them and their children. He financed the construction of nursing facilities for students interested in

the medical field. General Vang Pao also sponsored and sent outstanding students to study abroad, where it had only been possible for the wealthier class to attend. To improve the living conditions and welfare of his people, General Vang Pao established economic programs to assist them to become better entrepreneurs, farmers, etc. He started the Xieng Khouang Development Cooperation, which included a commercial airline to transport, import, and export goods and services throughout MR II. "General Vang Pao was a visionary,"

below
General Vang Pao took time off to spend with his children. Most of his time was consumed by the war in which he was mostly at the frontlines or with his soldiers; thus, moments like these were rare. Photo taken in early 1970s.

MOUA SUE COLLECTION

said former Major Cher Cha Vang, the General's personal guard. "He not only provided material goods and services, he also contributed his knowledge to help his Hmong people advance."

Aside from being an effective military commander, General Vang Pao was a political tactician. He had strong political influence. "Vang Pao was very connected to many politicians in Vientiane," said his brother-in-law former Colonel Ly Teng. "When he saw things that he didn't like in some policies, he was able to alter the decision of those politicians to vote against it." He met and worked with some of the most influential people of his generation in Southeast Asia. Moreover, he maintained good relationships with his American advisors and senior staff that were stationed in Laos. With his Hmong, he was a go-to leader for many clansmen who sought to resolve clan disputes and family affairs. He also made it known to the Lao Government to refer to his people as Hmong and not Meo, a derogative term the Hmong found offensive. A democratic moral philosophy General Vang Pao shared with the West was that he strongly believed no man should be ruled by a Communist state, but must live with the choice to exercise his and her freedom. However, when Laos fell into Communist control and the U.S. withdrew from Vietnam and no longer supported the war efforts in Laos, he along with his people were forced into living in exile abroad.

In May of 1975, General Vang Pao and 3,500 high ranking soldiers and their families were airlifted from his military base at Long Cheng to Thailand. "He did not leave immediately," said former Colonel Vang Geu. "His plane was [one of] the last to leave Long Cheng." General Vang Pao did not stay long in Thailand. On June 16, he was flown to France. On July 15, General Vang Pao and his family arrived in Washington, D.C., then relocated to Woodside, Montana. By 1977, he started the non-profit organization Lao Family Community, Inc. which was based in Santa Ana, California, to help with the resettlement process for his people coming

Brief Introduction 38

Brief Introduction

from the refugee camps in Thailand to the U.S. The non-profit organization's mission statement he drafted reads:

> *To empower refugees with the knowledge and skills to adapt to their new lives in America and to give them full assistance in their journey towards achieving their fullest potential in becoming self-sufficient and self-reliant in this society.*

General Vang Pao also went on to organize several other prominent non-profit organizations, including the Hmong 18 Councils, led by elected clan leaders, which in its charter states that it exists to preserve the Hmong culture and rituals, marriage traditions, resolve internal disputes, and mediate between the Hmong and American legal systems. General Vang Pao continued to lend his indispensable knowledge to many other areas where it was needed. He served as a senior advisor to several other Hmong and Lao groups to put an end to the inhumane treatment of his Hmong and Lao people hidden in the jungles of Laos. He traveled to the United Nations in New York several times to bring attention to the atrocity done by the Lao People's Democratic Republic, a government that killed more than 100,000 Hmong and Lao in Laos. For the veterans of the secret army he once led, he committed effort and resources to seek VA benefits for them by working closely with congressional leaders in the states where his Hmong and Lao veterans resided.

With the future still weighing on his shoulders, General Vang Pao rarely declined invitations to make speeches at annual conferences, high schools, and universities across the U.S. and abroad. Whichever state he traveled to he promoted the importance of higher education and cultural preservation. He also led discussions with Hmong community leaders about the creation of academic and economic programs and organizations to network, support, and share ideas about Hmong development in a civilized society. These conversations led to the creation of the Hmong-American National Development, which was later renamed the Hmong National Development, a national advocacy organization based in Washington, D.C. As for education, General Vang Pao emphasized that every child must have a good, quality education because this will lead to better employment opportunities. He encouraged families to work hard so they could provide for themselves rather than relying on government support. "I want my Hmong people to set an example for others," a remark he strongly claimed. His message about culture was for the Hmong to retain the uniqueness of their culture because it provides them a distinguished identity among the people on earth.

Each year, General Vang Pao's birthday was celebrated in selected cities across the nation. His first out-of-state birthday celebration was held in Wisconsin. In 2005, the Hmong community honored his 76th birthday at the Prom Center in Oakdale, Minnesota. There he expressed his gratitude to the community for their

> "My father-in-law dedicated his whole career to his people. He loved everyone, and this fulfilled his life to the fullest."

—Kong M. Xiong
General Vang Pao's son-in-law

kindness and love over the years. In 2006, he was reunited with former CIA agent James W. Lair in St. Paul, Minnesota. This marked their first reunion since they both left Laos.

In June 2007, General Vang Pao went to Wisconsin to pay tribute to the Secret War fallen soldiers event organized by the Lao Veterans of America-Wisconsin Chapter. Several weeks later, General Vang Pao along with 11 others were put under house arrest when the U.S. implicated them in an attempt to overthrow the Lao government. This arrest caused massive Hmong demonstrations across the nation that voiced for their innocence. By late 2009, the office of the U.S. attorney in Sacramento dropped the case, specifically against General Vang Pao, citing "in the interest of justice." He then toured Hmong-American communities across the U.S. to promote the importance of community leadership and civic engagement, and asked them to set examples for others. He also gave them good blessings.

On December 24, 2010, General Vang Pao was the honorable keynote speaker at the New Millennium Hmong-American Nationality Development Convention in Fresno, California, which was organized by Hmong-American community leaders nationwide. More than 300 people attended the conference. There he unveiled his vision as to how his people could become more successful by sharing resources and information; how they could resolve difficult community issues through consensus and unification; and that when there is a strong family foundation and values, this leads to fewer family problems and divorces within the Hmong population. Two days after speaking at the Hmong International New Year Celebration at the Fresno Fair Grounds, he was hospitalized due to pneumonia. He fought the illness for ten days. On January 6, 2011, General Vang Pao passed away at the Clovis Community Medical Center. He is survived by widows Mrs. Pai Lor and Mrs. May Song Vang, his 25 children, 68 grandchildren, and 17 great grandchildren.

During the late General Vang Pao's six-day funeral service at the Fresno Convention Center, more than 30,000 people, including his American veteran friends, came to pay their tribute and celebrate the life and legacy he left behind. His life may be best summarized by his son-in-law, Kong Xiong. "My father-in-law dedicated his whole career to his people," said the emotional Kong Xiong, who is married to the late General's daughter, Mai Kou Vang. "He loved everyone, and this fulfilled his life to the fullest."

To mark the first anniversary of General Vang Pao's passing, the Hmong communities across the nation gathered to remember his life. In California, several statues were erected to honor his legacy. In Minnesota, they gathered at the state Capitol's rotunda in St. Paul to remember him. In February 2012, the trustees of the Fresno Unified School District approved an elementary school to be named after him; and in September, they officially held an opening ceremony to welcome the new students to the Vang Pao Elementary School. ◆

Medals

The following were some of the medals and accomplishments General Vang Pao received throughout his lifetime. By 1965, he already had been awarded more than 35 military honors and accolades.

Grand Officer of the Order of the Million Elephants and the White Parasol

Phagna Norapamok 'Lord Protector of the Land'

Commander of the U.S. Legion of Merit

Knight of the French Legion d'Honneur

Grand Officer of the Thai Order of the White Elephant

Medal for Combatants from King Sisavang Vong

Medal of the Reign of King Sisavang Vatthana

French Croix de la Guerre des Opérations Extérieures, four bronze stars and 1 bronze palm

French Foreign Legion Indochina Vietnam Colonial Medal

French Foreign Legion Indochina Campaign Dien Bien Phu

The U.S. Central Intelligence Agency's Distinguished Intelligence Medal

front  *back*

The U.S. Central Intelligence Agency's Distinguished Intelligence Medal & Citation awarded to Major General Vang Pao by the CIA Director William Colby on December 15, 1975.

KONG XIONG COLLECTION

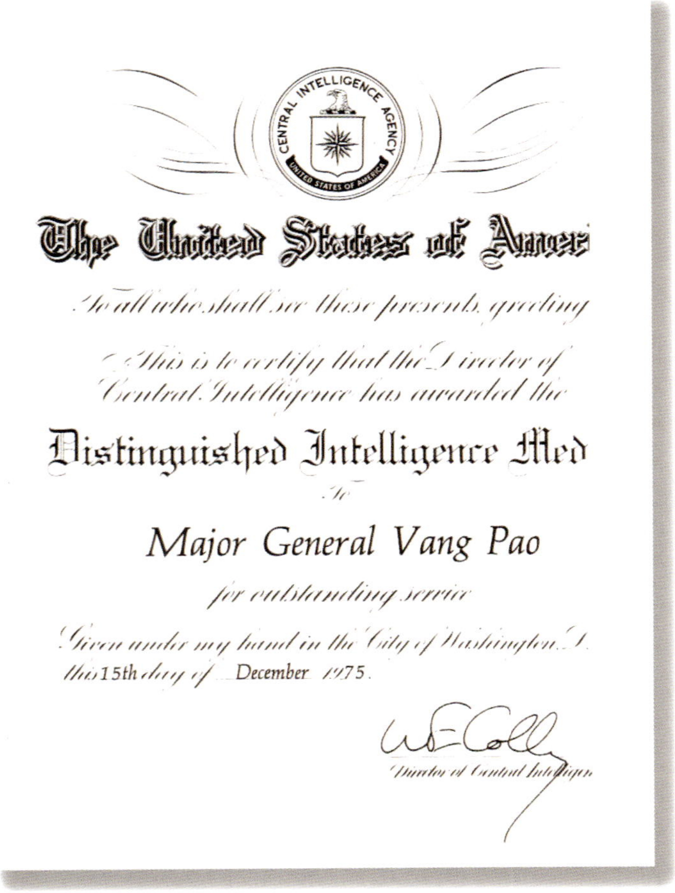

The United States of America

To all who shall see these presents, greeting

This is to certify that the Director of Central Intelligence has awarded the

Distinguished Intelligence Medal

to

Major General Vang Pao

for outstanding service

Given under my hand in the City of Washington, D.C. this 15th day of December 1975.

W.E. Colby
Director of Central Intelligence

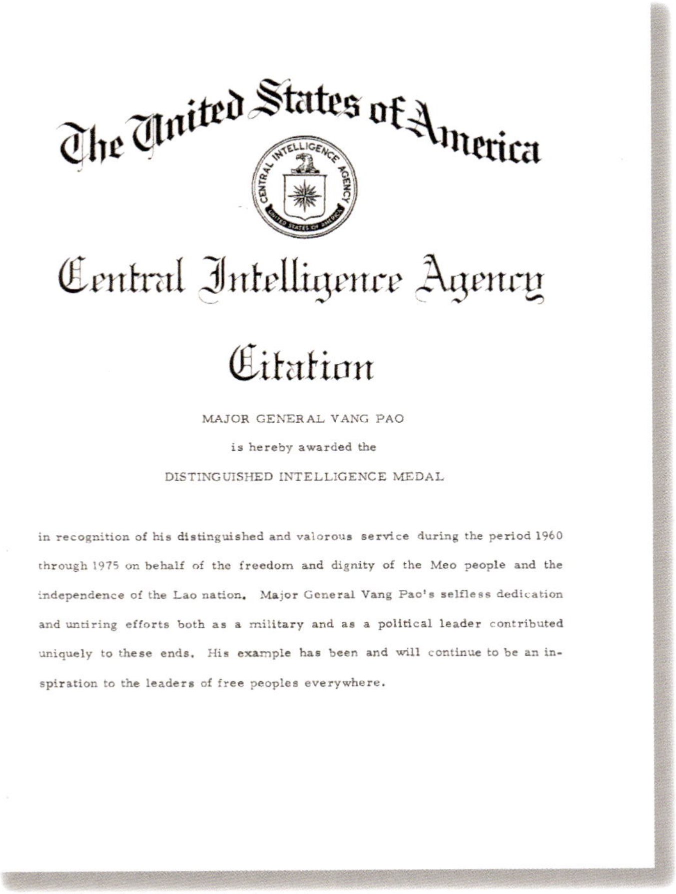

The United States of America

Central Intelligence Agency

Citation

MAJOR GENERAL VANG PAO

is hereby awarded the

DISTINGUISHED INTELLIGENCE MEDAL

in recognition of his distinguished and valorous service during the period 1960 through 1975 on behalf of the freedom and dignity of the Meo people and the independence of the Lao nation. Major General Vang Pao's selfless dedication and untiring efforts both as a military and as a political leader contributed uniquely to these ends. His example has been and will continue to be an inspiration to the leaders of free peoples everywhere.

BRIEF CHRONOLOGY

1929 - 1950

1929

December 8, birth of Vang Pao. He was born in Phou Kong Khao, Muang Khan Disttrict, Xieng Khouang Province, Laos, to Phutong Neng Chu Vang and Song Thao. Vang Pao's father's second wife was Va Lor; he married her after her previous husband, from the Yang clan, had passed away. Va Lor brought with her three sons and a daughter, but the daughter was already married to her husband from the Lor clan. They had a daughter named Chao Vang.

Neng Chu Vang was a local official, or *Phutong*, who represented the people in his town and handled all of their family and social disputes. In the early 1920s, Vang Pao's family farmed for a living. Like most Hmong families, they owned a parcel of land where they grew crops and raised livestock.

1930s

This was the end of an era for two respected Hmong leaders, Kiatong Lor Bliayao and Ly Xia Foung. *Kiatong* is a sub-district chief title used by the Chinese and Vietnamese. Ly Xia Foung was Bliayao's son-in-law and secretary. Their sons, Lor Faydang and Touby Lyfoung, would later become well-known politicians in Laos. Bliayao's son, Lor Faydang, was the Vice President of the Pathet Lao Government in 1975 while Ly Xia's son, Touby Lyfoung, was given the highest honorary title of *Phagna* by the King of Laos for his public service. Late in his career, he was appointed as an advisor to the King's Council.

Phutong Neng Chu Vang with a relative in Laos in early 1940s.

THE GVP FAMILY COLLECTION

1942

Vang Pao attended an elementary school that was built near his hometown. Prior to that, his education was taught through a private tutor paid for by his parents.

1943-1944

Vang Pao received some Lao education in his hometown; he only finished 3rd grade. He left school to work as a courier for Hmong leader *Tasseng* (or sub-district chief) Touby Lyfoung, Prince Saykham Southakakoumal, and the French.

1945

In World War II, Japan invaded Laos. Vang Pao was assigned to gather information on the Japanese for his French superiors. Because of his successful information-gathering tactics, the French hired him to work with them until his late teens.

During this time, Lor Faydang, Touby Lyfoung's uncle (or his mother Mai Lor's brother), sided with the Communist Pathet Lao after the two clans had a bitter confrontation over who should have the title of Tasseng in the Nong Het region. Touby Lyfoung remained loyal to the French and to the King of Laos.

1946
> Vang Pao and his step-brother, Pa Ger Yang, attended the same military training school. French Captains Bichelot and Fret recognized Vang Pao's leadership potential.
>
> Vang Pao also joined a column of soldiers sent to rescue King Sisavang Vong, who was under house arrest by the Pathet Lao forces, at the Royal Palace in Luang Prabang.

1947
> Laos gained partial independence from France. The majority of Hmong under the leadership of Touby Lyfoung sided with the Royal Lao Government and the French. Vang Pao had an interest in French Lieutenant Ticot's newly created provincial police force in Xieng Khouang. He soon was recruited into a police unit.
>
> On May 11, Congressman Toulia Lyfoung, the younger brother of Touby Lyfoung, championed a law under the new Lao constitution that granted Hmong full citizenship in Laos.

1948
> Vang Pao was promoted to Corporal and was enrolled in the Gendarmerie NCO school run by the French officers in Luang Prabang.
>
> Vang Pao disrupted a band of eleven North Vietnamese Viet Minh, which eventually earned him a reputation as a tough fighter and the trust of the French commanders. The French had tried several times to get rid of the eleven Viet Minh soldiers who were occupying a village. With each try they were unsuccessful. The French decided to test Vang Pao's military skills and sent him with a handful of other soldiers to this village. The enemy was caught off guard, and Vang Pao captured all eleven rifles and returned them to his superiors.
>
> Vang Pao also began networking, organizing, and recruiting other Hmong men throughout the Xieng Khouang Province to join the military.

1949
> Vang Pao was promoted to Master Corporal and attended school in Luang Prabang to advance his military knowledge. In training, he stood out among his classmates for his bravery and tactical abilities. The following year, Vang Pao received sergeant training in Vientiane, the administrative capital city of Laos.

1950
> While Vang Pao was away for his military career, his father Phutong Neng Chu Vang died from an unknown illness. Vang Pao never saw his funeral service. His family wrote a letter to inform him of his father's death.

1951

Vang Pao joined the Mixed Airborne Commando Group, which operated under the umbrella of the Groupement de Commandos Mixtes Aéroportés. He served in the Commando 200, commanded by Captain Jean Sassi. The two became close comrades in their efforts to fight against the North Vietnamese's Viet Minh. Vang Pao was in charge of a 34-man Hmong platoon.

1952

Vang Pao was the only Hmong who attended the ANL Officer Candidate School in Dong Hene, Savannakhet. He graduated in 7th place out of 56 students. While at the academy, Vang Pao was promoted to Second Lieutenant.

By March of 1952, 2nd Lt. Vang Pao was in charge of the Garde Nationale company called CGN 14 in Mouang Hiem, Sam Neua Province. Months after his promotion, the Viet Minh attacked Sam Neua, forcing him and his troops to retreat to the Plain of Jars (also known as Thong Hai Hin in Lao). His military unit was No. 3067.

1953

The Kingdom of Laos gained independence from France. 2nd Lt. Vang Pao earned the rank of 1st Lieutenant and was sent to Moung Hiem to resolve racial disputes between Hmong and Lao.

He commanded 74 soldiers to fight 1,000 North Vietnamese troops at a garrison on Colonial Route 7, near Nong Het. The enemy Viet Minh retreated after two years of combat, then Vang Pao returned to the Plain of Jars. On November 16, Vang Pao was wounded while trying to save his nephew, Thong Vang, during an enemy pursuit in Nong Het. The bullet went through Thong's abdomen and hit Vang Pao's belt, then strayed left. Thong died instantly.

right
Hmong soldiers/warriors in Xieng Khouang Province, Laos, 1953.

VTSY COLLECTION

1954
Laos had about 20,272 men in the army. The country was declared a neutral and sovereign state at the Geneva Conference. The International Control Commission (ICC) was set up to monitor the ceasefire agreement between Cambodia, France, Laos, and Vietnam. The ICC was comprised of three countries: Canada, India, and Poland.

In the U.S., President Dwight D. Eisenhower emphasized America's priority to halt the spread of communism in Southeast Asia in what was known as the Domino Theory. This meant that if Vietnam and Laos were to fall to communism, the rest of the Southeast Asian countries would be at risk.

In the previous year, the French began training their soldiers in *Operation CASTOR* to prepare for the battle at Dien Bien Phu between the French Far East Expeditionary Corps and North Vietnamese communist revolutionaries, the Viet Minh.

1st Lt. Vang Pao ousted a band of Viet Minh troops from a post from Nong Het. He was promoted to Captain. His French commanders ordered him to return to their Headquarters in Khang Khay to organize and prepare a group of 500 soldiers to serve as reinforcements at Dien Bien Phu. He was the commander of the group that was made up of mostly Hmong troops. When they reached Mouang Fern, near the Laos and North Vietnamese border, the French already had been defeated by the Viet Minh. This ended with the French military's tactical failure against the Viet Minh.

1955-1956
Captain Vang Pao received battalion commander training and the company he commanded was converted into Volunteer Battalion 21. France's last troops exited Laos.

In 1955, the U.S. Operations Mission established the Program Evaluation Office (PEO), which usually consisted of retired U.S. military personnel, to serve as advisors and manage the military aid in Laos.

1957
The Royal Lao Government and the Communist Pathet Lao formed their first Coalition Government. The Coalition Government requested that Captain Vang Pao be sent to Mouang Peune for military duty. He then was given the rank of Major.

1958 - 1961

1958

Major Vang Pao attended a battalion commander training course in Chinaimo in Vientiane. Later, he was sent to a 29-day counterinsurgency training in the Philippines. He also toured other nearby countries before he returned to Khang Khay, the old French military Headquarters in Laos. He was also sent to the administrative capital of Vientiane, Laos, for more military training.

Major Vang Pao finalized all the paperwork to acquire a rental property in Vientiane for himself and his family.

1959

Death of His Royal Highness King Sisavang Vong, who had ruled the country since 1946. His son Sisavang Vatthana succeeded him as King of Laos. Major Vang Pao was made the director of a Non-Commissioned Officer school to be established in Khang Khay. Laos had three major political parties: the Royal Lao Government, the Neutralist Government, and the Communist Pathet Lao.

As for the Hmong, a coalition between the Hmong leaders from the pro-Royal Lao Government, led by Phagna Touby Lyfoung, and Lor Faydang, of the Communist Pathet Lao Party, convened in Xieng Khouang.

Major Vang Pao was called back to secure the airport on the Plain of Jars, which was beginning to be occupied by communist forces. On May 25, Major Vang Pao commanded Captain Ly Pao to lead a battalion to pursue antagonist troops led by Lt. Colonel Thaotou Yang, a member of the Communist Pathet Lao Party. Major Vang Pao's soldiers were successful and drove their enemies from the Plain of Jars. The first American Major Vang Pao met in Laos was Jack Mathews, a PEO advisor in Laos.

By this time, Indiana farmer Edgar Buell had arrived in Laos through the International Voluntary Services, a program sponsored by the U.S. Buell, known as "Pop" or father, to the Hmong and Lao, helped them with agricultural productivity and humanitarian assistance throughout the war. He first came to work with the Hmong and Lao people in Lat Houang before they were relocated to Sam Thong, the medical center.

right
Lt. Colonel Vang Pao distributing money to his soldiers in Pa Dong in 1961. The money was directly paid by the U.S. through an office in Thailand. Thao Chai managed all transactions between Thailand and Long Cheng. He was later promoted to the rank of Colonel. Far left on the receiving end is Toulu Moua, who was later promoted to a Full Colonel and held the position as Budgetary Director in MR II.

JAMES W. LAIR COLLECTION

1960
Laos had become a strategic marker in halting the spread of Communism in Southeast Asia. About 300,000 Hmong lived in Laos, with 70,000 Hmong located on the Plain of Jars.

U.S. President John F. Kennedy increased U.S. military advisors and trainers, doubling the 100 already training the Laotian army. Neutralist Captain Kong Le launched a coup d'état to take over Laos and ordered Major Vang Pao and Rightist Lao military personnel to surrender. Major Vang Pao refused because Captain Kong Le had no royal authority to rule Laos. However, in the final days of December, Prince Saykham Southakakoumal and Major Vang Pao, fearing for the safety of their families and people that Kong Le might launch a surprise assault, headed south toward Savannkhet to get reinforcements from General Phoumi Nosavan. Soon Major Vang Pao received an order from Nosavan and General Ouane Ratikoune to return and secure the Plain of Jars.

Major Vang Pao was promoted to Lieutenant Colonel and commander of Infantry Battalion 10. A Lao soldier within Major Vang Pao's battalion attempted to assassinate him, but failed. Prime Minister Souvanna Phouma sent General Amkha Soukhavong to the Plain of Jars to collect food to nourish the Communist troops in Vientiane, but Major Vang Pao, who by then was promoted to Lieutenant Colonel, arrested him for treason and sent him to General Nosavan in Savannakhet.

1961
On January 3, U.S. CIA operative James W. Lair met with Lt. Colonel Vang Pao to form an alliance in Tha Vieng. Accompanying Lair to Tha Vieng was Thai PARU Commander Colonel Pranet Ritruechai. Lair knew immediately that the Hmong would fight against the Communist forces, because, according to Lair, "The Hmong would not get along with the Communists." Lair, Ritruechai, and Lt. Colonel Vang Pao formed a three-way alliance to fight in a covert operation known as the *Secret War* in Laos. This clandestine military operation was paid for and sponsored directly by the U.S. Government. Their alliance resulted in the launch of Operation Momentum, a name designated for the Hmong paramilitary guerrilla operations.

On January 24, Lair and Lt. Colonel Vang Pao arranged military supply drops to the 300 Hmong in Pa Dong. The drops were done by Air America planes. President Kennedy authorized the CIA to recruit 2,000 more Hmong soldiers. Kennedy also ordered an increase of the U.S. military trainers to 500 men in Laos. The first U.S. troops arrived in South Vietnam.

Lt. Colonel Vang Pao was promoted to a full Colonel. With his commitment to the war efforts inside Laos, the Royal Lao Army decorated him as the Deputy Commander of Military Region II, which was comprised of the Xieng Khouang and Sam Neua provinces. His temporary Headquarters was established at Pa Dong. While combating in Pa Dong, Communist Pathet Lao suffered 700 casualties while Colonel Vang Pao and his men lost only a couple dozen. By the end of the year, the number of Hmong casualties stood at 60 men.

1962 - 1965

1962

The Geneva Accord of 1962 was signed to establish Laos as a neutral nation and forbade foreign military interference during the Vietnam War. Prince Souvanna Phouma was named the country's Prime Minister.

Colonel Vang Pao and his irregular forces increased from 9,000 to 18,000. Many soldiers were given weapons and uniforms. At the end of the year Pa Dong was destroyed, forcing Colonel Vang Pao to relocate temporarily to Pha Khao. Since the previous year, between 700 and 1,000 Hmong soldiers were trained mainly by the Thai PARU in Hua Hin, Thailand; the first Hmong group consisted of 52 soldiers. They were trained in running radio nets, weapons, parachuting, intelligence, communications, and map reading. After their graduation in August, Colonel Vang Pao delivered a congratulatory speech, reminding them to return to defend their country from the Communists. On their return to MR II, they reformed into Battalion 201 with Major Youa Vang Lee as commander. The North Vietnamese Army (NVA) in Laos increased from 5,000 to 10,000.

1963

King Sisavang Vatthana and several of his top advisors visited the White House in Washington, D. C.

Colonel Vang Pao was awarded the rank of Brigadier General and his Headquarters was moved to Pha Khao for a short period, then it moved to the Long Cheng airstrip, which became the permanent Headquarters of Military Region II (MR II). When they first resettled at their new Headquarters, the Long Cheng valley only had a few Lao-Theung families living there.

King Sisavang Vatthana, his wife Queen Kham Phoui, and members of his higher courts made a visit to Sam Thong, Lima Site 20, the new medical center for MR II, and awarded medals to the public servants and soldiers there. This visit by the King marked an important point in Hmong history, by demonstrating respect for and integration of the Hmong into Lao society.

By this time the Hmong soldiers who were trained in Thailand were organized into Special Guerrilla Unit One, or SGU 1. 20,000 Hmong soldiers were armed. 19,000 Hmong were soldiers enlisted as Auto Defense de Choc (ADC) or civilian troops. Air America dropped food supplies averaging 40 tons per month to families in remote villages that were affected by the war.

Brig. General Vang Pao's personal chef was Tong Pao Lee and his brother-in-law Pa Nou Thao. Tong Pao Lee was among the Hmong soldiers who had escaped to Laos from Dien Bien Phu after the French were defeated in 1954.

1964

Brig. General Vang Pao's soldiers were estimated at 30,000. MR II was an area the NVA placed highest priority on controlling. The CIA's paramilitary budget increased from $11.6M to $14M in Laos.

Communist military actions displaced 200,000 civilians, mostly Hmong, from northern Laos. Hmong soldiers were paid 3,000 *kip*, equivalent to $3US, per month. As a Brig. General, General Vang Pao's monthly salary was 90,000 *kip*, equivalent to $90US.

Brig. General Vang Pao identified education, handicrafts, health, livestock production, and road building as the key areas that needed development to help the Hmong economically.

1965

Brig. General Vang Pao was popularly known as General Vang Pao, or 'Nai Phoo Vaj Pov.' His troops gained strength with support from the U.S. The wet and dry seasons in Laos became important strategic attacking times for both sides of the Secret War. Since he relied on airpower supported by the U.S., Brig. General Vang Pao used the wet season to execute his offenses against the NVA and Pathet Lao troops. During the dry season, his enemies moved over the dry ground to attack his forces.

Brig. General Vang Pao was named the Commander of Military Region II. He and his soldiers captured Na Khang, Lima Site 36, after several months of intense fighting. This site was important to the NVA in controlling Route 6.

U.S. Ambassador William Sullivan assumed control of the Secret War operations with more lenient funding and air support. The U.S. dispersed CIA training and supplies to some 30,000 Laotian military fighters from all ethnic groups at the height of the war. President Lyndon B. Johnson escalated U.S. forces in Vietnam from 75,000 to 125,000 and doubled the monthly draft from 17,000 to 35,000.

Seeing that opium had become a drug problem in Laos, especially among his Laotian counterparts, General Vang Pao ordered the termination of opium production in MR II. Instead, he encouraged his people to seek other opportunities to make a living. Moreover, the U.S. Agency for International Development (USAID) assisted many of these families to raise livestock as a business. General Vang Pao then established the Xieng Khouang Development Corporation, which included the commercial airline Xieng Khouang Air Transport, in Long Cheng. The primary purpose of the airline was to import commercial goods such as textiles, sugar, and salt from countries like Indonesia, Malaysia, and Thailand, to be sold in the Hmong and Laotian markets. In addition, Xieng Khouang Air Transport provided passenger air service in and out of Long Cheng. This company was managed by General Vang Pao's brother, Pa Vu Vang.

1966 - 1970

1966

The U.S. started Project 404, a program operated by the U.S. Air Force advisors to provide support and training to the Royal Lao Army.

General Vang Pao's code name was "1-2-5," which was assigned to him by his brother-in-law Ly Teng, who is married to Der Vang.

In May, General Vang Pao was badly wounded in the shoulder in combat at Na Khang, Lima Site 36. He was taken to Thailand and then to Hawaii for recovery. This wound was among a dozen serious injuries he suffered throughout his military career. The NVA dispatched 14,000 more troops into Laos, now totalling 50,000.

King Sisavang Vatthana and his family members visited Long Cheng.

Some 20,000 Hmong lived in Long Cheng, which later became the second most populated city in Laos, next to Vientiane, the country's administrative capital city.

1967

General Vang Pao reshuffled his three SGU battalions to form the first military regiment called Groupement Mobile 21 (GM 21). Hmong soldiers were estimated at 40,000 fighting in the war. Some soldiers were recruited from the Auto Defense de Choc (ADC), a civilian defense team.

USAID provided aid to 88,000 war-torn Hmong refugees in Xieng Khouang. General Vang Pao built the first college in Sam Thong. 75 Hmong men and women were trained as medics in Sam Thong, Lima Site 20.

1968

Brig. General Vang Pao received the rank of Major General.

The U.S. radar site installed on the mountaintop of Phou Pha Thi in 1967 fell under enemy control, costing between 11 to 13 American lives, and forcing about 16,000 Hmong soldiers and their families to seek refuge in Xieng Khouang. General Vang Pao exhausted almost everything he had to defend the radar site, but his troops were outnumbered and outgunned by the NVA and Pathet Lao forces. By now, Hanoi and the NVA were more in control of the war than their Communist Pathet Lao counterparts.

In November, General Vang Pao launched an offensive attack named *Operation Pigfat*. The total number of people involved in the war in MR II, including SGU, ADC, and civilian staff, equalled more than 40,000 people. By now there were eight GMs (or regiments) in MR II, with an average of three to five battalions per regiment, with about 500 soldiers per battalion. The eight GMs were GM21 through GM28. Thus far, 18,000 Hmong soldiers had been killed in combat. The number of civilian casualties was unknown.

General Vang Pao visited France and then made his way to Washington, D.C. He gave a flintlock gun as a gift to U.S. President Lyndon B. Johnson.

1969

General Vang Pao launched *Operation About Face*. With this operation, he recaptured Mouang Soui and Khang Khay, which had been occupied by the NVA and Pathet Lao forces since 1964.

With Operation Stronghold, General Vang Pao and his forces took back the Plain of Jars from NVA and Pathet Lao troops.

Former U.S. Ambassador Sullivan admitted at a U.S. Senate hearing that the current number of Americans employed in Laos was about 558, including 338 working with USAID and 127 military attachés.

Renowned T-28 pilot Captain Lee Lue was shot down by enemy anti-aircraft artillery at Mouang Soui, Lima Site 108, and died.

1970

During *Operation Kou Kiet*, General Vang Pao with his 15,000 soldiers succeeded in taking the Plain of Jars from the NVA who had some 45,000 troops.

In March, Military Region II soldiers at Long Cheng defended the military base by shelling several positions occupied by the enemy NVA and Pathet Lao troops.

Between 20 and 30 percent of the Hmong population in MR II had been killed since the war began. Twenty-seven thousand Hmong soldiers remained in Xieng Khouang Province. In the Royal Lao army, there were some 63,000 soldiers. In contrast, the NVA had about 50,000 soldiers in Laos, with some 16,000 around the Plain of Jars.

The medical center at Sam Thong suffered heavy enemy attacks. B-52 bombings began on the Plain of Jars. Of the 150,000 people who lived in the Plain of Jars region in 1960, only 9,000 remained.

Most Hmong soldiers' weapons were upgraded to M-16s.

In 1969, General Vang Pao started construction to build a Buddhist Temple in Long Cheng. The entire project was estimated between 14 and 15 million *kip*, equivalent to $1,400 and $1,500US. The cost for the King's house in Long Cheng was around 7 to 8 million *kip*, equivalent to $700 to $800US.

Since the 1960s, more than 400 Lima Sites, or landing sites, had been built throughout Laos for helicopters and short-takeoff and landing aircrafts. These sites were used for supplying logistical needs to troops at the frontlines, delivery of aid to displaced war victims, served as refugee evacuation centers, etc.

left
General Vang Pao respected all religions in Laos. In 1970, he built this temple Wat Chum Chen in Long Cheng as a sacred worshipping place for those who believed and followed Buddhism, which was the country's main religion. Personally, he believed in shamanism, which is widely practiced by the majority of the Hmong in Laos.

TUA VANG COLLECTION

1971

General Vang Pao sent several of his children, including Chai Vang, Cha Vang, Sisouk Vang, and Colonel Toulu Moua's son Chong Moua Jones, to school in Missoula, Montana. Some of them stayed with Jerry 'Hog' Daniels' family. Daniels was a CIA paramilitary advisor in Laos and worked closely with General Vang Pao.

Operation About Face II was launched on the Plain of Jars. The NVA had about two divisions, or 16,500 soldiers, in MR II, with 3,000 at the frontline. Later, the NVA pursued Long Cheng as their target. They attacked the Headquarters' large artillery positions, using tanks and 130-mm guns. However, in defense, massive airstrikes caused the NVA to retreat.

At this point in time, the average age of Hmong soldier recruits was 15 (while some were as young as 10). An estimate of 3,000 Hmong soldiers were killed and 6,000 wounded in the war during this year alone; between 18,000 and 20,000 Hmong soldiers were killed from 1961 to 1971.

1972

Operation Phou Phiang. General Vang Pao increased his support for education throughout Laos by purchasing and distributing books and school supplies to Hmong and Lao children. General Vang Pao with other Hmong leaders helped established colleges and universities for Hmong and Lao students. To further General Vang Pao's commitment to education, he also built a nursing facility in Long Cheng to treat the wounded soldiers, as well as hiring professional nurses to train others interested in nursing.

In 1971-1972, Long Cheng came under heavy enemy military assaults. In 1972, General Vang Pao learned of a peace treaty to be signed to end the war. This meant that his soldiers would return to their civilian lifestyles. To prepare them for readjustment back to their agricultural lifestyles, he implemented numerous economic development projects that provided courses in using modern farm tools, irrigation techniques, the basics of importing and exporting of goods and services, and banking.

In July, General Vang Pao visited the U.S., where he attended a dinner in Washington, D.C., with members from the CIA. Prior to his returne, he visited his children in Montana where they attended school. Later on, he also led a Hmong delegation to France to visit Hmong students who attended post-secondary schools there, including in Paris.

General Vang Pao's brother, Pa Vu Vang, passed away after his car rolled over on his way to his farm in Na Xue, Laos. Because of threats to the General's life, Battalion 205 was formed with Major Cher Cha Vang as commander to officially provide heavier security and protection for him and his family.

There were many key CIA advisors who worked closely with General Vang Pao, including Pat Landry, Dick Johnson, Vince Shields, and Burr Smith. Some Lao ethnic military personnel who assisted him were Brigadier General Chao Monivong, Captain Chaomai Srisongfa, Captain Kham Seth, Colonel Thong, and Colonel Khamhoung Pravongviengkham.

1973

A cease-fire Peace Treaty agreement was signed between the Royal Lao Government and Communist Pathet Lao. Even with the signing of the treaty between the two sides, the Communist Pathet Lao continued to attack General Vang Pao's positions on the Plain of Jars. In September, the NVA and Pathet Lao forces attacked Long Cheng.

Since 1968, the U.S. had continued the air campaign *BARREL ROLL* in support of General Vang Pao's forces and the Royal Lao Army in northern Laos. Since 1964 more than two million tons of bombs were dumped on Laos, a world record, especially along the Ho Chi Minh Trail.

Only 3,000 of 15,000 Thai military personnel remained in Laos. The Royal Lao Army had about 74,000 soldiers. About 120,000 Hmong became internal war refugees.

General Vang Pao purchased three airplanes for personal use. One of them was code named "Papa Uniform" and later was flown by his personal assistant, Moua Song, out of Long Cheng the day Long Cheng collapsed, May 14, 1975.

General Vang Pao and two of his personal staff, Lt. Colonel Vang Geu and Major Vang Neng, toured a farmland and chicken production facility in Chiang Rai, Thailand. Their intention was to explore the possibility of agriculture and economic development in MR II. The King of Thailand, Bhumibol Adulyadej, also invited them for a visit.

left
Special guests at a celebration at General Vang Pao's residence in Long Cheng in the 1960s.

THE GVP FAMILY COLLECTION

Brief Chronology

1974 - 1976

1974

Fighting decreased. The U.S. defunded its war efforts to Laos. Air America, civilian contractors, CIA advisors, and USAID staff began exiting Laos. By June, only about 40 U.S. military personnel were still in Laos. All the Thai military personnel had returned to Thailand. The Thai had lost about 2,500 soldiers. All the GMs were dissolved and SGU soldiers were combined into the Royal Lao Army. The Communist Pathet Lao political party garnered key positions in the Lao Government as a result of the Peace Treaty. Many MR II Hmong soldiers were discharged and returned to their villages. General Vang Pao pleaded with the U.S. to provide more funds because he had to provide care for 12,000 war widows, 16,000 orphans, 2,000 disabled veterans, and 250,000 refugees.

General Vang Pao visited Chiang Mai, Thailand, to observe various agricultural projects that might apply to Laos. In late December, General Vang Pao was invited to attend a forum in Vientiane, hosted by the Royal Lao and Pathet Lao, to discuss the future of Laos. However, he knew that this could be a trap to capture him so he brought along his CIA advisor, Jerry Daniels. General Vang Pao did not stay long at the meeting and returned to Long Cheng.

Since the beginning of the 1960s, General Vang Pao had become a revered and respected Hmong leader and military commander. He also helped promote civilian and military personnel to higher posts in MR II. His son, Wa Chong Vang, was enrolled at the West Point Military Academy in New York.

below
Hmong soldiers and their families waiting to be evacuated out of Long Cheng on May 14, 1975, the day that brought an end to the fighting of the Secret War and with Communist Pathet Lao taken complete control of the country. About 3,500 soldiers and their families were airlifted into Thailand for safety.

MOUA SUE COLLECTION

1975

The Secret War ended. The Pathet Lao slowly seized control of the central government. From May 12–14, about 3,500 of General Vang Pao's top military soldiers and their families were airlifted out of Long Cheng to an outdated Thai military base in Nam Phong, Thailand, for safety concerns. This mission was organized by the CIA, especially by Jerry Daniels, General Aderholt, and Colonel Vang Geu, and comprised of flying in two C-46s, a C-130, a Turbo Porter and a Bell 205 to evacuate the Hmong from Long Cheng to Thailand.

Between 30,000 and 40,000 Hmong soldiers were killed trying to prevent some 70,000 NVA from over-running Laos since the start of the Secret War. More than 50,000 Hmong civilians were also killed, some 50,000 to 58,000 were wounded; and 2,500 to 3,000 soldiers were missing in action. About 10 percent of Laos' population sought political refuge elsewhere.

While in Thailand, General Vang Pao faced political pressure to leave the country because the Thai Government feared an invasion of Communist forces from Laos. The Thai government sent two top military personnel, one of them under the code name of 'Thon', to ask General Vang Pao to leave Thailand as soon as possible. On June 17, Thailand Prime Minister Kukrit invited General Vang Pao for dinner. Several days later, the General and his family flew to France. Joe Glasgow, a CIA employee, accompanied them from France to the U.S. On July 5, they arrived in Washington, D.C. On July 15, the General and his family resettled in Victor, Montana. When General Vang Pao arrived in Montana, a CIA agent named Sam came to help him and his family with their resettlement process. Soon, Sam was replaced by Norm Larum. Later that year, Moua Song, a close associate of the General's family, fully assumed the role that was held by Sam and Larum.

1976

General Vang Pao chose to live in Montana not only because his children lived there, but because the landscape was also similar to that of his old military Headquarters, Long Cheng. He purchased a 400-acre farm for about $380,000. On this parcel of land, they grew barley as the main crop. General Vang Pao and his family typically made about $60,000 annually selling their harvest. However, the cost of production was $40,000 yearly, which left the family with only $20,000.

In March, General Vang Pao was interviewed by the Select Committee On Missing Persons In Southeast Asia, of the U.S. House of Representatives, pertaining to U.S. prisoners in Laos.

General Vang Pao's first vehicle in the U.S. was a yellow Dodge truck. General Vang Pao returned to farming after many years of fighting on the frontlines for the Americans during the Secret War in Laos. He stayed there with his family until 1984 when he officially moved to Santa Ana, California.

1977 - 1982

1977

Since 1976, hundreds of thousands of Hmong and Lao poured into Thailand seeking political refuge.

On General Vang Pao's first visit to St. Paul, Minnesota in the spring, his first meal with the Hmong Minnesota community consisted of Whoppers from Burger King.

1978

General Vang Pao met with U.S. President Jimmy Carter's Administration to address the plight and resettlement of the Hmong and Laotian refugees coming to the U.S. As more and more Hmong and Laotians started making their way to the U.S., he wanted to make sure that there were programs available to assist them in integrating in their new country, America.

General Vang Pao established Lao Family Community, Inc. in Santa Ana, California, a non-profit organization that provided assistance to his people adjusting to the challenges that faced them in the U.S. General Vang Pao served as the President while Vang Shur Wangyi served as the first Executive Director. With the Hmong and Laotian populations being scattered throughout the U.S., the non-profit organization also expanded to states where they resettled in large numbers, such as Minnesota, Wisconsin, Rhode Island, Michigan, Kansas, Utah, Alabama, and Georgia. At one point, Lao Family Community, Inc. had 28 branch offices nationwide.

Early 1980s

General Vang Pao was a revered public speaker at Hmong New Year celebrations, summer festivals, political, and social gatherings. His words were often said to restore hope and encourage his people to build their new lives with confidence.

He also founded several other well-known organizations, was a strong advocate for human rights in Laos, and encouraged Lao councils to unite Hmong and Laotian communities in the U.S.

right
General Vang Pao discussed the resettlement process and what the Hmong needed to do in order to adapt and overcome challenges facing them as new immigrants to Minnesota and throughout other states. Photo taken at the Lao Family Community Center n St. Paul, Minn., in 1982.

THE GVP FAMILY COLLECTION

1980

A defector reported that between 1975 and 1980 some 50,000 Hmong civilians died from Vietnamese and Lao chemical poisoning, starvation, diseases, or were killed while trying to escape across the Mekong River to Thailand. Thousands of refugees claimed they were forced to flee Laos when their villages were suddenly attacked with chemical poisons delivered by Soviet and Vietnamese aircraft, causing the death of hundreds of women, children, and elderly.

In California, General Vang Pao created the United Lao Development Cooperation (ULDC) to provide imported goods and services from Asian countries to the growing Hmong and Laotian communities in the U.S. The corporation served as an information resource center, wholesaler, distributor, and opened small retail grocery stores from Rhode Island to California. The grocery store he managed in Santa Ana, California, was called Best Food. To boost the entrepreneurship of his people, General Vang Pao had his staff travel to different communities to teach and assist those interested in starting small retail businesses. This dissemination of resource and training resulted in many successful Hmong businesses.

1981

On December 3, General Vang Pao was sworn in as a U.S. citizen in the District Court of Montana. He and his son Vang Chong also visited many Laotian leaders in Australia.

General Vang Pao co-founded the United Lao National Liberation Front, or Neo Hom Kou Xat, with Laotian political leaders living in exile. One of the organization's primary missions was to provide security and humanitarian aid to the incoming refugees in Thailand from Laos. Secondly, the supreme committee of ULNLF restored the Royal Lao Family. They appointed Chao (Prince) Sauryavong Savang as The Regent. The Prince was the youngest son of King Sisavang Vatthana. This organization's name was later shortened to just Neo Hom. The first president of the organization was Chao Phagna Luang Muang Chanh Outhong Souvannavong. General Vang Pao served as the Vice President and was in charge of security operations for the organization.

1982

General Vang Pao was a special guest speaker at Harvard University. He spoke for two hours regarding his military career and the economic, social, and political factors that he faced in Laos and in the U.S.

General Vang Pao along with Hmong leaders established the first Hmong 18 Councils in Fresno, California. According to the General, the non-profit organization started based on the "ideas of self-support, self-determination, and community leadership development." Later that year, General Vang Pao's mother Song Thao passed away in Montana of old age while he was on a diplomatic trip to Singapore. He did not see either of his parents' funeral services.

1983 - 1994

1983

General Vang Pao opened a financial institution called the Lao Hmong Security Federal Credit Union to offer financial services to entrepreneurs and families. He also encouraged business-minded individuals to capitalize on the financial sectors by getting into the real estate market as brokers or to become auto or life insurance agents.

1984

General Vang Pao and his family attended the senior high school graduations of his son Cha Vang and nephew Xa Vang.

General Vang Pao met former CIA director William Colby in Washington, D.C., where he had a family dinner with Colby and his wife at their residence. Colby then scheduled a private meeting with General Vang Pao and former U.S. President Richard Nixon. Their conversation was brief. According to General Vang Pao's personal aide Moua Song, who accompanied the General, "They didn't discuss much. They just updated each other's lives and how things went for Vang Pao in Montana."

Almost a decade after his involvement in the war ended, General Vang Pao still received death threats from Hanoi's agents.

1985

General Vang Pao led the newly developed organization United Lao Movement for Democracy, with former Colonel Ly Teng serving as the Vice President. He also created the ULD financial services to provide a banking system for the community.

1986

General Vang Pao helped establish the Lao Human Rights Council. Dr. Pobzeb Vang became the leading member of the Council and dedicated his life to advocating for protection and humanitarian efforts for the Hmong hiding in the jungles of Laos.

General Vang Pao was a fervent supporter of the organization Hmong-American National Development, which existed to advocate and educate the federal government regarding state and local Hmong social resettlement needs. Later it was renamed Hmong National Development, based in Washington, D.C.

General Vang Pao closed his 400-acre ranch in Montana and moved his entire family to California.

1987

General Vang Pao and his family went on a personal trip to China.

1990
General Vang Pao and his family purchased a two-story home in Westminster, Orange County, California, and moved there from Santa Ana.

During the 1990s, General Vang Pao was active in advocating for human rights in Laos and in diplomatically working to develop peace, freedom, and democracy in the impoverished country of Laos.

1991
With Hmong and Laotian youth violence growing in the Twin Cities, Lee Pao Xiong and Bob Fletcher, the head of the juvenile unit with the City of St. Paul, brought these gang issues to the attention of General Vang Pao and explained how it was negatively affecting the Hmong and Southeast Asian communities. This effort led to state and federal funding of $1.5M to address gang-related activities in the Asian-American communities.

1992
Hmong community leaders and members organized an event for General Vang Pao and his former soldiers of the Secret War at the 144th Fighter Wing in Fresno, the California Air National Guard Base. Throughout the program, retired American pilots and staff at the base toured and educated General Vang Pao and his veterans on many of the displayed aircraft that were used in World War II as well as modern war planes.

1993
On April 9, General Vang Pao was a keynote speaker at the Hmong Stout Student Organization's Sixth Annual Educational Conference at the University of Wisconsin-Stout. The topic of his speech focused on the "Unity of Hmong in Higher Education."

In November, General Vang Pao, his wife Mrs. May Song Vang, Colonel Ly Toupao, Lt. Colonel Vang Fong, and Moua Ge attended the Hmong Michigan New Year Celebration in Detroit, Michigan.

1994
General Vang Pao authorized Dr. Pobzeb Vang to officially register the word "Hmong" to replace "Miao" and "Meo" at the United Nations in New York.

In April, General Vang Pao attended the National Lao Human Rights Conference. There he met and discussed the Hmong human rights and refugee issues in Thailand with key leaders and politicians, including U.S. Representative Toby Roth (R-WI).

1995 - 2003

1995

In August, General Vang Pao attended the Second International Symposium on the Hmong People held in St. Paul, Minnesota. Its goal was to promote the awareness of Hmong culture around the world. The First International Symposium on the Hmong People was held in Jishou, Hunan Province, China, in 1994.

General Vang Pao was part of a honorary delegation called the Committee For A Free Laos: Toward A Post-Communist Laos and the Hmong/Lao Refugee Crisis that went to Washington, D.C., to discuss the refugee issues and human rights violations committed by the LPDR to staff and members of Congress. The rest of the delegation included members of the Royal Lao Family, General Thonglith Chokbengoun, Lao Veterans of America, the Lao Human Rights Council, and the United Lao Movement for Democracy.

1996

In April, General Vang Pao addressed an audience at the Vietnam Center Conference organized by the Texas Tech University Vietnam Center and Archive. He briefly mentioned the dire effect of the chemical Agent Orange used by the Vietnamese and Lao governments on the Hmong and Lao refugees in Southeast Asia.

General Vang Pao attended an event organized by the Lao Veterans of America in Fresno, California, honoring those who served and sacrificed their lives during the Secret War. About 5,000 Hmong and Laotian veterans attended the ceremony.

General Vang Pao signed the by-laws that implemented the Hmong 18 Councils chapter in Minnesota.

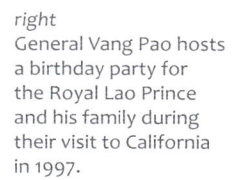

right
General Vang Pao hosts a birthday party for the Royal Lao Prince and his family during their visit to California in 1997.

THE GVP FAMILY COLLECTION

1997

On May 15, 1997 through the efforts of the Lao Veterans of America, a memorial plaque honoring the "Hmong and Lao Combat Veterans and their American Advisors Who Served Freedom's Cause in Southeast Asia" was unveiled at Arlington National Cemetery in Washington, D.C. Hmong veterans living in the U.S. were estimated at more than 20,000.

General Vang Pao and the Hmong community leaders of California officially invited members of the Royal Lao Family, including Crown Prince Soulivong Savang and Prince Sauryavong Savang, to attend the Hmong International New Year Celebration at the Fresno Fairgrounds. This was the first year the new year event was held at the Fair Grounds.

1998

General Vang Pao along with the members of the Lao Veterans of America went to Washington, D.C., to lobby Congress to pass the House Resolution 371, which would grant Hmong and Laotian veterans an easier path to becoming U.S. citizens. On May 26, 2000, President William J. Clinton signed H.R. 371, known as the "Hmong Veterans' Naturalization Act of 2000," into law in the 106th Congress, 2D Session. The two main points were: 1) "Removes naturalization barriers for certain Hmong by waiving the English language requirements and providing special consideration for the civics requirement. To qualify, the Hmong must have been admitted into the United States as a refugee from Laos and served with a Laotian-based special guerrilla or irregular unit in support of U.S. forces at any time from February 28, 1961 through September 18, 1978"; and 2) "Allows up to 45,000 Hmongs to apply for naturalization under these special provisions no later than 18 months after May 26, 2000."

2001

The Vang Pao Foundation was established, with the mission to support the non-profit organizaitons through a foundational block grant. However, in 2005, the foundation was closed down by the Minnesota Attorney General's office.

2002

In April, General Vang Pao was the keynote speaker at the University of Wisconsin-Eau Claire during a special session on Hmong history.

2003

General Vang Pao, some members of the Asian-American entrepreneurs, U.S. Secretary of Labor Elaine L. Chao, and her staff toured small Asian-American businesses along University Avenue in St. Paul, Minnesota. Their visit was part of the Bush Administration's minority business economic initiatives.

General Vang Pao and several of his advisors met with some Vietnamese Government officials in Switzerland. The purpose was to ask Hanoi to intervene with the Lao Government about rebuilding peaceful efforts between the current and former governments and military leaders abroad.

2004

General Vang Pao met with U.S. Senator Norm Coleman and Matt Daley, Deputy Assistant Secretary of State for East Asia and Pacific Affairs, to discuss his "efforts to bring peace to Laos, the refugee resettlement program for Hmong in Thailand, and the humanitarian crisis facing many Hmong living in Laos." Coleman stated: "I have some serious concerns about the way the Hmong people are being treated today in Southeast Asia. It's critical that the U.S. State Department does all it can to bring peace to Laos and an end to the humanitarian and refugee crises facing many Hmong in Southeast Asia."

General Vang Pao was a special guest at the opening of the new Hmong-American charter school, New Millennium Academy, in North Minneapolis, Minnesota.

With the leadership of Dr. Khamphay Abhay, President, and General Vang Pao, Vice President, the United Lao Council for Peace, Freedom, and Reconstruction organization was formed, with the Headquarters in Fresno, California. Also, the non-profit veterans organization Special Guerrilla Units Veterans & Families of USA, Inc., was established to serve former Hmong soldiers and their families.

2005

General Vang Pao attended the funeral service of his step-brother Sia Cheng Yang in Maplewood, Minnesota.

In April, he was a special guest speaker at the Center for Hmong Studies' Open House at Concordia University in St. Paul, Minnesota. He emphasized to the Hmong students and scholars the importance of preserving Hmong culture, history, and values. At the Open House, Vang Xang, executive director of the Hmong American Mutual Assistance Association, donated $20,000 to the Center to preserve and collect Hmong history and artifacts.

In Fresno, California, General Vang Pao helped unveil a 6-foot bronze statue commemorating the sacrifices of Hmong and Lao soldiers during the Secret War. General Vang Pao ardently stressed the hope that Hmong and other Laotians in exile would be able to return to Laos safely.

An activity General Vang Pao enjoyed was reading the morning newspaper to keep up-to-date with current events. He also liked to watch the Miss Universe pageant and basketball. In May, General Vang Pao picked the San Antonio Spurs over the Detroit Pistons during the National Basketball Association Championship game. The Spurs defeated the Pistons in the series 4-3.

2006

One of General Vang Pao's favorite places to dine was in Redondo Beach, California.

In November, General Vang Pao and former CIA operative James W. Lair were reunited in St. Paul, Minnesota. During their visits, they both celebrated the Hmong New Year Celebration and helped draft a resolution to honor and recognize the SGU veterans. "I know the Hmong very well. They can adapt very quickly to different situations. I believe that when we take them here in the U.S. they will become very useful citizens," recounted Lair at the Hmong New Year Banquet in Oakdale, Minnesota, regarding his past experience working with the Hmong during the Secret War. "They are largely uneducated; they're very bright, adaptable people. Now that I observe [the Hmong in] Minnesota and other places, I am very pleased to say that my words were true."

General Vang Pao led a delegation of Hmong-Americans to the United Nations in New York, asking that the United Nations address the human rights violations against the Hmong who were still hiding in the jungles of Laos in fear of persecution by the Lao Government (LPDR).

2007

General Vang Pao attended the Wisconsin-Chapter's Lao Veterans of America event where he laid a wreath to honor the fallen Hmong and Laotian soldiers of the Secret War.

An elementary school in the Madison, Wisconsin, area was to be named after General Vang Pao. This was abandoned in the wake of the arrest of General Vang Pao along with 11 others charged with attempting to overthrow the Lao Government. The criminal complaint was Case No. 207-MJ-0178. Following their arrests, supporters across the U.S. rallied for their release.

2008

General Vang Pao traveled throughout the United States to give speeches to remind his people to love and support each other.

2009

In October, General Vang Pao's 2007 case was dismissed in Sacramento, California, where about 10,000 Hmong of all ages came to voice their support for his innocence. This was also a turning point for the Hmong communities worldwide—especially among the younger generations—who started to realize the inhumane struggle of their people in Laos and Thailand since 1975.

General Vang Pao traveled to different states to promote the well being of his Hmong people and encouraged them to stay strong in times of economic hardships. He also started the Hmong National Foundation, based in Milwaukee, Wisconsin. Its purpose was to find ways to assist the Hmong people worldwide.

In July, General Vang Pao launched the Core Committee of Hmong 18 Council of Wisconsin, which was to bring gender equality and equal opportunity for women and free election of the 18-clan members to represent the Council. This work, led by Mrs. Houa Vang, began in 2007 in order to address the social problems and gender issues within the Hmong community.

2010

In January, General Vang Pao announced his plan to return to Laos; however, he cancelled the trip due to political reasons. On April 11, General Vang Pao and James W. Lair met at the SGU office in St. Paul, Minnesota, to discuss future advocacy work to get VA benefits for Hmong and Laotian veterans.

On October 30, General Vang Pao attended the Grand Opening of the new business and shopping center Hmong Village, or Zos Hmoob, on the Eastside of St. Paul.

On December 26, General Vang Pao gave his last speech at the opening of the Hmong International New Year Celebration at Fresno's Fair Grounds in California.

2011

In January 6, General Vang Pao passed away at Clovis Community Medical Center. He died of pneumonia at the age of 81 surrounded by family members and personal friends. Following General Vang Pao's death, the charges against the remaining defendants in the 2007 case alleging they sought to overthrow the Lao Government were dropped.

The late General Vang Pao's funeral service was held from February 4 to 9 at the Fresno Convention Center, Fresno, California, and was attended by more than 30,000 people. From May 27 to 29, General Vang Pao's Soul Release 'Tso-Plig' Ceremony was held in St. Paul, Minnesota.

In Fresno, a statue of the late General Vang Pao was unveiled at the Hmong International New Year. On December 8, Hmong-Americans gathered in their states to remember and celebrate his birthday. They also planned to lobby Congress to recognize this day as a national holiday to honor him. On December 14, Time Magazine nominated General Vang Pao as one of its Persons of the Year under the category of *Fond Farewells*.

2012

The first edition of this book was published and distributed throughout the United States.

In February, the Fresno Unified School District approved an elementary school to be named after General Vang Pao. "This is a great day for the people, for our elders. It means a great step forward for the next generation, but also an important legacy for the Hmong community," said Fresno City Council Member Blong Xiong. In September, Vang Pao Elementary School was officially opened, and many local community leaders and members attended the event. The late general's son, Chineng Vang, said, "[General Vang Pao] lectured over and over wherever he went that education is the key to success. That is sort of the school motto. That statement was taken directly from him. The importance of education will empower his people to gain more knowledge and experience to better themselves."

In California, several statues were built to honor the late General Vang Pao's legacy.

2013

Many Hmong-Americans continue to celebrate and honor the late General Vang Pao for his lifelong public services that impacted their lives and the Hmong and Lao societies in the United States and abroad.

below
On January 6, 2012, the Hmong Minnesota Leadership Council organized a special event marking the first anniversary of the late General Vang Pao's death at the Minnesota State Capitol Rotunda in St. Paul. It was attended by politicians and community leaders and members. Addressing the audience from the podium was one of the late General's sons, Neng Chu Vang.

ETHAN VANG COLLECTION

CHRONOLOGY SOURCES

- Anne Fadiman's *The Spirit Catches You and You Fall Down: A Hmong Child, Her American Doctor, and the Collision of Two Cultures*. Farrar, Straus, and Giroux: New York, 1997.
- Arthur J. Dommen's *Conflict in Laos: The politics of neutralization*. Praeger: London, 1971.
- Arthur J. Dommen's *The Indochinese Experience of the French and the Americans: Nationalism and Communism in Cambodia, Laos, and Vietnam*. Indiana University Press: Bloomington and Indianapolis, 2001.
- Captain Vang Neng. *Interview*. Minnesota, 2000s.
- Captain Vang Xai Nou. *Interview*. Minnesota, 2011.
- Cha Vang. *Interview*. Minnesota, 2010.
- Chai Vang. *Interview*. California, 2010.
- Christopher Robbin's *The Ravens: The Men Who Flew in America's Secret War in Laos*. Crown: New York, 1987.
- Colonel James W. Lair. *Interview*. Texas, 2009 & 2010.
- Colonel Ly Toupao. *Interview*. Minnesota, 2006.
- Colonel Ly Teng. *Interview*. Minnesota, 2000s.
- Colonel Vang Geu. *Interview*. North Carolina, 2000s.
- Colonel Xiong Shong Leng. *Interview*. Minnesota, 2010.
- Dale Yurong. "Fresno Unified opens Vang Pao Elementary." ABC 30, Fresno, California. August 20, 2012.
- Dr. Charles Weldon's *Tragedy in Paradise: A Country Doctor At War In Laos*. Asia Books, Bangkok: 1999.
- Dr. Yang Dao's *Hmong at the Turning Point*. WorldBridge Associates: Minneapolis, 1993.
- Eric Chevreuil's *Our Meos and French Indochina*. Presentation at GVP's Funeral Service, Fresno, Ca. February 2011.
- Gayle L. Morrison's *Sky Is Falling: An Oral History of the CIA's Evacuation of the Hmong from Laos*. McFarland & Company: North Carolina, 1999.
- General Vang Pao. *Interview*. California & Minnesota, late 2000s.
- Grant Evans' *A Short History of Laos: The Land in Between*. Allen & Unwin: Australia, 2002.
- Jack F. Mathews. *Personal files*. Retrieved from Kong M. Xiong, 2011.
- Jane Hamilton-Meritt's *Tragic Mountains: The Hmong, the Americans, and the Secret Wars for Laos, 1942-1992*. Indiana University Press: Indianapolis, 1993.
- Kenneth Conboy's *Shadow War: The CIA's Secret War in Laos*. Paladin Press: Colorado, 1995.
- Kenneth Conboy's *War in Laos, 1945-1975*. Squadron Signal Publications: Texas, 1994.
- Kong N. Xiong. General Vang Pao's son-in-law. *Interview*. California, April 2011.
- Lao Veterans of America. St. Paul, Minnesota.
- Lee Pao Xiong. *Interview*. St. Paul, Minnesota, 2011.
- Lt. Col. Nenglo Yang. *Interview*. Minnesota, June 2011.
- Lt. Colonel Vang Toufu. *Interview*. California, 2010 & 2011.
- Lt. Colonel Wangyee Vang. *Interview*. California, April 2011.
- Lieutenant-colonel Jean-Vincent BERTE's *Indochine : les supplétifs militaires et les maquis autochtones*. Retrieved from http://taktika.cesat.terre.defense.gouv.fr. in June 2012.
- Major Cher Cha Vang. *Interview*. Minnesota, 2010.
- Major Neng Sho Xiong. *Interview*. Minnesota, 2000s.
- Moua Song. *Interview*. California, April 2011.
- Declassified/Released US Department of State EO Systematic Review 30 JUN 2005. *VANG PAO IN THAILAND*. Retrieved from the National Archives, May 2011.
- Neng Chu Vang. *Interview*. Minnesota, 2005.
- Nicholas Tapp's *The Hmong of China*. Brill: Boston, 2001.
- Noah Vang. *Personal experience with General Vang Pao*. 2000s.
- Pacyinz Lyfoung's *Phagna Norapamok General Vang Pao*. An eulogy of the late General Vang Pao, which was printed during his funeral service. Fresno, Ca., Feb. 2011.
- Perry L. Lamy's *Barrel Roll, 1963-73: An Air Campaign in Support of National Policy*. Air War College: Alabama, 1995.
- Richard Reeves' *President Kennedy: Profile of Power*. Simon and Schuster: New York, 1994.
- Roger Warner's *Back Fire: The CIA's Secret War in Laos and Its Link to the War in Vietnam*. Simon and Schuster: New York, 1995.
- Sandra Millett's *The Hmong of Southeast Asia*. Lerner Publications: Minneapolis, 2002.
- Sisouk Vang. *Interview*. Minnesota, 2011.
- *Special Guerrilla Units Veterans & Families of USA*. St. Paul, Minnesota, 2010.
- Thomas L. Ahern's *Undercover Armies: CIA and Surrogate Warfare in Laos, 1961-1973*. Center for the Study of Intelligence, CIA, 2006.
- Thua Vang. *Interview*. California, 2010.
- W. Courtland Robinson's *Terms of Refugee: Indochinese Exodus and International Response*. Zed Books, 2000.
- William M. Leary's *CIA Air Operations in Laos, 1955-1975*. Center for the Study of Intelligence, CIA. Retrieved from www.cia.gov in 2006.
- U.S. Senator Norm Coleman. "Coleman hosts first ever meeting between Hmong leader General Vang Pao and senior State Department official." January 2004. Retrieved from www.coleman.state.gov.
- Wa Chong Vang. *Interview*. California, 2012.
- Xang Vang. *Interview*. Minnesota, 2000s.
- Zong Lia Vang. *Interview*. Texas, 2010.
- Newspapers: *Bangkok Post, Fresno Bee, Hmong Times, Hmong Today, Sacramento Bee, St. Paul Pioneer Press, [Minneapolis] Star Tribune, The New York Times*.

Vang Pao Elementary School was opened for
student enrollment in 2012 in Fresno, California.

AN ILLUSTRATION OF HIS REMARKABLE LIFE

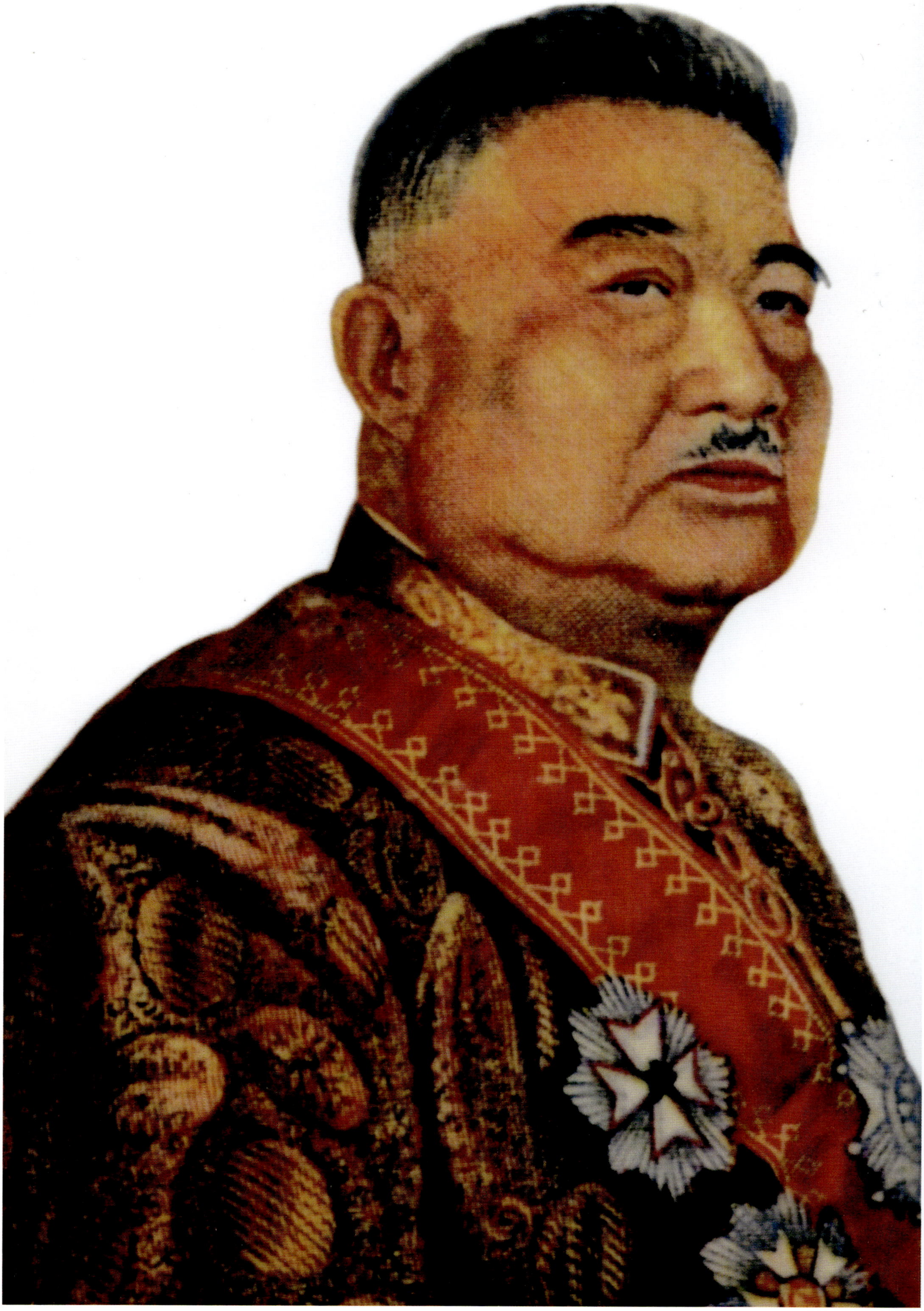

King Sisavang Phoulivong

left
King Sisavang Phoulivong, *also known as King Sisavang Vong*, was born in Luang Prabang, Laos, in 1888 and ruled the entire country from 1946 to 1959. After his death in 1959 his son, Sisavang Vatthana, was crowned King of Laos. The first King of Laos was King Fa Ngum, then known as the Kingdom of Lan Xang (or land of "Million Elephants"), founded around 1353. King Setthathirat ruled the country after King Ngum and promoted the establishment of Buddhism in the country in the 16th century. Laos then was divided into three kingdoms: Champassak (1700-1946), Vientiane (1707-1828), and Luang Prabang (1707-1946). Each kingdom was ruled by a different king until 1946 when the three kingdoms were unified under one monarch, King Sisavang Vong, with the Royal Lao Capital located in Luang Prabang. The three-headed elephant flag, *above*, symbolized the unity of the three kingdoms of Laos.

NOAH VANG COLLECTION

King Sisavang Vatthana

"The Lao People reject Communist ideology because it runs counter to their soul and assaults their principles, their institutions and culture."

* * *

HIS MAJESTY SISAVANG VATTHANA
KING OF LAOS
LETTER TO PRESIDENT JOHN F. KENNEDY
VIENTIANE, LAOS
MARCH 27, 1962
WWW.JFKLIBRARY.ORG

right
King Sisavang Vatthana was born on November 13, 1907, and became the 6th and last king to rule Laos, from 1959 until 1975 when Royalty was abolished by the incoming Communist Pathet Lao regime. The majority of the Royal Lao family members were forced into exile; those remaining, including the King's wife Queen Khamphoui and Crown Prince Vong Savang, were captured and sent to re-education camps in Sam Neua Province, Laos, where they died from torture or chronic illness.

LT. COLONEL YANG NENGLO COLLECTION

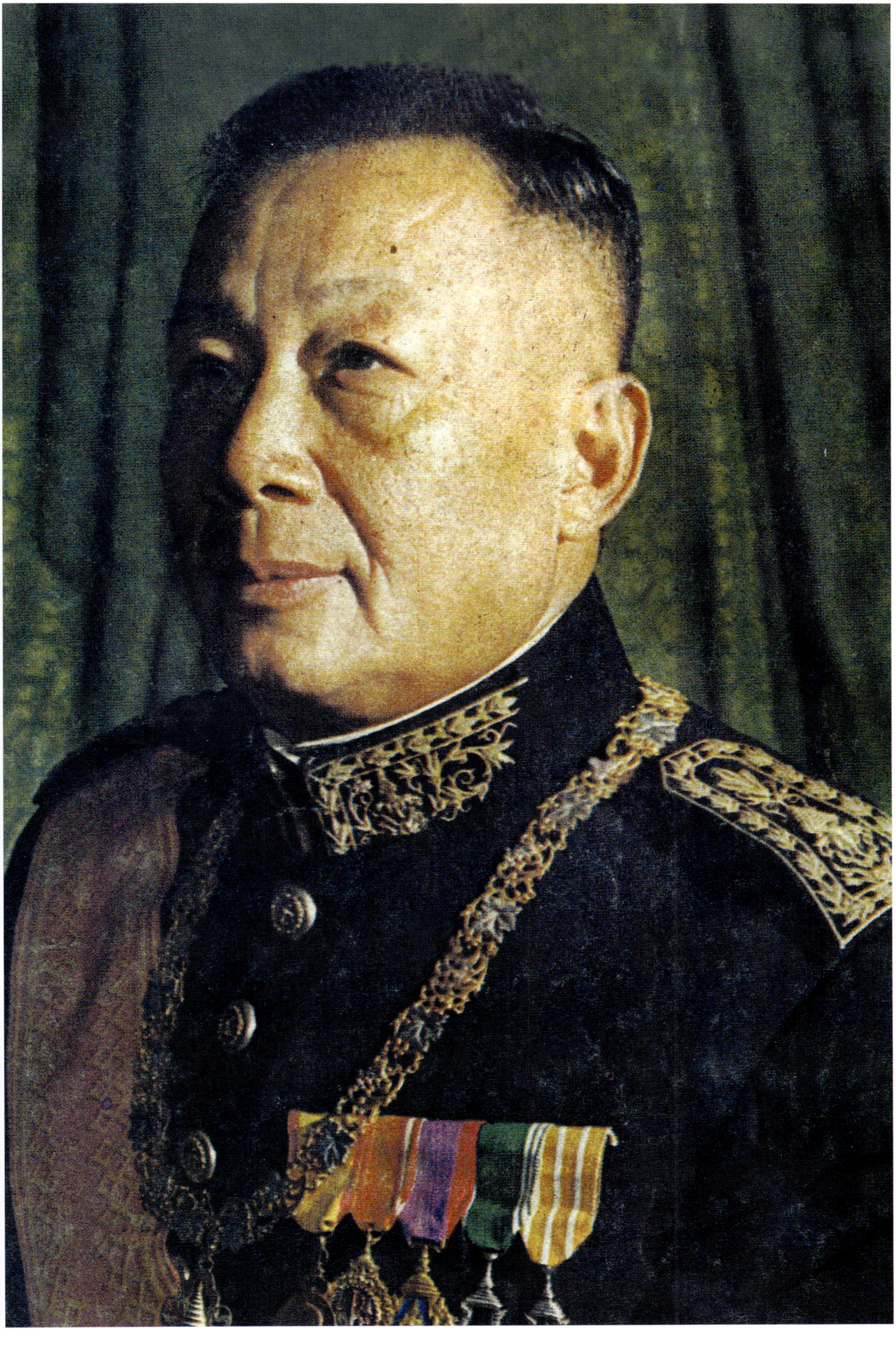

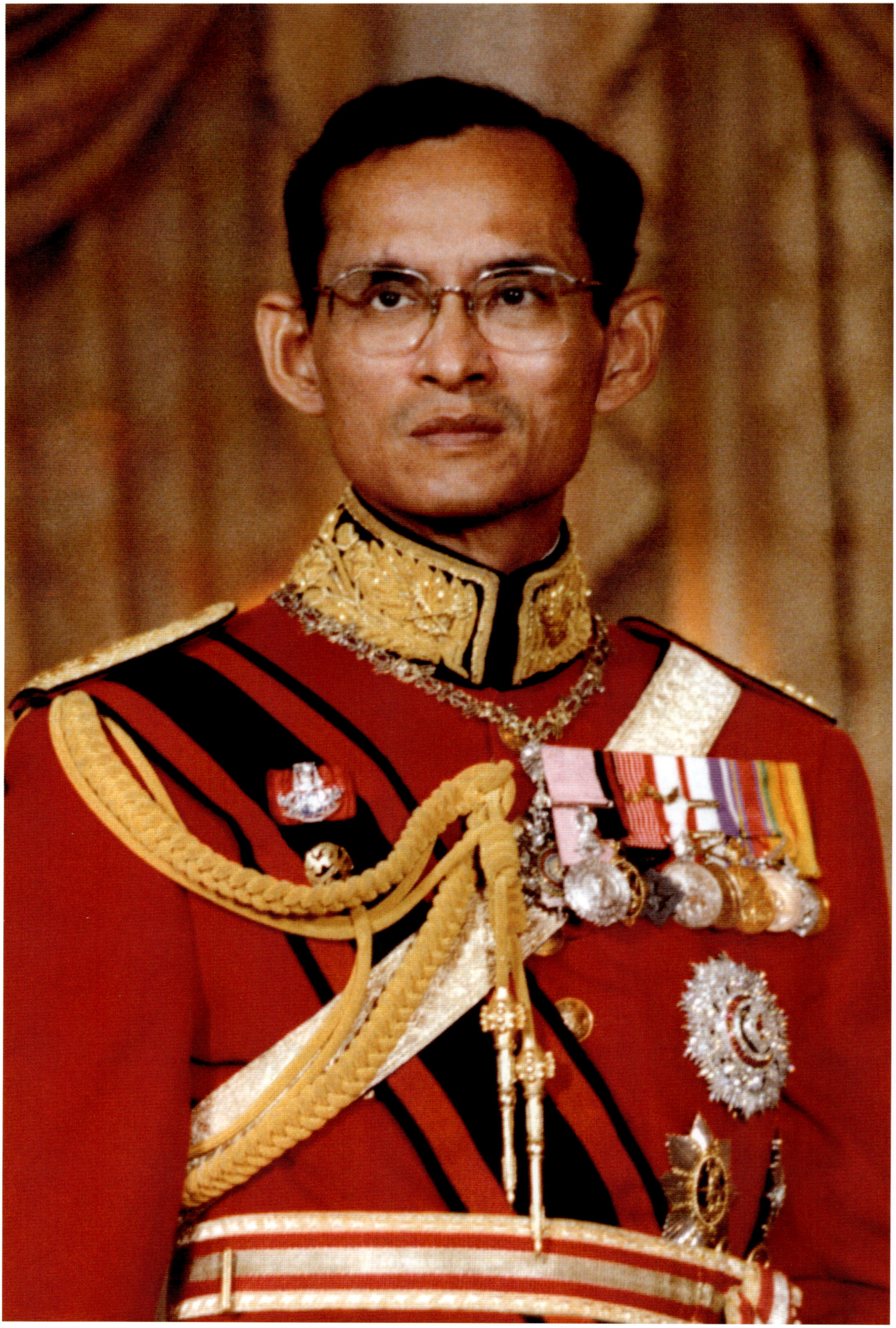

King Bhumibol Adulyadej

"His Majesty of Thailand [King Bhumibol Adulyadej] supported General Vang Pao's efforts in Laos. Freedom was important to them both. The King stated that Communism was wrong for Laos and absolutely wrong for his country. He didn't want Communists spilling over into his kingdom. The King had granted his Thai troops to help us because he knew Vang Pao would defend Laos completely, the best he could...

"The King and our Hmong leader General Vang Pao shared a special relationship. Vang Pao had helped the King before in dealing with the Hmong issues in his country. Vang Pao traveled to Thailand and told his Hmong of Thailand to be loyal to the kingdom, country and be productive citizens. They cooperated."

* * *

COLONEL VANG GEU
REPHRASING H.R.H. KING BHUMIBOL ADULYADEJ'S
CONVERSATION WITH GENERAL VANG PAO DURING THEIR VISIT
TO THAILAND IN 1972
AUTHOR'S INTERVIEW
NORTH CAROLINA
RETRIEVED ON JULY 2012

left
King Bhumibol Adulyadej of the Kingdom of Thailand. *Above*, the flag of Thailand.

ASSOCIATED PRESS COLLECTION

An Illustration of His Remarkable Life

THE PHUTONG NENG CHU VANG FAMILY TREE

1ST GENERATION
Lived and farmed in China.
Late 1700s

Xia Chai Vang — married — Unknown

children

2ND GENERATION
Migrated from China to Laos. Many left China due to wars and oppressions.
Early 1800s

Pa Ker Vang
son, wife is unknown

children

3RD GENERATION
First generation of children born and/or raised in Laos. They were part of the beginning of French occupation in Indochina. Many men in their generation were involved in and witnessed the Madman's War, led by Pa Chay Vue (1919-1921) that had a ripple effect on the borders of Laos and Vietnam.
Late 1800s to mid-1900s

Nhia Gao Vang	Chue Lue Vang	Phutong Chia Long Vang	Blia Vue Vang
son	son	son	son

4TH GENERATION
General Vang Pao's generation. They were children of World Wars I & II and the Cold War. Laos gained independence from France. They were involved in the Secret War in Laos, a part of the Vietnam conflict that affected the entire Southeast Asian region.
Early 1900s to 1975

Song Thao

children

Doua Vang	Nao Tou Vang	Gen. Vang Pao	Pa Vu Vang	Mao Vang	Chia Vang	Ying Vang	Cha Vang	Va Vang
son	son, married to Miss Mai Nao Lyfoung	son	son, married to Miss Shoua Thao	daughter, married Mr. Nhia Teng Yang	daughter, married to Mr. Pa Xao Thao	daughter, married to Mr. Bliatou Vue	daughter, married to Col. Neng Chue Thao	daughter, married to Mr. Cha Ger Yang

79

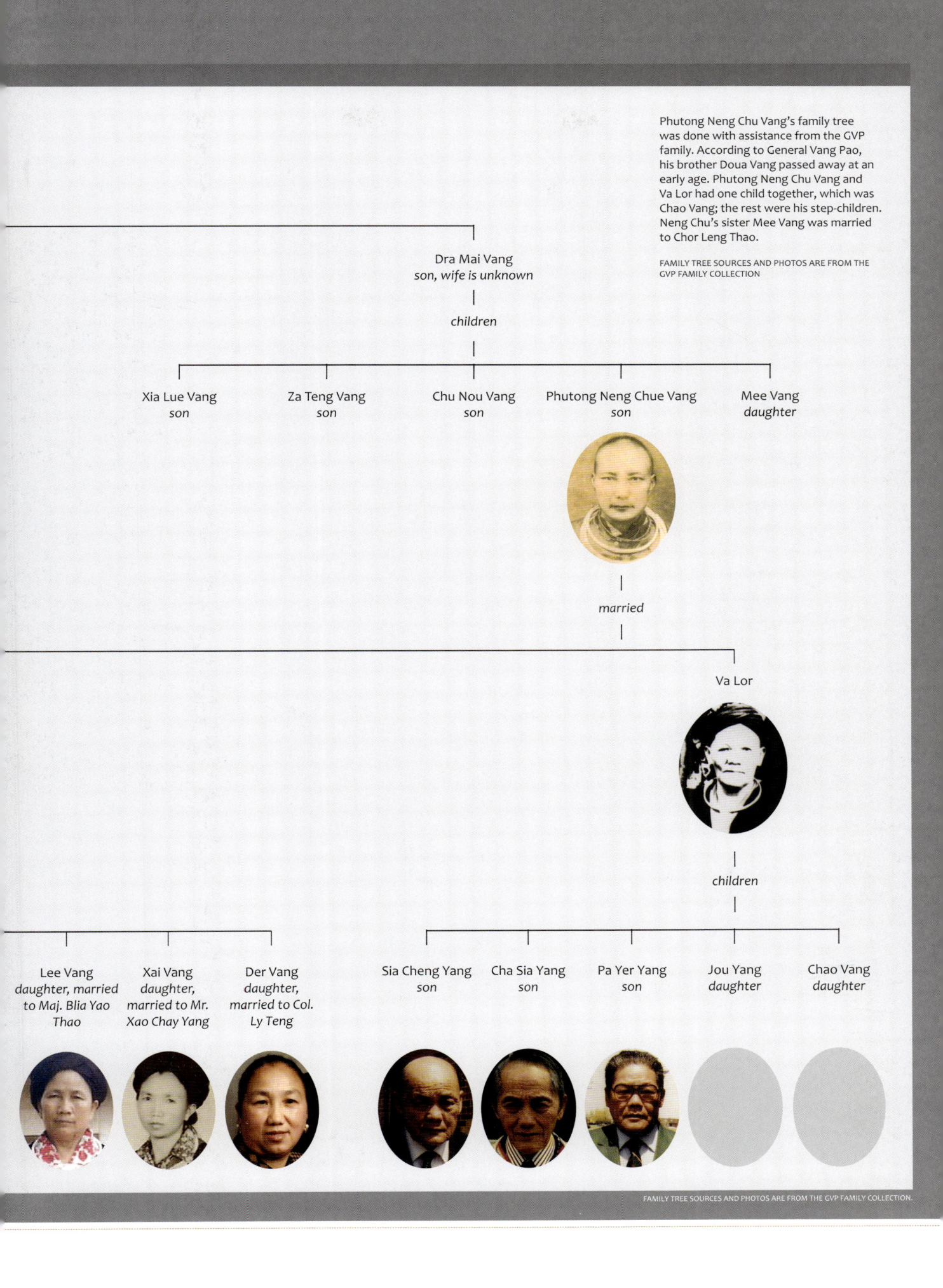

Phutong Neng Chu Vang's family tree was done with assistance from the GVP family. According to General Vang Pao, his brother Doua Vang passed away at an early age. Phutong Neng Chu Vang and Va Lor had one child together, which was Chao Vang; the rest were his step-children. Neng Chu's sister Mee Vang was married to Chor Leng Thao.

FAMILY TREE SOURCES AND PHOTOS ARE FROM THE GVP FAMILY COLLECTION

Dra Mai Vang
son, wife is unknown

children

- **Xia Lue Vang** *son*
- **Za Teng Vang** *son*
- **Chu Nou Vang** *son*
- **Phutong Neng Chue Vang** *son*
- **Mee Vang** *daughter*

married

Va Lor

children

- **Lee Vang** *daughter, married to Maj. Blia Yao Thao*
- **Xai Vang** *daughter, married to Mr. Xao Chay Yang*
- **Der Vang** *daughter, married to Col. Ly Teng*
- **Sia Cheng Yang** *son*
- **Cha Sia Yang** *son*
- **Pa Yer Yang** *son*
- **Jou Yang** *daughter*
- **Chao Vang** *daughter*

FAMILY TREE SOURCES AND PHOTOS ARE FROM THE GVP FAMILY COLLECTION.

An Illustration of His Remarkable Life

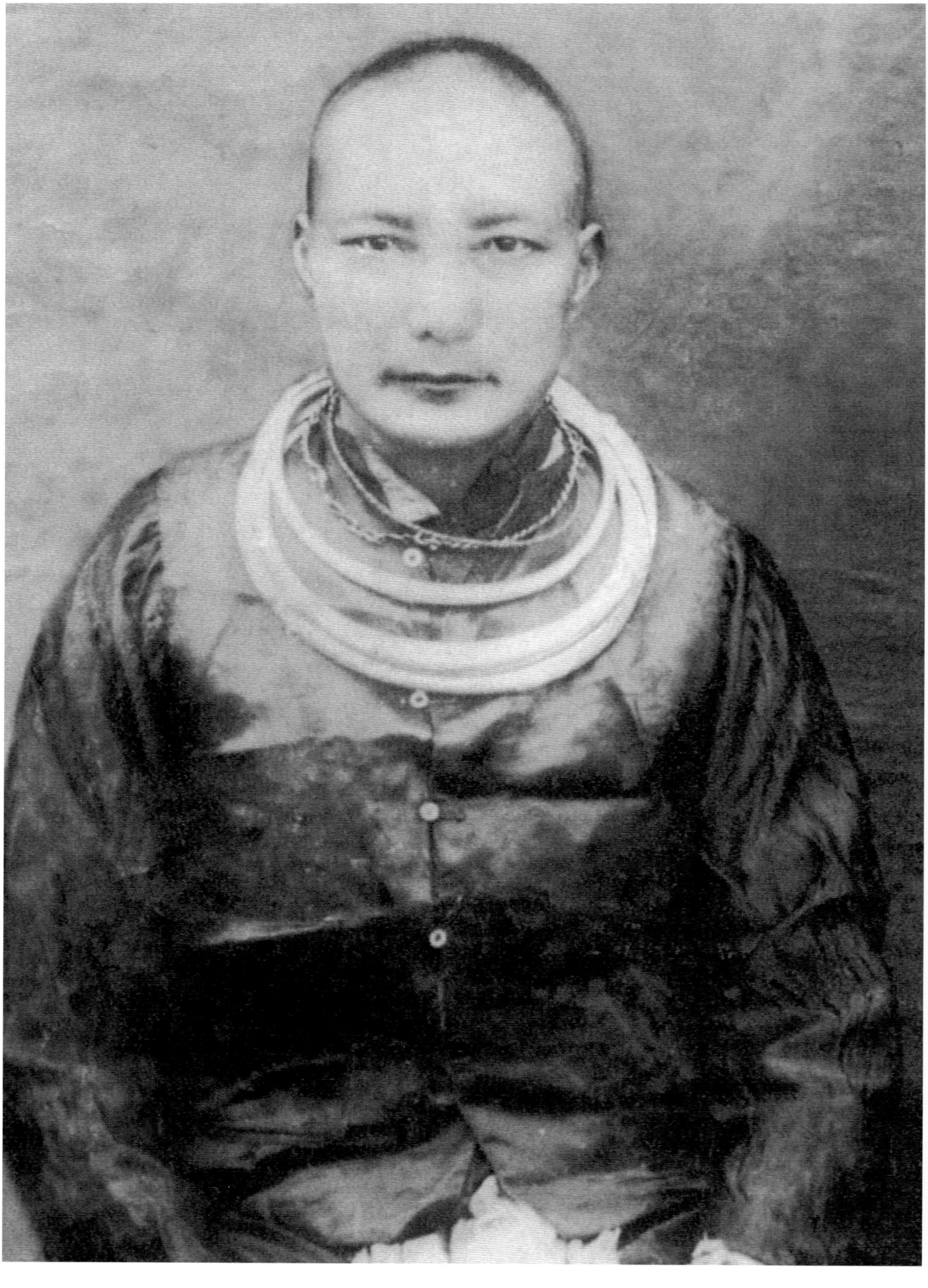

"My best friend in the family was my father. After my father had a second wife [Va Lor], who was the descendant of Kiatong Lor Bliayao and had a previous marriage with the Hmong Yang, she had four children and brought them to my family. Her youngest son who also had the same age as I did, we were considered the best brothers and friends like who shared the same biological parents.

"In our family, we did not plan to lead the Hmong people. However, since one is born as a Hmong, one has the desire to help the Hmong people. Because after the Hmong fled from China, there were so many problems. It was not like when the Hmong once lived in China. Since I grew up and realized how the Hmong life had been, I began to trace the Hmong life. One needs to know how Hmong life came about. So first, that is the priority.

"My father was not literate. However, he knew the law. He knew the difference between supreme laws and statutes. He was an honest man. He never helps these cousins or outsiders when it comes to justice. One who is found guilty must be punished. Who is innocent must be innocent. The only help he could do was to provide rice, animals, and other property values to help the guilty to relief his punishment, but never to arbitrarily help anyone in order to win a case. He never did... Therefore, regardless of good or bad, one must try to be good citizen role model to lead the Hmong people. Therefore, one must try to lead the Hmong in every possible way so that everybody can have a life."

* * *

GENERAL VANG PAO
INTERVIEW
MAY 1999
RETRIEVED FROM THE HMONG ARCHIVES
DECEMBER 5, 2010

Kuv tus phooj ywg zoo tshaj hauv kuv tsev neeg yog kuv txiv. Tom qab kuv txiv muaj niam yau lawm, uas yog Vab Lauj, yog Kiab Toom Lauj Npliaj Yob tus ntxhais; nws tus txiv tom ntej ub yog xeem Yaj ces nws tau coj plaub tug me nyuam los nrog peb tsev neeg nyob thaum nws yuav kuv txiv lawm. Nws tus tub yau muaj hnub nyoog ib yam li kuv. Wb yog ob tug zoo phooj ywg thiab kwv tij tam li yog niam txiv ib plab yug.

Nyob hauv peb tsev neeg, peb tsis xav tias yuav muaj tus tau ua Hmoob tus thawj coj, tab sis vim tias yug los ua ib tug Hmoob lawm yus yuav tsum muaj lub siab los pab Hmoob. Yav tom qab Hmoob khiav tawm hauv tebchaws Tuamtshoj los lawm kuj muaj teeb meem ntau heev thiab. Lub neej tsis zoo li thaum Hmoob nyob Tuamtshoj teb lawm. Txij thaum ntawd los, kuv loj hlob tuaj thiaj paub meej tias qhov tseeb ntawm Hmoob lub neej zoo li cas tiag. Kuv thiaj pib taug Hmoob keeb kwm. Yus yuav tsum paub tias Hmoob tawm qhov twg los, ntawd yog thawj kauj ruam.

Kuv txiv yeej tsis paub ntaub paub ntawv, tab sis nws paub txog lub tebchaws txoj cai thiab paub txog txoj cai tswj tib neeg. Nws yog ib tug neeg ncaj ncees. Nws yeej tsis pab cov txheeb ze los yog cov sab nraud yog thaum txiav txim tuaj lawm. Tus tsis txhaum yeej tsis raug txim, tus txhaum ces yeej raug txim, tiamsi yog tus raug txim lawm ces nws yeej pab lawv tsev neeg kom tau noj tau haus thiab. Li ntawd, txawm yuav zoo thiab phem los nws yeej ua ib tug pej xeem zoo thiab ua tus qauv zoo los coj haiv neeg Hmoob rau txhua txoj kev kom txhua tus muaj lub neej ua.

(TRANSLATION - LUS TXHAIS)

left
Phutong Neng Chu Vang, General Vang Pao's father. Photo taken in the mid-1940s.

THE GVP FAMILY COLLEaCTION VIA LANG VANG

"Making a living is very hard. At that time, our Hmong were very poor. It was not just our family. The whole Hmong population in Nong Het area was very poor. After I came back from school, I talked to my mom. I said, 'Mom, you and dad, your way of life seems very difficult. When your children, all of us, grow up we will be poor too because when we grow up we want to have adequate subsistence needs like food and clothing. We also want to have money. We cannot even grow banana plants. We cannot even grow sugar cane. We can only grow maize and opium poppy.'

"As for the elderly, they all grew opium poppy more than anything else because there were no other alternatives. No idea. Only grow opium to trade for fabrics, silk, candies, and other food items with the Vietnamese merchants. That was the elderly's idea.

"My mother worked very hard. My mother worked the most and was skilled in every area including the men's roles. What did she do the most? She could do things like wood bucket, rice cooking pot, make dust pan and broom, use axes to cut giant trees, she could do all.

"Her crop field covered about the length of three mountains and three valleys. It was not a small field at all."

* * *
GENERAL VANG PAO
INTERVIEW
MAY 1999
RETRIEVED FROM THE HMONG ARCHIVES
DECEMBER 5, 2010

Ua lub neej nyob tsis yog yooj yim. Thaum lub caij ntawd peb Hmoob tseem txom txom nyem. Kuj tsis yog peb tsev neeg xwb, tag nrho tsoom Hmoob nyob rau Looj Hej (Nong Het) kuj txom nyem heev. Tom qab kuv mus kawm ntawv los, kuv nrog kuv niam tham, kuv hais rau kuv niam tias, 'Koj thiab txiv neb txoj kev ua neej ntxim li nyuaj heev - thaum neb cov me nyuam uas yog peb sawv daws loj tuaj peb yuav txom nyeem li neb thiab, vim thaum peb loj hlob tuaj peb xav kom peb muaj noj muaj haus muaj nyiaj muaj txiaj thiab pab tau peb tus kheej.'

Raws lis cov laus lub neej feem coob lawv tsuas xav txog qhov cog maj thiab yaj yeeb coj los mus pauv ntawm Mab Suav thiab Nyab Laj kom tau ntaub xo, mov noj thiab nyiaj txiag xwb. Tom ntej no peb yuav tsum hloov es los mus cog lwm yam qoob loo xws li plej los mus rau txiv hmab txiv ntoo.

Kuv niam yog ib tug niam tsev zoo, nws paub ua txhua yam, nws ua tau txiv neej tej luag hauj lwm tib si. Nws txawj txua thoob, txawj txua tsu cub mov, txawj hiab khaub hruab, txawj txhib taws thiab txawj siv taus ntov ntoo vajkhaum tib si. Kuv niam thaj teb los loj kawg li, muaj peb roob peb ha, tsis yog me kiag li.

(TRANSLATION - LUS TXHAIS)

right
Song Thao, General Vang Pao's mother. Photo taken in the late 1960s. According to General Vang Pao, he said that his tenacity and diligence were from his mother.

THE GVP FAMILY COLLECTION VIA LANG VANG

An Illustration of His Remarkable Life 84

"I was born in 1929. In 1940, I went to a school, but it was not a formal school. I only paid the teacher to teach me. At that time, there were no teachers. There were only very few paid Laotian teachers. Even you pay, very few paid teachers were willing to come to tutor. After that, in 1942 a new school was built so I could go to that school. Before that, one only paid a tutor."

* * *

GENERAL VANG PAO
INTERVIEW
MAY 1999
RETRIEVED FROM THE HMONG ARCHIVES
DECEMBER 5, 2010

right
Vang Pao at the age of 17 or 18. At an early age he saw the struggle for equality of the Hmong, and this became his conviction to make a difference.

CHALEUNSOUK VANG COLLECTION

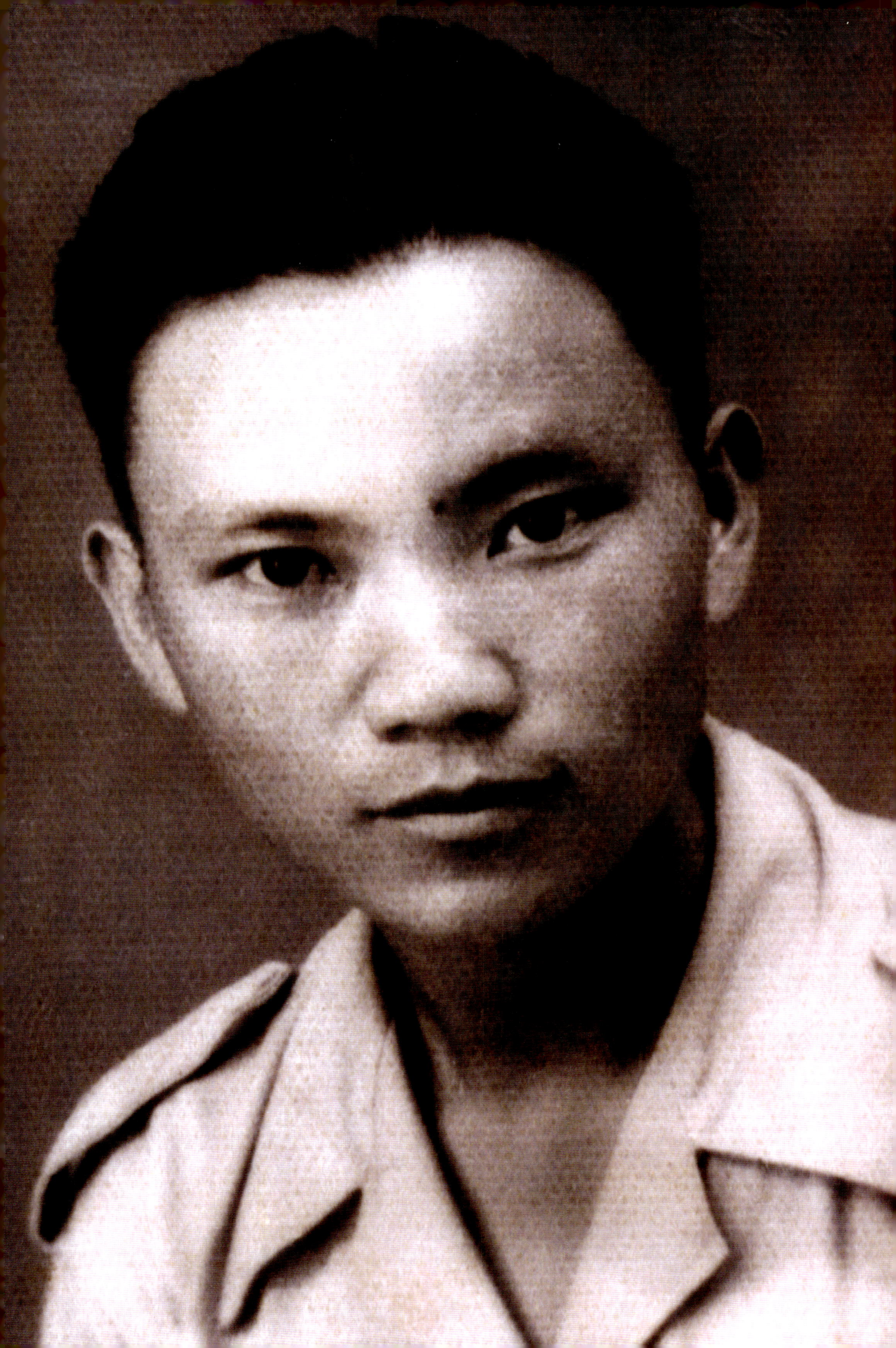

"My brother Vang Pao has always been brave. With my father's leadership, he tried to be a role model to his children. He took Vang Pao everywhere he went. By the time my brother was 13 or 14 years old, he was already handling some local Hmong problems.

"As for my oldest brother Doua, he died young. We never got the chance to know him. My brothers Nao Tou Vang and Pa Vu Vang were not really into military. Nao Tou became a Nai Ban [local village chief]. Pa Vu Vang was a devoted farmer who farmed his entire life.

"As for my brother Vang Pao, he always wanted to do the best for the people. We had a big family growing up. Each meal we cooked was like cooking to feed three families. We farmed. We raised livestock. We had horses. My dad had a favorite horse that he rode to many places. There were very limited opportunities.

"As girls, we stayed back and helped our parents. The boys were granted the chance to go to school. Plus, school was not close, so our parents did not let us attend. My father sent the boys to school."

* * *

MRS. CHAI VANG
WIFE OF MR. XAO CHAY YANG
GENERAL VANG PAO'S SISTER
NOVEMBER 2010

General Vang Pao's sister Chai Vang, her husband, Xao Chay Yang, and their children in Laos in early 1970s. Their children's names are, *left to right*, Ze Yang, Kou Yang, Kia Yang, Kao Yang, and Chao Yang.

CHAI VANG COLLECTION

Song Thao and her daughter Der Vang in Montana in 1981. Der Vang took this photo with her mother while she visited her ailing mother in Woodside, Montana.

COLONEL LY TENG COLLECTION

"As a child, my brother Vang Pao was a talkative and extremely outgoing person. Our father taught him to have good manners in and around the house when we had guests over. He was very good at receiving house guests. He shook their hands. He directed them to sit. He was polite. On the other hand, he joked a lot. I heard people refer to him as 'Pov Dag', or Pao the Joker. He never liked school much. When we packed him lunch for school, he usually took it somewhere else and finished his food before he came home.

"Things changed when he joined the French army. We hardly saw him anymore. Maybe once or twice a year. He was very dedicated to the military. He always stayed in Xieng Khouang; that was the city where the soldiers were trained. When he had gone away to Mouang Hiem to fight, the Vietnamese soldiers were scared of him and the French armies. They had guns. The Vietnamese soldiers did not, only a few had weapons. They were poor and underprivileged soldiers. When the Vietnamese soldiers retreated back to Nong Het, they would say that they had killed Vang Pao, or he was dead. We never believed them nor replied to anything. They would gossip to the locals, 'The Hmong have no more Vang Pao.' But in our hearts, we knew that they were not telling the truth. As the war in Laos progressed, my brother cared a lot for our safety and moved us from our old city of Nong Het, which borders Vietnam, to Xieng Khouang."

* * *

MRS. DER VANG
GENERAL VANG PAO'S SISTER &
WIFE OF COLONEL LY TENG
AUTHOR'S INTERVIEW
NOVEMBER 2010

"My father Phutong Neng Chu Vang saw how poor and how uneducated the Hmong people were in Nong Het. He didn't want his family and children to be poor. This motivated him to become a Hmong leader. He also sent us to school so we could be smart and care for our family when we were older."

**
GENERAL VANG PAO
AUTHOR'S INTERVIEW
SEPTEMBER 2005

Kuv txiv Phub Toom Neej Tswb Vaj hais tias tsoom Hmoob nyob Looj Hej (Nong Het) txom nyem thiab tsis muaj kev kawm. Nws tsis xav kom nws tsev neeg thiab tej me nyuam txom nyem. Vim pom Hmoob tej kev txom nyem no thiaj ua rau nws mob siab hlo los peem thiaj tsheej los ua Hmoob ib tug thawj coj. Tsis tas li ntawd, kuv txiv thiaj xa peb mus kawm ntawv kom peb txawj ntse thiaj pab tau peb tsev neeg thaum peb loj hlob tuaj.

(TRANSLATION - LUS TXHAIS)

After Touby Lyfoung was nominated as the Chaomouang Hmong (Mayor of the Hmong) and with the newly appointed Hmong Tassengs and Phutongs (local government officials), they were invited by the French Administration to be introduced and inauguarated in the town of Xiengkhouangville, Xieng Kouang Province, Laos, in 1948.

Standing, left to right: Nai Kong Youa Pao Yang, Chong Vue Chang (Phutong Nong Het), Lee Vang, Chue Chao Lee (Phutong Phavene), Xai Chao Yang (Naiban Hintong), Nai Kong Xia Xang Moua, Nao Yee Yang (Tasseng Phou Fa), Shoua Toua Lee (Tasseng Keng Khouay), Chia Vang Xiong (Tasseng Phak Leung), and Tong Kai Xiong (Tasseng Phou Sa Ngob). *Sitting, left to right*: Pa Lue Lee (Phutong Phak Boun), Neng Chu Vang, Tasseng Touby Lyfoung, Nao Chao Lee (Tasseng Phak Boun), Lee Xiong (Tasseng Phou Da Pho), and Youa Chao Xiong (Tasseng Navang).

COLONEL LY TENG COLLECTION

An Illustration of His Remarkable Life

"My second in command is a rather tall and cumbersome guy with a triangular face below a wide forehead. First Lieutenant Vang Pao has greatly changed since his first day with the Foreign Legion as a tracker against the Japanese along the colonial route 7. After 9 years of guerrilla [training], he has become as hard and ascetic as the enemy. The young '[Hmong]' officer barely smiles, don't eat much and almost never sleeps. Cold, almost rigid, with a little despising fold on his thin lips, his arms often crossed, he looks like one of these mystical warriors. Despite an obvious humility, he is actually a tiger ready to attack."

* * *

MAX MESNIER
1953
PRESENTATION BY ERIC CHEVREUIL
RETRIEVED FROM KACHOUAZ LYFOUNG
FEBRUARY 2011

right
Vang Pao being promoted to a Lieutenant in the French Army.

ERIC CHEVREUIL COLLECTION

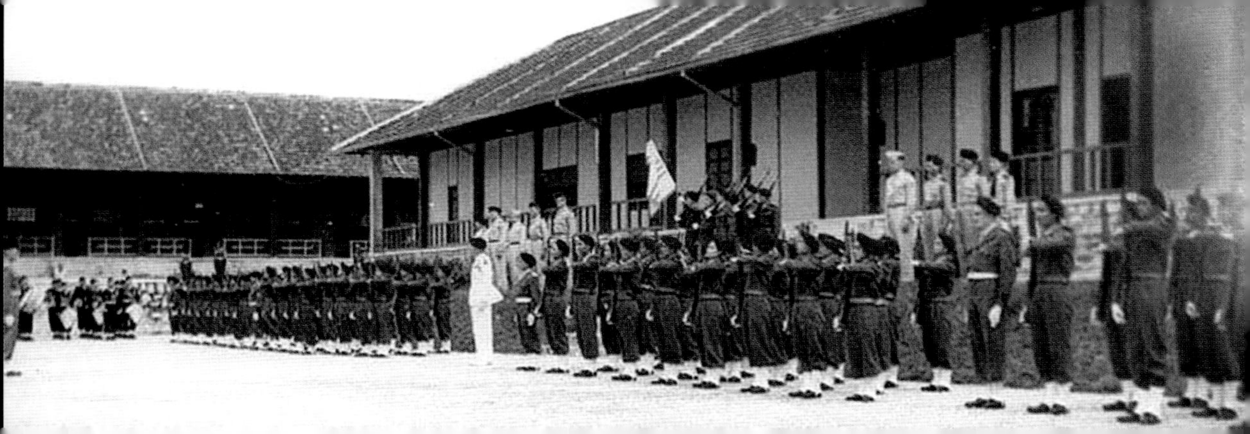

This banner represented Vang Pao's French military unit Group Commandos No. 200 in the early 1950s. After the French left Laos, Colonel Max Mesnier took this flag with him. In 2010, he returned this flag to Vang Pao at their reunion in St. Paul, Minnesota. The inner symbol is a Hmong men's necklace encircling a black cougar, which represented strength.

SGU—MINNESOTA CHAPTER COLLECTION

"The history of the Hmong is long, rich, and exciting. But before the Vietnam War era the Hmong's history and the Hmong were 'little known' to anyone in the civilized world. We lived very simple lives throughout Southern China and into Southeast Asia."

* * *

GENERAL VANG PAO
SPEECH AT THE CENTER FOR HMONG STUDIES
CONCORDIA UNIVERSITY
JUNE 28, 2005
RETRIEVED FROM LEE PAO XIONG
OCTOBER 2010

Haiv neeg Hmoob thiab peb tej txheej txheem keeb kwm kab lis kev cai yeej muaj los ntev tau ntau txhiab xyoo lawm nyob rau hauv Tuamtshoj tebchaws yav qab teb thiab hauv cov tebchaws Asia yav qab teb hnub tuaj. Ua ntej thaum nthwv tsov nrog Nyab Laj Cob Tsib, neeg Hmoob ua lub neej yooj yim nyob ntsiag to, tim lo lis ntawd lwm haiv neeg vam meej nyob ntiaj teb thiaj tsis paub txog peb Hmoob.

(TRANSLATION - LUS TXHAIS)

In Laos, with the assistance of the French military officers, Touby Lyfoung was able to recruit Hmong and Laotian soldiers into the French Army in the Nong Het region. Among those who Touby saw that had potential in the army was Vang Pao. *From left to right*: Commandant Sang, Captain Vang Pao, Governor of Xieng Khouang Province Prince Saykham Southakakoumal, and Hmong Mayor Touby Lyfoung inspecting Hmong soldiers in the city of Xieng Khouang in 1954.

VAJTSUA SHOUA YANG COLLECTION

An Illustration of His Remarkable Life

Lt. Vang Pao and his squad of Hmong soldiers readied to pursue North Vietnamese Viet Minh troops in the Nong Het district in 1953. His nephew Thong Vang, *in white hat*, was shot and killed at Phou Nong Sam Che. Vang Pao was wounded by a gun shot while attempting to save his nephew.

        Since the day Vang Pao joined the French military, he had earned himself a reputation as being a fearless fighter and willing to lead into combat against the Pathet Lao and North Vietnamese Viet Minh forces. His fighting skills even earned him praise from the Viet Minh leader, Ho Chi Minh.

VAJTSUAS SHOUA YANG COLLECTION

"Vang Pao is a great fighter."

* * *

HO CHI MINH
LEADER OF THE NORTH VIETNAMESE COMMUNIST PARTY
"THE 1945-1975 WAR IN LAOS & THE PLIGHT OF THE LAO REFUGEES"
WRITTEN BY GEU VANG
FORMER COLONEL OF THE ROYAL LAO ARMY
PAGE 37

"It has been so long that I forgot their names. But for every men who had fought alongside me, they were warriors."

**
GENERAL VANG PAO
AUTHOR'S INTERVIEW
NOVEMBER 2010

Nws ntev heev los lawm uas kuv nco tsis tau sawv daws cov npe, tab sis txhua txhua tus uas tau nrog kuv ua tsov ua rog, lawv yog Hmoob cov neeg muaj peev xwm, tshaj lij thiab muaj nuj nqi.

(TRANSLATION - LUS TXHAIS)

Captain Vang Pao along with two Hmong soldiers prepared to head to Dien Bien Phu in 1954.

YANG ENG COLLECTION

right
After the Hmong soldiers completed their military trainings in the French army, each soldier received a postcard, signed by French General Jean de Lattre, expressing his well wishes for their future military careers. General Lattre was the commander of the French troops during the First Indochina War. This postcard was issued to Nenglo Yang, whose nickname was Ba Pha Lao, in late 1954. Nenglo Yang later fought in the Secret War and was promoted to the rank of a Lieutenant Colonel.

LT. COLONEL NENGLO YANG COLLECTION

Le général de Lattre vous envoie, mon cher BA.pha.Lao ses vœux affectueux et les meilleurs.

J. de Lattre

Noël 1951
1er Janvier 1952

Jean Sassi was a former French Army Colonel, who led Captain Vang Pao and his troops to assist the French Expeditionary Force at Dien Bien Phu in 1954. Sassi was the maquis chief through the Groupement de Commandos Mixtes Aéroportés in French Indochina.

VAJTSUA SHOUA YANG COLLECTION

"Under the command of Captain Sassi, I left with four hundred Hmong and regular supporters to Sam Neua. Objective: Dien Bien Phu."

* * *
VANG PAO
"LES HMONG DU LAOS 1945-1975
LEUR ENGAGEMENT DANS LES GUERRES D'INDOCHINE AUX
CÔTÉS DES OCCIDENTAUX : ENJEUX ET RÉALITÉS"
BY GRALL TIPHANIE
16 JUIN 2006

Major Vang Pao with Jack F. Mathews, an advisor to the Program Evaluation Office (PEO) and military advisor of the Royal Lao Army in Nong Het, Xieng Khouang Province, Laos in July 1960. Major Vang Pao was the 10th Infantry Battalion Commander. The two met in December 1958.

KONG XIONG COLLECTION

"The first American I met was Jack Mathews. He came from the Program Evaluation Office. He arrived before the country was in full scale civil war. He first came to meet me and asked if I needed anything. I asked him to bring clothes and transistor communication radios. That was how I got those radios. He also donated some Carbine rifles. He also asked if the Hmong needed any winter jackets. I said, 'Yes.' The Hmong were poor and had no clothing.

"I would greatly appreciate and thank you for those gifts, if you could bring them in,' I told him. Then he distributed salt and clothes to the villagers. In doing so, the Hmong rallied into one unified voice."

＊＊

GENERAL VANG PAO
INTERVIEW MAY 1999
RETRIEVED FROM THE HMONG ARCHIVES
DECEMBER 5, 2010

Thawj tus Asmeliskas uas kuv tau ntsib yog Jack Mathews. Nws txoj hauj lwm yog tuaj soj ntsuam. Nws tuaj txog ua ntej thaum lub tebchaws Lostsuas tsis tau muaj tsov rog hnyav. Zaum xub thawj wb sib ntsib nws nug kuv tias kuv xav tau kev pab dab tsi. Kuv thov nws hais tias kom nws pab ris tsho hnav thiab xov tooj tuaj rau peb. Yog li ntawd, kuv thiaj li tau cov xov tooj coj los siv. Tsis tas li ntawd, nws kuj pub tau ib cov phom Carbine thiab. Ntxiv ntawd, nws nug seb Hmoob puas xav tau cov tsho tiv no. Kuv teb tias, 'Xav tau.' Vim Hmoob txom nyem thiab tsis muaj ris tsho sov hnav. Kuv hais rau Jack tias kuv yuav zoo siab heev thiab ua tsaug ntau rau koj tej khoom pub, yog tias koj nqa tau tuaj pab rau peb.

Ces nws thiaj thauj ntsev thiab ris tsho hnav tuaj rau cov zos Hmoob. Vim li ntawd, tsoom Hmoob thiaj li los sib koom tes ua ib pab ib pawg hais ib lo lus lawm xwb.

(TRANSLATION - LUS TXHAIS)

An Illustration of His Remarkable Life

Throughout 1960, this Air America aircraft Helio Courier #183 was used by PEO Advisor Jack Mathews and Major Vang Pao to travel to remote regions in MR II to meet with ally forces. Their pilot was Ron Sutphin. Upon Major Vang Pao's meeting with Hmong clan leaders in these different places, he addressed the importance of banding into paramilitary groups to fight against the Communist NVA and Pathet Lao forces invading their homeland.

KONG XIONG COLLECTION

Several days after the conversation between Major Vang Pao and PEO Advisor Jack F. Mathews, Mathews ordered an AAM C-47 to drop off clothes, rice, and salt to the Hmong villages as requested by Major Vang Pao. This delivery of supplies earned Major Vang Pao the trust and support of the Hmong, for which they later became his soldiers in MR II.

KONG XIONG COLLECTION

An Illustration of His Remarkable Life 104

The day Vang came into power: "On October 7, 1960, Vang Pao came to me, Toulu Moua Chongtoua, Nai Kong (local government official) over the three districts of Xieng Khouang Province, and said, 'Toulu, take the jeep and Lee Wakai with you and go to the airport. Soon there is going to be a very important military man coming from Vientiane. When he arrives I want you to arrest him and bring him to the mess hall.'

"I then dispatched Nai Kong Xiong Pao Lee and his 100 soldiers to the airport. At 9:00AM General Amkha Soukhavong, Commander of the Laotian Army Northern Zone, arrived in a Dakota DC-3.

"When the plane landed, I approached the entrance. As the door opened, General Amkha appeared with two guards at his side.

"Although I noticed that the General had a pistol strapped to his waist, I instructed, 'General, I need you to get into my jeep as there has been a change of plan.' The General reached for his revolver. Swiftly, Lee Wakai slapped the gun out of his hand. Amkha's two guards rushed to his defense.

"Lee Wakai back-handed one and punched the other sending them both tumbling backwards. Xiong Pao's soldiers quickly wrestled them to the ground. I then ordered the General to sit in the front passenger side of the jeep. I told Lee Wakai to get in the back seat with a rifle, an eight shooter (*phom yim teg*), and hold it to the General's head. I ordered, 'If he doesn't move nothing will happen but if he flinches … shoot him.'

"The General inquired, 'Who wants to meet with me?' I replied, 'Soon enough a very important man will come to speak with you.'

"I left Xiong Pao and his men to secure the plane and drove the General to the mess hall. I met up with Vang Pao and informed him that I've arrested General Amkha. Vang Pao stood up and rushed to telephone General Phoumi Nosavan that General Amkha was under house arrest.

"From that moment on, news of the coup d'état had quickly spread throughout the mountains. Hmong men arrived from all corners of Northern Laos requesting guns and knives."

* * *

COLONEL TOULU MOUA CHONGTOUA
FORMER CHIEF FINANCIAL OFFICER, MILITARY INSPECTOR AND ADVISOR IN MILITARY REGION II
RETRIEVED FROM CHONG JONES
APRIL 2013

In late 1960, Kong Le's coup and Communist movement on the Plain of Jars caused Vang Pao and his men to retreat to Tha Vieng to regroup. This location was where CIA operative James W. Lair and Thai PARU Colonel Pranet Ritruechai met with Vang Pao to form an alliance to fight against Communist forces. Left to right (front row): Toulu Moua Chongtoua, Lo Seng, Vang Pao, Youa Pao Xiong, and Cher Pao Moua. They all became military leaders throughout the war.

THE GVP FAMILY COLLECTION

An Illustration of His Remarkable Life

"I had my first contact with the Hmong when I worked in Thailand. They came from the mountains to the cities during the day, and returned [home] before dusk. They never stayed overnight. They said they were scared of the devil. At first, I didn't know what they meant. Soon I found out that one of the main causes of death in their population were from contacts with diseases passed by mosquitoes.

"However, their ability to trek back home impressed me. They were quick and durable people. And I knew they would be good guerrilla fighters because of their lifestyle, living up in the mountains. With the Lao leaders, there were too many quarrels between them. We needed someone who was willing to fight. We knew the Hmong well. Then we heard about Vang Pao through the Lao and Thai merchants along the Mekong River in the 1950s.

"When I met Vang Pao and the Hmong, Communism was too much against their will. I knew I needed to get there with some of my Thai personnel to assist the Hmong to resist the Communist [in Laos]. I asked Vang Pao, 'Now that the situation is as it is, what are you going to do?' Vang Pao replied, 'We cannot live with the Communist. We must fight them or run away, move to Thailand. If you would give us the weapon, we would fight them.'

"I believed him. I went to the U.S. Government to do my best to fight for the weapons they wanted. It was all extremely successful."

* * *

COLONEL JAMES W. LAIR, RETIRED
CIA OPERATIVE
SPEECH AT HMONG NEW YEAR IN 2006 &
AUTHOR'S INTERVIEW
MAY 2010

CIA operative James W. Lair in his early military career. Lair went to Thailand in 1951. His assignment was to train the Thai national police in guerrilla warfare skills. Soon, Lair converted those in his training group into the Thai Police Aerial Resupply Unit (PARU). He was very well informed of the Communist activities inside Laos. His Thai counterpart was Colonel Pranet Ritchenchai, who, in 1961, flew with Lair to meet Major Vang Pao in Ta Vieng. Throughout the Secret War in Laos, Lair's Thai PARU played a critical role supporting military and communications for the Royal Lao Army and General Vang Pao's MR II soldiers. *Right*, Lair receives one of the highest medals from H.R.H. King Bhumibol Adulyadej for his completed work with the Thai PARU and operations in Laos.

JAMES W. LAIR COLLECTION

An Illustration of His Remarkable Life 108

"Communism was spreading in our part of the world—pouring into Laos, Cambodia, and South Vietnam. We had to find a way to stop them. The U.S. had the vision to stop them from spreading into these countries.

"I aligned with the U.S. because they were the most powerful country in the world at that time. The United States had won World War I and World War II, and I assumed that winning the Vietnam War would be no problem."

**

GENERAL VANG PAO
AUTHOR'S INTERVIEW
OAKDALE, MINNESOTA
NOVEMBER 2006

"Vang Pao was naturally intelligent, an expert guerrilla fighter. That's why I sought after him."

**

COLONEL JAMES W. LAIR, RETIRED
CIA OPERATIVE DURING THE SECRET WAR
AUTHOR'S INTERVIEW
JUNE 2011

Kev cai Kooj Sam (Communist) twb hnov ncha thoob ib ncig los mus rau peb tej teb chaws tag lawm—yuav kis los rau tebchaws Lostsuas (Laos), Qhab Meem (Cambodia), thiab Nyab Laj qab teb. Peb yuav tsum nrhiav kev pab cheem kom tau. Tebchaws Ameliskas muaj zeem muag uas yuav cheem kom tau txoj kev Kooj Sam.

Kuv txiav txim siab koom tes nrog tebchaws Ameliskas, vim tias lawv yog lub tebchaws uas muaj zog tshaj nyob rau hauv ntiaj teb lub caij ntawd. Tebchaws Ameliskas twb yeej nthwv Rog Ntiaj Teb Zaum 1 (WW I) thiab Rog Ntiaj Teb Zaum 2 (WW II), kuv xav tias kev yuav yeej nthwv rog Nyab Laj Cob Tsib zaum no yuav tsis muaj teeb meem.

(TRANSLATION - LUS TXHAIS)

right
Lt. Colonel Vang Pao in Pa Dong, Laos in January 1961. This was the temporary Headquarters of Military Region II. Within several days after meeting with CIA operative James W. Lair and Thai PARU Colonel Pranet Ritruechai in Ta Vieng, at which they promised military supplies, arms, and training to Vang Pao and his soldiers, this became the start of the Hmong and the U.S. relationship in fighting a clandestine war inside Laos.

GETTYIMAGES/ JOHN DOMINIS COLLECTION

An Illustration of His Remarkable Life 110

"[James W. 'Bill'] Lair first became involved in a major way in November 1960 when he was asked to provide PARU teams to work with [General] Phoumi during his attempt to capture Vientiane. Lair and his brother-in-law, PARU Colonel Pranet Ritruechai, had intelligence teams all along the border and knew about Vang Pao and the Hmong, and their potential for guerrilla warfare. In Vientiane, after Phoumi captured the city on December 17, Lair wanted to find Vang Pao, but no one knew his location. On the morning of December 21, Lair ran into Ron Sutphin at the airport. Sutphin told Lair that he had landed the day before at a recently constructed airstrip at Ta Vieng, south of the [Plain of Jars], and that Vang Pao was there. Lair went to see [CIA Chief of Station Gordon L.] Jorgensen. The first UH-34 had arrived in Bangkok that morning, and Lair wanted to use one to find Vang Pao. Jorgensen agreed... It was nearly dark when they reached the strip that Sutphin had identified, and there was only one old farmer in sight. He said that Vang Pao was there but was in the countryside at the moment. Pranet and his team remained overnight while Lair went back to Vientiane. Pranet sent a CW message the next morning that he had found Vang Pao. Lair flew out and spoke with Vang Pao. VP told Lair that he could not live with the Communists. He had two choices: fight or leave the country. If the U.S. supplied weapons, he would fight. Lair asked VP how many people he could raise. VP said that he easily could raise 10,000. Both Lair and Pranet were impressed with VP...

"Lair outlined a program to support the Hmong. Although he 'never thought that they would do it,' the next day [Chief of the Far East Division in the Clandestine Service] Des Fitzgerald asked him to write up the proposal, and send it to Washington... Lair drafted an 18-page cable. The answer came back 'surprisingly soon' that the idea was worth trying. [Lair] was authorized to arm the first 1,000 Hmong and see how it was working out...

"Lair went to see Vang Pao again to set up a location for the arms drop and training. Vang Pao said that he would go to [Pa Dong]. In January, weapons for the first 300 Hmong troops were dropped. A PARU team led by Pranet did a three-day training program, involving use of the weapons and basic ambush techniques. The helicopter carrying Lair, Pranet, and the PARU team, flown by Abadie, crashed. No one was injured, but it was a close call. Lair asked VP to select 20 men out of the first 300 for training as radio operators. They were sent to Hua Hin [in Thailand]. This gave VP the beginning of an efficient, secure communications sysetms."

* * *

"INTERVIEW WITH JAMES W. (BILL) LAIR AND LLYOD (PAT) LANDRY, BANGKOK, THAILAND, JULY 3, 1993"
RETRIEVED FROM WWW.UTDALLAS.EDU
JUNE 2012

CIA operative James W. Lair in Thailand in 1962.

JAMES W. LAIR COLLECTION

Thai Colonel Pranet Ritruechai, commander of the Thai's Police Aerial Resupply Unit (PARU), which was established with the help of his brother-in-law, CIA operative James W. Lair. The PARU became an integral part of the fighting against Communist forces during the Secret War in Laos.

JAMES W. LAIR COLLECTION

THE JOINT CHIEFS OF STAFF
OPERATIONS DIRECTORATE
JOINT STAFF
Washington 25, D. C.

COPY NO. _____

1961 MAR 20 08 13

OFF SECY OF DEFENSE

19 March 1961

MEMORANDUM FOR THE JOINT CHIEFS OF STAFF

Subject: Laos Situation Report (U)

Attached hereto is the Situation Report 74-61, on the current situation in Laos, based on information available in the Laos Situation Room as of 0630 EST Sunday, 19 March 1961.

FOR THE DIRECTOR FOR OPERATIONS:

L. W. JOHNSON
Colonel, USAF
JCS Duty Officer

DISTRIBUTION:

White House (General Clifton)	(1)
White House (Situation Room)	(1)
Secretary of State (Room 6310, New State Bldg. Msg Center, Bureau FE Affairs)	(7)
Secretary of Defense	(1)
Deputy Secretary of Defense	(1)
Asst Secretary of Defense (ISA)	(3)
Asst Secretary of Defense (PA)	(2)
Asst to SECDEF (Special Operations)	(1)
Regional Director, Far East ASD/ISA	(1)
Chairman, Joint Chiefs of Staff	(6)
Chief of Staff, USA	(18)
Chief of Naval Operations	(12)
Chief of Staff, USAF	(17)
Commandant of the Marine Corps	(7)
Director, Joint Staff	(1)
Deputy Director, Joint Staff	(1)
Director, J-1	(1)
Director, J-2	(2)
Director, J-3	(6)
Director, J-4	(6)
Director, J-5	(5)
Director, J-6	(1)
Director, JMAA	(1)
Director, JPO	(1)
Secretary, JCS	(3)
Secretary, JSSC	(3)
Special Asst to JCS to NMC	(1)
Director, NSA	(4)
CIA (Mr. Fitzgerald)	(10)
CID (J-2)	(1)
JIOA (J-2)	(1)
JCS (R&RA)	(1)

TOP SECRET
SPECIAL HANDLING REQUIRED
NOT RELEASABLE TO FOREIGN NATIONALS

SPECIAL HANDLING REQUIRED;
NOT RELEASABLE TO FOREIGN NATIONALS

THE JOINT CHIEFS OF STAFF
OPERATIONS DIRECTORATE
JOINT STAFF
Washington 25, D. C.

LAOS SITUATION REPORT   19 March 1961
74-61

PERIOD COVERED: 180630-190630 local based on information available in the Joint War Room as of 0630 EST Sunday, 19 March 1961.

1. INTELLIGENCE:

a. The enemy continues to consolidate and strengthen his positions north and south of the junction of Routes 7 and 13. Lao Army units repulsed enemy probing attacks in the vicinity of Kui Kha Cham, about 24 miles south of Luang Prabang, and at Ban Pho Home, about 15 miles north of Vang Vieng. In the Kui Kha Cham encounter, effective use of artillery was credited with dispersing the enemy.

b. Enemy guerrilla operations continue to harass friendly rear areas. Two ambushes of a Lao Army convoy and a guerrilla attack on a Lao Army post occurred along Route 13 between Vientiane and Vang Vieng.

c. South of the Plaine des Jarres, about 18 miles northeast of Ban Ta Viang, Mobile Group "C" has been ordered to withdraw 18 miles south to Tha Thom. In the same general area, the enemy maintained close contact with Mobile Group "A" which continued its withdrawal from Ban Ta Viang to Tha Thom. The withdrawal of these two groups will leave only Lieutenant Colonel Vang Pao's Mobile Group "B" with 1100 in mixed Army units and about 3-4000 Meo tribesmen in Xieng Khouang province. Vang Pao's headquarters is located about 15 miles southwest of Xieng Khouang.

2. OPERATIONS:

a. Chief, PEO, reports that Phoumi is now rather desperate and that he cannot be persuaded to go on the offensive on any front. His concept now is to dig in and to hold what

TOP SECRET   - 2 -
SPECIAL HANDLING REQUIRED
NOT RELEASABLE TO FOREIGN NATIONALS

he has. Chief, PEO, believes it is only a matter of time before the enemy gets the necessary build-up for another push. Chief, PEO, says Phoumi plans on committing the last three of his six relatively untrained special battalions. The first three were recently committed to Luang Prabang. Phoumi also plans to commit, after the barest minimum training, the newly organized infantry battalions scheduled for training in Thailand. Chief, PEO, stressed that these untrained units can be a liability in combat instead of an asset. Phoumi counters that he took Vientiane with untrained troops. Phoumi feels we have overrated the MEO, and in fact he now blames the MEO for the original loss of the Plaine des Jarres. Chief, PEO, states the LTAG teams with the four infantry battalions will give them the best training they can in the time available. Chief, PEO, assures he will expend every effort to salvage some part of the training plan for Thailand.

b. Chief, PEO, reports that bombs are now in Vientiane. Phoumi claims his pilots are willing and able to employ them. Chief, PEO, has not informed FAL that the bombs are there. In consequence, the FAL has not been able to go through the mechanics of arming the planes. Chief, PEO, foresees no difficulties and feels that, except for this, the FAL is ready in all respects to undertake bombing with T-6 aircraft.

3. LOGISTICS:

JCS has authorized establishment of a logistic group to support the PEO mission in Laos. The US Army, Pacific and US Air Force, Pacific have been levied by CINCPAC to provide personnel as soon as possible for 180 days TDY to fill this requirement, with the USARPAC providing the largest part of the logistic group augmentation.

4. WEATHER:

Valid 191200Z to 201200Z March 1961. Scattered lower clouds at 2000-3000 feet and variable layers of middle and high clouds. Visibility 7 miles and better except locally in higher terrain where visibility will be 1-2 miles in ground fog and haze. Visibility will improve in afternoon hours with scattered to broken middle and cirrus layers.

President John F. Kennedy

"I want to make it clear to the American people, and to all of the world, that all we want in Laos is peace, not war—a truly neutral government, not a cold war pawn, a settlement concluded at the conference table and not on the battlefield.

"Our response will be made in close cooperation with our allies and the wishes of the Laotian government. We will not be provoked, trapped, or drawn into this or any other situation but I know that every American will want his country to honor its obligations to the point that freedom and security of the free world and ourselves may be achieved."

* * *

PRESIDENT JOHN F. KENNEDY
PRESS CONFERENCE AT THE STATE DEPARTMENT AUDITORIUM
MARCH 23, 1961
RETRIEVED FROM THE WWW.JFKLIBRARY.ORG
SEPTEMBER 2010

right
President John F. Kennedy in March 1961. Kennedy was elected as the 35th President of the United States. In the early years of his presidency, he also dispatched CIA personnel to Laos. The maroon-color shaded region on the map was MR II, commanded by General Vang Pao, and was the area where the heaviest fighting in Laos took place. On November 22, 1963, Kennedy was assassinated in Dallas, Texas.

THE JFK LIBRARY COLLECTION VIA SGU-MINNESOTA CHAPTER

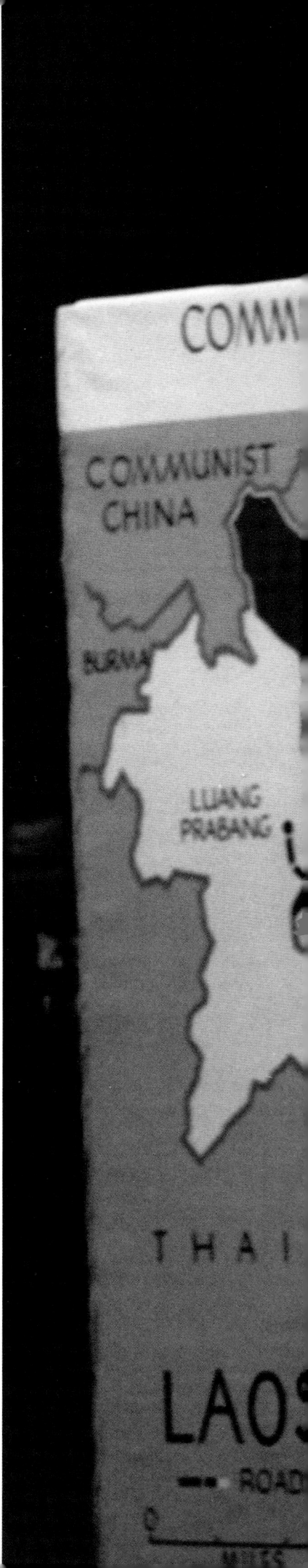

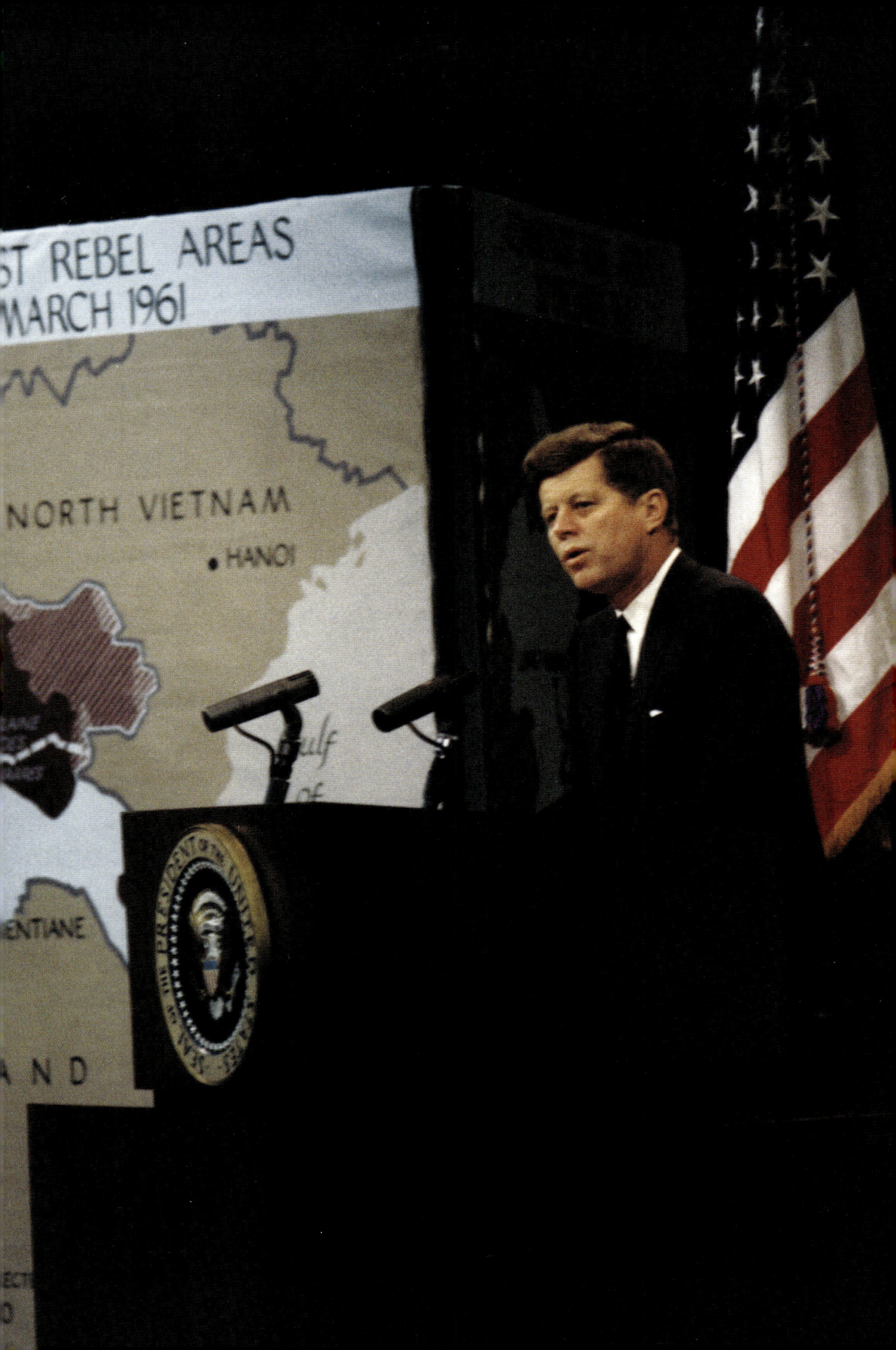
ST REBEL AREAS
MARCH 1961
NORTH VIETNAM
HANOI
ENTIANE
AND

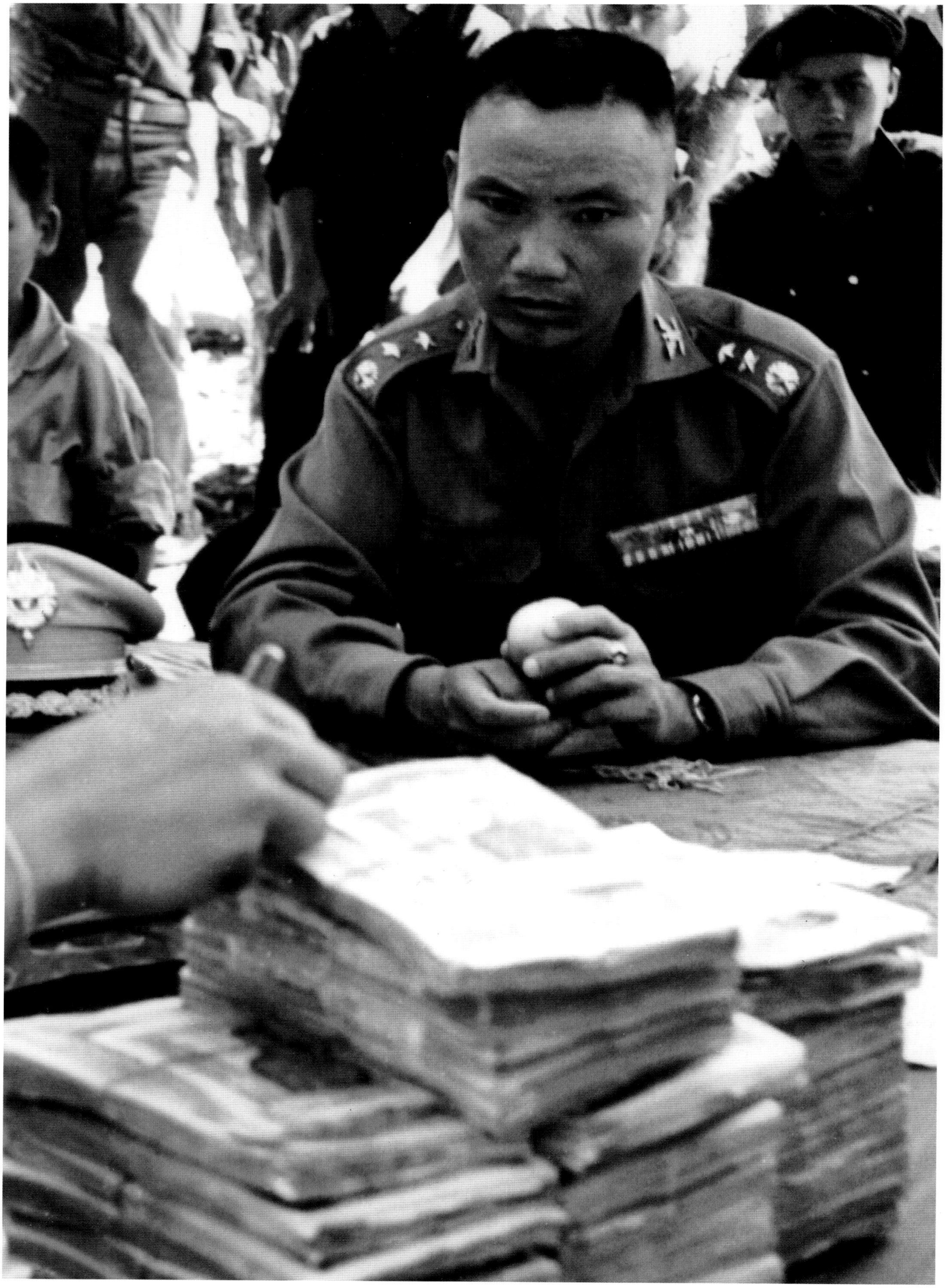

"Vang Pao certainly was not a creation of the [CIA] agency. Vang Pao came to where he was by his own abilities... He was an amazingly dynamic man...

"[By] the time the agency got to Vang Pao he was already vying with Touby Lyfoung for political control, and as the military operations increased and ... the political side of the struggle became less important, his role became much more important.

"So, Vang Pao was in no way a creation of the agency. Now, perhaps, you can say that the Americans made him more powerful, but, ... he was a leader long before we got there and his sense ... of political leadership was really quite astute."

* * *

VINTON (VINT) LAWRENCE
"INTERVIEW WITH J. VINTON (VINT) LAWRENCE, 1981"
SERIES VIETNAM: A TELEVISION HISTORY
PROGRAM CAMBODIA AND LAOS
JULY 17, 1981
RETRIEVED FROM OPENVAULT.WGBH.ORG
FEBURARY 2012

left
Lt. Colonel Vang Pao prepares to pay his soldiers in Pa Dong, Laos in 1961.

JAMES W. LAIR COLLECTION

right
On May 22, 1961, after the U.S. had agreed to drop military supplies to Lt. Colonel Vang Pao and his 300-strong Hmong army in Pa Dong, Vang Pao already was aware of enemy positions around the Plain of Jars. Using his combat knife, Lt. Colonel Vang Pao pointed to the area of Pheun Thang that could potentially be occupied by Communist NVA and Pathet Lao troops. Pa Dong was his temporary Headquarters in MR II. Standing next to him is Ly Toupao, who later became the Chief of Staff in MR II.

SOMSANOUK VANG COLLECTION

An Illustration of His Remarkable Life 120

President Kennedy held a private talk with Laos King Sisavang Vatthana during an official trip to Washington, D.C., in 1963. According to General Vang Pao's longtime interpreter Vang Xang, he said that the General told him that "[when] the Laos King traveled to Washington to meet with President Kennedy, the two accepted and agreed to a strategy that we must attack the Communist from expanding to Laos. Part of the responsibility was handed to General Vang Pao to protect the vital interests of the United States and their country."

SGU—MINNESOTA CHAPTER COLLECTION VIA THE JFK LIBRARY

right
Colonel Vang Pao in Pa Dong, Laos, in 1962.

UNIVERSITY OF TEXAS AT DALLAS COLLECTION VIA PAT LANDRY

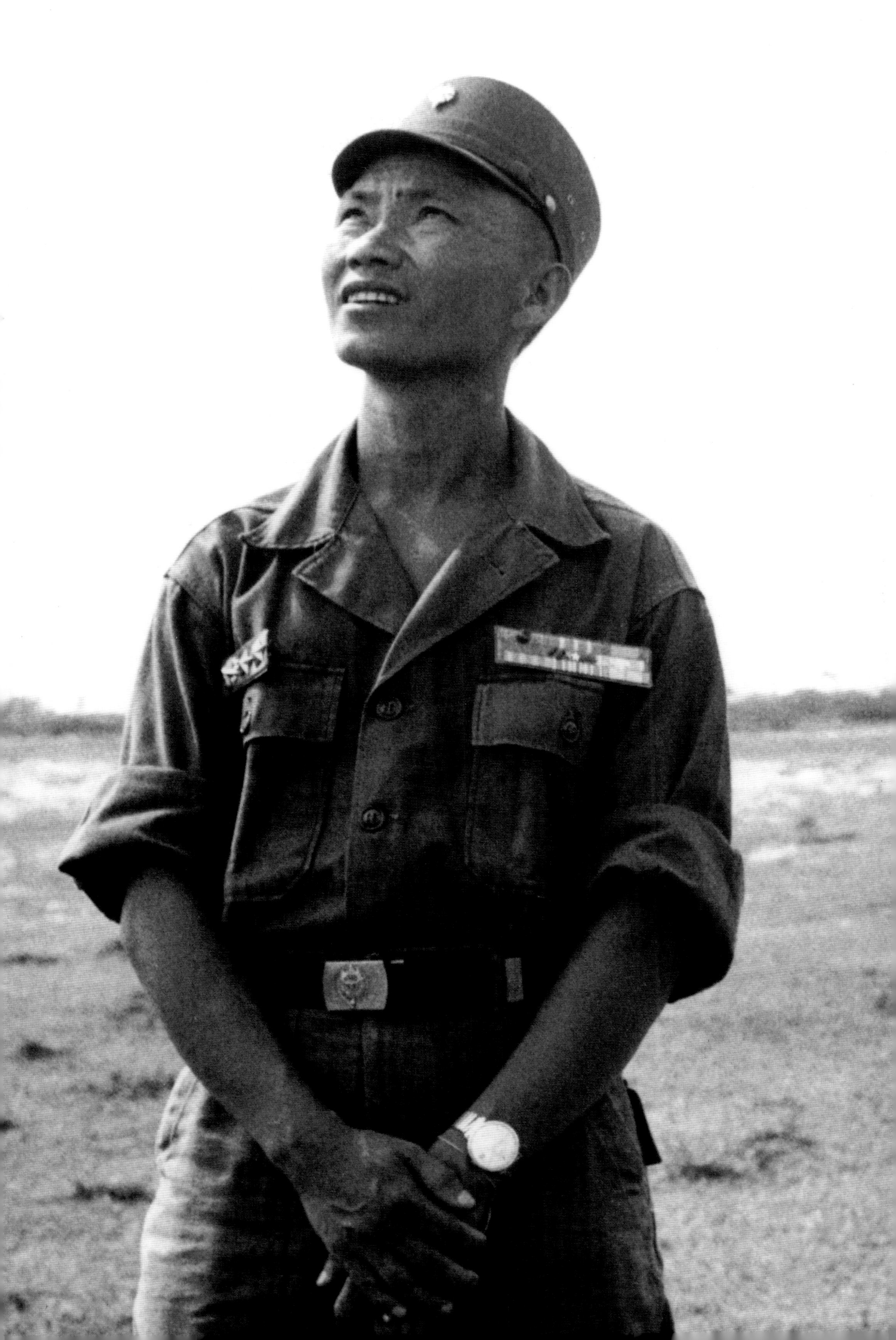

"In Xieng Khouang, the Hmong once again blew up the bridges on Route 7 in a desperate effort to interfere with North Vietnamese truck convoys rolling westward. The [U.S.] had been quietly supplying arms to the Hmong since at least March 1957 to enable them to resist the Pathet Lao, but the North Vietnamese influx created a sudden need for arms far in excess of what the Laotians could supply, even with the help of Thailand. The Hmong, under their military leader Vang Pao, had taken up positions in the mountains surrounding the Plain of Jars and asked to talk to United States officials. Vang Pao requested quick delivery of arms, but United States officials were concerned that the Hmong would not fight, and the arms might fall into communist hands. Vang Pao said all 7,000 volunteers would fight, but they needed the arms in three days or they would have to fall back to more exposed positions. United States airdrops of arms from stocks in Okinawa began three days later, signaling the beginning of a heroic Hmong resistance."

* * *

"LAOS: THE WIDENING WAR"
DATA AS OF JULY 1994
RETRIEVED LIBRARY OF CONGRESS
DECEMBER 12, 2010

right
Vang Pao and Thao Chai, who later became a Colonel and acted as the Finance Director based in Thailand, in 1963.

HOWARD BUELL COLLECTION

An Illustration of His Remarkable Life   124

Brig. General Vang Pao congratulates a newly trained company as they prepare to combat Captain Kong Le's Neutralist and Communist Pathet Lao forces in Pa Dong in 1962. Pa Dong was the temporary Headquarters for Vang Pao and his troops.

JAMES W. LAIR COLLECTION

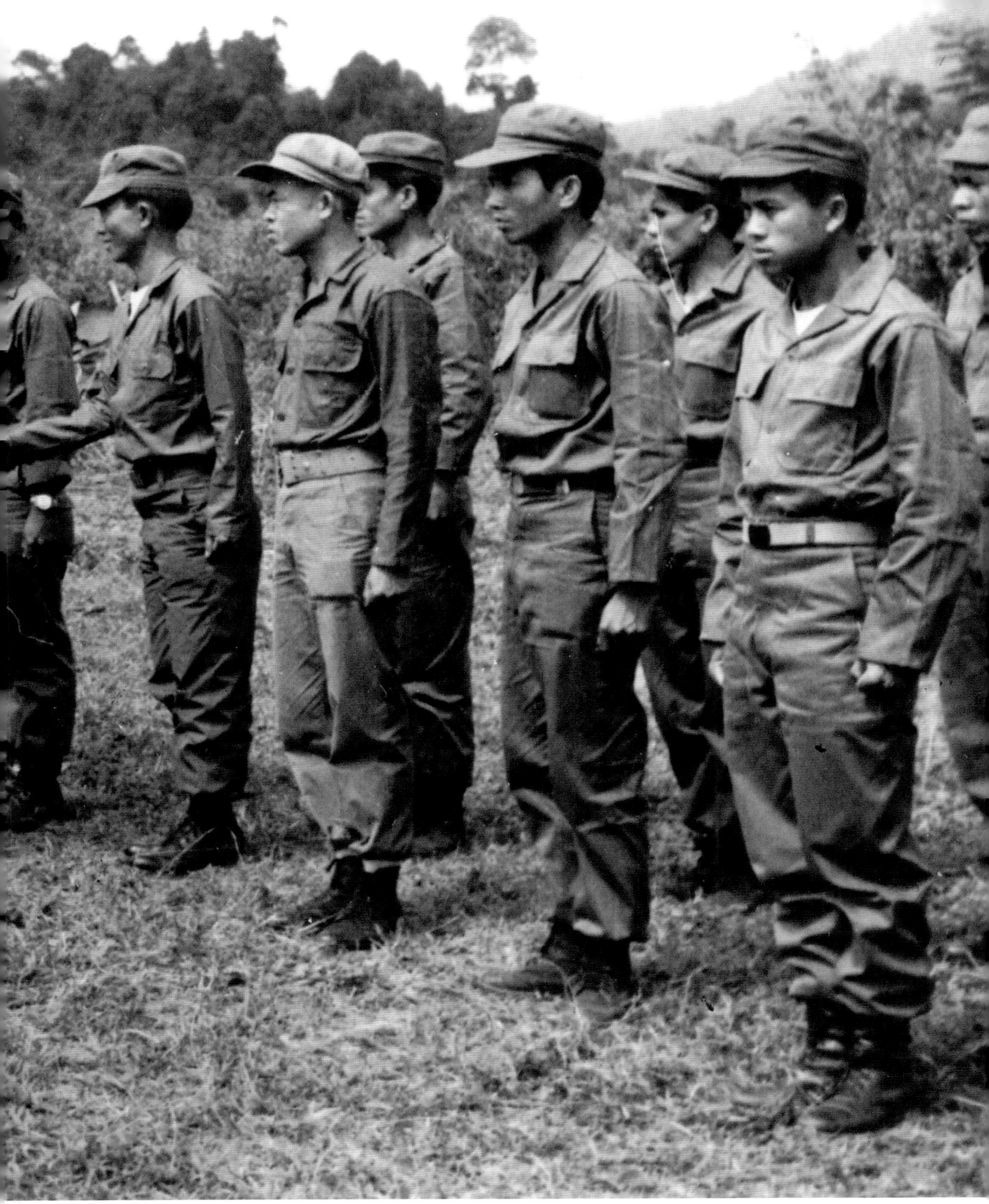

G-4
MAJOR NAO
GAO LY

G-2
LT. HANG
SAO

BATTAL-
ION
COMDR.
CAPT. YU
VANG LY

"Then, our objectives in supporting the United States to fight the war in Laos were: first, we had to stop the North Vietnamese from sending troops and supplies into South Vietnam using the Ho Chi Minh Trail; second, to rescue downed American pilots; and third, to defend and protect the radar site at Phou Pha Thi."

**

COLONEL LY TOUPAO, RETIRED
AUTHOR'S INTERVIEW
ST. PAUL, MINNESOTA
OCTOBER 2006

left
These were among the very first Hmong military officers along with Lt. Colonel Vang Pao that fought and defended their country and the United States' interests in Laos. Later on they all earned the rank of colonel and held key positions in managing the war in Military Region II and in Hmong society. Correct name spellings are *Nao Kao Lyfoung* and *Youa Vang Ly*. Photo taken in early 1960s.

VINT LAWRENCE COLLECTION VIA ROGER WARNER

NLK 01-203-19-3

APPROVED FOR RELEASE
DATE: MAR 2001

Copy 1 of 14

STATUS REPORT
OF THE
TASK FORCE SOUTHEAST ASIA
COVERT ANNEX - LAOS
(13-27 JUNE 1962)

1. Plans for an extensive reorganization for the CIA-directed Meo operation in north Laos, which were submitted in early May, are now being implemented ▓▓▓▓ with the assistance of MAAG/Laos. This reorganization calls for the division of the Meo forces of approximately 14,500 into three basic types of units:

   a. Special Units which will be volunteer, full-time, and mobile,

   b. Ordinary Units which will be volunteer, full-time, local area or defense forces and,

   c. Reserve units which will be volunteer, part-time duty reserve units responsible for local area security and initial defense.

This organization also touches on the command structure of the Meo operation, communications, and special operations. ▓▓▓▓ has reported that this reorganization is now under way and is being implemented.

2. CIA ▓▓▓▓ continues to maintain its present capabilities in intelligence collection which are primarily in two fields:

   a. ▓▓▓▓▓▓▓▓▓▓▓▓▓▓▓▓▓▓▓▓▓▓

   b. ▓▓▓▓▓▓▓▓▓▓▓▓▓▓▓▓▓▓▓▓▓▓

is further envisaged that military intelligence capabilities will cover to some extent compliance with or violation of the Geneva Agreements by enemy forces. The latter would include such items as withdrawal of Vietnamese troops from Laos and possible violations of the cease fire by enemy forces.

3. On 16 June Colonel Vang Pao, the Meo commander, addressed a number of Meo commanders and members of his own staff. Colonel Vang Pao spoke of the accomplishments of the Meos in the past 18 months and spoke of the current situation. Colonel Vang Pao told his commanders that Meo troops should keep their unit integrity and retain their organization and weapons. However, the Meos should not launch attacks of any kind against the Communists or Kong Le forces except as ordered by Vang Pao. If a Souvanna government were replaced by a Communist government, the Meos should, said Vang Pao, if the Meo-held area became completely untenable, be prepared to relocate to other parts of Laos, Thailand, or South Vietnam.

4. Plans are continuing for a Laos staybehind headquarters in Thailand in implementation of previous policy guidance. These plans call for a staybehind headquarters in northeast or central Thailand with radio communication from Meo intelligence cadres in Laos to the staybehind command post in Thailand.

5. ███

6. A total of approximately 700 Lao and tribal people formed into six counterguerrilla groups are currently operating ███████████ in areas of central and south central Laos. The groups, based at Thakhek, have the mission of harassing enemy supply lines on and near Routes 8 and 12 in central Laos and collecting intelligence on enemy activities. Heavy enemy pressure forced three groups to return to Thakhek from the Route 12 area in early June, and these groups are being retrained. One group which is in process of establishing a base north of Tchepone (in south central Laos) appears better qualified to fulfill its mission because of better leadership and motivation. The other groups have a limited capability for harassment and intelligence collection which it is hoped can be improved with training and better leadership.

An aerial view of Long Cheng, Lima Site 98 or commonly called Lima Site 20 Alternate (LS20A), in 1962. Long Cheng eventually became the Headquarters of MR II, commanded and operated by General Vang Pao. In the beginning, there were only a few Lao Theung families living in the valley. By the late 1960s, Long Cheng was the busiest air transportation hub in the world, and had the second largest population in Laos, with more than 40,000 people. The administrative capital city, Vientiane, was ranked first. The military base is also spelled by many as *Long Tieng*.

WA CHONG VANG COLLECTION

right
When Long Cheng was finally determined as the Headquarters of Military Region II, many of Vang Pao's Hmong soldiers began relocating their families to the area. Here, clothes and supplies were delivered and readied to be distributed to the people arriving at Long Cheng in late 1962. This was arranged by the Indiana farmer Edgar 'Pop' Buell, of the International Voluntary Services, stationed in Laos.

HOWARD BUELL COLLECTION

"On January 1, 1961 everybody left Xieng Khoung from the Plain of Jars because, we, the Rightist party, could no longer fight against the Neutralist party under the leadership of Captain Kong Le and the Leftist, which served under [Prince] Souphanouvong. During this period, the two parties [Neutralist and Leftist] joined together and we were outnumbered.

"As we met with ... Vang Pao in a small village, he was still celebrating his new promotion to Lieutenant Colonel. He was very upset to see that we were outnumbered by the two parties. He left in a truck and returned with a truckload of weapons. He gave out these weapons and told us to head to Savannaket to join our leader [General] Phoumi Nosavan. On the way there, we stopped at Ta Vieng and were told to build an airport. On the third day, Colonel Bill Lair landed at this new airport to meet with General Vang Pao. Ten days later, we were chased off with Kong Le and his troops. We left to Pa Dong and regrouped by ... Vang Pao. He ordered everyone from different services to join in as CIA soldiers on January 25, 1961. I was in charge of distributing all military supplies with my friend Lee Nou."

* * *
LT. COLONEL VANG CHOU, RETIRED
"THE SPOTTER"
VETERANS MAGAZINE, INC.
FRESNO, CALIFORNIA
VOLUME 1, NUMBER 1
APRIL 2008, PAGE 14

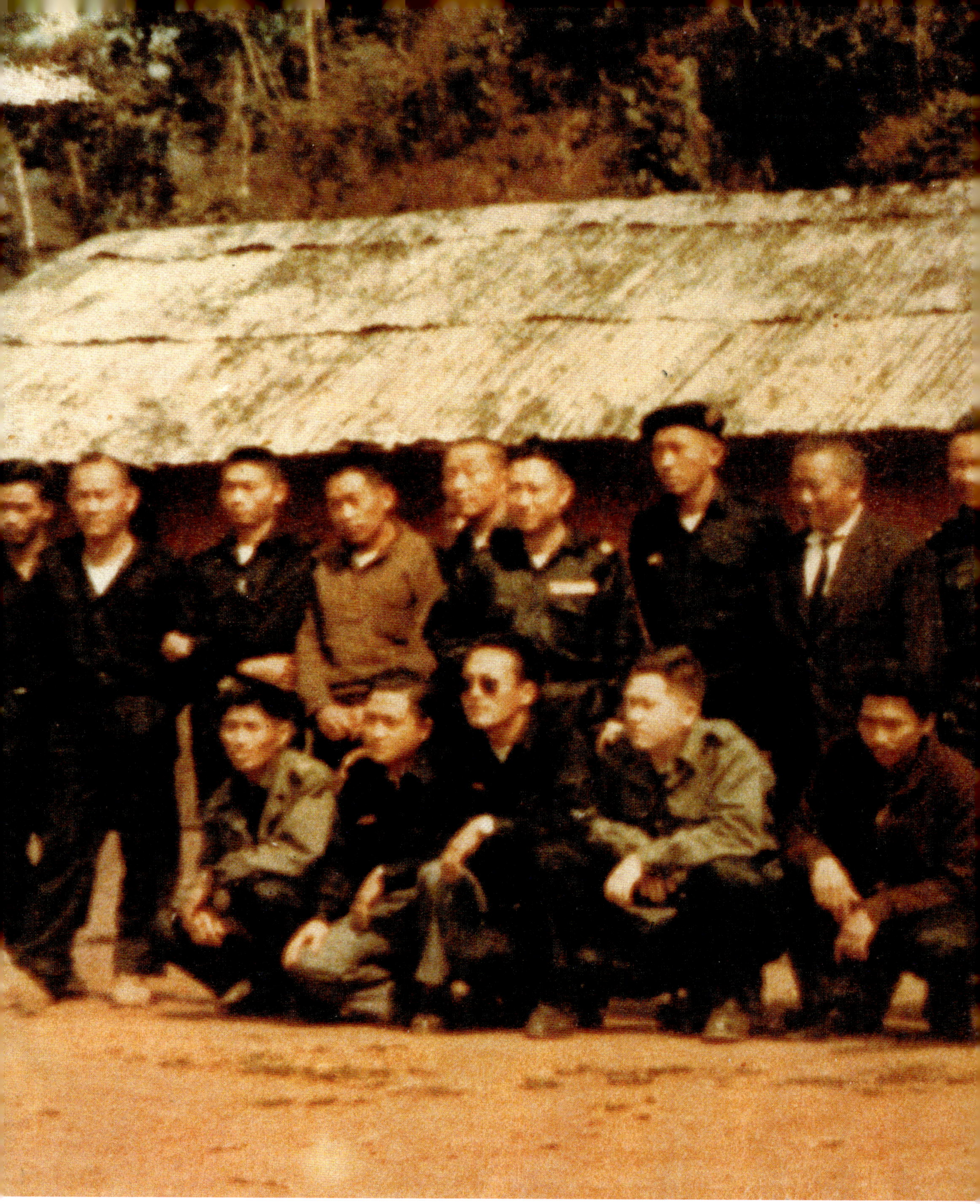

First group of Hmong civilian and military leaders to establish Long Cheng, the Headquarters of MR II, in early 1963. MR II was composed of the provinces of Houa Phan (or Sam Neua) and Xieng Khouang. *Standing, left to right*: Unknown, Unknown, Colonel Yang Shoua, Nai Kong Nao Ying Lee, Colonel Thao Neng Chue, Colonel Ly Toupao, Mayor Tong Pao Lee, Brig. General Vang Pao, Mayor Lee Neng Thong, Lt. Colonel Vue Chong Kua, Nai Kong Vang Xai Shoua, and Colonel Moua Cher Pao. *Sitting, left to right*: Captain Lo Seng, Colonel Lyfoung Nao Kao, Major Lee Tong Chao, Colonel Lyfoung Sublong, Colonel Lee Xang, Major Lee Nao Pou, Unknown, and Colonel Lee Youa Vang.

YANG ENG COLLECTION

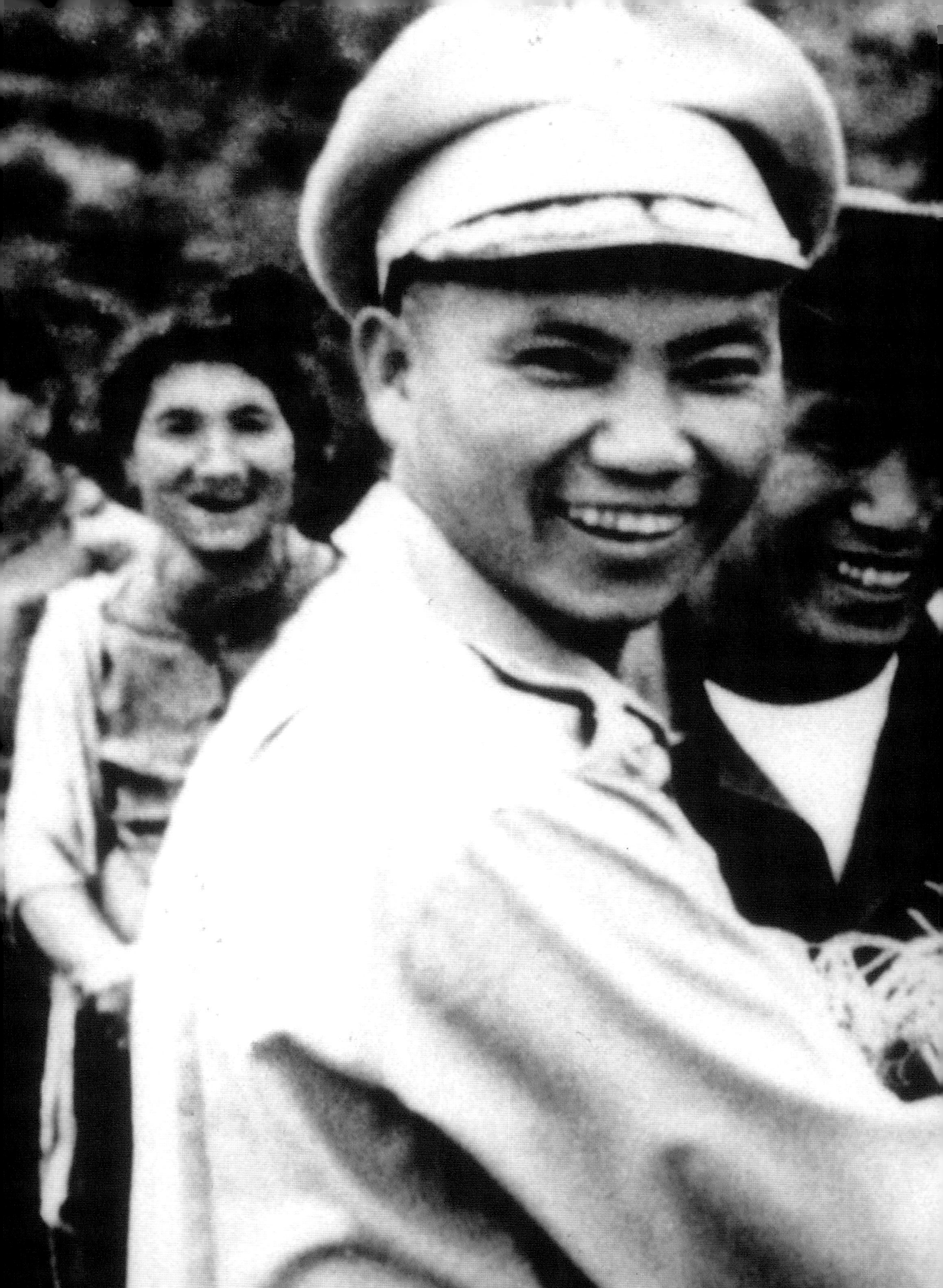

left
Brig. General Vang Pao at a celebration in a Lao ethnic Thai Dam village in 1963-1964.

THE GVP FAMILY COLLECTION

"General Vang Pao was the best field general I have ever met."

* * *
CAPTAIN D. L. "PAPPY" HICKS
RETIRED UNITED STATES ARMY
"A SECRET ARMY NO MORE"
TRI COUNTY LEADER
WHITEHOUSE, TEXAS
JUNE 12, 1997

Civilians welcomed King Sisavang Vatthana and members of his council during their first tour of the medical center at Sam Thong in 1963. The King was also accompanied by Hmong leaders Brig. General Vang Pao and Phagna Touby Lyfoung, *far right*.

HOWARD BUELL COLLECTION

"Everything turns in time, and it'll turn again in Laos some day. Maybe it's turning now, maybe it'll be 10 years or 50 years before there's peace.

"But when that day comes, these people will remember what Pop stood for, whether they remember me or not.

"They'll be just a little better off for my being here, and that's the only thing that keeps me going. No man is big enough or brave enough to go on working like this without some kind of purpose. I'm sowing seeds that someday are gonna grow."

* * *
EDGAR 'POP' BUELL
"THE BLAD MAGAZINE"
MAY 3, 1970
RETRIEVED FROM HOWARD BUELL
JULY 2010

Edgar 'Pop' Buell dressed in traditional Hmong costume. Buell worked for the International Voluntary Services (IVS) in Laos starting in June 1960. He was committed to the people, especially with the humanitarian efforts in relocating the displaced war victims from the Plain of Jars. "My father loved the people," said Howard Buell, Pop's son, in a 2010 interview, "he considered himself Hmong."

HOWARD BUELL COLLECTION

"The victory [between the Hmong and Americans] that we were most proud of was [that] we were only a small ethnic minority in Laos, yet the superpower, the American people, asked us to help them to fight in this great war. Yet we were outnumbered ten to one by the enemy [the Communists] and were able to stand up against them [for 15 years]. We felt that we have this victory that no one else has had."

* * *

GENERAL VANG PAO
"GENERAL VANG PAO'S LAST WAR"
THE NEW YORK TIMES
BY TIM WEINER
FEBRUARY 2008

Brig. General Vang Pao in 1963.

CHAI VANG COLLECTION

next page
General Vang Pao and Edgar 'Pop' Buell at a Hmong village on the Plain of Jars, Xieng Khouang Province, Laos, in the early 1960s.

ROGERS PHOTO ARCHIVE/ARGENTA IMAGES COLLECTION

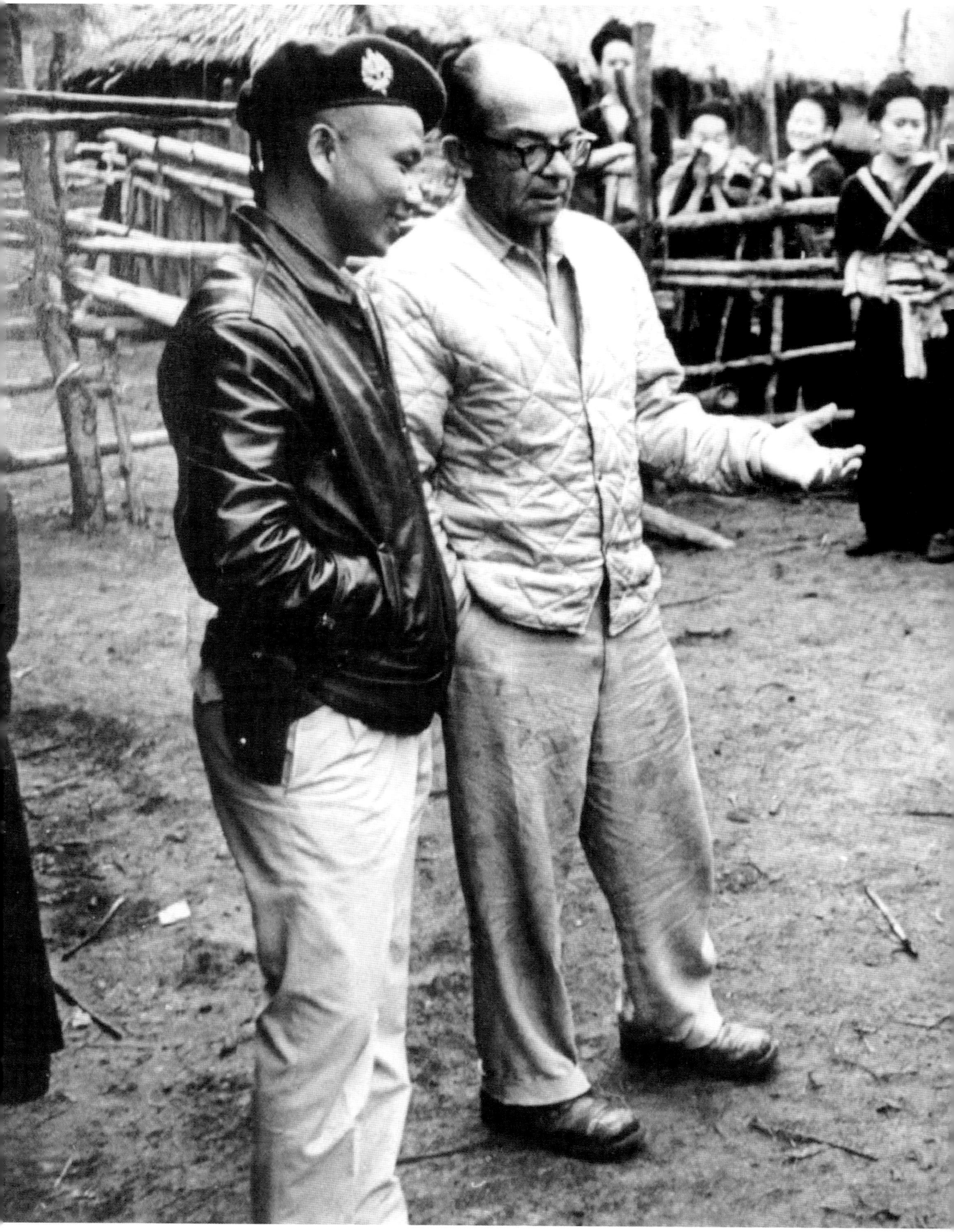

An Illustration of His Remarkable Life 144

Father Luc Bouchard, Brig. General Vang Pao, and Dr. Charles Weldon (in white surgical uniform) in Mouang Cha in 1964. Bouchard was a Catholic missionary. Dr. Weldon was the medical chief officer for USAID in Laos and spent 11 years working there. They both went beyond their ordinary roles to ensure the safety and security of the Hmong and Laotian citizens who had fled their towns and villages due to the war.

HOWARD BUELL COLLECTION

SUBJECT: Report of Recent Activities in Regard to Cholera Outbreak in Sam Neua

ITINERARY:

Place	Date
Sam Neua	August 10-11, 14-20, 1963

On August 10, 1963, the Chief Public Health Advisor was in Sam Neua province for the opening of a new bamboo hospital at Hong Nong. This hospital was built on the decision of Colonel Vang Pao and Pop Buell for several reasons but primarily to reduce the problem of transportation of sick and wounded from this isolated area. Previously the seriously ill and wounded were evacuated to Sam Thong and Vientiane by air. Under the supervision of the excellent Lao medic, Sam, at Hong Nong, a beautiful 14-bed dispensary has been built with a surgery, treatment room, consultation room and waiting room. This facility is adequate to perform all the functions of a field hospital. It is clean, light and airy and has an esthetic appeal in keeping with the environment. The total cost involved was zero. Since the hospital's opening I have performed surgery and treated desperately ill patients in it without feeling that any essentials were lacking. This facility epitomizes one of the many ways Colonel Vang Pao, Pop and the people are working together.

While at Hong Nong on this occasion an American missionary whom I had seen several times previously, described to me an outbreak of a fatal disease in the area which we both felt was cholera. Pop, the Colonel and I discussed the situation briefly and we were all agreed that we should make every effort to contain the disease as quickly as possible, not only from the humanitarian view-point, but also from the aspect of the potential danger to the over-all operation in this area.

Dr. Charles Weldon's field notes on a cholera outbreak in Sam Neua, Laos.

President Lyndon B. Johnson

"Our policy in Southeast Asia has been consistent and unchanged since 1954. I summarized it on June 2 in four simple propositions:

> "1. *America keeps her word. Here as elsewhere, we must and shall honor our commitments.*
>
> "2. *The issue is the future of Southeast Asia as a whole. A threat to any nation in that region is a threat to all, and a threat to us.*
>
> "3. *Our purpose is peace. We have no military, political, or territorial ambitions in the area.*
>
> "4. *This is not just a jungle war, but a struggle for freedom on every front of human activity. Our military and economic assistance to South Vietnam and Laos in particular has the purpose of helping these countries to repel aggression and strengthen their independence.*

"The threat to the three nations of Southeast Asia has long been clear. The North Vietnamese regime has constantly sought to take over South Vietnam and Laos. This Communist regime has violated the Geneva accords for Vietnam. It has systematically conducted a campaign of subversion, which includes the direction, training, and supply of personnel and arms for the conduct of guerrilla warfare in South Vietnamese territory. In Laos, the North Vietnamese regime has maintained military forces, used Laotian territory for infiltration into South Vietnam, and most recently carried out combat operations—all in direct violation of the Geneva agreements of 1962."

* * *

PRESIDENT LYNDON B. JOHNSON
"PRESIDENT'S MESSAGE TO CONGRESS"
AUGUST 5, 1964
RETRIEVED FROM HTTP://TEACHINGAMERICANHISTORY.ORG
JUNE 2012

right
On August 10, 1964, U.S. President Lyndon B. Johnson signed the "Gulf of Tonkin" Resolution (H.J. RES 1145), authorizing him the power to increase U.S. engagement in the Vietnam conflict. On August 4, there was a report that the North Vietnamese had attacked the USS Maddox off the coast of North Vietnam. This triggered the U.S. to respond with this joint resolution, which stated that "Congress approves and supports the determination of the President, as Commander-in-Chief, to take all necessary measures to repeal any armed attack against the forces of the United States and to prevent any further aggression." Johnson was the 36th President of the United States.

LBJ LIBRARY/WHITE HOUSE PHOTO OFFICE COLLECTION

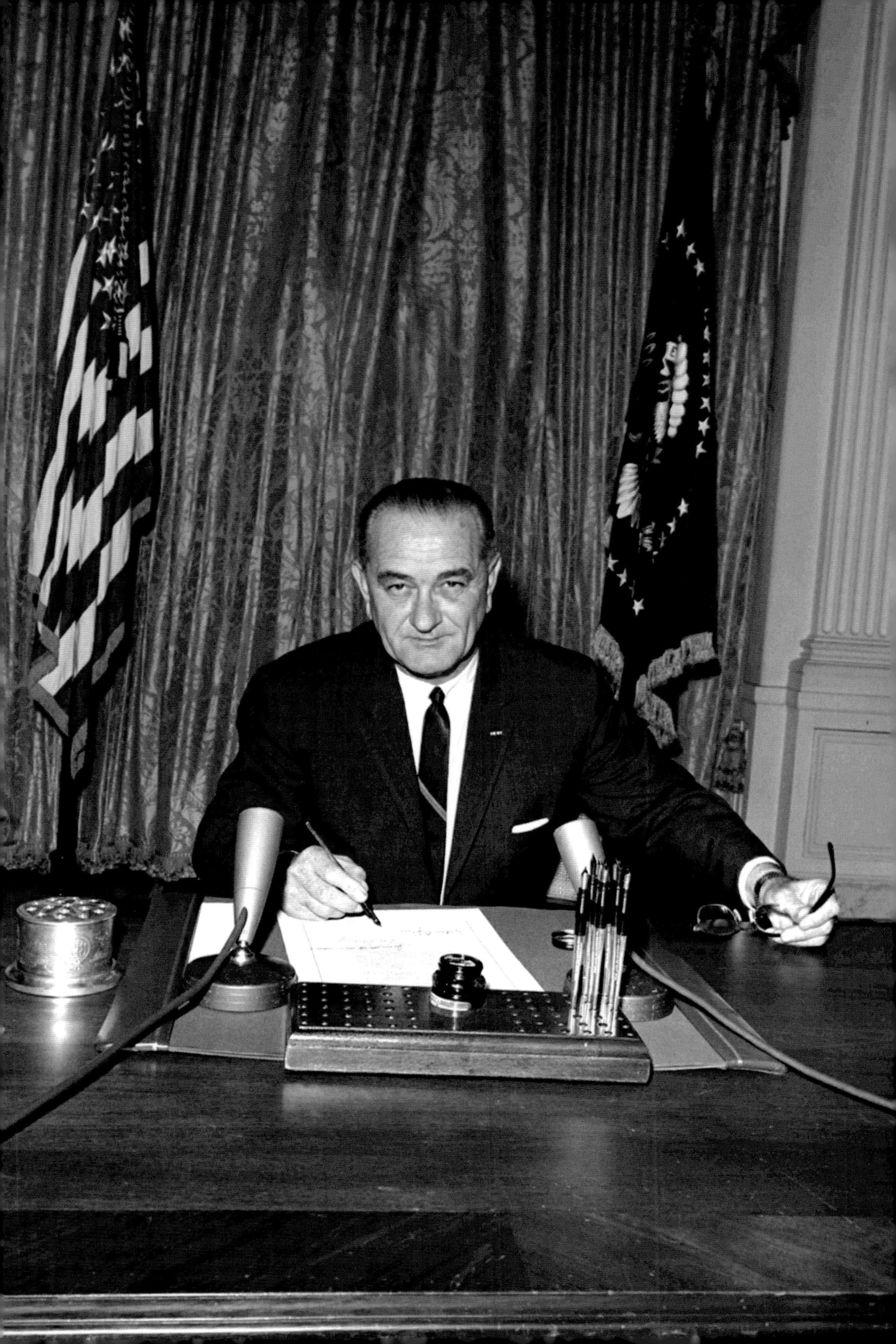

Friday, December 17, 1965 — BANGKOK WORLD

Personality Spotlight
General Vang Pao
By United Press International

GENERAL Vang Pao—Commander of the Meo tribal forces integrated into the Force Armée Royale of Laos, is one of the strongest anticommunist leaders in that country, or perhaps the world. Almost single-handedly, the Meos under his command have for three years stopped the advance of the combined Pathet Lao/Viet Minh forces and have even succeeded in recapturing large portions of Sam Neua Province from the communists.

Who is this man who has become almost a legend in his own time? He is a small, mild-mannered soldier, only 35 years old. But, he personally has a most incredible record of bravery and adventure gained in fighting for the freedom of his people and his country.

He was born in Ban Phou Kong Khao, Laos, on July 4, 1930, the son of a minor official in the Government. His childhood, up until 1945 was normal for a Meo-Lao youth of that era. In early 1945, he was a schoolboy when the attempted Free French coup against the Japanese took place. Many of the Meo tribesmen, under their chief Touby Ly Foung supported the French. When the Japanese entered Laos in force to restore their control, though only 13 years old, Vang Pao left school to serve his people. He served as a scout collecting information on Japanese troops, which allowed Touby and others to escape capture.

At the end of the Second World War, the Viet Minh revolt against the French erupted. The Meos sided with the French against the Vietnamese, who all through recent history and until the present, have tried to dominate their home region in Northeastern Laos. At first, the young adventurer served as an interpreter for French troops fighting Viet Minh invaders and their Pathet Lao satellites. In 1946 he joined the column which marched from Nong Het to Luang Prabang and liberated the King who had been imprisoned by a group of Pathet Lao and Chinese.

In 1947 Touby Ly Foreng wished to reward his services by preparing him for a government career, but having tasted adventure, the young man would be nothing but a soldier. Therefore, Touby arranged for his appointment to the Gendarmerie, and at the age of 17 he found himself in command of a 12-man squad of Meos in the service of the Royal Lao Government. This same year, he was sent for training in Luang Prabang, and in 1948 he attended another six month NCO course in Vientiane. By 1949 he was a Sgt. Chef, commanding a 34-man Meo platoon.

In 1950 he greatly distinguished himself when his platoon was sent to the Nam Mo area, where for two years the French had unsuccessfully tried to wipe out a mixed Viet Minh-Pathet Lao company. Contacting loyal Meos, Vang Pao surrounded the house where 13 Viet Minh, including the company commander, were staying. He attacked, killing seven and capturing three prisoners. He also captured a notebook giving a list of Pathet Lao agents, whom he liquidated. Thus, he thwarted the Viet Minh plan for infiltrating and taking over the entire area. As a result, he was recommended for an officer's school, which he attended all through 1951 and 1952.

In 1953 aspirant Vang Pao was third in command of the 40th Indepenendent Company made up of Meos. That same summer a government battalion of Hua Moung was routed by the Viet Minh. Vang Pao's company joined the remnants at Noung Him which by October was completely surrounded by Vietnamese communist troops. A breakout to the Plaine des Jarres was planned, but most of the troops threw away their arms and fled in small groups. Vang Pao took 74 Meos of his company and four French and struck out fully armed for the Plaine des Jarres. After ten days, in spite of all assistance, the Frenchmen gave out. Vang Pao arranged with friendly Meos to hide them. Then he split his command into small groups, and, avoiding the Viet Minsh, made his way out of the area.

Ten days later the entire group, including the French, reassembled and without casualties made their way to Phou San where they rejoined the Royal Lao Forces. This action greatly increased his reputation as the company had been believed to be wiped out. In recognition, in early 1954, he was made full Lieutenant and given permanent command of his unit now renamed the 4th Special Commando Company. He served in combat with this force until the conclusion of the Indo China war.

During the lull in fighting from 1954 through 1957, he served in FAR, rising rapidly to the rank of Major. He commanded (at that time) the Second Commando Group which consisted of 18 companies of Meos in Sam Neua and Xieng Khouang Provinces. These were the nucleus of those powerful forces which today form the first line of defense and the main bulwark of the Royal Army and Government against the People's Army of Vietnam and their Pathet Lao lackeys.

As the fighting increased, Vang Pao's forces took a more and more active part, and he quickly earned his General's stars. Time and again, by cutting their line of communications and attacking their bases and supply depots, Vang Pao and his men frustrated the communist plans, and enabled the Lao forces to turn back major offensives.

Regularly, he has proved that the Communists are not the only master of guerrilla warfare. Repeatedly his fierce tribesmen, fighting for their freedom and traditional way of life under his skilled leadership, have recorded victories with exactly those tactics which made Gen. Giap's Viet Minh forces so formidable.

During his adventurous career, this doughty little warrior has earned no less than 17 decorations, almost all of which were given directly for bravery and exceptional combat performance.

There has been no lack of brave and talented men in Laos to guard that small country's independence through the years of unrelenting communist attack. Yet, it is hard to see how Laos could have been thus far saved without Vang Pao and his thousands of staunch anti-communist Meo fighters.

---

top
On December 17, 1965, Brig. General Vang Pao was featured in the Personality Spotlight of the United Press International.

HOWARD BUELL COLLECTION

right
Brig. General Vang Pao in 1965. The sword was a gift given to him by H.R.H. King Sisavang Vatthana.

FRANCOIS VANG COLLECTION

next page
Brig. General Vang Pao practiced shooting an M80 in 1965.

JOHN WILLHEIM COLLECTION

An Illustration of His Remarkable Life 150

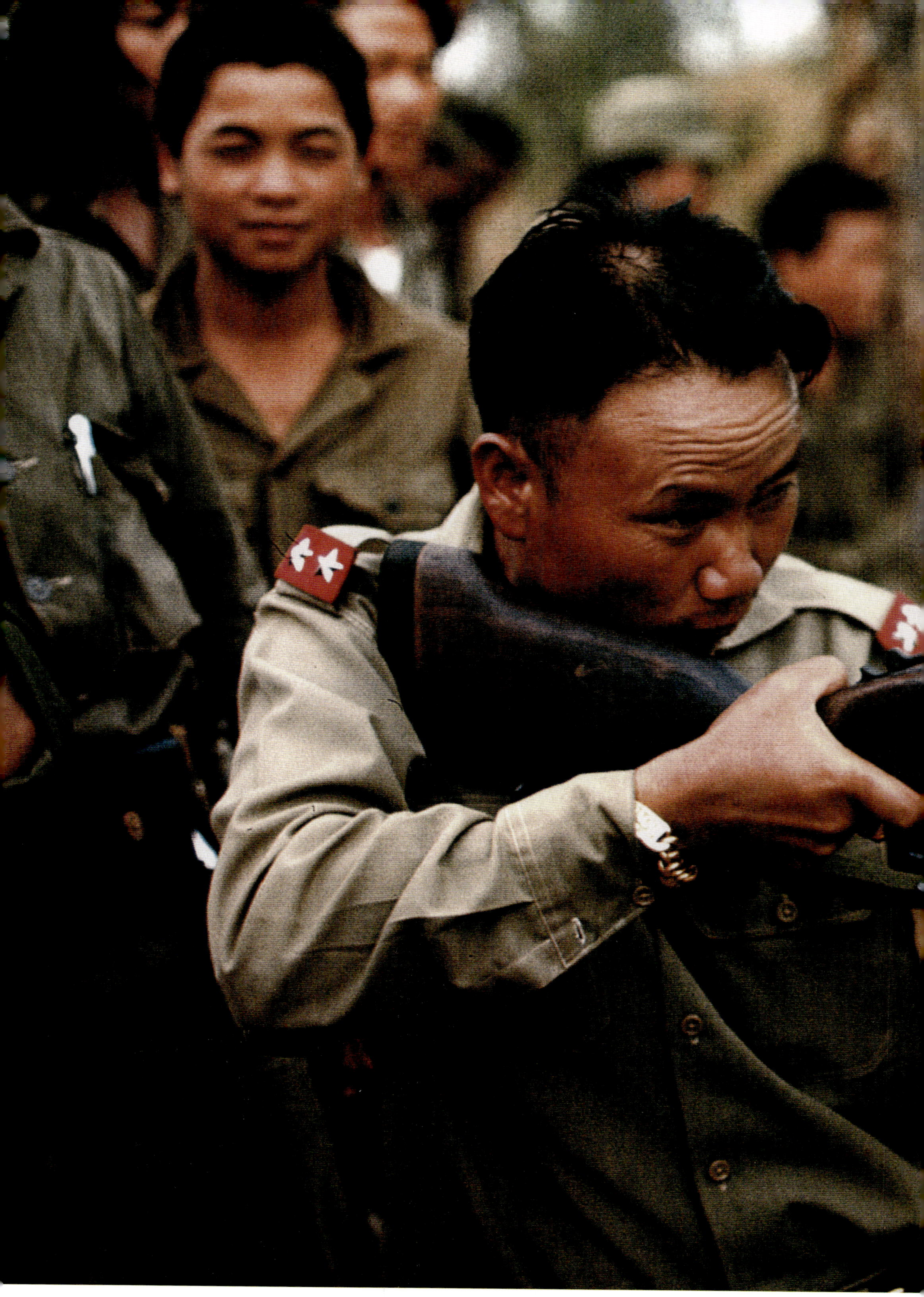

An Illustration of His Remarkable Life 152

153

General Phoumi Nosavan, of the Royal Lao Army, delivered a speech to his soldiers on the Plain of Jars in the early 1960s

THE GVP FAMILY COLLECTION

"No question about Lima 36's importance to the enemy [North Vietnamese Army]. It is a keystone in the control of Route 6 and is subject to attack any time they want to assert control over the entire route. Also, apparently, they had some emotional involvement with Site 36—probably because they tried not only to re-take it, but to annihilate the defenders. When they took it a year ago it was at a prohibitive cost, and then [General Vang Pao] took it away from them last May. They really wanted a decisive win in this one, and they thought they had it, and then the fighters came in and took it away from them."

* * *
COLONEL JOHN E. BRIDGE
U.S. AIR FORCE
"LIMA SITE 36"
APRIL 28, 1967
PROJECT CHECO SOUTHEAST ASIA REPORT

Na Khang, or Lima Site 36, was among dozens of strategic Lima Sites the NVA was most interested in controlling during the Secret War. This site was also the place General Vang Pao was seriously wounded during an enemy attack. He was taken to Thailand and Hawaii for recovery. LS 36 was used as the search and rescue staging location for downed American pilots.

JAMES W. LAIR COLLECTION

General Vang Pao with four-star U.S. Admiral Grant Sharp in Honolulu in 1966. He was wearing a sling from being wounded in combat in Na Khang, Lima Site 36. While recovering in the U.S., he met Sharp, the Commander in Chief of the U.S. Pacific Command from 1964 to 1968. He presented Sharp with a Hmong machete.

SISOUK VANG COLLECTION

An Illustration of His Remarkable Life 156

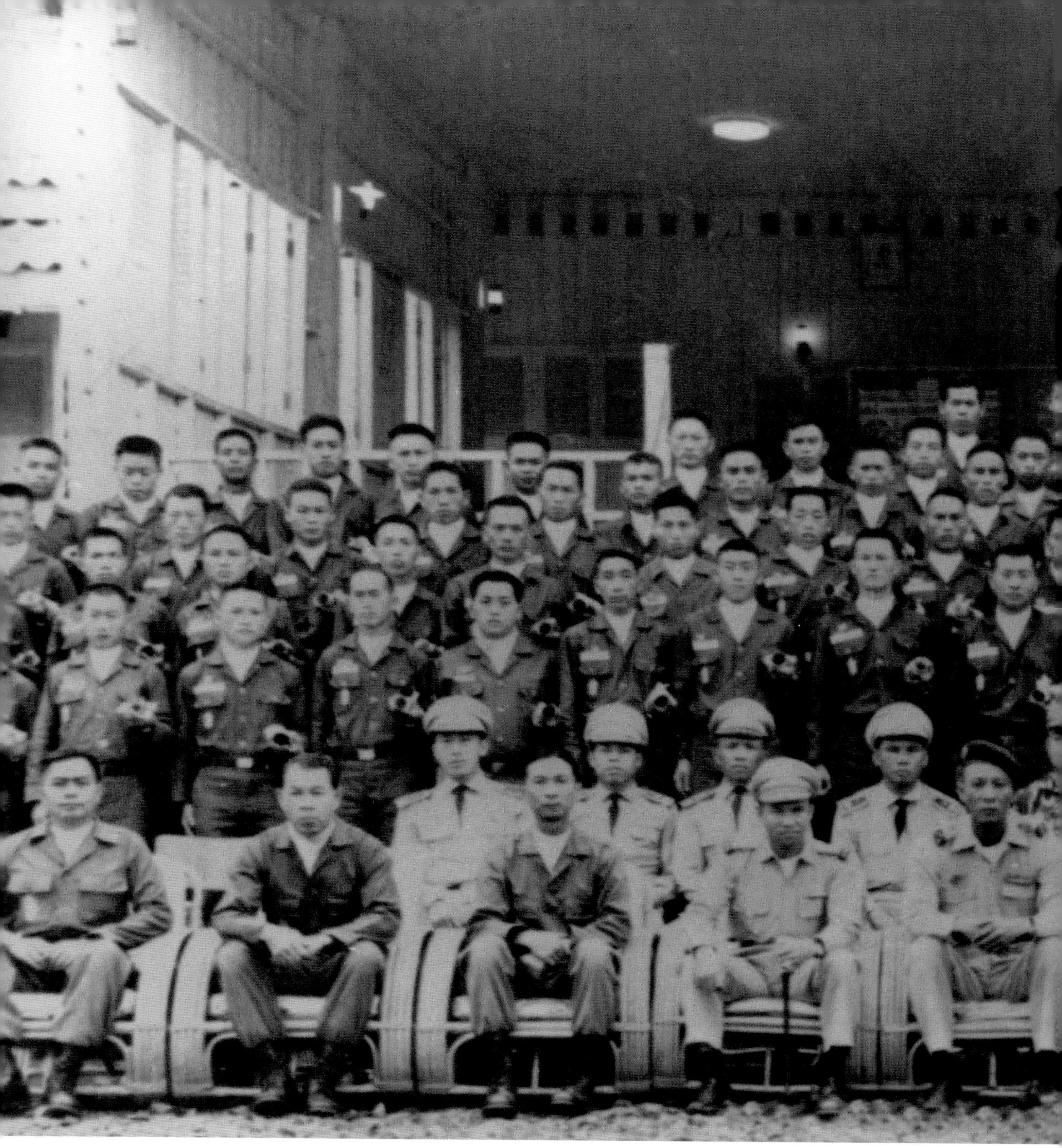

General Ouane Rattikone, commander-in-chief of the Royal Lao Army, *center in camouflage uniform*, and General Vang Pao with top military and civilian leaders during a leadership training in Vientiane, Laos, in 1966.

VAJTSUAS SHOUA YANG COLLECTION

"Everyone thought that one's country must have its own territory, a nation, and independence; it was the responsibility of the national defense forces to protect the people so that they can enjoy life and prosperity. By then the North Vietnamese Army (NVA) had taken over the Plain of Jars, one of the most important ancient civilizations of Laos. Our goal was to retake this ancient natural beauty and to not let the enemy hold control of it.

"Therefore, I planned the operation to retake the Plain of Jars. The NVA miscalculated us. They were well equipped with heavy armored tanks and long-range artillery with the exception of air power. They never worried about us. They were only concerned about the American bombings. They were fully confident that they would never be defeated by us. Yet the enemies suffered enormous casualties.

"We captured about $2 to $3 billion worth of military supplies. We did not use a lot of troops, dying, to achieve this victory. It was from our brilliant military planning strategies. I used only eight companies.

"When I met several senior NVA officers here in the United States, they told me that I deserved honor and credit for that victory. They congratulated me. 'We never thought that you were going to defeat us, but you did,' they told me. 'We would like to congratulate you.'"

* * *

GENERAL VANG PAO
INTERVIEW
MAY 1999
RETRIEVED FROM THE HMONG ARCHIVES
DECEMBER 5, 2010

Txhua tus yeej xav tias ib lub tebchaws yuav tsum muaj nws ciam teb chaws, muaj nws haiv neeg, thiab kev nyob ywj pheej. Lub luag hauj lwm ntawm cov tub rog yog tiv thaiv lub tebchaws kom cov pej xeem nyob muaj kev kaj siab thiab muaj lub neej ua. Tub rog Nyab Laj Qaum Teb (NVA) tau tuaj txeeb lub Tiaj Rhawv Zeb. Lub Tiaj Rhawv Zeb yog ib thaj chaw uas muaj txiaj ntsig rau haiv neeg Lostsuas heev. Peb lub hom phiaj yog yuav rov txeeb kom tau rov qab, txhob cia yeeb ncuab tuaj ua tus tswj.

Vim li ntawd, kuv thiaj ntaus tswv yim yuav txeeb kom tau lub Tiaj Rhawv Zeb. Cov tub rog Nyab Laj Qaum Teb xav tsis txog tias peb yuav npaj tau li ntawd. Lawv tsuas npaj tej phom loj txais dav hlau thiab phom loj tua deb nrog rau tsheb hlau loj thauj tub rog sib tua nruab ntug xwb. Lawv tsis nco ceev faj txog peb cov Hmoob li. Lawv tsuas txhawj tsam dav hlau Ameliskas tuaj tso foob pob (bombs) rau lawv xwb. Lawm ntseeg tias lawm yuav tsis swb nrog rau peb cov Hmoob li. Tabsis zaum ntawd cov yeeb ncuab kuj raug mob hnyav thiab muaj kev ploj tuag lawm ntau heev. Peb muab tau cov cuab yeej riam phom tub rog ntau uas raug nyiaj li ntawm $2 - $3 billion. Peb kuj tsis siv tub rog coob, los yog muaj ploj tuag ntau. Kev yeej nthwv rog zaum no yog los ntawm peb muaj tswv yim tob thiab cov tub rog sib pab npaj zoo. Kuv tsuas siv li yim pab tub rog xwb.

Thaum kuv ntsib ntau tus qub tub rog Nyab Laj theem siab nyob rau tebchaws Ameliskas no, lawv hais rau kuv tias kuv tsim nyog tau txais txoj kev hwm, kev qhuas, thiab nco txog txiaj ntsig rau qhov uas peb tau yeej kob rog zaum ntawd. Lawv thov qhuas kuv thiab hais tias peb tsis xav tias koj yuav yeej tau peb li, tab sis koj yeej lawm tiag, lawv hais li rau kuv.

(TRANSLATION - LUS TXHAIS)

right
General Vang Pao in 1966.

THE CENTER FOR HMONG STUDIES COLLECTION VIA LEE PAO XIONG

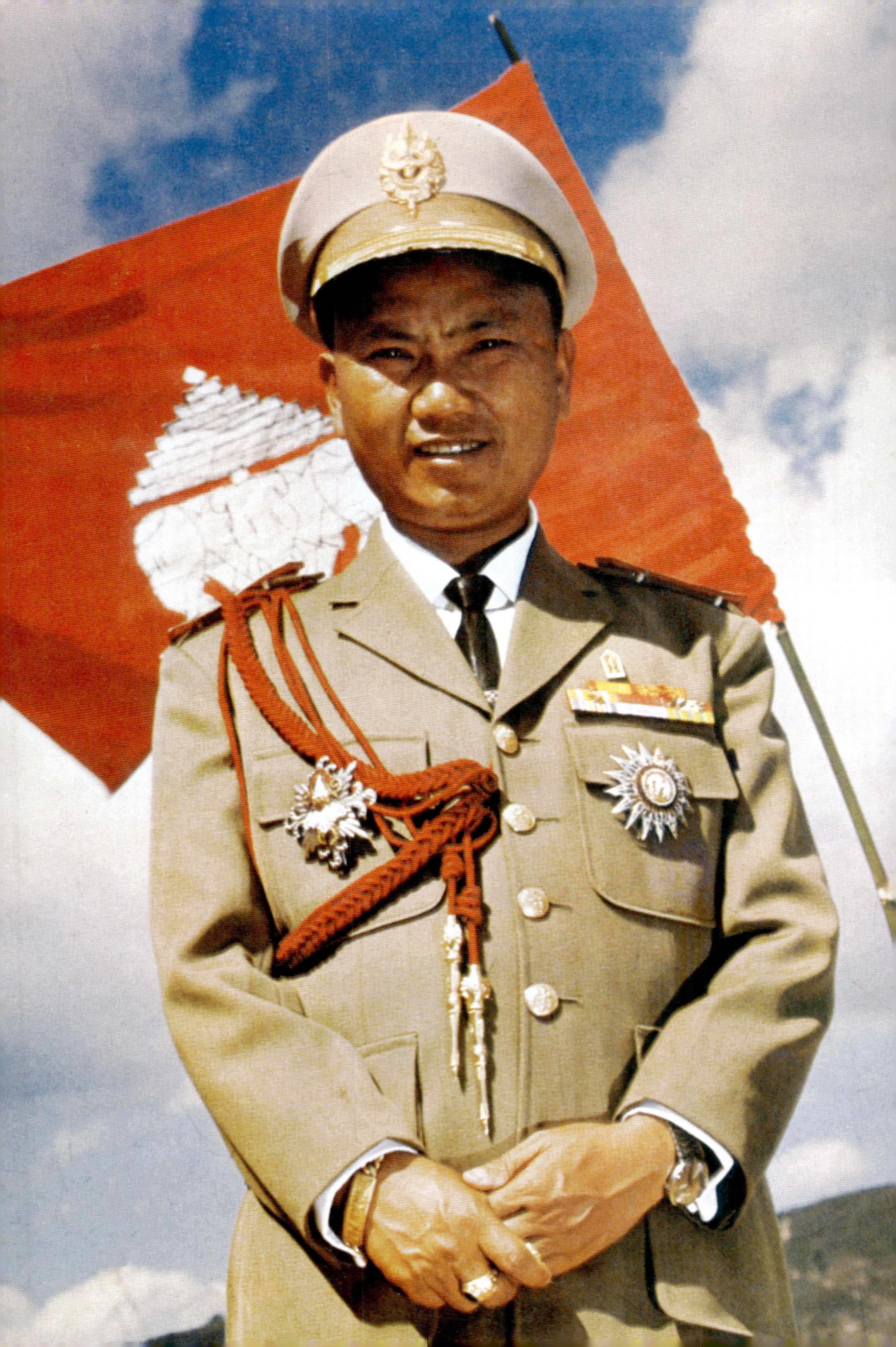

Left to right: General Vang Pao, U.S. Ambassador William Sullivan, CIA Operative James W. Lair, U.S. air attache in Laos Colonel 'Pappy' Pettigrew, and General Harry C. (Heinie) Aderholt in 1967.

JAMES W. LAIR COLLECTION

"[General Vang Pao] was the only person capable of leading the Hmong forces. Without his devotion, his talent, the Hmong would have gone under years ago."

* * *
GENERAL HARRY CHANEY "HEINIE" ADERHOLT
"THE COVERT WARS OF VANG PAO"
[MINNEAPOLIS] STAR TRIBUNE
TONY KENNEDY AND PAUL MCENROE
JULY 2, 2005

"I will fly 'til I die."

* * *
T-28 PILOT CAPTAIN LEE LUE
LEE LUE'S FAMOUS MOTTO, 1968
RETRIEVED FROM NHIA VUE LEE
OAKDALE, MINNESOTA
JUNE 2005

right
T-28 pilots Captain Vang Toua, *left*, and Captain Lee Lue, *right*, of the Royal Lao Air Force with General Vang Pao at the 'Waterpump' graduation in Nakhom Phanom, Thailand in 1967. Nakhom Phanom was home to the Royal Thai Air Force Base and was used by the U.S. to supply military and air support to the war in Vietnam and Laos. Vang Toua and Lee Lue were the first Hmong T-28 pilots. Soon after Vang Toua returned to Laos, his plane went down while on a combat mission and he was never found. Many veterans said that bad weather conditions may have caused his aircraft to crash. As for Lee Lue, he was shot down by North Vietnamese anti-aircraft fire in Mouang Soui in July 1969. In his flight career, he flew more than 5,000 combat missions. He was revered by a whole new generation of T-28 pilots before and after his death.

AIR COMMANDO ASSOCIATION COLLECTION VIA MAJOR GENERAL RICHARD SECORD

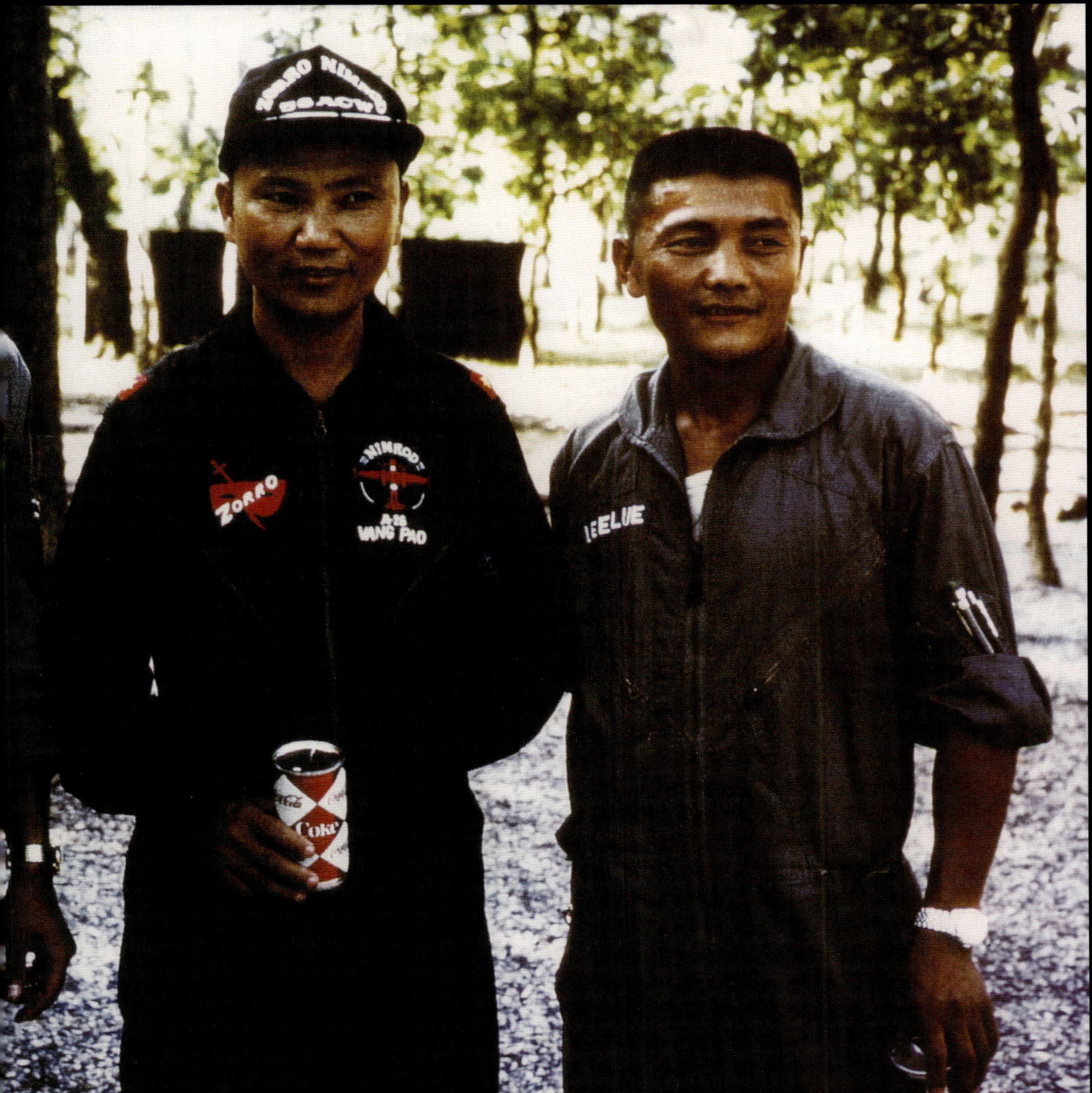
ZORRO
NIMROD
VANG PAO
LEELUE
Coke

Some of Hmong's T-28 pilots. They were all trained at the U.S. Air Force stationed in Udorn and at the Civil Aviation Training Center of Bangkok, Thailand. In the mid-1960s, General Vang Pao envisioned that to win the war, he will need air supports. Thus, with the help from the CIA, he created one of the most successful air programs in Laos.

MRS. NHIA HER LOR COLLECTION

right
H.R.H. King Sisavang Vatthana awarding nurses with medals for their courageous services during the Secret War at the medical center in Sam Thong, Lima Site 20, in early 1960s. The nursing program was founded by Edgar 'Pop' Buell and Dr. Charles Weldon, of the USAID, which had trained some of the best nurses where they had saved hundreds of thousands of lives. General Vang Pao also built facilities in Long Cheng for these nurses to train and treat the sick and wounded.

ROGER WARNER COLLECTION

"I love my job because I saved lives."

* * *
CHOUA THAO
ONE OF THE LEADING NURSES DURING THE SECRET WAR IN LAOS
STATIONED IN SAM THONG, LIMA SITE 20
AUTHOR'S INTERVIEW
MINNEAPOLIS, MINNESOTA
JUNE 2006

Prince Boun Oum of Na Champassak (with hat in both hands), former Prime Minister of Laos from 1948-1950 and 1960-1962, visited General Vang Pao and his soldiers in Long Cheng in 1966.

COLONEL LY TENG COLLECTION

"Between 1964 and 1967, the CIA-supported Hmong army in northern Laos, the main area of conflict, fought a highly successful guerrilla war against a mixed force of Pathet Lao and North Vietnamese troops. The high point of this phase of the war came in the summer of 1967. Royal Lao Army and Hmong units had blunted the enemy's dry season offensive of winter-spring 1966-67, causing local CIA officials to issue an optimistic appraisal of the situation in Laos. Hmong forces, a CIA Intelligence Information Cable argued, had gained the upper hand in the war: 'They now have the option of attempting a permanent change in the tactical balance of power in North Laos.'"

* * *
WILLIAM M. LEARY
PROFESSOR OF HISTORY AT UNIVERSITY OF GEORGIA
"THE CIA AND THE 'SECRET' WAR IN LAOS:
THE BATTLE FOR SKYLINE RIDGE, 1971-72"
THE VIETNAM CENTER AND ARCHIVE
RETRIEVED ON JUNE 2012

"Phou Pha Thi was our home. We were born and raised there. I could never imagine we would leave our home.

"Soon when the Americans came and built a radar there, suddenly our villages were unsafe. General Vang Pao had ordered all families to move to Long Cheng. He promised us shelter. We didn't want to go. However, after our leader Captain Kia Tou Vang was shot and killed at Phou Pha Thi in 1966 while making his usual flight routines, this convinced us that our villages would soon be raided by the North Vietnamese.

"My husband stayed back with the Americans to fight the North Vietnamese. We moved to Long Cheng. He said he would meet us in Long Cheng. Sadly, I never saw him again. One day while at home with my two young children, three of General Vang Pao's men delivered a note stating that my husband had been killed. Their faces looked hard with tired eyes. I didn't want to believe them. They said that some Americans also died at Phou Pha Thi. They apologized for my loss.

"I dropped to my knees and cried. My children rushed to comfort me. but they were too young to understand the pain thrusting inside me and the tragedy caused by wars.

"Several days later a cousin of mine came and explained that General Vang Pao did everything he could to save his men. 'We tried to bring home everyone, even the last man,' he said, 'but the enemy was too strong. They took them. They killed those that we couldn't get to.'"

* * *
MRS. XEE YANG
AUTHOR'S INTERVIEW
MINNEAPOLIS, MINNESOTA
OCTOBER 2009

"Since June 1966, I became a close subordinate to our leader General Vang Pao, and whatever he ordered me to do, I did. I was disciplined. I respected him. He trusted me. And for the nine years that I was General Vang Pao's bodyguard, I hardly had my boots off. I even slept with my boots on. I had to be ready at all time. His schedule was random. The country was at war. I didn't know when my leader was going to leave the house, day or night or whenever. I couldn't slow him down. Not one bit. When he came from his room upstairs, he was always dressed and ready to go on his daily routines. I was always prepared to go guard him. Whether to the frontlines, meet people, or go to see the King, I went with him.'

* * *
MAJOR YANG PA SUE
AUTHOR'S INTERVIEW
ST. PAUL, MINNESOTA
NOVEMBER 2010

Phou Pha Thi, Lima Site 85, where the U.S. radar site was installed. It was completely destroyed in March 1968 when the NVA attacked the site.

JAMES W. LAIR COLLECTION

left
To defend Phou Pha Thi, Lima Site 85, the 105mm howitzers were placed in nearby bunkers to keep the NVA from closing in on the radar site. This 105mm howitzer was placed at Houa Ma, which was located at the foot of Phou Pha Thi. At the waning moment of the fight against the NVA and Pathet Lao, General Vang Pao and his soldiers were unsuccessful and retreated to Long Cheng, causing massive civilian evacuation from the region westward. Picture was taken in 1968.

MAJOR YANG PA SUE COLLECTION

An Illustration of His Remarkable Life 170

right
MR II military leaders examine enemy movement in Phou Kong, near Phou Pha Thi. *Front to back:* Radio Operator Vang Vang, Lt. Colonel Toufu Vang, General Vang Pao, Colonel Yang Shoua, Colonel Yang Yong Chue, unknown, and unknown.

LT. COLONEL TOUFU VANG COLLECTION

An Illustration of His Remarkable Life   172

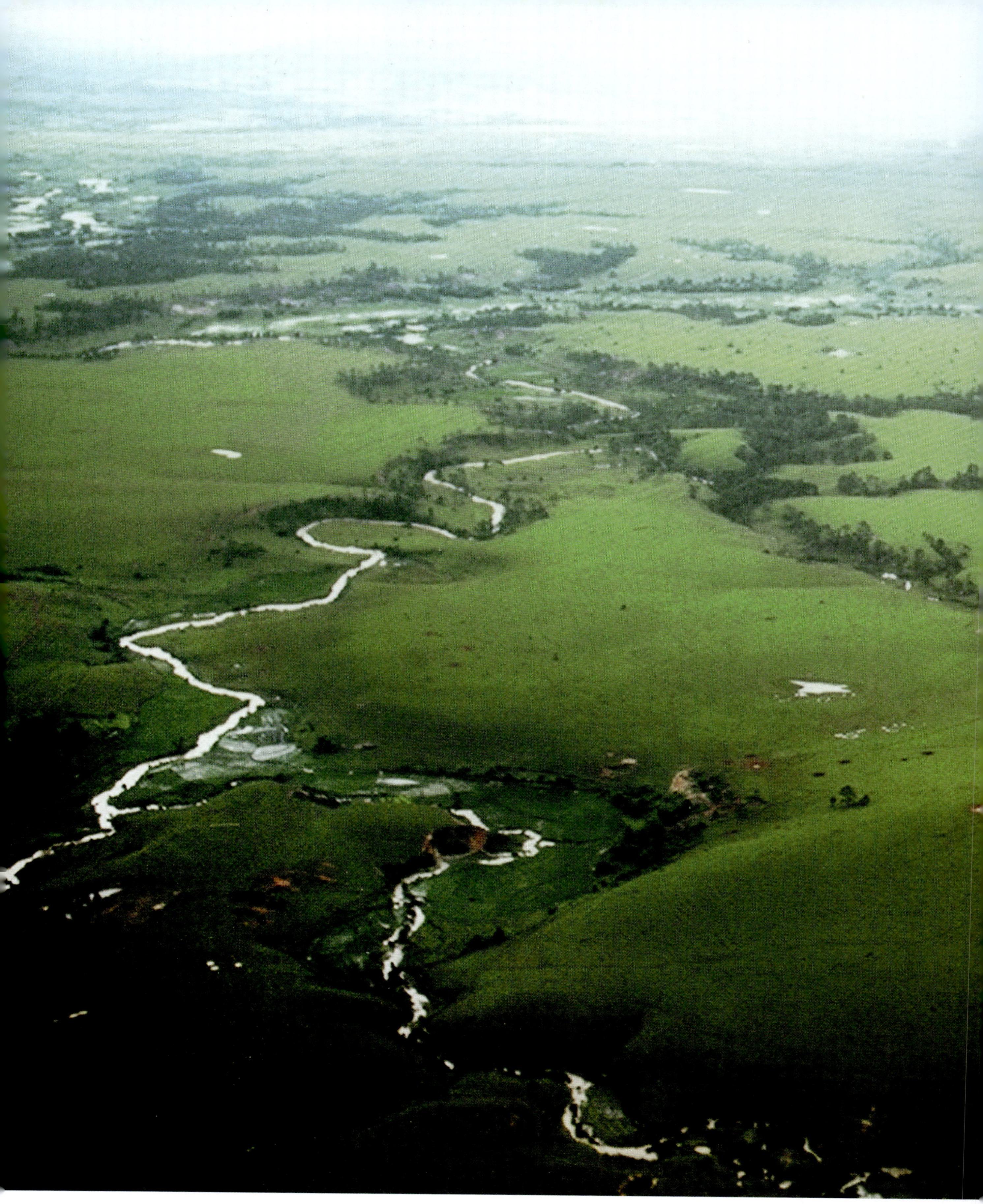

In 1966, the Plain of Jars, located in MR II, became one of the heaviest bombed areas, besides the Ho Chi Minh Trail, in Laos. The scattered brown spots are bomb craters.

JOHN MERZ COLLECTION

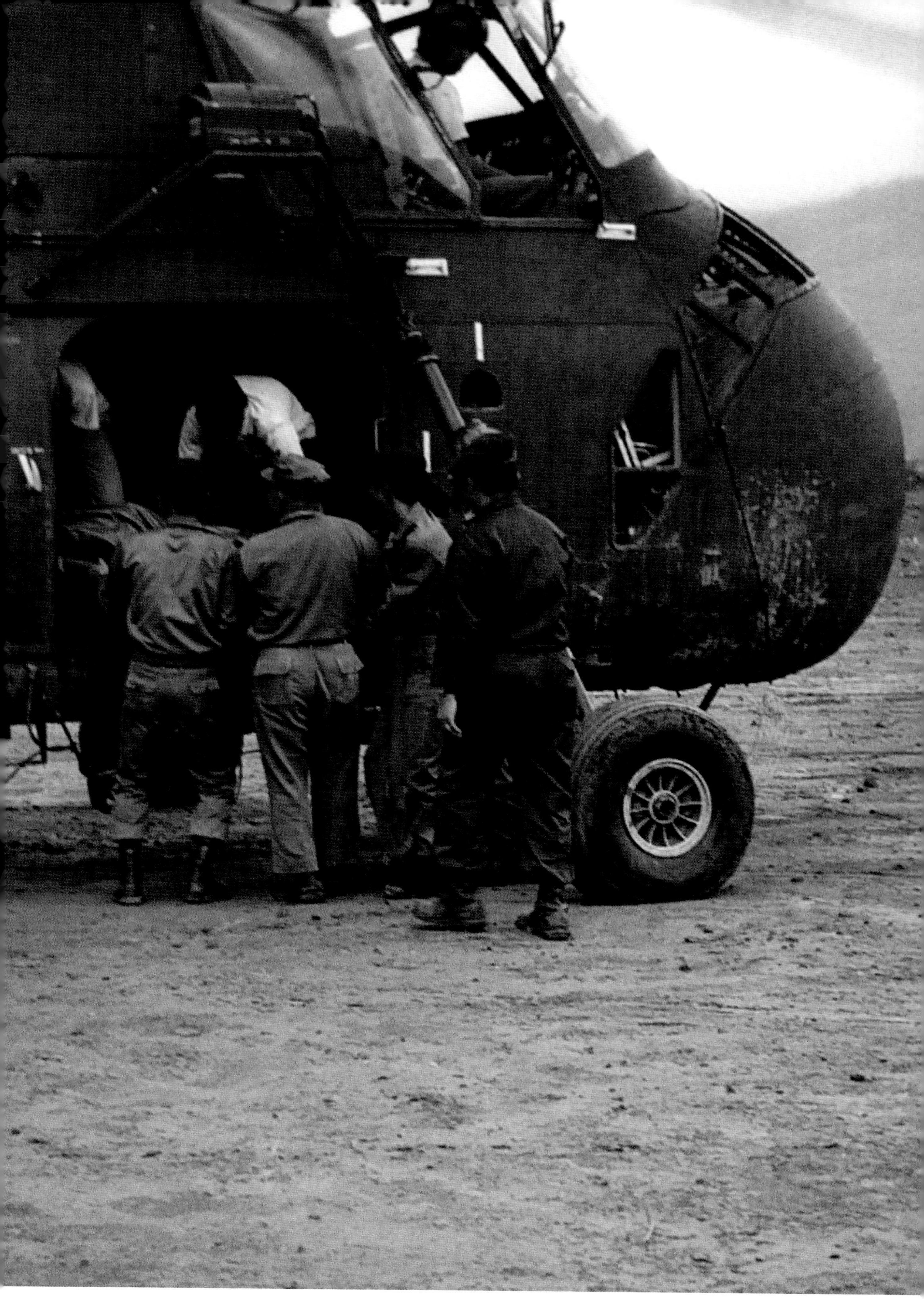

left
General Vang Pao salutes the body of Major Thongvong Rasamy, who was killed in action in Sam Neua, Laos, in 1966.

TUA VANG COLLECTION

"One of General Vang Pao's grand visions that he has accomplished for the people of Laos was he built schools for everyone, for children from all walks of life. At first, students from the upper class and wealthy families were the [only] ones who had access to good education. This was not what he wanted. General Vang Pao envisioned everyone being educated. So he built schools for the poor; he even built schools and hired teachers to teach in remote villages where no teachers had ever thought of going to teach so the children there could get a good education."

* * *

MAJOR VANG CHER CHA, RETIRED
GENERAL VANG PAO'S BODYGUARD
MINNEAPOLIS, MINNESOTA
AUTHOR'S INTERVIEW
NOVEMBER 4, 2010

Major Vang Cher Cha served as commander of Battalion 205, which was in charge of providing security measures to General Vang Pao's personal family members and his house.

MAJOR VANG CHER CHA COLLECTION

General Vang Pao with his soldiers and a CIA case officer in the late 1960s.

CHENG LENG VANG COLLECTION

"[During] the war years, I began sending my people abroad to become educated. It was my intention to have those who were educated abroad to return and implement their knowledge into those that did not get an opportunity to be educated. At that time, the majority of the people were not educated. [As] we fought to preserve our independence …, we also planned for the future our the country and our people."

* * *

GENERAL VANG PAO
"PEACE DOCTRINE ON LAOS"
WRITTEN ON NOVEMBER 26, 2003
RETRIEVED FROM XANG VANG
JANUARY 2012

Thaum tebchaws tseem muaj tsov rog, kuv pib xa kuv cov neeg mus kawm ntaub kawm ntawv, kawm txawj kawm tse rau txawv tebchaws. Kuv npaj cia kom cov tau mus kawm rov qab los qhia tej txuj ci uas lawm mus kawm los rau cov neeg tom qab uas tsis tau raug xa mus kawm. Thaum lub caij ntawd, cov neeg feem coob tsis tau mus kawm txawj kawm tse. Lub sij hawm peb ua rog tiv thaiv peb lub tebchaws kom tau kev ywj pheej …, peb tseem npaj lub neej pem suab rau peb lub tebchaws thiab cov pej xeem tib si.

(TRANSLATION - LUS TXHAIS)

top & below right
General Vang Pao handed out school supplies to children in MR II in the late 1960s.

PHOTOS FROM LT. COLONEL VANG GEU COLLECTION

top right
Sam Thong College was one of the schools General Vang Pao funded. The construction was completed in 1967. He also paid all the instructors. These students were second-year college students with their instructor Bounmi in April 1968. Students enrolled at the college were from all backgrounds.

VANG XANG COLLECTION

An Illustration of His Remarkable Life   180

General Vang Pao always found ways to entertain his guests in Long Cheng. He organized a *baci* ceremony, or string tying ritual, for his Laotian counterparts and honorary guests at his house in mid-1960s.

COLONEL LY TENG COLLECTION

top right
A small gathering with CIA case officers in Long Cheng in 1971. Person holding the cigarette was Colonel Lair's deputy, Pat Landry. General Vang Pao toasted drinks with Thai PARU commanders, *right middle*.

COLONEL LY TENG COLLECTION
SUSAN FINN COLLECTION VIA YEU TONG HLAO VU

below right
A U.S. diplomat, General Vang Pao, and Colonel Boun Noi.

COLONEL VANG GEU COLLECTION

An Illustration of His Remarkable Life 182

"In our country, we have our own territorial boundary and independence. When another country is trying to invade your country, this is the responsibility of all Lao people to fight and hold our country and territorial boundary. When someone is trying to change your outcome or to invade your country, it is necessary even to fight until the last man."

***
GENERAL VANG PAO
"THE MEO - DISAPPEARING WORLD"
DR. JACQUES LEMOINE, 1971
RETRIEVED FROM THE HMONG CULTURAL CENTER
JUNE 2006

Nyob peb tebchaws, peb muaj peb ciam av thiab kev nyob ywj pheej. Thaum uas muaj lwm lub tebchaws yuav tuaj caij tsuj peb lub tebchaws, nov yog lub luag hauj lwm ntawm txhua tus pej xeem yuav tsum tau los sib pab tiv thaiv tswj yus lub tebchaws. Yog muaj neeg yuav tuaj hloov koj lub hom phiaj los yog tuaj caij tsuj koj lub tebchaws, nws yeej tsim nyog uas koj yuav tsum tau sib ntaus sib tua kom txog thaum kawg txawm tias yuav tshuav yus ib leeg lawm xwb los xij peem.

(TRANSLATION - LUS TXHAIS)

right
General Vang Pao in 1968.

CHAI VANG COLLECTION

next page
General Vang Pao with Laotian military leaders.

THE GVP FAMILY & LANG VANG COLLECTION

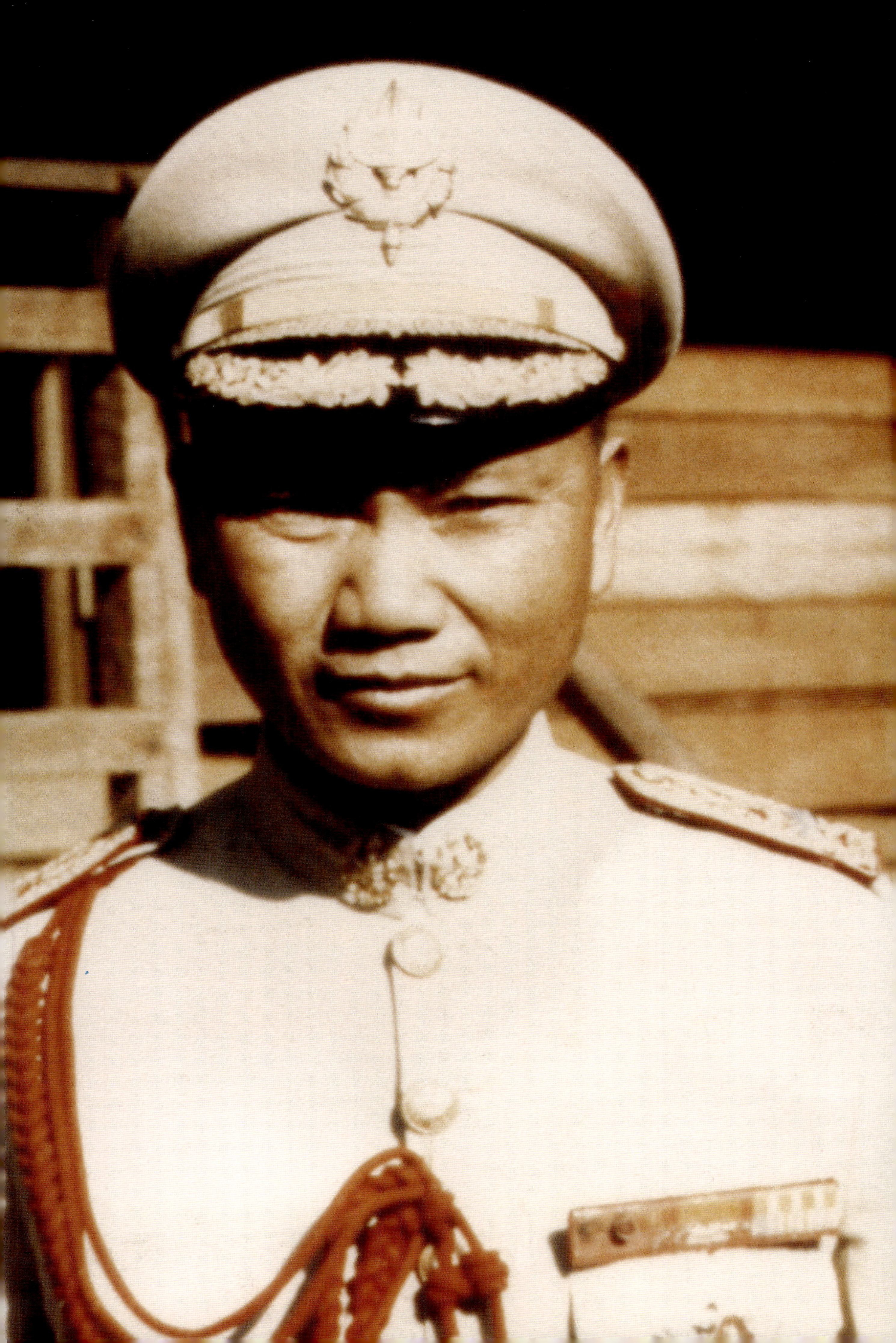

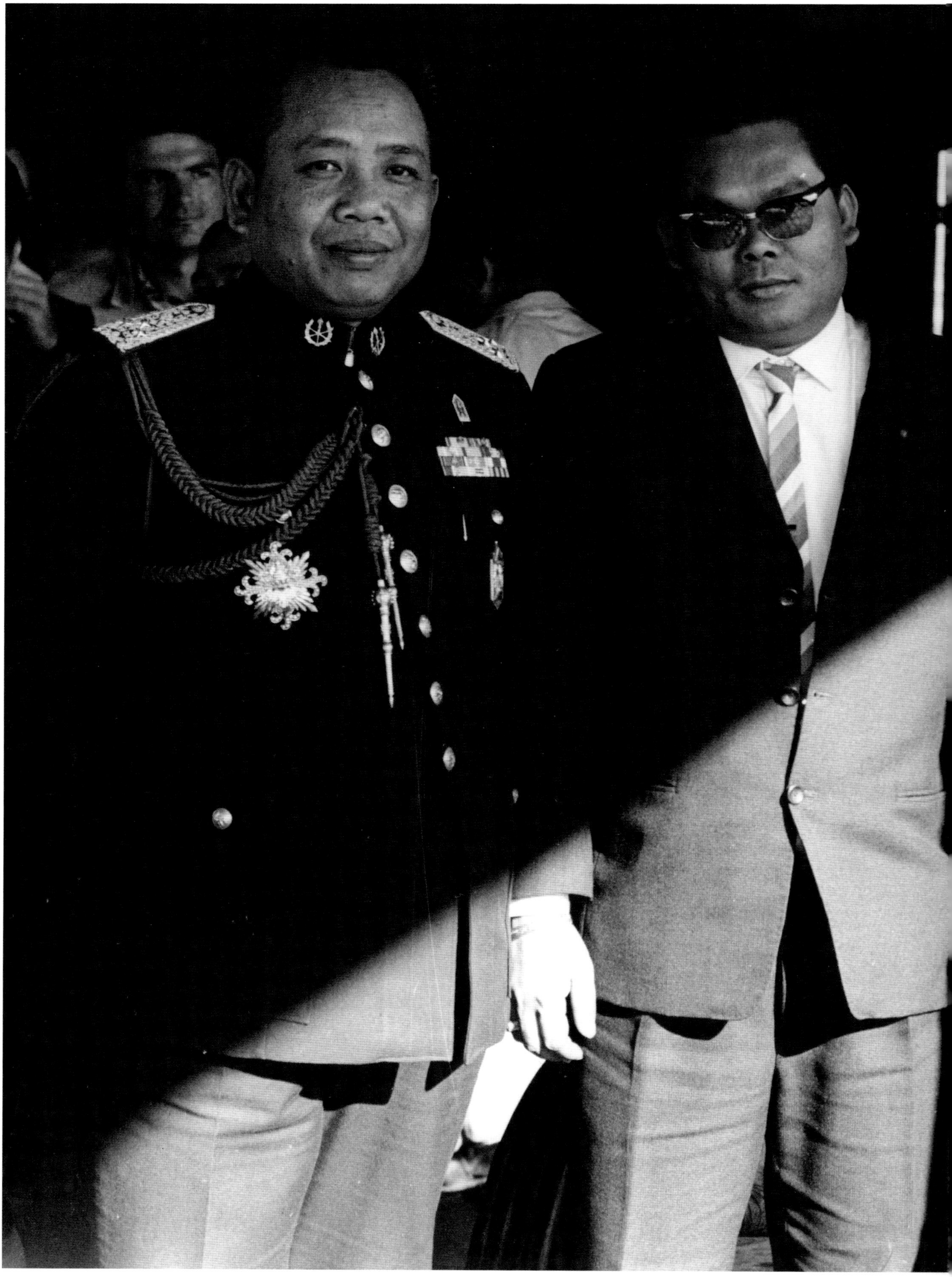

An Illustration of His Remarkable Life 186

"I thought you would be interested to know that General Vang Pao, the [Hmong] General from Laos, will be in the White House from 8:45 o'clock until 9:30 a.m. on 1 October for a private tour of the public rooms. General Vang Pao ... will also be received in State and Defense. If you have time I suggest you might find it interesting to take a few minutes to meet him while he is at the White House.

"As you know, Vang Pao is the head of the [Hmong] irregular forces, now consisting of over 22,000 men, which have been the backbone of the resistance to Communist infiltration in Northern Laos. Although Vang Pao and his forces have suffered some considerable loss of territory during the enemy dry season offensive, they are now in the process of regaining a significant amount. They have killed or wounded during the nine months to 1 August 1968 a total of some 3,500 enemy at losses of 1,500 to themselves. Vang Pao is one of the two Lao 'fighting generals' as well as being a most effective leader of his people. He is well thought of by both the King and [Prime Minister] Souvanna Phouma. Although he is primarily interested in the defense of his people and their highland living areas, he recognizes that in the long run the [Hmong] will have to become integrated with the rest of Laos society and has already taken considerable steps to this end, including educating the young children in the Lao language and teaching them allegiance to the King.

"General Vang Pao speaks fluent French and understands English, speaking it with a considerable accent..."

* * *

RICHARD HELMS
LETTER FROM THE OFFICE OF THE DIRECTOR, CIA
TO THE HONORABLE WALT W. ROSTOW
SPECIAL ASSISTANT TO THE PRESIDENT
SEPTEMBER 25, 1968
"TRAGIC MOUNTAINS" BY JANE HAMILTON-MERRITT
DECEMBER 4, 2010

A cross-stitch symbol of the U.S. CIA-Air America involvement in the Secret War in Laos.

FRED EISENHAUER COLLECTION

right
General Vang Pao with a U.S. Army General at the Pentagon during his official visit in 1968.

CHER CHANG VANG COLLECTION

An Illustration of His Remarkable Life   188

From left to right: CIA officers Burr Smith, Lawrence Devlin, Theodore G. Shackley, U.S. Ambassador William H. Sullivan, and General Vang Pao in Long Cheng, late 1960s. Sullivan was the ambassador to Laos from 1964-1969. His predecessor was Leonard S. Unger (1962-1964) and successor was G. McMurtrie Godley (1969-1973).

SUSAN FINN COLLECTION

"The Geneva Accords of 1962 for Laos had a territorial premise... [These] Lao agreements had hardly been signed, and hardly been put into effect in 1962 before the North Vietnamese began to break them. In fact they never withdrew their forces from Laos, as had been required by those agreements. They enhanced and expanded the Ho Chi Minh Trail, and they maintained an attitude of some provocation with respect to the Vientiane government, as well as the other forces in Laos.

"Eventually they assassinated one of the young military officers who was fairly senior in the neutralist command. This in turn resulted in the execution or the assassination of the foreign minister, who had close links with Peking, rather than with Hanoi, and in general the substance of the agreements began to break down. Our choice as the United States at that stage was either to declare that the agreements were no longer valid, and revert to a confrontation which presumably would result in the re-introduction of United States military forces into Thailand and all the other elements of the confrontation that existed prior to the agreements.

"Or else we could attempt to maintain the façade of the agreements but to shore up the neutralist government and try to really resolve the basic issue on the territory of Vietnam, rather than in Laos. Laos after all was really ancillary to Vietnam. The main thrust of the North Vietnamese, or the Lao Dong party, was to take over Vietnam first, all of Vietnam, and then only after that to expand over into Laos and Cambodia.

"They were using Lao territory primarily as a transit point to South Vietnam, and that was the principal preoccupation of Hanoi. So rather than re-establishing the confrontation overtly in Laos, a decision was made in 1963 and early 1964 to re-establish some logistic support to the [Hmong] tribe people up in the hills of the north-eastern quadrant of Laos, in order to slow down the advance of the Vietnamese across Lao territory, and in order to bring that measure under some control.

"It was decided to do this clandestinely, rather than overtly, because by doing it clandestinely we could still maintain the presumption that the Lao agreements were intact, and if and when a settlement was reached in Vietnam, then we could revert back to the status quo of having an agreement that did not require renegotiation, and which basically accepted a buffer arrangement for Laos..."

* * *

WILLIAM H. SULLIVAN
U.S. AMBASSADOR TO LAOS, 1964-1969
"SULLIVAN'S DISCOVERY OF THE SECRET NEGOTIATIONS," 1981
RETRIEVED FROM WGBH MEDIA LIBRARY AND ARCHIVES
DECEMBER 4, 2010

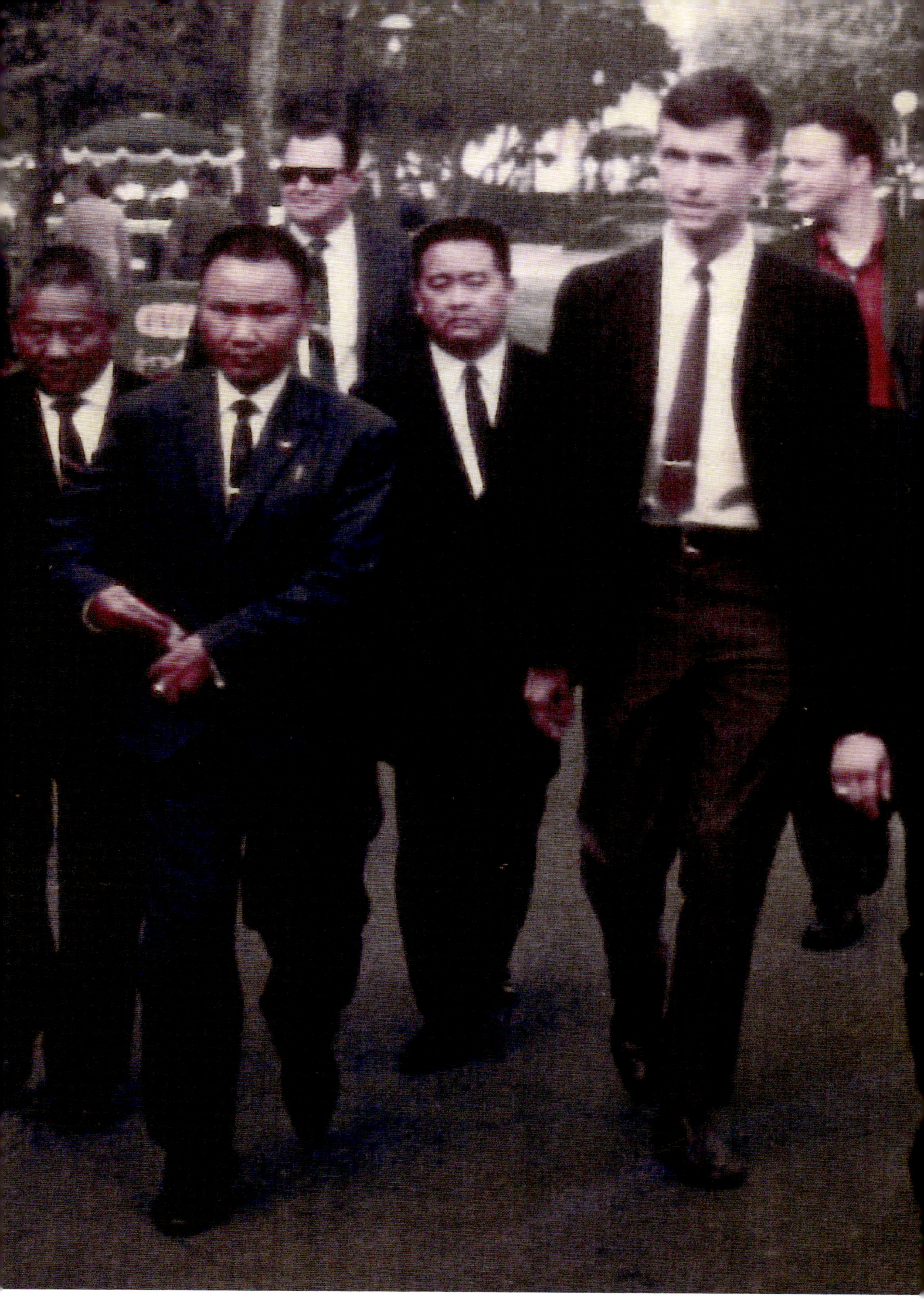

"Since 1962, this Agency has played a major role in support of United States policy in Laos. Specifically, we have developed and maintained a covert irregular force of a total of 39,000 men which has borne a major share of the active fighting, particularly in Northeast Laos. In this latter area, under the leadership of General Vang Pao, guerrilla units formed of [Hmong] tribesmen have been engaged for more than eight years in a seesaw battle with the North Vietnamese Army and Pathet Lao troops."

* * *

RICHARD HELMS
"MEMORANDUM FROM DIRECTOR OF CENTRAL INTELLIGENCE
HELMS TO PRESIDENT NIXON"
WASHINGTON, JULY 18, 1969
RETRIEVED FROM
FOREIGN RELATIONS OF THE UNITED STATES, 1969–1976
VOLUME VI, VIETNAM, JANUARY 1969–JULY 1970
JUNE 2012

left
Hmong leaders with State Department personnel in Washington, D.C., in 1968. *From left to right*: Chaomouang (Mayor) Tong Pao Lee, General Vang Pao, Colonel Toulu Moua, unknown American, and Congressman Tou Yia Lee.

WA JOE VUE COLLECTION

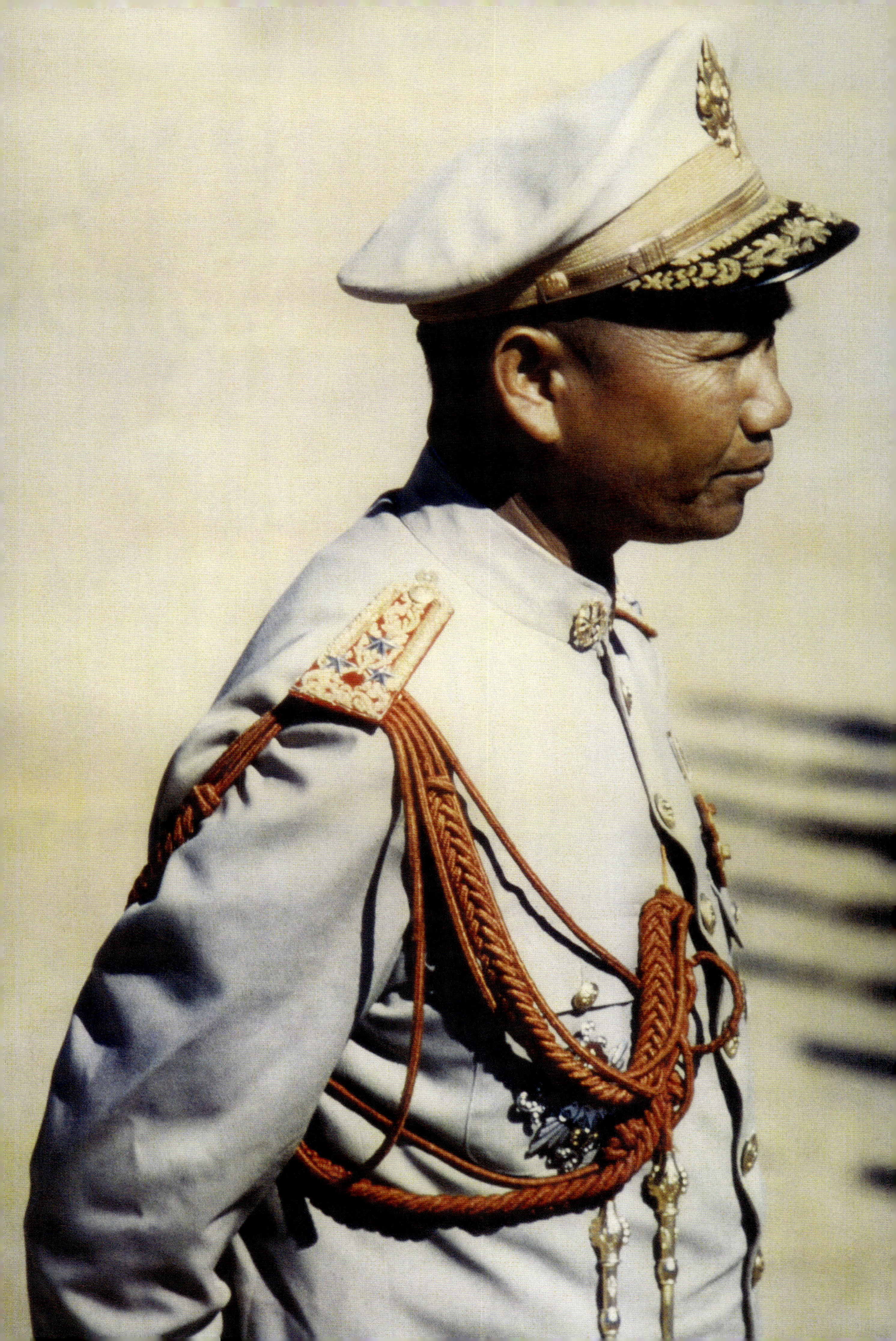

"[I was Commander of Military Region Two and Commander of the Special Guerrilla Units, a special forces of the United States. During the war, my first priority was to defend my country.] At any given time, I had 22,000 soldiers under my command and also about 450,000 civilians. In addition, I was in charge of the ten minority hill-tribes in Laos. My duties at that time were to stop North Vietnamese from supplying war materials to the Viet Cong in the South by way of the Ho Chi Minh Trail, which cut through Laos, and also to rescue downed American pilots. The Hmong sacrificed and suffered the most in the war."

**
GENERAL VANG PAO
SPEECH AT THE HERITAGE FOUNDATION
FEBRUARY 5, 1987
ISSN 0727-1155

Kuv yog tus Tuam Thawj Coj ntawm tsoom tub rog nqe 2 thiab Tuam Thawj Coj rau pawg tub rog hav zoov tshwjxeeb (Special Guerrilla Units). Thaum tseem ua rog, kuv lub homphiaj tsuas yog tivthaiv kuv lub tebchaws. Lub caij ntawd, kuv muaj tub rog txog 22,000 leej nyob rau kuv kev tswjfwm, thiab muaj kwv yees li 450,000 tus pejxeem. Dhau li ntawd, kuv tseem tau saib xyuas 10 haiv neeg tojsiab nyob rau hauv lub tebchaws Lostsuas. Kuv txoj dej num yog txiav kom tau Tub Rog Nyablaj Qaum teb txoj kev xa riam phom ua rog tuaj mus rau cov Viet Cong nyob rau Nyablaj Qab Teb uas yog nyob rau ntawd txoj kev Ho Chi Minh Trail, uas yog hla hauv tebchaws Lostsuas. Thiab kuv tseem pab cawm cov tub rog Ameliskas tsav davhlau poob. Kuv cov Hmoob yog cov uas muab roj ntsha pua tebchaws thiab rau tsim txom nyhav tshaj nyob rau nthwv rog zaum no.

(TRANSLATION - LUS TXHAIS)

This rare Military Region II Ring of Merits was awarded personally by General Vang Pao to his soldiers and American personnel in Laos for their heroism, bravery, commitment to service, and successful leadership during battles. The silver-gold centerpiece was the symbol of Military Region II.

CAPTAIN XAI NOU VANG COLLECTION

left
General Vang Pao in his three-star major general uniform in 1968.

DR. YANG LONG COLLECTION

An Illustration of His Remarkable Life   194

King Sisavang Vatthana and his council members visited General Vang Pao in Long Cheng, late 1960s.

COLONEL LY TENG COLLECTION

"The future well-being, happiness, prosperity, and unity of all the people of Laos must remain the first priority and above all else."

* * *
GENERAL VANG PAO
"PEACE DOCTRINE ON LAOS"
WRITTEN ON NOVEMBER 26, 2003
RETRIEVED FROM XANG VANG
JANUARY 2012

Lub neej zoo yav peb suab, kev zoo siab, kev vam meej thiab kev sib koom tes ntawm cov pej xeem nyob tebchaws Lostsuas yuav tsuj muab ua qhov tseem nceeb tshaj txhua yam.

(TRANSLATION - LUS TXHAIS)

General Vang Pao and an American official celebrate with one of the pageant contestant runner-ups. According to the General, the pageant competition was incorporated into the Hmong New Year Celebration was 1970s. This has been a popular tradition ever since.

COLONEL LY TENG COLLECTION

During the Hmong New Year Celebration in Long Cheng, one of General Vang Pao's favorite sports to watch was bull-fighting. He also owned several bulls. This was the most popular sport among men at the New Year sporting events. Although it is unknown when bull-fighting was introduced as entertainment during the Hmong New Year Celebration, many believe it had existed for many centuries.

XIONG PAO LOR COLLECTION

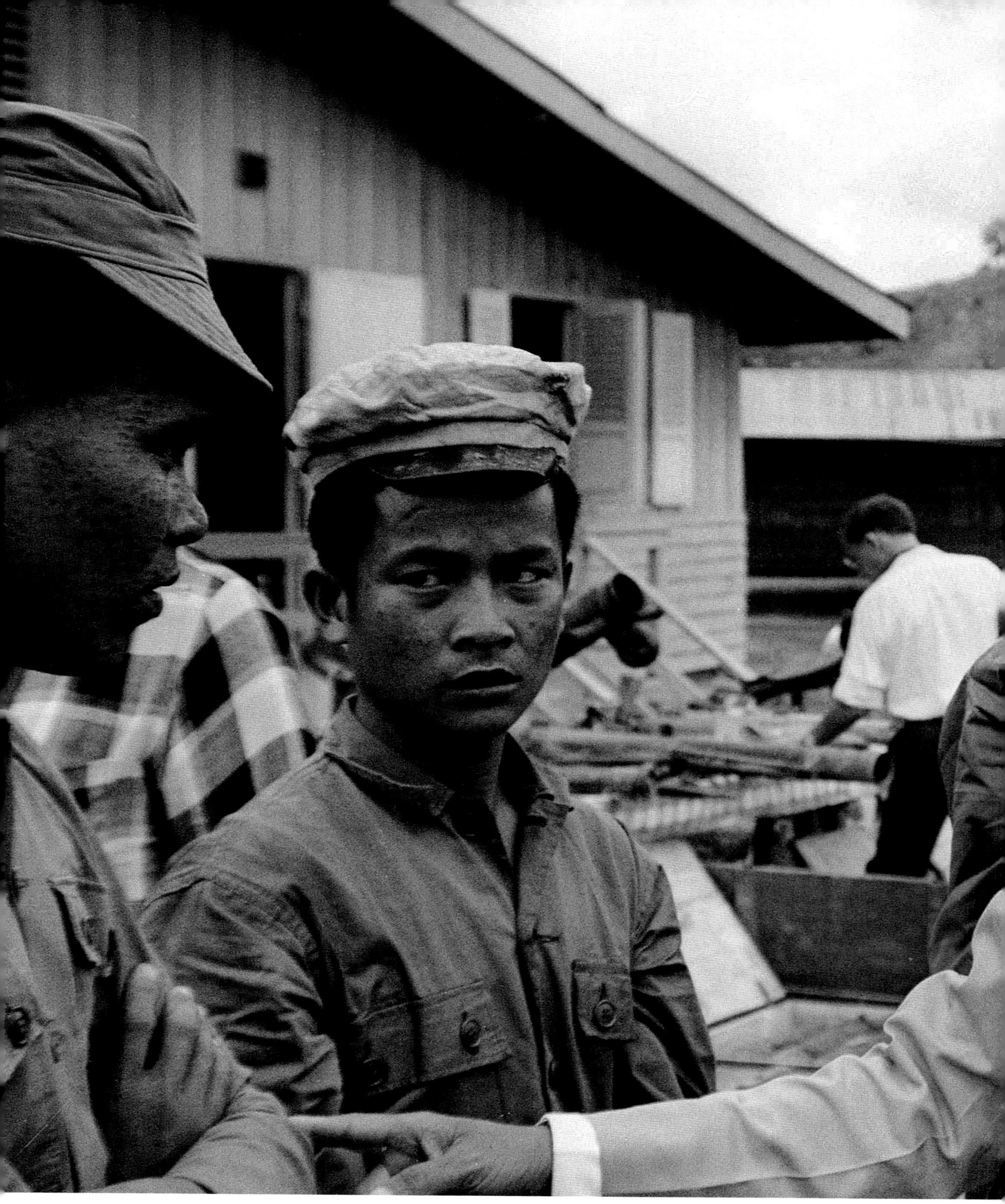

General Vang Pao questions two Communist North Vietnamese prisoners, who claim themselves as Communist Pathet Lao, in Sam Thong on October 17, 1969. They were captured during a fight near the Plain of Jars. During the war, more than 70,000 North Vietnamese soldiers fought in Laos.

ASSOCIATED PRESS COLLECTION

HMONG T-28 PILOTS

FIRST PROMOTION
Lt. Colonel Vang Chou
Major Lee Lue
Major Lee Ying
Captain Vang Ge
Lt. Xiong Kou, C47 Pilot
Lt. Vang Toua

SECOND PROMOTION
Major Yang Xiong
Captain Moua Va, C47 Pilot
Captain Lee Teng, c47 Pilot
Captain Vang Xue
Lt. Hang Ger
Lt. Moua Teng
Lt. Thao Nhia
Lt. Vang Cheng
Lt. Vang Dao
Lt. Vue Ger
2nd Lt. Her Ying
2nd Lt. Lor Neng

THIRD PROMOTION
Major Thao Xao
Captain Lee Tou Xiong
Captain Vang Bee
Captain Yang Pao
Lt. Bounchanh Sayavong, Khumu
Lt. Moua Chue, C47 Pilot
Lt. Vue Long
Lt. Vang Xeng
Lt. Yang Bee
Lt. Xiong Koua

FOURTH PROMOTION
Major Kha Vang, Commercial Pilot
Captain Vang Bee, Commercial Pilot
Lt. Kha Yia
Lt. Ly Moua
Lt. Vang Chong, Commercial Pilot
Lt. Vang Fong, Cessna Pilot
Lt. Vang Teng
Lt. Vang Tou
Lt. Yang Ge
2nd Lt. Moua Chue, Cessna Pilot

FIFTH PROMOTION
Captain Vang Foua
Lt. Moua Shoua
2nd Lt. Yang Phong
2nd Lt. Lee Ya
Her Nai, Cessna Pilot
Her Ying, Cessna Pilot
Lee Yi, Cessna Pilot
Moua Tong, Cessna Pilot
Thao Teng, Cessna Pilot
Xiong Song, Cessna Pilot
Xiong Yeng, Cessna Pilot

HMONG AIRCRAFT MECHANICS
Moua Ge
Moua Song
Lee Tou
Lee Ying
Vue Koua
Xiong Xeng

"We did not fight for fame or glory, we fought for the freedom of our country."

* * *

2ND LT. PHONG YANG
FORMER T-28 PILOT
"FORMER HMONG AND KHUMU T-28 PILOTS FIRST REUNION"
MAPLEWOOD, MINNESOTA
JUNE 16, 2012

General Vang Pao with some T-28 pilots in Long Cheng in 1972. Several of GVP's personal pilots include Captain Vang Bee, Lt. Xiong Koua, and Lt. Yia Kha. Out of all the Hmong pilots, three were commercial pilots and three were with the Ravens. At the end, some were killed and some were wounded while in combat.

NHIA BEE LEE, SON OF FORMER T-28 PILOT MAJOR LEE YING, COLLECTION
RIGHT, LIST RETRIEVED FROM YANG ENG COLLECTION

An Illustration of His Remarkable Life 202

General Vang Pao, CIA case-officer Burr Smith, along with MR II soldiers paying respect at the death of a soldier being buried at Long Cheng. *Far left* is Col. Neng Chue Thao, General Vang Pao's brother-in-law.

SUSAN FINN COLLECTION VIA YEU TONG HLAO VU

right
One thing that discomforted General Vang Pao most was attending his deceased soldiers' funerals. Although thousands were unaccounted for, the lucky ones were brought back and received proper burial traditions. Here, General Vang Pao helped lower the coffin of the late T-28 Pilot Major Vang Sue, who was killed in action in 1972, into his resting place.

DR. TONY VANG COLLECTION

"By 1968, there were nearly 600,000 refugees in Laos, many of whom had tried to set out on long marches and many of whom were brutally murdered when fallen into enemy hands. And while the civilian dependents of the Hmong soldiers had to endure constant relocation or even death, Vang Pao's army was also decimated dramatically: First, Air America helicopters had the grisly task of transporting the dead Hmong soldiers back to their villages. Then, as Vang Pao had lost more than 1,000 men since January 68, Air America helicopters flew again to native villages to recruit soldiers for the irregular army. But these recruitment drives turned up only 300 replacements, all very young (16 years or below) or over 35, so that the Hmong were threatened to be pushed out of their mountaintop posts surrounding the Plain of Jars."

* * *

DR. JOE F. LEEKER
"AIR AMERICA IN LAOS II —MILITARY AID"
UNIVERSITY OF TEXAS AT DALLAS
AUGUST 11, 2008
RETRIEVED IN MARCH 2011

"General Vang Pao, the leader of the hill-tribe irregulars in Laos, was recently in the United States on a visit. He is a real asset to us, a feisty little fighter who has led his [Hmong] people into a courageous battle against the Communists in Laos. He is an admirer of you--and of the United States-- and is deeply grateful for the American assistance provided his force.

"As a token of his and the [Hmong] people's appreciation, he has sent to you an old handmade flintlock rifle of the kind commonly used by his soldiers when they first began their resistance. (I think you will find it an interesting gift.) Attached is a letter of thanks which I recommend you sign."

* * *
WALT WHITMAN ROSTOW
SPECIAL ASSISTANT TO PRESIDENT LYNDON B. JOHSON
WHITE HOUSE MEMORANDUM TO THE PRESIDENT
NOVEMBER, 14, 1968
"TRAGIC MOUNTAINS" BY JANE HAMILTON-MERRITT
DECEMBER 4, 2010

"The Hmong are fiercely independent people... Despite ten years of defeat and suffering, most have remained staunch allies of America. Today with other hilltribes, they are still the backbone of the secret army... They have paid dearly for their commitment..."

* * *
"SECRET WAR IN LAOS: 1961-1975"
CBS DOCUMENTARY VIDEO OF THE WAR IN LAOS
RETRIEVED FROM HTTP://WWW.YOUTUBE.COM/
WATCH?V=AJ1CXGOIMZO
SEPTEMBER 2012

right
General Vang Pao gave a Hmong flintlock as a friendship gift to an American advisor to strengthen their commitment and efforts to fighting the Secret War in Laos.

CAPTAIN VANG NOU COLLECTION

An Illustration of His Remarkable Life 206

1.

2.

1. PAUL E. WHITE COLLECTION
2. ROGER WARNER COLLECTION
3. WA CHONG VANG COLLECTION
4. SUSAN FINN COLLECTION VIA YEU TONG HLAO VU
5. THE GVP FAMILY COLLECTION
6. TOUA VANG COLLECTION

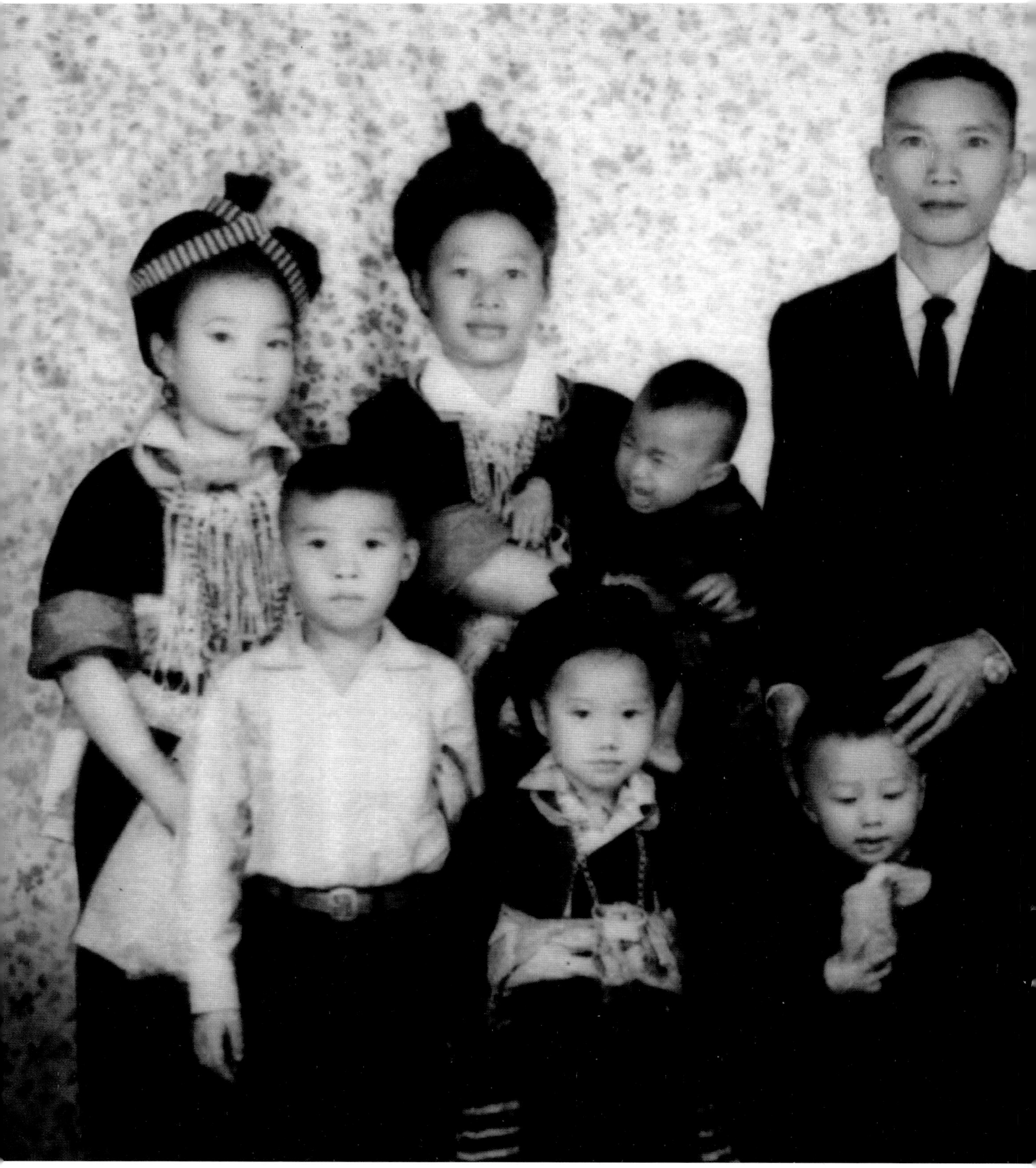

"My father Pa Vu was a quiet person. Although many people did not see him being actively involved in his brother General Vang Pao's political and military affairs, he was a key, behind-the-scene person who handled many of Vang Pao's projects; namely all the logistic for both military and civilian needs, and he also was responsible for Hmong economic development in MR II."

* * *
LIA VANG
SON OF MR. PA VU VANG & MRS. SHOUA THAO
AUTHOR'S INTERVIEW
NOVEMBER 2010

left
General Vang Pao's brother Pa Vu Vang's family in Long Cheng, Laos, early 1960s. At this time, the population in Long Cheng had about 4,000 people.

LIA VANG COLLECTION

"I do consider General Vang Pao as the greatest General the Kingdom of Laos has ever seen. I believe that a number of other Laotian generals would agree with me. Vang Pao undeniably has the qualities of a great military leader...

"In each of his visits to Paris, Prince Souvanna Phouma, himself, then Prime Minister, publicly praised General Vang Pao as a good soldier and a good public servant of the nation, before all the Laotian students in France. I did not hear the Prince make such complimentary comments regarding any other military leader. At the time, I was still a student in Bordeaux. I often went up to Paris to attend the press conferences given by the Prime Minister at the Lao Embassy, because I had much interest in my country's affairs."

* * *
DR. TOUXOUA LYFOUNG
SON OF THE HONORABLE PHAGNA TOUBY LYFOUNG
INTERVIEW WITH "HMOOB VAM MEEJ"
RETRIEVED FROM THE WWW.LAOSNET.ORG
NOVEMBER 2010

MR II soldiers combat enemy troops by shelling 155mm guns on the Plain of Jars in the late 1960s.

THE GVP FAMILY COLLECTION VIA LANG VANG

right
General Vang Pao surveys damages from a USAF strike against a NVA artillery position on the Plain of Jars in Fall 1970.

COLONEL TOM LUM COLLECTION

"General Vang Pao was, in my opinion, the best combat commander in Southeast Asia during the war against North Vietnam. But he was more than that. He was a tremendous Statesman and leader of the Hmong people. I observed him frequently while in action and during operational planning sessions from 1966 through August of 1969. This encompassed a number of actions and reactions to NVA campaigns aimed at eliminating the Hmong forces. General Vang Pao led from the front and had a feel for the fight that I have never seen before or since. He was both a strategic planner and a masterful tactician and could be a model for study at military academies. General Vang Pao's forces were still in the fight and undefeated in 1975 when the U.S. completely terminated its participation in the war. The U.S. never adequately recognized or supported General Vang Pao's people after the defeat in Southeast Asia. I was on detail from the USAF to duty with CIA during my years of association with General Vang Pao and served as the CIA officer in charge of combat air support for Laos."

* * *

MAJOR GENERAL RV SECORD, USAF, RETIRED
AUTHOR'S EMAIL INTERVIEW
AUGUST 9, 2011

~~TOP SECRET~~/SENSITIVE/EYES ONLY

RECORD OF PRESIDENT'S MEETING WITH
THE FOREIGN INTELLIGENCE ADVISORY BOARD

DATE: July 18, 1970: 10:45 a.m. - 12:15 p.m.

PARTICIPANTS: The President
Board Members:
  Chairman, George W. Anderson, Jr.
  Members: Gordan Gray
         Franklin B. Lincoln, Jr.
         (Dr.) Franklin D. Murphy
         Robert D. Murphy
Other:
  Henry A. Kissinger
  B/Gen. Alexander M. Haig
  Gerard P. Burke (Exec. Sec. PFIAB)

SUBJECT: Southeast Asia

The members of the PFIAB met with the President to report on their recent visits to Southeast Asia. Following is a summary record of the highlights of the meeting.

<u>Intelligence for Cambodia.</u> The Board members believed there had been no significant improvement in our intelligence capabilities in Cambodia as of their July 5 visit, and the President expressed his displeasure. Dr. Kissinger noted interagency disagreements on the facilities required; he said that local communications had been improved but those between Phnom Penh and the outside were still unresolved due to State's desire to maintain a low-US visibility. The President stated that more COMINT on Cambodia was needed and that Mr. Fred Ladd's arrival in Phnom Penh had greatly improved the reporting from there.

<u>US Personnel in Cambodia.</u> The Board confirmed the President's impression that US Charge Rives was in over his head in Cambodia and that Mr. Ladd was doing an exceptionally good job, although overworked and needing

~~TOP SECRET~~/SENSITIVE/EYES ONLY

WL:jlj 8/6/70

TOP SECRET/SENSITIVE / Eyes Only

shown at last real teamwork among the various South Vietnamese forces. The Chairman noted that Vang Pao often risked his personal safety in combat, and the President said we should prevent him from doing this in view of his importance to the effort in Laos. The Chairman declared that our knowledge of the intentions of Peking and Hanoi were essentially non-existent, and, for example, we might be passing over too casually the possibility of Chinese communist volunteers in Southeast Asia. The Chairman also stated that the critical factor in Eastern Asia during the next few years will be the Russian decision about what to do about Chinese nuclear weapons developments. The President agreed with Dr. Murphy that Indonesia was a key country with whom we should maintain a good relationship.

Hmong girls dressed in their traditional costumes decorating the walkpath with flowers to receive King Sisavang Vatthana and Queen Khamphoui durng their visit to General Vang Pao's military base at Long Cheng in 1971.

CAPTAIN VANG XAI NOU COLLECTION

top right
King Sisavang Vatthana decorated General Vang Pao with a medal of valor in Long Cheng in 1971.

CAPTAIN VANG NENG COLLECTION

right
Wives of military and public officials wait to welcome the arrival of King Sisavang Vatthana and his family to Long Cheng. They are in front of the house General Vang Pao built for the King in 1970 for whenever his majesty visited Long Cheng. *Left to right:* Mrs. Hang Sao, Mrs. Thong, Mrs. Phan, Mrs. Xia Thao Vang, Mrs. Phimpha, Mrs. Saykham Southakakoumal (wife of Governor of Xiengkhouang), Mrs. Lyfoung Tougeu, Mrs. Phouthen Sam Neua, Mrs. Lyfoung Touby, Unknown, Mrs. Ly Xang, Mrs. Moua Toulu, and Mrs. Moua Thong. General Vang Pao always supported women participating in public events since he became a leading figure in Hmong and Lao societies in the early 1960s.

THE GVP FAMILY COLLECTION VIA LANG VANG

An Illustration of His Remarkable Life 218

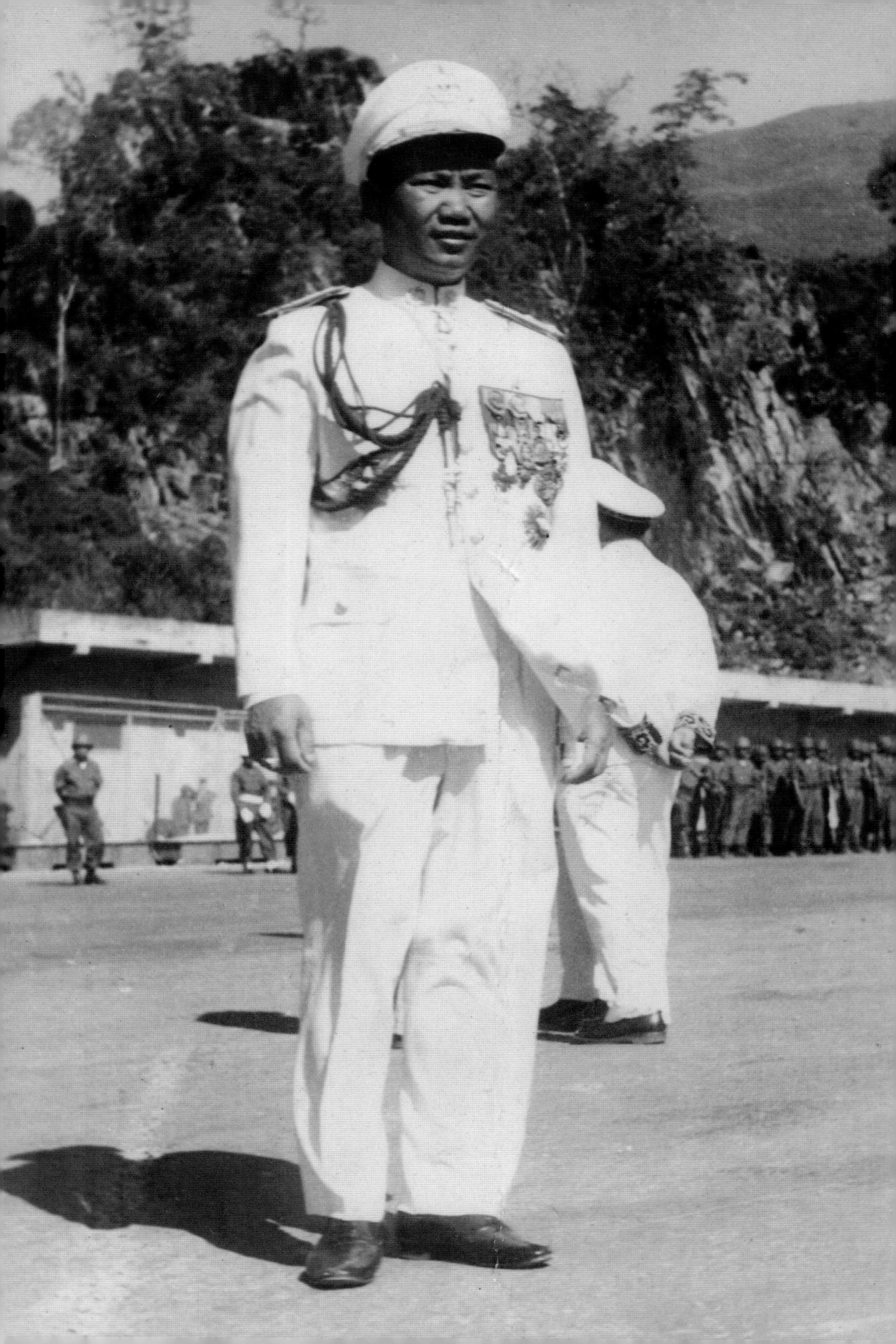

"Vang Pao was a type A personality, an enthusiastic and demanding leader, willing to do the ... work himself and more than willing to lead in combat. He was trusted by the Americans, who delivered to him something no Lao leader had ever possessed, massive logistical support and airpower. He expanded the number of Hmong personnel under arms until they eventually numbered some 40,000... [I]n a country where fighters were few and fighting leaders almost non-existent, Vang Pao established himself as the man to deal with, and he was generally admired by the Americans who flew in his support, whether with the CIA–operated airlines or with the Ravens, the covert US Air Force Forward Air Controllers."

* * *

WALTER J. BOYNE
"THE PLAIN OF JARS"
AIR FORCE MAGAZINE
JUNE 1999
WWW.AIRFORCE-MAGAZINE.COM

left
General Vang Pao in the late 1960s in Long Cheng, Laos.

MRS. XAI KOUA VANG COLLECTION

"I hope you all believe me when I say that your welfare has always been, is now, and will always continue to be of the highest priority interest for me and my fellow USA co-workers. I still remember that I and, perhaps, other Americans who are representatives of the United States government, have promised you, the Hmong People, that if you fight for us, if we win, things will be fine. But if we lose, we will take care of you...

"Admittedly we may not always be able to assist you as much as we would like, however, when we fall short it certainly is not because of forgetting or not trying, two things that none of us who have lived with you will ever be guilty of for the remainder of our days.."

* * *

JERRY 'HOG' DANIELS
CIA CASE OFFICER & GVP ADVISOR
"A LETTER FROM JERRY DANIELS (1941-1982)"
RETRIEVED FROM WWW.FS.FED.US
SEPTEMBER 2012

General Vang Pao and his CIA advisor Jerry 'Hog' Daniels, of Montana, on the Plain of Jars in 1971. Daniels was among many of General Vang Pao's CIA paramilitary advisors in Laos, including Bill Lair, Vint Lawrence, Pat Landry, Dick Johnson, Burr Smith, and Vince Shields.

VANG NHIA COLLECTION

"What scarred my heart most was to see many women and children lose their beloved husbands and fathers—especially the number of orphans increased as the war waged on. I never wanted any of these to occur. I never wanted to take their men from their families.

"There would be casualties in time of crisis, in time of wars. We were not given an option when our country was threatened by the communists and when our families were being coerced to live under a political system that worked against our wills. As a leader, I was not going to let this happen in my country. We must fight and defend our democratic principles, values.

"There was not a moment that I did not think about my wounded soldiers and those who died for our country's cause. In return, I took full responsibility for their lives. I promised their families food, money, shelter, and safety."

* * *
GENERAL VANG PAO
AUTHOR'S INTERVIEW
SEPTEMBER 2005

Qhov ua rau kuv txias siab tshaj mas yog vim tias kev tsov rog yuav ua rau kom me tub me nyuam thiab poj niam tub se ua ntsuag nos, tsis muaj txiv. Tseem ceeb yog cov me nyuam ntsuag coob heev, yog thaum kev ua rog tsis txawj xaus. Kuv yeej tsis xav kom muaj tej teeb meem no li, tab sis thaum tebchaws muaj tsov rog ces yeej yuav muaj kev puas tsuaj xwb.

Yog thaum peb lub tebchaws raug caij tsuj raws kev cai Kooj Sam thiab peb cov neeg raug quab yuam nyob rau ib txoj kev tswj fwm ua speb tsis nyiam, kuv yog ib tug thawj coj kuv yuav tsis pub tej kev tsim txom no tshwm sim. Peb yuav tsum sawv tua tiv thaiv kom tau txoj kev huaj vam ncaj ncees uas muaj nqis rau peb tsav neeg.

Yeej tsis muaj ib lub sij hawm uas kuv yuav tsis xav txog kuv cov tub rog uas tau raug mob thiab tuag vim lawv muab txoj sia los pauv peb lub tebchaws. Thaum kawg ces kuv ua tus ris txhua yam tag nrho nrog rau lawv txoj sia. Kuv cog lus yuav pab lawv tsev neeg kom tau noj tau haus, muaj vaj tsev nyob, thiab tsis muaj kev nyab xeeb (have safety).

(TRANSLATION - LUS TXHAIS)

General Vang Pao gives money to a woman. Most of them who came for his financial assistance were widows. Wherever he went, he usually carried along several pieces of luggage full of money to distribute to the wounded soldiers, elderly, women, and children. *From left to right*: An unknown woman, Lt. Colonel Vang Wangyee, Colonel Moua Sue, GVP, Captain Lee Tou, and Captain Va Yang Vang.

ZONG LIA VANG COLLECTION

right
General Vang Pao visits wounded soldiers at the medical center at Sam Thong, Lima Site 20, Laos, which was about seven miles northeast of Long Cheng. On every visit to the center, he always compensated his wounded soldiers for their services.

SUSAN FINN COLLECTION VIA YEU TONG HLAC VU

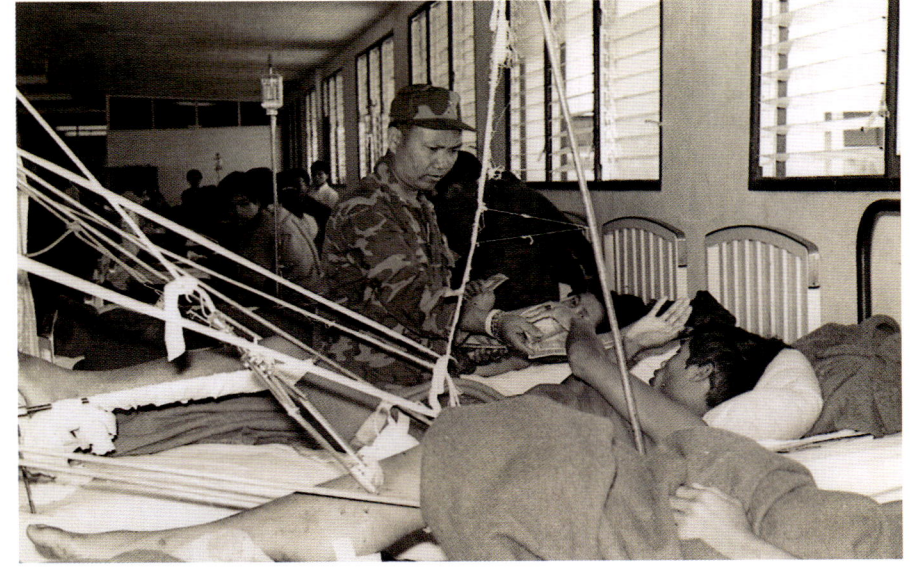

An Illustration of His Remarkable Life 224

President Richard Nixon

"There are no American combat forces in Laos. At the present time, we are concerned by the North Vietnamese move into Laos. There are 50,000 North Vietnamese there at the present time, and more perhaps are coming.

"As you know, the American participation in Laos is at the request of the neutralist government, which was set up in accordance with the 1969 Accords, which were agreed to, incidentally, by Hanoi, Peking, and the Soviet Union. That was during the administration of President Kennedy, negotiated by Mr. Harriman [Assistant Secretary of State for Far Eastern Affairs].

"We have been providing logistical support and some training for the neutralist government in order to avoid Laos falling under Communist domination. As far as American manpower in Laos is concerned, there are none there at the present time on a combat basis...

"When we consider the situation in Laos, I think President Kennedy in his first major television speech, which we all remember, in 1961, put it very well. He pointed out that Laos was potentially the key to what would happen in Thailand as well as in Vietnam and the balance of Southeast Asia.

"Now, Laos relates very much to Vietnam, because the Ho Chi Minh Trail runs through Laos. It is necessary, under those circumstances, that the United States take cognizance of that, and we do have aerial reconnaissance; we do have perhaps some other activities. I won't discuss those other activities at this time."

* * *

PRESIDENT RICHARD NIXON
THE PRESIDENT'S NEWS CONFERENCE
SEPTEMBER 26, 1969
RETRIEVED FROM THE WWW.NIXONLIBRARY.GOV
DECEMBER 4, 2010

Richard Nixon was the 37th President of the United States from 1969 to 1974. In 1973, America's involvement in the Vietnam War came to an end after his ceasefire negotiation with the North Vietnamese.

THE NIXON LIBRARY AND MUSEUM COLLECTION

right
General Vang Pao in the late 1960s.

THE GVP FAMILY COLLECTION

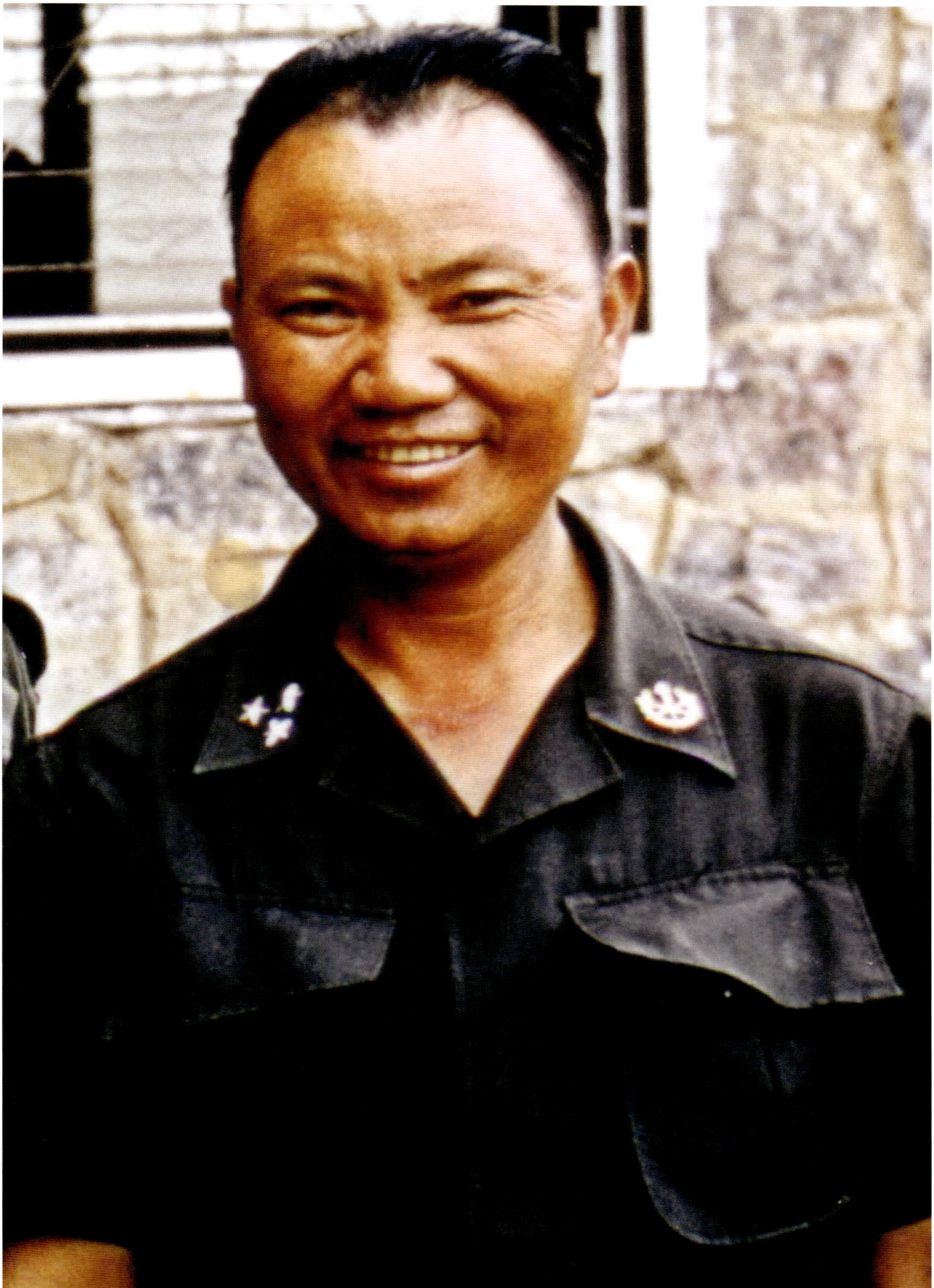

MEMORANDUM FOR: Dr. Henry A. Kissinger

I thought the President and you would be interested to get the recent flavor of the fighting in Laos.

Richard Helms

Attachment

11 October 1969
(DATE)

CENTRAL INTELLIGENCE AGENCY
WASHINGTON, D. C. 20505

OFFICE OF THE DIRECTOR

11 OCT 1969

MEMORANDUM FOR: The President

1. Since your trip to Thailand, the Laotian guerrilla forces under the command of General Vang Pao have fought a series of engagements with the North Vietnamese in north central Laos, and Vang Pao has successfully occupied the Plain of Jars. The Meo attempt to cut the main supply routes used by the North Vietnamese to support and resupply their troops in north central Laos was successful. The North Vietnamese retreated leaving behind large caches of arms, ammunition and medical supplies. My officers in Laos estimate these losses cost the North Vietnamese twelve million dollars. The Meos captured nine Soviet-built tanks, a field hospital with all its equipment, a radio station given to the Pathet Lao by the Chinese Communists and a number of assorted artillery pieces. The captured ammunition is estimated to be more than the North Vietnamese and Viet Cong forces used in South Vietnam in 1967. General Vang Pao's major victory, however, came in attracting to his side some 10,000 refugees in the Plain of Jars who have lived under communist rule since 1964. This has left the North Vietnamese in a difficult position. For years these people have been used as porters to move supplies down innumerable trails in central Laos to support the North Vietnamese offensives against the towns and cities of Laos. These people are now denied to the enemy, and he will have a more difficult time in future logistics operations in the Plain of Jars.

2. The key to this successful advance is General Vang Pao. Through the past eight years we have had a unique opportunity to watch the growth of a leader of an ethnic minority. Early this

week, Ambassador Godley and our station chief visited several areas in the Plain of Jars as guests of General Vang Pao. As a sidelight to the war my officer sent in some vignettes which I feel may interest you. I quote from a cable I received yesterday.

"When the Ambassador and I visited rear areas of the Plain of Jars on 7 October, we found that Vang Pao had organized old men and boys to police up the battlefield. They were collecting assorted ammunition and other supplies abandoned by friendly troops when they were launched on attack missions. As you are aware, troops going into the attack can carry only limited supplies and sometimes have to leave behind stocks of rifle ammunition, grenades, and rockets that were built up to permit them to resist attacks in forward positions. In one area we found a group of old men with a homemade wooden cart mounted on bicycle wheels, minus tires, busily sorting through the debris of battle in an effort to recover every last cartridge.

"A few weeks ago one of the irregular battalions was overrun at night and driven off a hill position. The following day when Vang Pao went out to insure that his troops were again on the offensive and endeavoring to retake the hill, he found the battalion commander busily engaged in repairing a sewing machine which he had 'liberated.' Vang Pao snatched up the sewing machine, smashed it on a rock, kicked it down the hill, and with a few well chosen words launched the acting battalion commander and his men back up the hill. They took it.

"A short time ago Vang Pao was at a command post on Phou Keng, a key hill position on the north-western side of the Plain of Jars when it came under counterattack by the enemy. Vang Pao, who was eating lunch at the time, dropped his sticky rice and was the first person to reach the 81 MM mortar located next to his command post. He personally fired the first twenty or thirty rounds into the enemy and then directed the troops into the final assault which captured and secured a strategic hilltop.

"A short time later Vang Pao stood on the trail leading to the summit of the hilltop and personally turned around his troops who had broken in the face of determined enemy resistance. Some he turned by cajolery, others by a show of anger, and some by mocking them for their fears. Others turned about of their own accord when they saw him standing, unafraid, in the path."

3. The Laotian Government, Vang Pao and the Meos are understandably elated with the success of their military offensive. Prime Minister Souvanna Phouma realizes, however, as do Vang Pao and the other officials in Laos, that this is just another stage in the battle for the kingdom. The Laotians are well aware that the North Vietnamese may now be mounting a counterattack to retake the Plain of Jars and continue the push to the west they began during last year's dry season. The Meo offensive has undoubtedly slowed the new Vietnamese attack. The Meo, however, are tired and greatly outnumbered. They cannot hope to withstand a determined enemy force.

4. The North Vietnamese 312th Division of approximately 12,000 soldiers has begun to enter Laos along Route 7 and various trails. This is the first time since 1954 and the battle of Dien Bien Phu that this Division has been deployed in combat. We expect the North Vietnamese troops who withdrew from the Plain of Jars to regroup will join this Division and counterattack the Meo forces. It seems clear that the Meos will not be able to stay in the areas they have taken, and may shortly be hard put to defend their base in the hills around Vang Pao's headquarters.

Dick
Richard Helms
Director

"What the Thai PARUs did to help us in Laos was remarkable. They supported us wholeheartedly. At the end, they also suffered enormously."

* * *
GENERAL VANG PAO
RETRIEVED FROM SGU–MINNESOTA CHAPTER
NOVEMBER 2011

Cov Thaib PARU tau pab peb nyob tebchaws Lostsuas yog ib qhov zoo heev. Lawv txhawb peb tag siab tag ntsws lis. Thaum kawg, lawv kuj tau txais kev ploj tuag puas tsuaj ntau heev thiab.

(TRANSLATION - LUS TXHAIS)

left
Logo of the Unknown Warrior Association 333, a veterans organization representing the Thai military personnel who served and fought alongside the Hmong and Laotian soldiers in the Secret War. During the conflict there were as many as 20 battalions of Thai troops, including 'volunteers,' stationed in Laos.

CAPTAIN VANG NENG COLLECTION

General Vang Pao and CIA case officer Burr Smith posing with some top Thai PARU leaders and trainers in Long Cheng in the early 1970s. The fourth person from the left was Rachen, General Vang Pao's personal Thai liaison. Names starting *left to right* from Smith were General Sukij Maiyalarb, GVP, General Thon, General Vithool Y. Pol, Colonel Rachen, and Major General Mungkorn (PARU Commander from 1965-1969). *Next page*,

SUSAN FINN COLLECTION VIA YEU TONG HLAO VU

next page
GVP shakes hand with General Thon, Deputy Commander Thai Forces, to establish stronger ties between the Hmong and Thai soldiers in Laos.

KONG XIONG COLLECTION

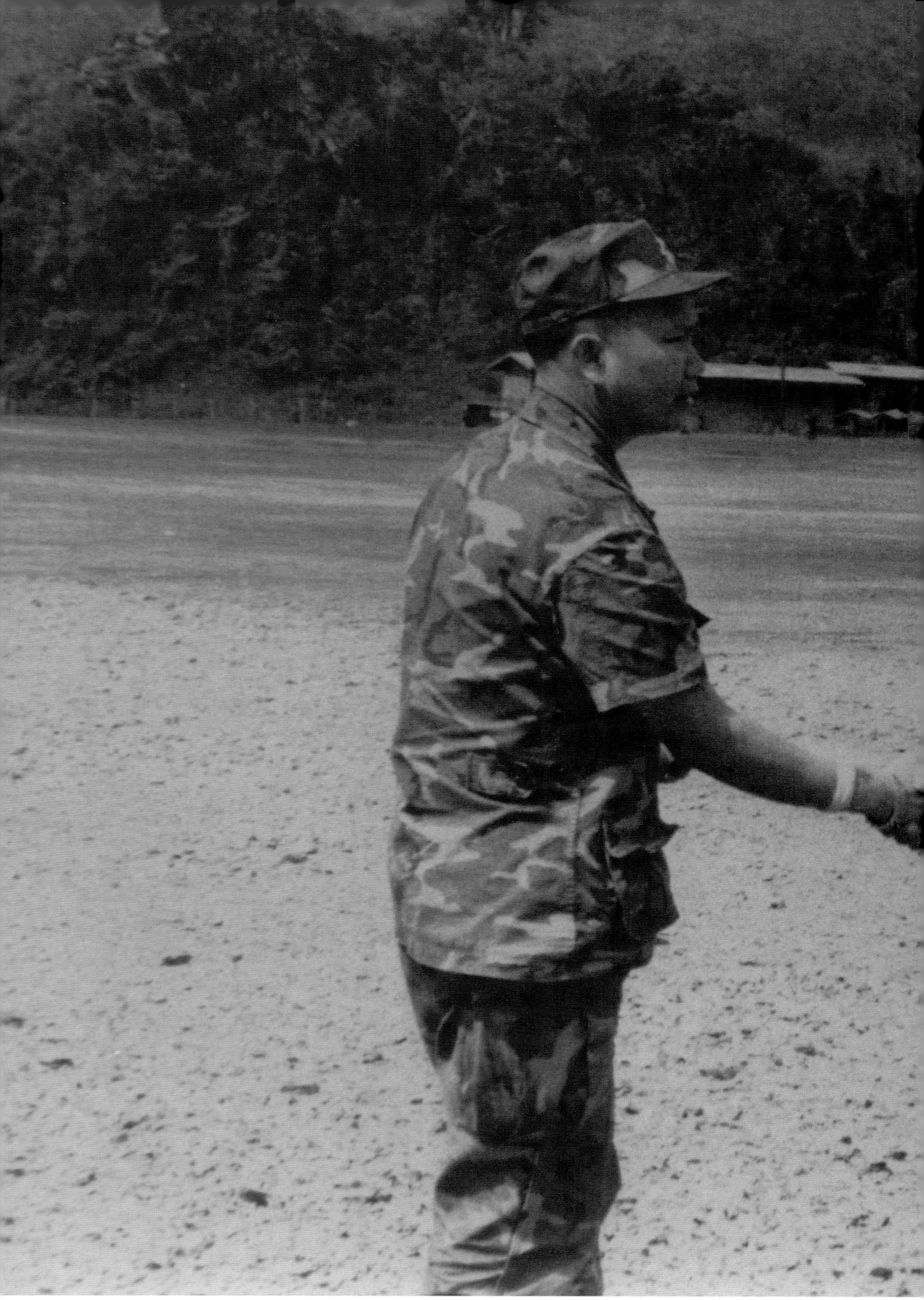

An Illustration of His Remarkable Life 234

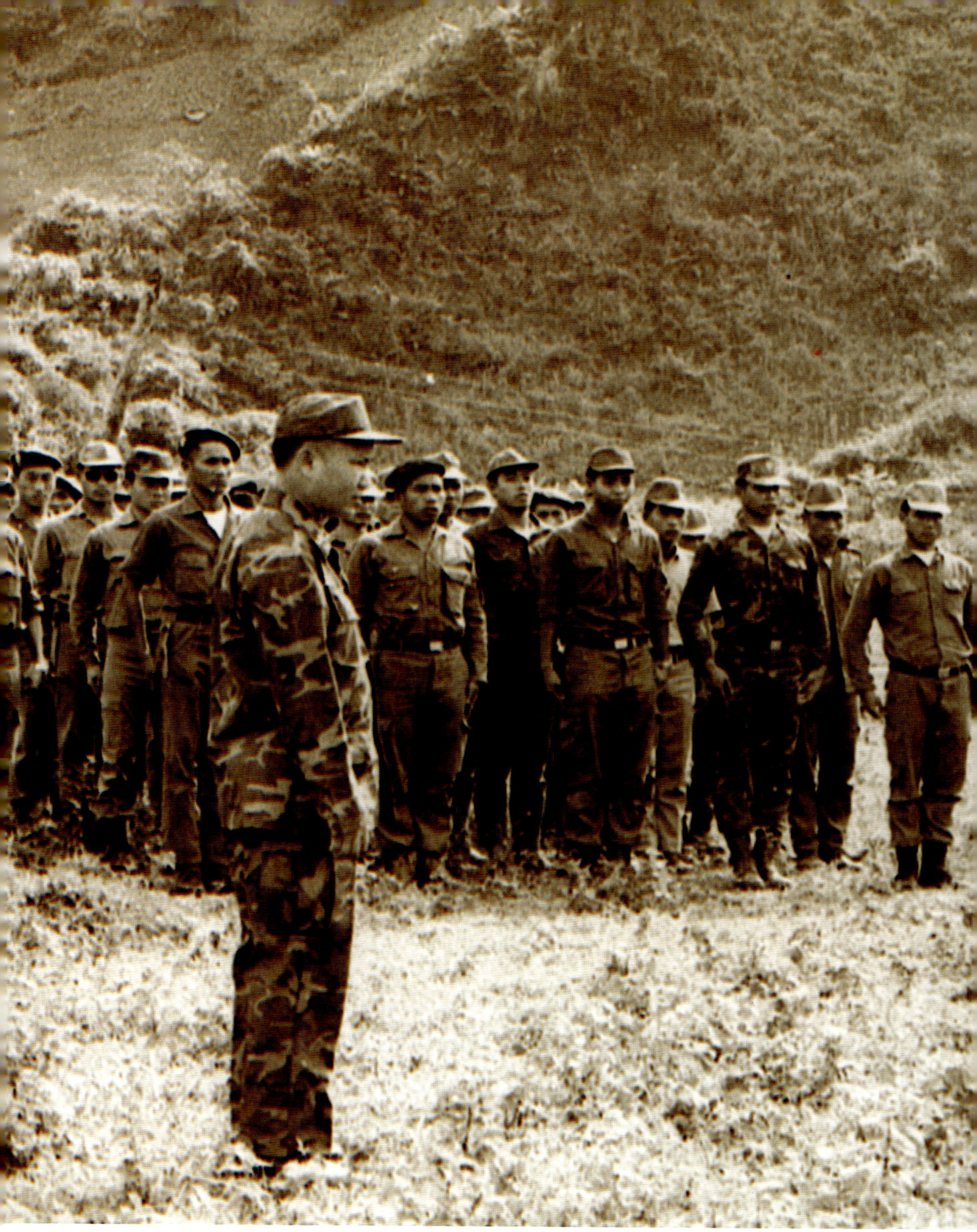

General Vang Pao makes a final motivational speech to Colonel Xang Dang Xiong, commander of GM 21, and his Battalion 206 soldiers before being sent to combat on the Plain of Jars in early 1971.

SUSAN FINN COLLECTION VIA YEU TONG HLAO VU

top
General Vang Pao's family at their house in Long Cheng in 1971 and, *above*, in 1969.

THE GVP FAMILY COLLECTION VIA LANG VANG.

General Vang Pao's house in Long Cheng. The first house was made out of wood. By 1965, he reconstructed the outside with concrete walls. The rooms on the second floor were designated for family members while the rooms on the first floor were for meetings and special guests. *Right*, General Vang Pao's residence in Vientiane, Laos.

THE GVP FAMILY COLLECTION VIA LANG VANG

An Illustration of His Remarkable Life 240

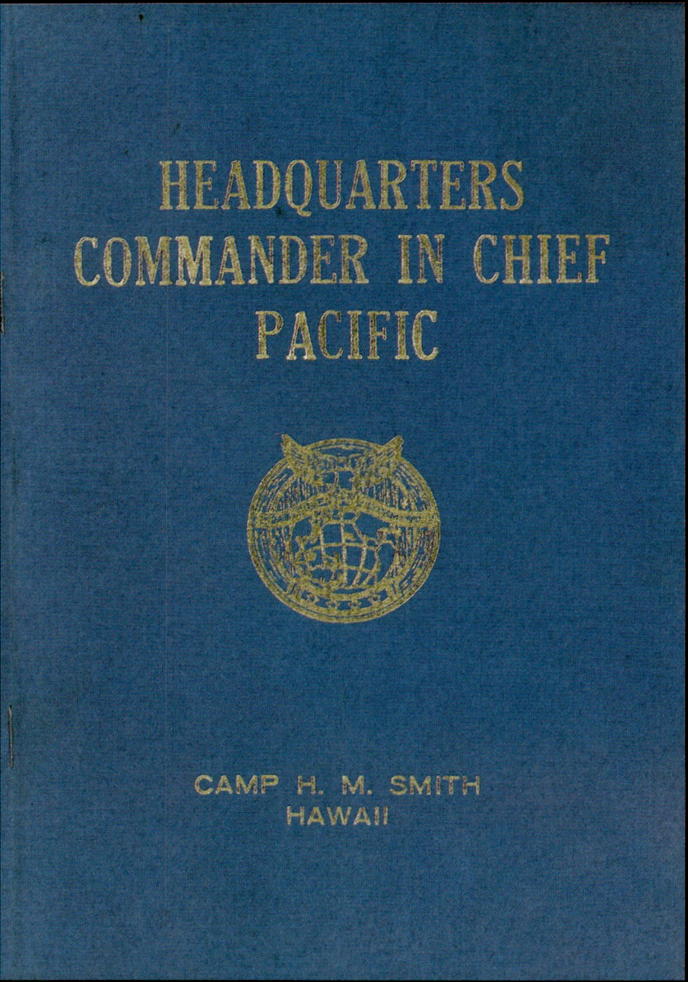

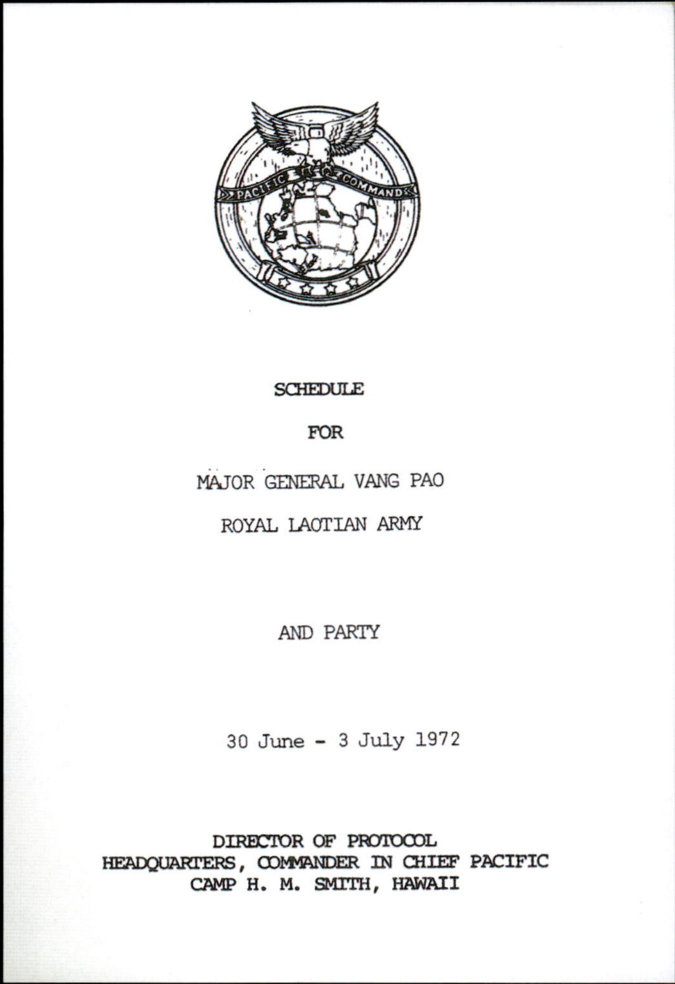

HEADQUARTERS COMMANDER IN CHIEF PACIFIC

CAMP H. M. SMITH
HAWAII

SCHEDULE

FOR

MAJOR GENERAL VANG PAO

ROYAL LAOTIAN ARMY

AND PARTY

30 June – 3 July 1972

DIRECTOR OF PROTOCOL
HEADQUARTERS, COMMANDER IN CHIEF PACIFIC
CAMP H. M. SMITH, HAWAII

General Vang Pao's itinerary for Camp H. M. Smith, Hawaii from June 30 to July 3, 1972.

THE CENTER FOR HMONG STUDIES COLLECTION VIA LEE PAO XIONG

On General Vang Pao's visit to the U.S. in July 1972, he met U.S. Admiral Thomas Moorer, *above left*, Chairman of the Joint Chiefs of Staff from 1970-1974. He also had dinner with U.S. Admiral John S. McCain, Jr., USN, Commander in Chief Pacific. Admiral McCain was U.S. Senator John McCain's father.

NICOLAS PHA COLLECTION

An Illustration of His Remarkable Life 242

"In General Vang Pao's speech, he described how long the Hmong people had been fighting against the North Vietnamese who were invading their homeland, and how in recent years the struggle had become so much more intense, and the sufferings of the Hmong people had increased. He expressed his thanks to the United States for their assistance in the war, and also for the economic aid to the civilian population which had been especially important to the care of the people who had lost their lands and their homes as the enemy forces had come closer to the populated areas. As a soldier and leader of the Hmong he said that he and his men were doing everything they could to support the Royal Government of Laos under the King."

* * *
B. HUGH TOVAR
CIA STATION CHIEF OF LAOS, 1970-1973
AUTHOR'S EMAIL INTERVIEW
MAY 2011

General Vang Pao spoke to members of the CIA in Washington, D.C., in July 1972. Accompanying him to the dinner were Hugh Tovar, CIA Chief of Station in Laos, and Colonel Ly Toupao. He gave his speech in English.

HUGH TOVAR COLLECTION

An Illustration of His Remarkable Life 244

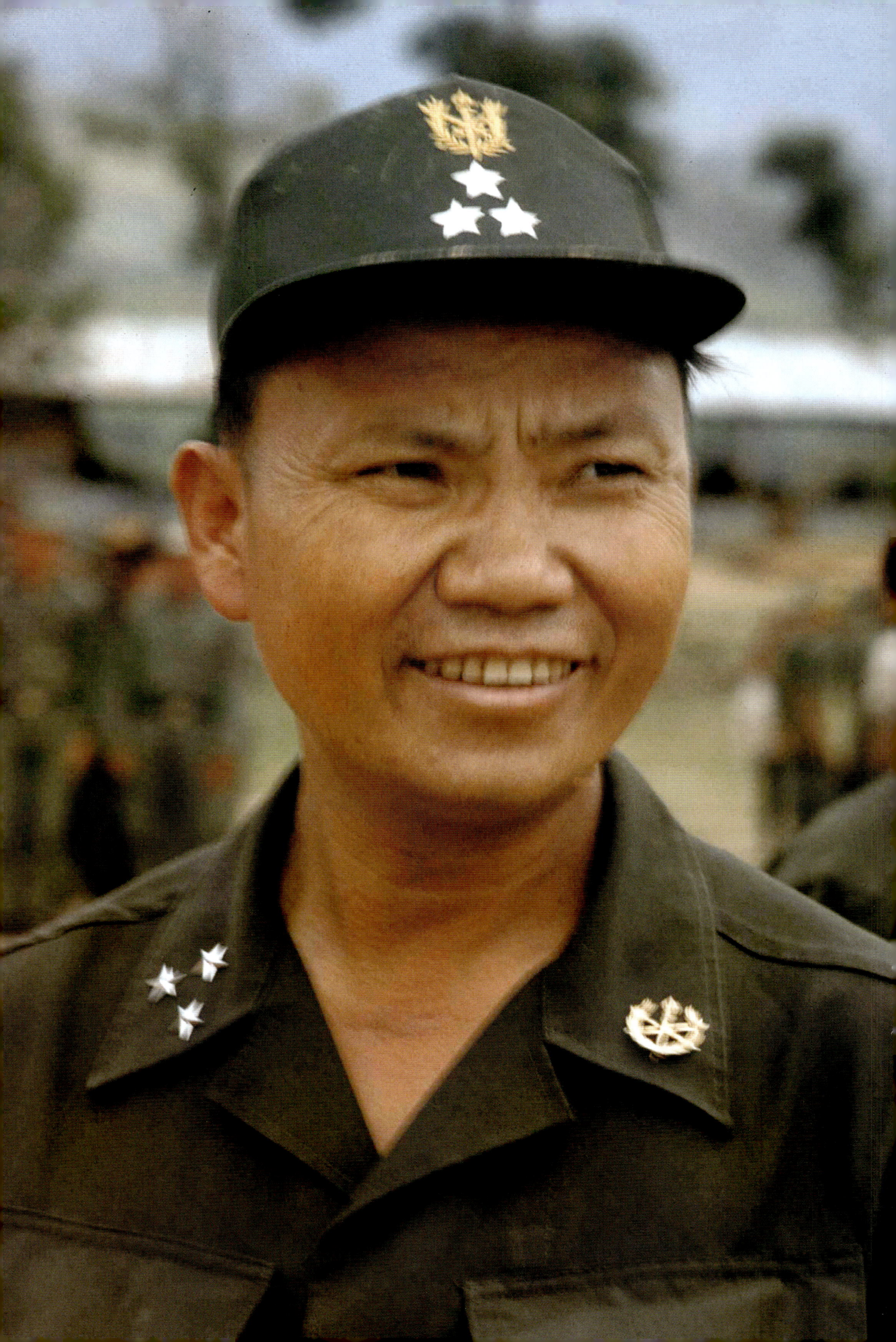

"[No] group of nationalists in Indochina was as closely tied as allies to the Americans as were the [Hmong]."

* * *

ARTHUR J. DOMMEN
"THE INDOCHINESE EXPERIENCE OF THE FRENCH AND THE AMERICANS"
INDIANA UNIVERSITY PRESS
BLOOMINGTON AND INDIANAPOLIS, 2001
PAGE 933

left
General Vang Pao in October 1972.

AP IMAGES COLLECTION

"I have worked with General Vang Pao as a soldier to defend our country from the Communists during the French occupation from 1953 to 1954 and the Vietnam War from 1968 to 1975. In those periods, I felt as he was like Moses who had the blessing from God to come and save his Hmong people.

"The Hmong lived remotely from the rest of Lao society and were treated unfairly. When General Vang Pao was 13, he already knew how to help people, and surrounded himself with leaders. He was optimistic about the future for all the people in Laos. He devoted his life to love and care for his country. He loved the Hmong people. He loved the Lao people. He sacrificed his life for them all. He gave all he could to every life he could touch. He impacted each person who came to his help.

"When our country fell into Communist Pathet Lao control, he evacuated us into Thailand. We were at our darkest moment. Our future was unknown. However, General Vang Pao reassured us and saw a bright future. He knew his people would do well in America. Soon, he left to America. This opened a new journey to our people, and many followed him to start their lives all over again in the U.S."

* * *
COLONEL VANG GEU
NORTH CAROLINA
EMAIL INTERVIEW WITH AUTHOR
NOVEMBER 17, 2010

Colonel Vang Geu was the Assistant Commander of Division 2 in MR II.

COLONEL VANG GEU COLLECTION

In 1973, the U.S. gave a $10M economic development package to General Vang Pao's MR II. Accompanying him to Thailand to learn more about the Thai's agricultural developments were Lt. Colonel Vang Geu, *left of GVP*, and Jerry 'Hog' Daniels, *far back on right*. Xuwicha Hiranpreuck, *next to Daniels*, was the General's liaison and contact person in Thailand. The rest of the people were Thai technicians. They also examined other modern farming technologies, such as plastic irrigation pipes, *right*.

COLONEL VANG GEU COLLECTION

An Illustration of His Remarkable Life 248

"The Pathet Lao were installed by the brutal military forces of the North Vietnamese military, armed largely by the Soviet Union. The Pathet Lao Communists, in cooperation with North Vietnam, established a one party Communist dictatorship—the LPDR (Lao People's Democratic Republic). They were quick to develop a genocidal dictatorship that eliminated all political enemies and apparently murdered the beloved King, Queen, and the Crown Prince [Vong Savang]—as well as some 46,000 [Royal Lao] government officials. Because of horrific and inhumane treatment by the LPDR, hundreds of thousands of Laotian people fled their beloved homeland to Thailand for asylum. Many were fortunately given the opportunity to settle in third countries, such as the US.

"For those who were not so fortunate to escape, many faced the unspeakable hardship and merciless persecution of the LPDR regime's Communist dictatorship. Many Laotian people, after only a few months under the jack-boot and control of the LPDR regime, could not endure the repression so decided to take arms and went to the jungle and fought until today.

"On the other hand, those who tried to resist the LPDR regime, or Communist forces from Vietnam, in a peaceful way—such as teachers, writers, poets, intellectuals, students or just good patriotic citizens—often paid a high price. Many were arrested, beaten or tortured, and thrown into terrible prison camps or jails. Tens of thousands of Lao and Hmong people suffered or died in these ways over the last 25 years."

* * *
GENERAL VANG PAO
STATEMENT AT THE U.S. CONGRESSIONAL FORUM
WASHINGTON, D.C.
OCTOBER 14, 1999
RETRIEVED FROM CAPTAIN VANG NENG
DECEMBER 4, 2010

Tsoom fwv Lostsuas tog Pathet Lao yog raug txib tsim tsa quab yuav los ntawm tsoom tub rog Nyab Laj Qaum Teb, cov tub rog txhawb nqa coob yog Xaus Viaj (Soviet). Tsoom fwv Pathet Lao kev cai Kooj Sam (Communist) yog koom tes nrog Nyab Laj Qaum Teb, teeb tsa kom tau ib pawg neeg coj kev cai Kooj Sam txoj kev cob qhia tsoom fwv LPDR (Lao's People Democratic Republic). Lawv maj nroos tsa tau ib lub tswv yim los tshem thiab tua cov neeg uas yog cov coj pab pawg kav tebchaws uas tawm tsam lawv, lawv tau quab yuam tua Huab Tais Lostsuas, Niam Huab Tais, thiab Tuam Thawj sawv cev huab tais (Crown Prince Sayvong Savang), tsis tag li xwb, nrog rau li ntawm 46,000 tus neeg ua hauj lwm rau tsoom fwv pab pawg sab xis puav leej raug tua tib si. Vim txoj kev tsim txom tsis ncaj ncees rau neeg ntiaj teb los ntawm tsoom fwv LPDR, muaj txog pua txhiab leej pej xeem Lostsuas thiaj tau khiav tawm hauv tebchaws Lostsuas tuaj mus nkaum nyob rau tebchaws Thaib. Muaj ntau yim neeg kuj muaj feem raug cai tawm tuaj mus ua lub neej tshiab nyob rau tebchaws thib 3, xws li tebchaws Ameliskas.

Cov pej xeem uas tsis muaj tswv yim yuav nrhiav kev tawm tau, muaj ntau leej raug quab yuam yam tsis muaj los lus yuam piav tau. Thaum cov pej xeem Lostsuas raug quab yuam tsim txom tau li ob peb hlis, lawv tsis nyiam kev cai kom sam uas tuaj quab yuam caij tsuj lawv, lawv thiaj li koom tes kwv riam phom khiav must nyob tom hav zoov tawm tsam sib tua rog Nyab Laj Liab los txog rau niaj hnub no.

Dua li cov uas ua tiag nyiaj koom tes nrog Nyab Laj Liab txoj kev cai Kooj Sam tuaj puag Nyab Laj Liab teb tuaj, xws li: Xib fwb qhia ntawv, tub xov xwm, kws sau paj huam, tub ntxhais txawj ntse, tub ntxhais kawm ntawv, los yog tej pej xeem neeg ncaj ncees, lawv los kuj tau txais kev cov nyom nyav kawg thiab. Coob leej kuj raug txhom, raug ntau tsim txom, thiab coj mus kaw tsev loj cuj (qhov taub). Muaj ntau caum txhiab tawm leej neeg Hmoob thiab Lostsuas raug tua tuag raws li tau hais los sau no nyob hauv 25 lub xyoo dhau los no.

(TRANSLATION - LUS TXHAIS)

His Royal Highness King Sisavang Vatthana and Queen Khamphoui being received by Pathet Lao soldiers in Vientiane, 1974.

CAPTAIN VANG NENG COLLECTION

Many of the military documents required General Vang Pao's signature and approval before any actions or orders could be taken. The enclosed seal was the official symbol of the MR II.

LT. COLONEL NENGLO YANG COLLECTION

Lt. Colonel Nenglo Yang received a certificate for completion of leadership training which was authorized and approved by General Vang Pao in 1968.

LT. COLONEL NENGLO YANG COLLECTION

right
A military discharge decree authorized by General Vang Pao. He knew that the war would soon end, so he honorably dismissed many soldiers to return home to their normal lives. Other soldiers decided to continue their military service by joining the Royal Lao Army in Vientiane, Laos.

THE GVP FAMILY COLLECTION

ກ້າລັງທັບແຫ່ງຊາດ
ກອງບັນຊາການກອງພັນປະຈັນບານທີ ໑
ເສນາທິການ ກ່ອງການທີ ໑

ເລກທີ 655 /ສບກ/ກພ໑/ທ໑

ໃບປົດປ່ອຍແລະສລະເສິກ

ຂ້າພະເຈົ້ານາຍພັນຕຣີ, ຜູ້ບັນຊາການກອງພັນປະຈັນບານທີ ໑ ແລະ ທະຫານ ພາກ ໒

ໄດ້ປົດປ່ອຍ ຈ່າມົວທ່ອ ຊັ້ນ ຕຣ ລ/ດ ໔໗໗-໔໐໐
ສັງກັດຢູ່ກອງພັນ ໑໗໘/໔ ກອງຮ້ອຍ ໔໗໘/໑ ເກີດເມື່ອວັນທີ ໓ / ໖ / ໑໓ ໔໓
ຢູ່ບ້ານ ບອກ ຕາແສງ ນຊ້າງາວ ເມືອງ ໂອມິນ ແຂວງ ຫົວພັນ
ທີ່ໄດ້ອາສາສມັກຣັບໃຊ້ປະເທດຊາດນັບແຕ່ວັນທີ ໑ / ໖ / ໑໓ ໖໑
ເຖິງ ມ້ອ / ໔ / ໑໗໗໕ ອອກຈາກລາຊການທະຫານເພື່ອກັບໄປເປັນພົນເມືອງດີ.

ເນື່ອງຈາກ ກອງທັບແຫ່ງຊາດໄດ້ຫຼຸດກຳລັງຕາມພະຣາຊໂອງການ ໙໕
ລົງວັນທີ ໑໐ ມີນາ ໑໗໗໕
ນັບແຕ່ວັນທີ່ / ໔ / ໑໗໗໕ ນີ້ ເປັນຕົ້ນໄປ, ຜູ້ກ່ຽວມີສິດເສຣີເພື່ອອອກໄປທຳມາຫາ
ກິນສ້າງຊາຕິ.

ຍ້ອຍາຍແລະສລະເສິກວ່າຜູ້ກ່ຽວເປັນວີຣະບຸຣຸດຜູ້ມີນ້ຳໃຈຣັກຊາດອັນແຮງ.
ດ້ວຍນັ້ນຈຶງໄດ້ອອກໃບປົດປ່ອຍ ແລະ ສລະເສິກນີ້ໃຫ້ຜູ້ກ່ຽວໄດ້ໃຊ້ ໃບທາງຣາຊການຕໍ່ໄປ.

ຂ.ປ. ໒໔.໒໗, ວັນທີ 14. 6. ໑໗໗4

ຜູ້ບັນຊາການກອງພັນປະຈັນບານທີ ໑ ແລະ ທະຫານພາກ ໒

(ພັນຕຣີ ວ່າງປ່າວ)

"War is difficult; peace is hell."

* * *
GENERAL VANG PAO
"THE HMONG OF LAOS: NO PLACE TO RUN"
BY W. E. GARRETT
NATIONAL GEOGRAPHIC
JANUARY 1974

General Vang Pao expressed frustration about the war in early 1970s.

HOWARD BUELL COLLECTION

"During the first week in May [1975], there was a meeting in Vientiane with VP, Prime Minister Souvanna Phouma, the rest of the generals, and the supreme commander. They were not happy with VP after VP ordered a bombing attack on Sala Phou Khoun. They told him they would send a new person to Long to assist VP. They gave the name of Chao Monivong and said he would be accompanied by coalition soldiers. VP rejected that. He said: 'Region II belongs to me! I am always against the communists, and I will not agree for someone else to come and help me run my people that way!' He warned Mr. Prime Minister: 'It's not going to be a fair game like the communist party says. They will not keep their promises.' VP told them that. But the rest of the high ranking Laotian officers saw it a different way. They said: 'Well, the Pathet Lao are also our relatives. We are all Laotian, and they will not do such things. Let's join hands and welcome them.' VP told them that there were only two ways to go—fight the communists or leave. When he asked the Prime Minister for permission to fight, they said: 'We will not fight, and we will not leave. We will stay together with them.' So VP told them: 'If you decide that way, I will be the one to leave. I cannot stay with the communists. I have fought against them for 30 years. If I am here, I have to drive them out. If they are here, I have to go somewhere else.' They told him, 'Vang Pao, if you don't like it, you can quit.' So VP pulled off his stars and quitted. He gave his final words to the Prime Minister, 'If I am gone, you are dead.'

"Mr. Sisouk Nachampassak was at that meeting of the high ranking officials. Mr. Sisouk was the Minister of Defense. When VP walked out of the meeting room, he went straight to Mr. Sisouk's office. VP said to Mr. Sisouk, 'Why don't you order me to defend the country rather than leave?' Mr. Sisouk said, 'Vang Pao, we are like brothers. When you die, I die. When our boss is not willing to fight, then we both must leave the country in peace.'

"After the meeting with the Vientiane government, VP realized they would not back him up in fighting. Still VP did not give up. VP went to Luang Prabang and asked the King [Sisavang Vatthana] to give a direct order to VP to defend the country. But the King said: 'Vang Pao, your people are dying. So many have died already. I don't want to see your people die anymore. I will not give you what you want.' VP wished him well and told the King he should take care of himself. I think the King knew exactly what was going to happen."

**
CHU VANG
ONE OF GENERAL VANG PAO'S SONS
"SKY IS FALLING"
BY GAYLE L. MORRISON
MCFARLAND & COMPANY, INC.
1999, PAGES 28-31

right
Souvanna Phouma, Prime Minister of Royal Lao Government of Laos from June 1962 to 1975. He also held this post several times earlier in his political career. His half-brother, Prince Souphanouvong, was the head of the Communist Pathet Lao. Their imperfect union was a deciding factor that caused the collapse of the Royal Lao Government and an end to the ruling of King Sisavang Vatthana.

HOWARD BUELL COLLECTION

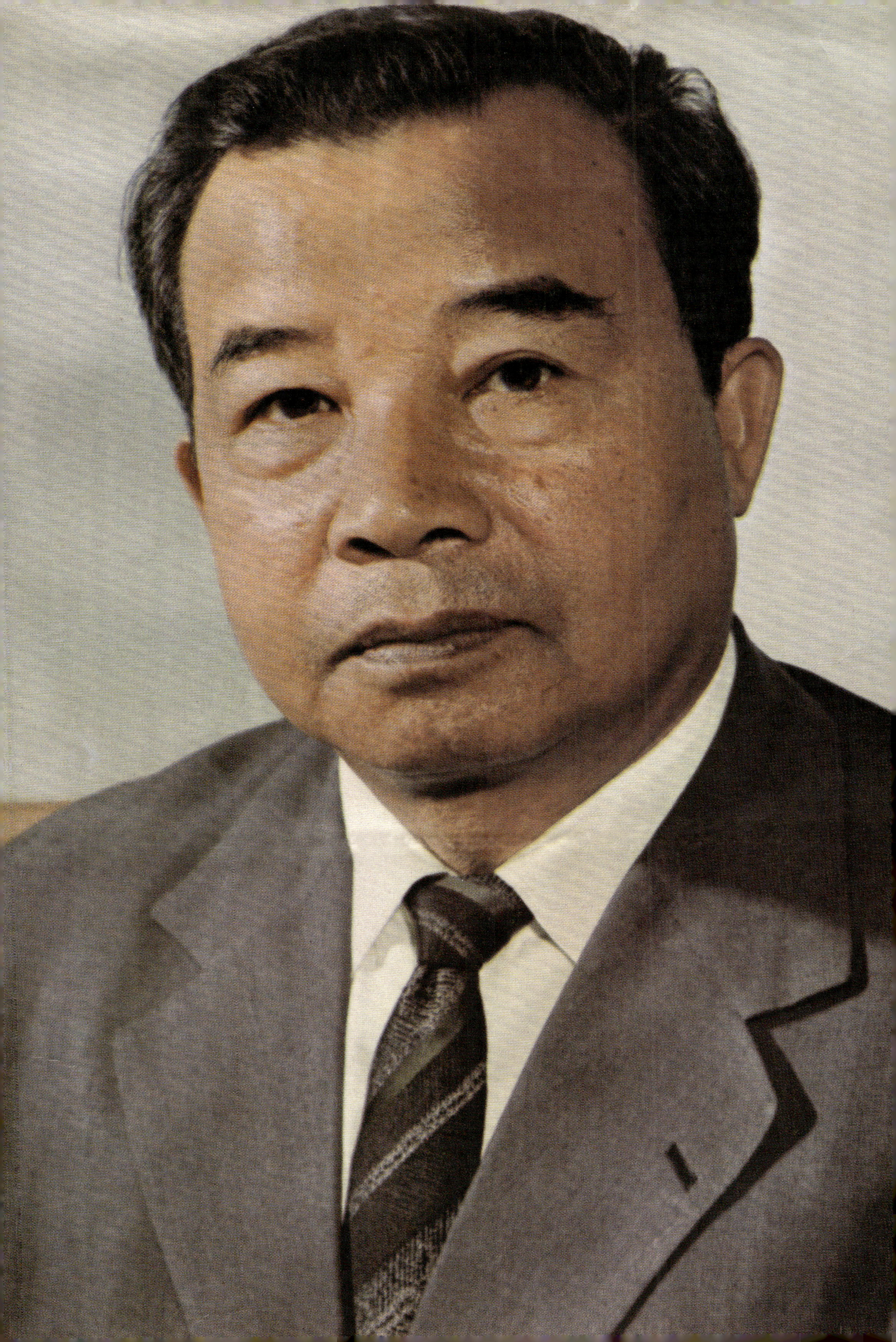

Prince Sisouk Na Champassak, Defense Minister of Laos. While living in exile in the U.S., he passed away in 1984 at General Vang Pao's house in Santa Ana, California.

PRINCE OPHAT NACHAMPASSAK COLLECTION

"When I took charge of the national defense, from June 1970 on, I had a very close relationship with [Vang Pao], full of trust. But the most important moment in our relationship, between Vang Pao and myself, was at the fall of Long [Cheng]. One day, in the morning, around 9 o'clock, 9:30, he came to my house and said, 'This is the end, Long [Cheng] has fallen. I have just seen the Prime Minister who has ordered me to withdraw from Long [Cheng] to Phu Khao Khuay.' These are the mountains behind Vientiane.

"The Prime Minister had already received the order from the mouth of the American ambassador to instruct Vang Pao to withdraw his troops. So he came to me almost in tears, and asked me, 'This is the end. The Prime Minister has ordered me to withdraw my troops, in a complete rout. So has the American ambassador. What should I do?'

"So I told him: 'Listen. I was not in charge of your business because it is the business of the CIA, etc. It was between you, the Prime Minister, and the CIA. I don't know anything about it. But now, can you tell me the truth? How many men do you have left who are able to carry weapons and go on with the struggle? I am like a physician, if you don't tell me your illness, and the truth is your illness, I can't cure you. So give me the exact number because you have inflated it elsewhere, I don't know, but people, rumors have it that you have inflated the number of your troops. Now I want to know the truth if one wants to defend Long [Cheng].'

"So he told me, 'I have left about three thousand, or 3,400 able to do something, to carry arms, but the morale is very low.' I said, 'If that is the way it is, we must do something. We must resist. With 3,000 you can resist. As for me, I am going, going to Bangkok to ask for reinforcement, two battalions of Thais, of Thai troops as reinforcement.' With this he left quite satisfied to go directly to Long [Cheng]. So, on that day, we did not follow the order of the Prime Minister.

"I told him, 'The two of us are taking the responsibility for this. If there is a hitch, we run the risk of a court martial because we have refused to obey orders which have been given. But we are going to do it.' I went to Bangkok to ask for two battalions of the Thai Special Forces. I met Marshal Thanom, Thavi, and Papat, etc. I asked them… I explained to them the situation. I told them that it is absolutely necessary to defend Long [Cheng], because if Long [Cheng] falls into the hands of the … North Vietnamese, then it is the end, it is the rout of Vientiane. Vientiane will be under siege, surrounded by the North Vietnamese forces. And after Vientiane, it will be the Thailand's turn, your turn, to be in charge.

"Fortunately, Thanom immediately gave the order to make ready one battalion, one battalion right away as reinforcement for Long [Cheng]. And before leaving for Bangkok, I had given the order to the government to dispatch two GM from the Third Military Region, that is from Savannakhet, to defend Long [Cheng]. To use these two GM, one had to ask the Americans, because one had to go through the Americans before using the Special Forces. So I went to the American ambassador and told him that we must do something to defend Long [Cheng].

"He said, 'But you are crazy? Long [Cheng] is gone.' I told him, 'No. It is not the end yet. There is Vang Pao who is defending it. We are going to do something. Do you realize the situation, to bring a population of 60,000, soldiers and everyone from Long [Cheng] to Phu Khao Khuay. It's a story without end. The retreat of these 60,000 men, this population, the children, etc., it's not possible. We must defend them.' He said, 'That's your opinion?' And I said, 'I would like to have the two mobile gendarmeries of Savannakhet.' After that, we discussed the situation and he gave his agreement. So I telephoned to Vang Pao and Vang Pao was completely on board.

"And at this point I left, and at the time I departed, the Americans had already bombarded their military base. What they had found next to the house of Vang Pao were telephone installations, installations of their equipment, which were very obvious and that they did not want to leave in the hands of the Viets. And for the Americans, Long [Cheng] was finished…"

* * *

PRINCE SISOUK NA CHAMPASSAK
INTERVIEW WITH SISOUK NA CHAMPASSAK, 1982
SERIES VIETNAM: A TELEVISION HISTORY
PROGRAM CAMBODIA AND LAOS, 1982
RETRIEVED FROM OPENVAULT.WGBH.ORG
FEB. 2012

"General Vang Pao's words were, 'If we die, we die together. Nobody will be left behind.' He never commanded from headquarters. Every day he was with his soldiers. He knew the soldiers were paid very little, so he would always share what food he had with them. They saw [him as] a regular guy, a very fair man. We called him 'Siab Loj.' A big-hearted man."

* * *

COLONEL LY TENG, RETIRED
GENERAL VANG PAO'S BROTHER-IN-LAW
"THE COVERT WARS OF VANG PAO"
BY TONY KENNEDY AND PAUL MCENROE
STAR TRIBUNE
JULY 2, 2005

"Before the war all the men in our village worked hard and supported their families. We had peace. There was no war. All the sudden, our lives changed. The men began to disappear. They went to fight for General Vang Pao, for the Americans. Most of our husbands never returned home.

"My husband died in the war. I cried many nights. I became sad. Extremely depressed. And ill. I told General Vang Pao to bring back my husband. He said to us widows that our husbands died for saving our country from the enemy. We told him we wanted the war to end and to end all the killing. He also wanted the war to end."

* * *

MRS. YOUA LEE
HER HUSBAND WAS KILLED IN 1967 DURING THE SECRET WAR
SHE AND HER CHILDREN WERE AMONG THOUSANDS OF WAR REFUGEES
AUTHOR'S INTERVIEW
ST. PAUL, MINNESOTA
JUNE 2011

Colonel Ly Teng was the Assistant Chief of Staff of Logistics. He oversaw five departments in Long Cheng: Department of Personnel; Department of Logistics Supplies, and Medications; Department of Transportation; Department of Ordinance such as weapons, ammunitions, tanks, cars, trucks, artilleries; and Department of Finances and Nutrition. He also assigned code names to specific military personnel so their real names would not be detected by the enemy. Ly Teng was among about two dozen Hmong men who earned the rank of colonel in Laos. He is married to General Vang Pao's sister, Der Vang.

COLONEL LY TENG COLLECTION

right
General Vang Pao hands money to two women during a visit to a in refugee camp in Laos in 1974. Many of them were widows whose husbands had died fighting in the Secret War.

W. E. GARRET/NATIONAL GEOGRAPHIC STOCK COLLECTION

An Illustration of His Remarkable Life 260

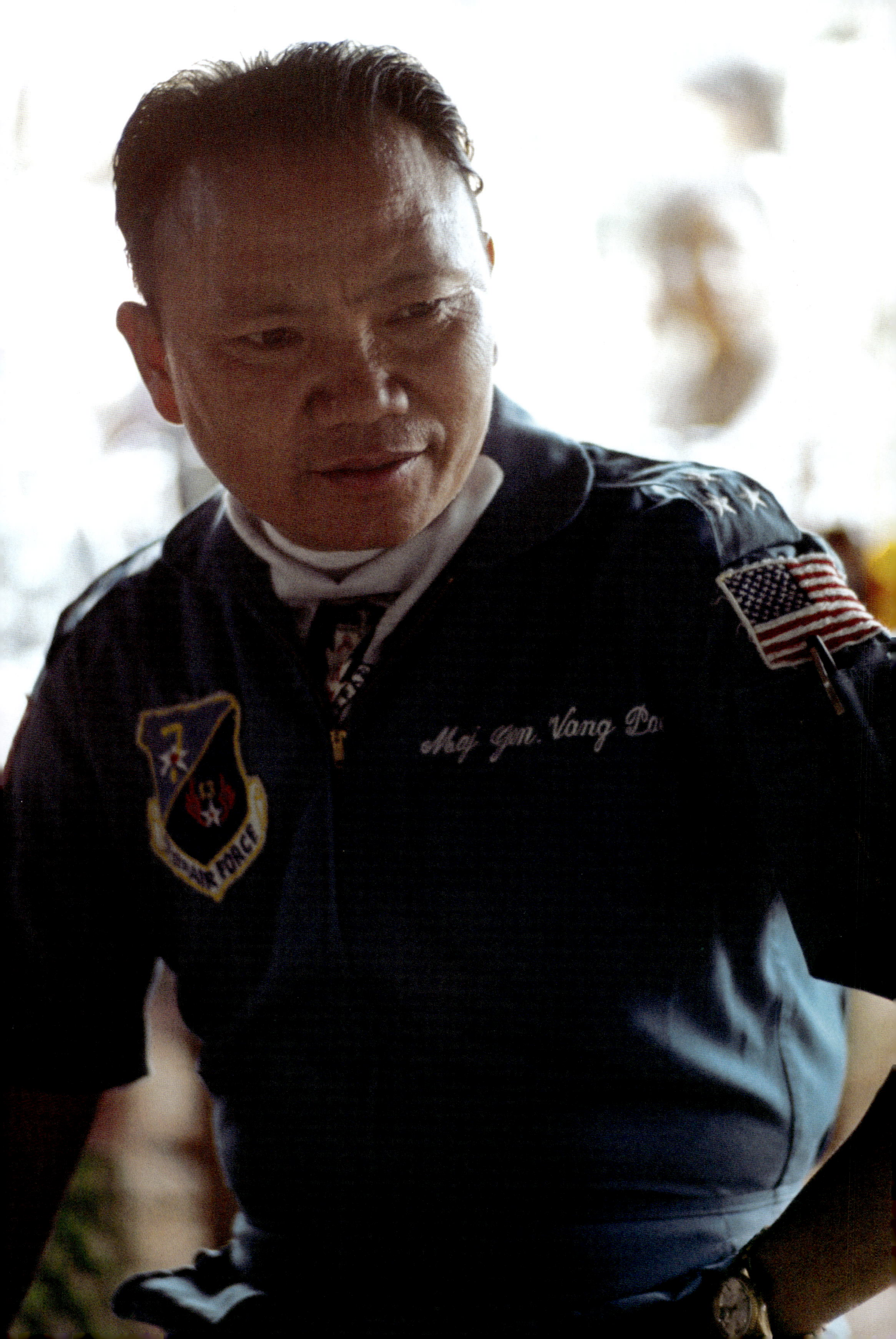
Maj. Gen. Vang
AIR FORCE

"The Americans had come to the aid of the [Hmong] in January 1961 with the CIA's program of furnishing arms and ammunition, run out of CIA headquarters in Washington. [U.S. Ambassador William] Sullivan might argue in a congressional hearing in Washington in 1969 that the Americans had no formal commitment to the [Hmong], but that was not the way it was perceived in Laos. The [Hmong] felt they had a commitment from the Americans, and that is why they sacrificed themselves willingly to snatch downed American fliers to safety under fire from the Pathet Lao and North Vietnamese. Americans in Laos, also, felt that there existed a strong American bond to the [Hmong]..."

* * *

ARTHUR J. DOMMEN
"THE INDOCHINESE EXPERIENCE OF THE FRENCH AND THE AMERICANS"
INDIANA UNIVERSITY PRESS
BLOOMINGTON AND INDIANAPOLIS, 2001
PAGE 933

left
General Vang Pao dressed in a light blue flight suit in Long Cheng, LS 20A, the Headquarters of MR II, Laos, in 1974.

W. E. GARRET/NATIONAL GEOGRAPHIC STOCK COLLECTION

"Take a close look at our country; this could be our last time seeing our country, our land."

***
GENERAL VANG PAO TOLD HIS FAMILY THE MORNING THEY WERE BEING AIRLIFTED OUT OF LONG CHENG BY CIA PILOT KNOTTS, MAY 14, 1975.

Ntsia peb lub tebchaws kom tseeb, tej zaum nov yuav yog zaum kawg uas peb pom peb lub tebchaws, peb thaj av.

(TRANSLATION - LUS TXHAIS)

Long Cheng, LS 20A, the Headquarters of MR II, in November 1974. 'SKY' was an alias used for the CIA compound and personnel stationed at Long Cheng.

PHOTO BY CAPTAIN DAVID H. KOUBA; CASI 1968-1975. ALSO IN THE COLLECTION OF TUA VANG.

Hmong soldiers and their families being evacuated by a C-130 from Long Cheng on May 14, 1975. There were intense military and political pressures for the top Hmong military personnel living in the city. The Pathet Lao had generated a blacklist of all the top Hmong commanders who had worked directly with the CIA and General Vang Pao to be captured and sent to re-education in Sam Neua. The majority of them escaped to Thailand on this day while some were captured and sent to prison camp.

THUA VANG COLLECTION

"People always ask me, 'General, how did you and the Hmong people get through those dark years toward the end of the war?'

"I always tell them that it was actually quite simple—through hope, through faith, and through unity.

"Because through those darkest moments we never lost hope, and we always believed that if somehow we could keep our people together we could rebuild our Hmong family! No matter what the obstacle was, if we could just stay together we could overcome anything!

"As we reflect back on our lives we can see clearly that because we never lost hope, we never lost faith in God, and we stayed unified and together, our people not only rebuilt our Hmong family, but we have grown to new heights."

* * *

GENERAL VANG PAO
JULY 4TH, 2008 SPEECH
RETRIEVED FROM CHA VANG
NOVEMBER 2010

Neeg nug kuv tias, 'Yawg Hlob Nai Phoo, pej xeem Hmoob thiab koj ncua coj dhau tej kev tsaus ntuj thaum muaj tsov rog los tau li cas?'

Kuv hais rau lawv tias nws yooj yim vim peb muaj kev cia siab, kev tseeg, thiab kev sib koom tes.

Vim thaum lub caij tau kev tsaus ntuj peb tsis tag kev vam, thiab peb tseeg tau tias yog peb sib koom tes ces peb Hmoob lub neej yeej yuav muaj xwb! Txawm phem li cas los yog peb sib koom tes ces peb yuav dhau tau txhua yam.

Yog tig mus saib peb lub neej yam dhau los ces peb yeej pom tau tseeb tseeb hais tias vim peb tsis tag kev cia siab, peb tsis tag kev ntseeg yawm saub, thiab peb sib koom siab thiab sib koom tes, twb tsis yog peb kho tau peb lub neej Hmoob xwb tab sis peb lub neej Hmoob twb nce siab lawm ib qib.

(TRANSLATION - LUS TXHAIS)

An Illustration of His Remarkable Life 266

"I never imagined that I would be a refugee, because the United States—the greatest country on earth which had saved Europe from the Nazis and Asia from the Japanese—supported me in my fight against the Communist takeover of my country."

* * *
GENERAL VANG PAO
"TRAGIC MOUNTAINS"
JANE HAMILTON-MERRITT
INDIANA UNIVERSITY PRESS
1999, PAGE 351

Kuv xav tsis txog tias yuav raug ua neeg thoj nam tawg rog li, vim tias Ameliskas yog ib lub tebchaws loj tshaj nyob rau ntiaj teb—uas lawv twb tau cawm yeej tebchaws Europe los ntawm cov Nazis thiab cov tebchaws Asia los ntawm Yib Pooj (Japanese) lawm—lawv pab txhawb nqa kuv thiab tiv thaiv tsis pub kom Nyab Laj Liab tuaj txeeb txhav kuv lub tebchaws.

(TRANSLATION - LUS TXHAIS)

General Vang Pao's 1975 Thai passport.

JANG CHENG VANG COLLECTION

right
Thai Prime Minister Kukrit Pramoj held a press conference on Vang Pao and other Laotian refugees in Thailand, May 12, 1975. The reporter was referring to the General's family. Two days prior to his arrival at Udon on May 14, 1975, there were already some 450 refugees at the military barracks.

RETRIEVED FROM THE NATIONAL ARCHIVES. MARGARET P. GRAFELD DECLASSIFIED/RELEASED U.S. DEPARTMENT OF STATE EO SYSTEMATIC REVIEW 05 JULY 2006

Prime Minister Kukrit Pramoj on Vang Pao and
other Lao refugees in Thailand
Press Conference
May 12, 1975

* * *

REPORTER: Turning to the subject of Laos, General Vang Pao has come to Udon ...
KUKRIT: He has come here, bringing his family with him. Since he has come here already, what can be done? He has been disarmed and he is in Udon at present.
REPORTER: What action will we take?
KUKRIT: Talks are being held with him to try to persuade him to return to Laos.
REPORTER: Has he brought his family only?
KUKRIT: He has a very big family, dozens of person, but ...
REPORTER: It is said that the Defense Minister came also.
KUKRIT: Chao (Prince) Sisouk [Nachampassak]? I heard some time ago that he would go abroad. He has passed through only. It was reported at first that he would go to attend a meeting or conference somewhere.
REPORTER: Who are we sending to hold talks with General Vang Pao and the persons accompanying him who have come here?
KUKRIT: Our military authorities are looking after him, finding a place for him to stay and disarming them if they have any weapons. But since his family is composed of women and small children, they will most probably not have anything much with them.
REPORTER: Should he ask for asylum, what action do you think ought to be taken?
KUKRIT: He hasn't made any such request yet, but it must be considered first. My personal view is that I would like him to return to Laos, and efforts are being made to try and persuade him. Should he return to Laos, it would be better.
REPORTER: Has the government drafted any rules and regulations in regard to Lao refugees yet, in preparation should the situation in Laos deteriorate further?

KUKRIT: I don't think that the same rules and regulations could be used as for Cambodians and Vietnamese, because of the long common border between Laos and Thailand. We have towns scattered widely along the bank of the Mekong River, as can be seen. Furthermore, the people along both banks of the Mekong River cross backwards and forwards all the time and they have close ties, because of inter-marriage and the fact that people on both banks are relatives. It has been usual when any violent incident occur on the Lao side for the people in Laos to cross over and come to the Thai side; then when the situation becomes quiet again they return to Laos. It would be difficult to close the border and to forbid Laos from crossing over into Thailand because they have become accustomed to coming here in the past, until it has become a custom. When any violence occurs in Laos, they cross over into Thailand and they come and stay with their relatives here, then they return to Laos later when it is safe. In addition, there are very large number of Thais who have gone to earn a living in Laos.
REPORTER: I meant high level Lao officials.
KUKRIT: Consideration would have to be paid to high level officials individually, how they have entered our country, etc. We will endeavor to put pressure on most of them to go to live in other countries. It would be utterly impossible for us to care for all Lao officials in our country.
REPORTER: We have refused to give political asylum to Vietnamese and Cambodians. Couldn't we use the same rules and regulations for Lao?
KUKRIT: Wait until the time is reached. The same rules and regulations will most probably have to be used for high level officials -- for them to pass through and go on to any country of their choice. We can't be expected to let them remain here.

"When I was born in 1970 in Long Cheng, five years before the Secret War ended, I only heard of General Vang Pao's name and his fame. At age 5 and close to the end of the war, I heard of his popularity and status as similar to that of the King of Laos. My parents and grandparents and the Hmong people talked about General Vang Pao's leadership as something special, derived from nature; he has supernatural military skills. Most importantly, he played a critical role in the Hmong history, which made us known to the world."

***

YENVISET XIONG
MINNEAPOLIS, MINNESOTA
AUTHOR'S INTERVIEW
NOVEMBER 10, 2010

"General Vang Pao was very sad when he received an order to leave Nam Phong, Thailand, from the Thai generals right after he had just arrived. He didn't want to leave his people to the United States. He wanted to stay behind so much, but he couldn't because of the political risk with him being in Thailand for the Thai."

***

MRS. HOUA YANG
WIFE OF COLONEL SHONG LENG XIONG
AUTHOR'S INTERVIEW
MINNEAPOLIS, MINNESOTA
DECEMBER 2010

H.H. Kukrit Pramoj
Prime Minister of Thailand
Bangkok, Thailand.
                     Missoula, Montana, U.S.A.
                     July 25, 1975

General Vang Pao
c/o 1701 Cooly # 1
Missoula, Montana, U.S.A.

Your Honorable:

    We, the Royal Lao Government side, had tried very hard to maintain the equilibrium of the Peace Agreement in Laos in 1973. However, the enemy, who could not win in battle, have resorted to use force to take over the country in violation of the Agreement after the collapse of the former regimes in South Vietnam and Cambodia. Thus as a result of this, a large number of Lao population of Mhong (Meo) tribe have fled to Thailand to take temporary refuge under the protections of Their Majesties the King and the Queen, your government, and the Thai people. This is because we, Lao people, look toward Thailand which is linguistically, culturally, and socially similar to Laos, as its big brother.
    I have left Thailand for the United States in order to visit my children and to take a brief political asylum. The time, however, has been quite sufficient now and I would like to request your honorable's permission to return to Thailand to assist my people to resettle on the new land that you so graciously give us and to insure that the Mhong abide to the Thai laws.
    Hoping that you will kindly consider my request, may I express to you my humble sentiment and high consideration.

                     Yours faithfully,

                     General VANG PAO

H.H. Kukrit Pramoj
Prime Minister of Thailand
Bangkok, Thailand.
                     Missoula, Montana, U.S.A.
                     July, 25, 1975

General Vang Pao
C/O 1701 Cooly # 1
Missoula, Montana, U.S.A.

Your Honorable:

    The Lao population of Mhong (Meo) tribe who have taken refuge in the northeast of Thailand are mostly farmers. Therefore, on behalf of these refugees, may I request you to reconsider some land in the region of Mae Hong Son instead of Nan where it will offer them a more peaceful and profitable life.

    Hoping that Their Majesties the King and the Queen, your honorable's government, and the Thai people will show compassion to the Mhong refugees, may I request you to accept our sincere sentiments and high consideration.

                     Yours faithfully,

                     General VANG PAO.

Within a month after General Vang Pao arrived in Montana, he sent a personal letter to the Prime Minister of Thailand, Kukrit Pramoj, asking him to provide safety and security to his people as they were coming from their war-torn country of Laos.

DOCUMENT FROM THE CENTER FOR HMONG STUDIES VIA LEE PAO XIONG

right
A drawing depicting General Vang Pao's commitment to fight for freedom.

CAPTAIN VANG NENG COLLECTION

"WE WILL ALWAYS FIGHT FOR FREEDOM EVEN IF IT IS FOR A 100 YEARS." GENERAL: *Vang Pao*

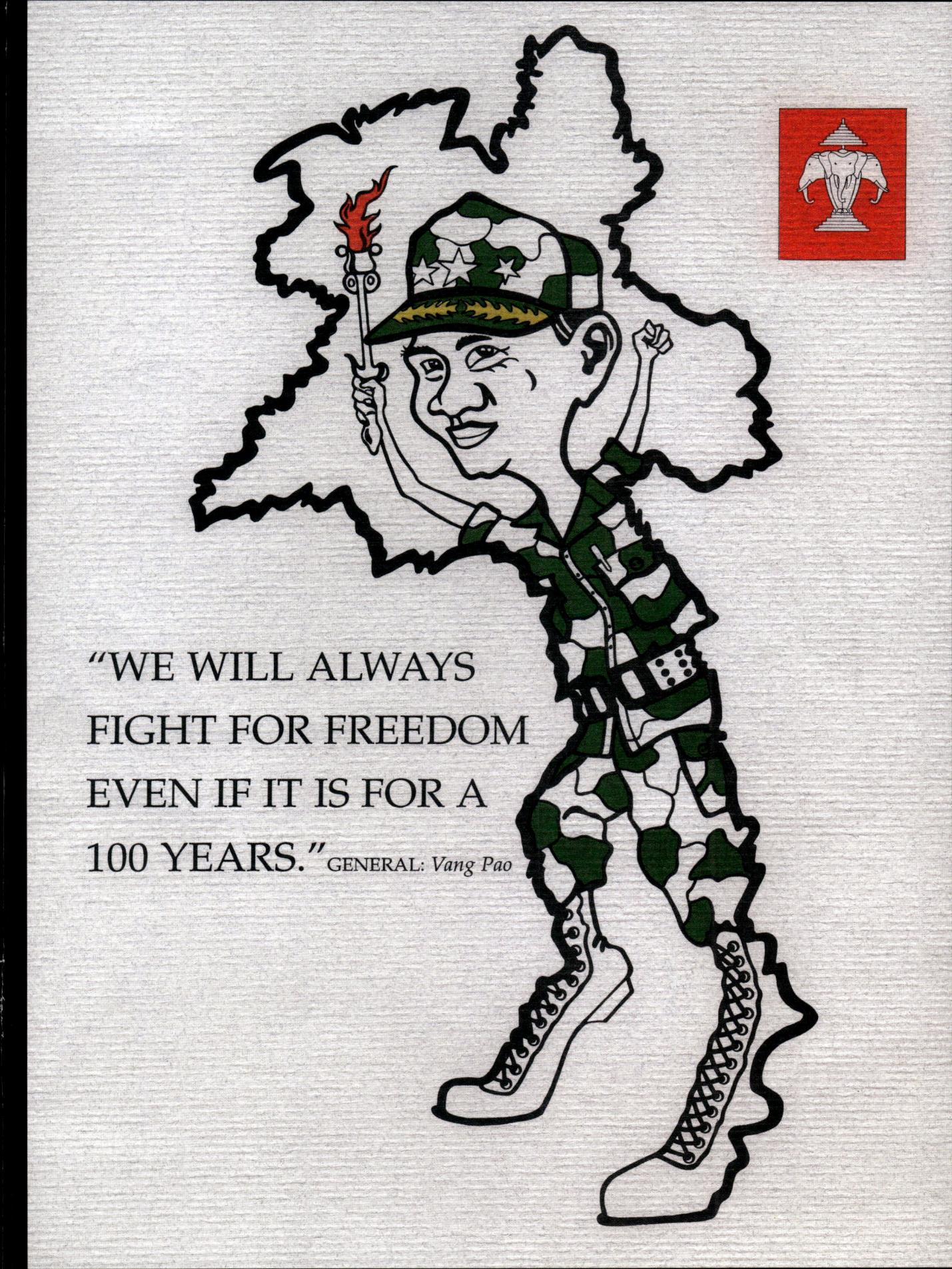

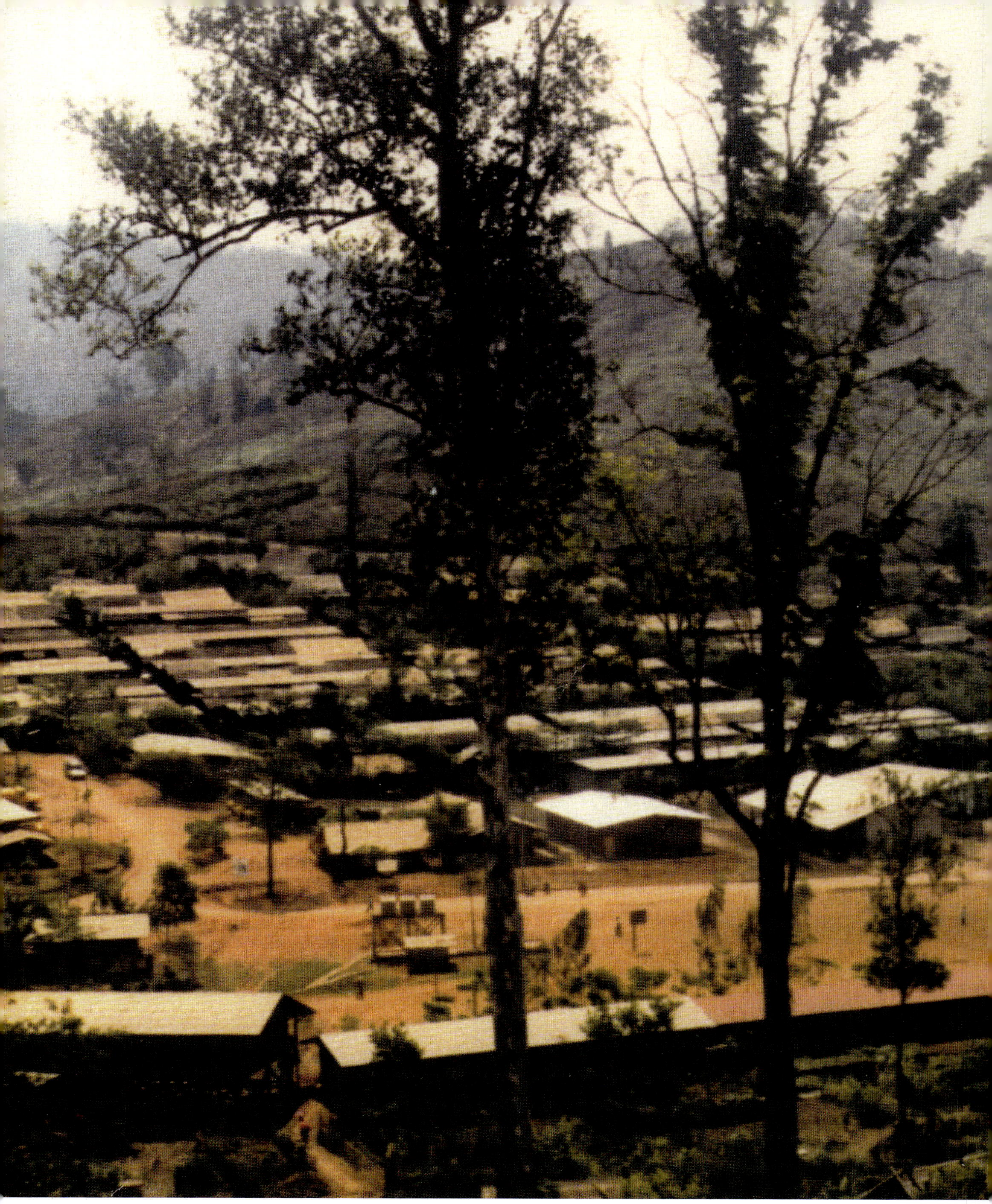

This is a picture of the Ban Vinai Refugee Camp in Loei Province, Thailand, in the early 1980s. Ban Vinai was among a handful of refugee camps located along the northeast borders of Thailand and Laos that provided temporary shelters for the war-torn people from Laos. In 1976, Ban Vinai was built on a 400-acre land that eventually became home to more than 40,000 people, with Hmong being the largest population among all ethnic people coming from Laos. This camp was closed in 1992.

CAPTAIN VANG NENG COLLECTION

IN THE UNITED STATES OF AMERICA

"In Montana, I was no longer a military commander. I had to make a living and support my family. I farmed. I raised livestock."

* * *
GENERAL VANG PAO
AUTHOR'S INTERVIEW
MAY 2007

Nyob rau xeev Montana, kuv tsis yog thawj tub rog lawm. Kuv yuav tsum khwv thiaj tau noj tau haus los yug kuv tsev neeg. Kuv tau ua liaj ua teb thiab yug tsiaj txhu.

(TRANSLATION - LUS TXHAIS)

General Vang Pao with his family and nieces and nephews at their first home in Victor, Montana. When his children came, they stayed with Jerry 'Hog' Daniels' family. The Vang families were very closed because Jerry was an advisor and personal friend to General Vang Pao during the Secret War. In Montana, the family raised livestock and farmed for a living.

THE GVP FAMILY & CHU VANG COLLECTIONS

An Illustration of His Remarkable Life 280

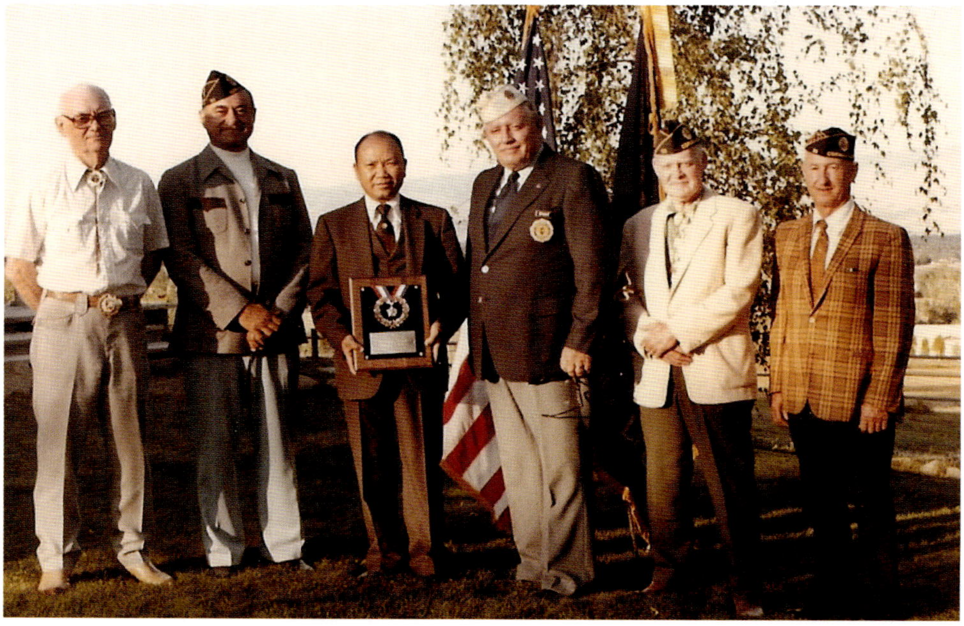

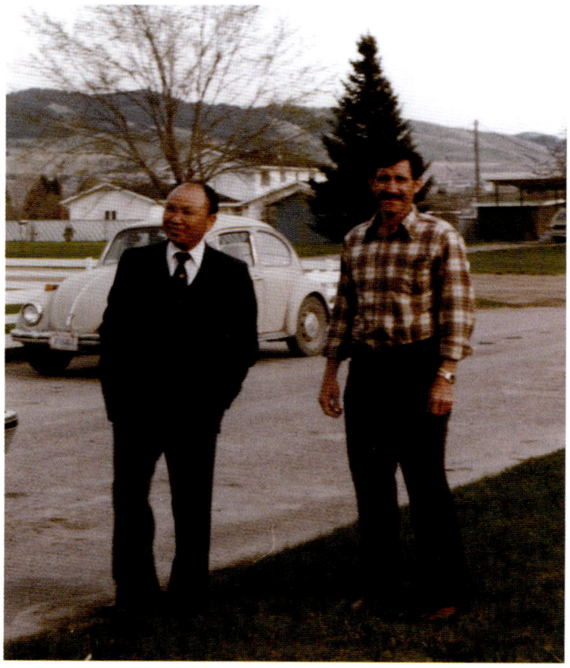

General Vang Pao with Hmong community leaders and members in Santa Ana, California, in the early 1980s. Dr. Vang Shur, *far left*, became the first Executive Director for the newly established non-profit organization, Lao Family Community of California.

THE GVP FAMILY COLLECTION

top left
General Vang Pao with some American friends in Woodside, Montana, in the early 1980s.

THE GVP FAMILY COLLECTION

bottom left
GVP and Jerry 'Hog' Daniels in Montana in the late 1970s.

THE GVP FAMILY COLLECTION

An Illustration of His Remarkable Life 282

While on Her Majesty Queen Sirikit of Thailand's trip to New York City, New York, in the summer of 1979, her majesty also had an audience with General Vang Pao. The reason for this meeting was to discuss activities related to the Hmong in Thailand. Accompanying the General was his personal assistant, Nhia Ying Vang, *center*. *Right*, Nhia Ying Vang shakes hands with Queen Sirikit.

CHER CHENG VANG COLLECTION

top, far right
General Vang Pao and Prince Sisouk Nachampassak had an audience with H.R.H. King Norodom Sihanouk, of Cambodia.

WA CHONG VANG COLLECTION

bottom, far right
GVP with a Japanese top government official (second from left).

WA CHONG VANG COLLECTION

An Illustration of His Remarkable Life 284

ຂ່າວສານ
ແຜ່ນດິນໄກຫ້

ສບັບທີ ໄ ປີທີ ໑   ມັງກະຣາ-ກຸມພາ ໑໬๗໴

ອົງການສາມັກຄີຄົນລັາວ   1423 S. Mohawk Drive, Santa Ana
California 92704
ໂທຣ: (714) 979-2022

ແຜ່ນດິນໃໝ່

ອົງການສາມັກຄີຄອບຄົວລາວ
ເລກທີ ໐໐໕ / ອ.ສ.ຄ.ລ
ວັນທີ ໓ ກຸມພາ ໑໙໗໮

ໜ້າ ໑

ຈົດ

ຖານ..

ເຮື່ອງ : ຄ່າບຳລຸງອົງການສາມັກຄີຄອບຄົວລາວ ຈາກຖານສະມາຊິກທີ່ກຸ່ມແຂງ.

ກອນອື່ນອາພະເຈົ້າຂໍສະແດງຄວາມຊອບໃຈຕໍ່ຖານສະມາຊິກທັງຫຼາຍທີ່ມີໃຈເອື້ອເຝື້ອເຜື່ອແຜ່ເຂົ້າມາເປັນສະມາຊິກເພື່ອປະກອບຜົນປະໂຫຍດສ່ວນຮວມ ແລະ ຍັງໄດ້ສຽສະຫຼະສັບສົມບັດເວັນເວລາມາຊ່ວຍປັບປຸງອົງການ ໃຫ້ຈະເລີນກ້າວໜ້າ ໃຫ້ສາມາດປົກປັກຮັກສາຊີວິດຂອງປະຊາຊົນ ແລະ ສັງຄົມຂອງລາວເຮົາເຮົາໄວ້ໃຫ້ລຸກຫຼາບ ແລະ ລົບ ຂອງເຮົາໄດ້ສຽຕາຍໃຫມ່ວັນລົມ.

ອາພະເຈົ້າຊ້າຍງານໃຫ້ຖານສະມາຊິກ ແລະ ຜູ້ແຜ່ນຂອງຢາກວ່າ ຕລົງຈາກພອກເຮົາໄດ້ພາກັນມາທຳການເລືອກຕັ້ງອົງມະນາມອຍຍຳການ ແລະຄະນະບໍລິຫານ ຜ່ານມາບໍລິຫານງານຂອງອົງການສາມັກຄີຄອບຄົວລາວ ສຸດທ້າຍນີ້ ອຍ່າງຖີ່ຍ່ານໃດໜຶ່ງນ້ອມ ຕລົງຈາກບົນອາພະເຈົ້າກໍໄດ້ທຳຄຳຮ້ອງອຳການຊ່ວຍເຫຼືອອອກຈາກອົງຍົກຄົບຄຸຈີນ ສະເພາະຢ່າງຢຽມນບຂາງຊົມຍົກລາງເຮົາ ຕໍ່ຢຶກບານອາກາເຮັງກາ ເພື່ອໃຫ້ຜູ້ຍົກລາງເຮົາໄດ້ຮັບການຊ່ວຍເຫຼືອຕໍ່ໄປໃນອານາຄົດ ນ້ອຍຈາກວ່າ ແຜນການຊ່ວຍເຫຼືອສອງ (໒) ປີ ກຳລັງຈະໜົດໃສ່ວັນທີ ໑໐ ຄືນເຄືອນສີຍຕາມ ໙ພຶກ ແລະອາພະເຈົ້າມີຄວາມຢ້ານກົດຄດກຄ້ອນ ສຽຕາມ ໙ພຶກ ຖ້າໄດ້ການຊ່ວຍ ເຫຼືອຕຳລອງຂາງຍົກລາງເຮົາຈະຄ້ອງມີນັບຕາ ແບບວນ ຊ່ວຽຈັນເປັນຕອງນຳຄຳຮ້ອງໃໝ່ໃຫ້ກົດຫຼືສັງກອນ ຕລົງຈາກ ຊັກຢາມ ແລະ ສະພາສຸຂະພາພຂຳໄດ້ອາງມັດການຊ່ວຍຫຼາງ ໔ (ສີ່) ປີ ຕໍ່ແຫຼງ ອາພະເຈົ້າຈຶ່ງໄດ້ວາງແຜນໄປປຶຜານຢາມຊາງຍົກລາງເຮົາແຕ່ລະຕິດ ເພື່ອທຳການຈັດຕັ້ງສາຂາຂອງອົງການສາມັກຄີຄອບຄົວລາວຂຶ້ນໃນແຕ່ລະຕິດ ຕລົງຈາກກັບມາປະຈຳການຢູ່ຄາລີຟໍເນຍ ເພື່ອດຳເນີນງານຂອງອົງການຕໍ່ໄປ.

ສຸດທ້າຍນີ້ ຂ້າພະເຈົ້າຂໍໃຫ້ຖານສະມາຊິກທັງຫຼາຍ ຈົງໃຫ້ການຮ່ວມມີ ກະຊຸມສ່ວຽເວົ້າຄຳບຳລຸງທີ່ ຄ້າງຄາ ຕລຄຊຸດຢ່ວຍໄດ້ສົ່ງມາຈັກຕອບນີ້ໃຫ້ສົ່ງມາສະບັບສະໜຸບ ໃຫ້ອົງການຂອງພອກເຮົາດຳສຫອດຕໍ່ໄປ.
ຂໍ ຊອບໃຈ.

ພຍາບຳຊະປະໂມດ ວ່າງ ປາວ
ປະຖານ ອ.ສ.ຄ.ລ

Board of Directors and advisors of the Lao Family Community of Fresno in 1984-1985. *Back row, left to right:* Wang Xang Her, Shong Ying Lo, Ge Xiong, Chong Ying Moua, Cha Yang, Lee Chong Yang, Vang Kao, and Pa Chong Vue. *Front row, left to right:* Wang Kay Kong, Blia Ying Cha, Wang Kay Fang, Colonel Youa True Vang, Moua Koua, General Vang Pao, Dr. Tony Vang, Nyia Zoua Thao, Chai Pha Cha, Say Lang Her, Bounma Phimmavong, Youa Pao Lee, and Tong Ger Vang.

DR. TONY VANG COLLECTION

right
Logo of General Vang Pao's non-profit organization Lao Family Community, which was a standardized logo used in all states. The four women represent the Lao, Hmong, Mien (Yao) and Khumu (Lao-Theung) people.

LAO FAMILY COMMUNITY OF MINNESOTA COLLECTION

Board members and staff of the Lao Family Community of Minnesota in 1984.

COLONEL LY TENG COLLECTION

"Now that we are in America we must teach our culture and traditions to everyone. This is how we can pass on our culture to the next generation. In exchange we are not only preserving ours, but learning the unique cultural values of others."

* * *
GENERAL VANG PAO
AUTHOR'S INTERVIEW
MAY 2007

Tsam no peb nyob tebchaws Ameliskas lawm, peb yuav tsum qhia peb tej kab lis kev cai rau txhua leej txhua tus. Li no peb thiaj yuav ceev tau tej kab lis kev cai rau peb cov me nyuam mus lawm yav tom ntev. Qhov sib qhia nov tsis yog ua kom peb khaws tau peb tej kab lis kev cai xwb, tiamsi peb tseem kawm tau luag tej kab lis kev cai zoo los ntxiv rau peb li thiab.

(TRANSLATION - LUS TXHAIS)

General Vang Pao spoke to an audience at the first Hmong New Year celebration in the U.S. in Woodside, Montana, in 1977. *Right,* General Vang Pao demonstrated a traditional Lao dance called *Salavan* to some of his American friends at the Hmong New Year Celebration.

THE GVP FAMILY COLLECTION VIA LANG VANG

An Illustration of His Remarkable Life 290

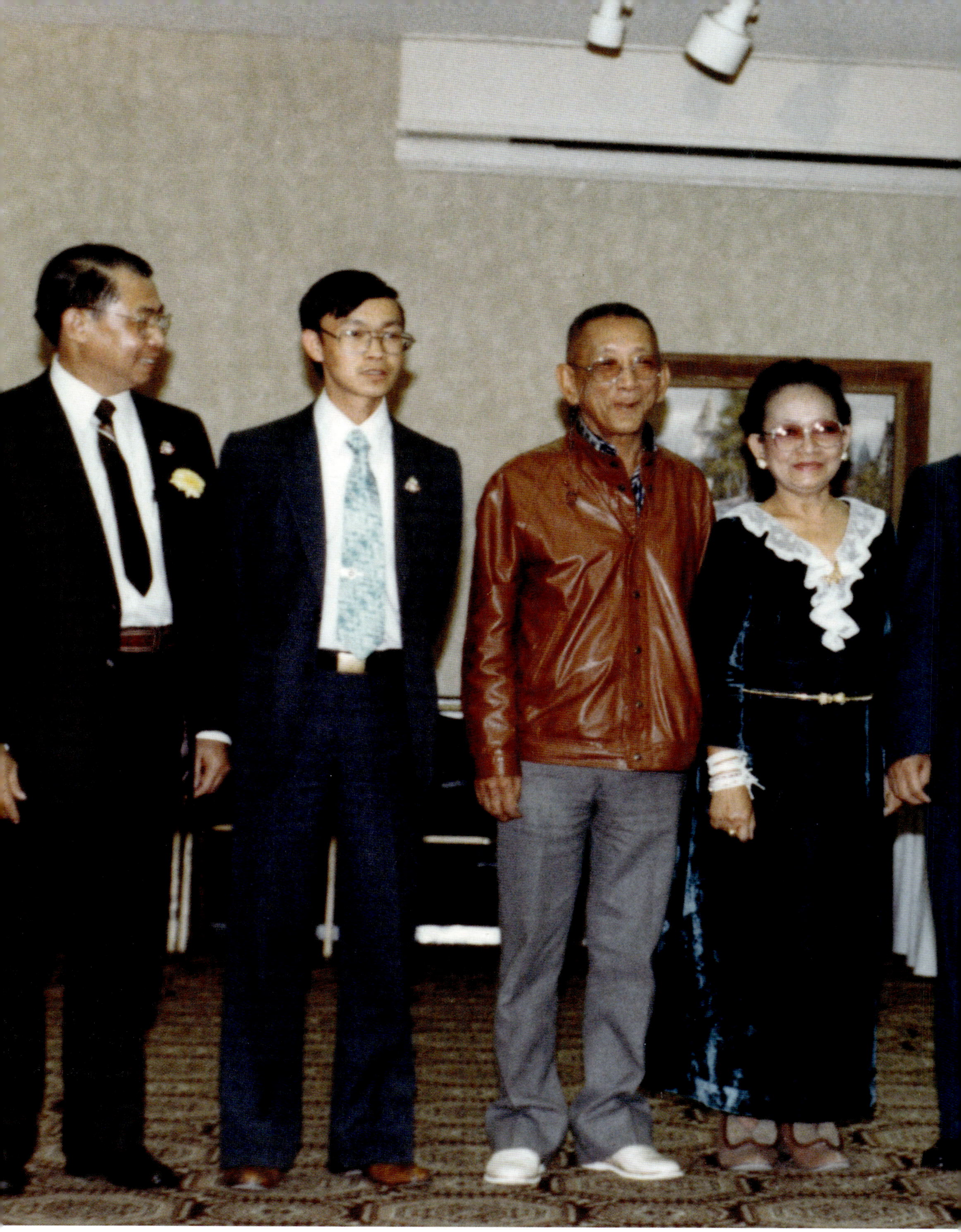

General Vang Pao with his family members and friends in Thailand in early 1980s.

THE GVP FAMILY COLLECTION VIA LANG VANG

An Illustration of His Remarkable Life 292

PACTE D'UNION NATIONALE

POUR LA LIBERATION DU PEUPLE LAO

****

-Considérant que l'Union Nationale pour la Paix, la Neutralité et l'Indépendance en vue de sauvegarder la pérennité de notre Peuple est un acte suprême du patriotisme de tous les Lao,

-Reconnaissant que, pour assurer la continuté de la légitimité Monarchique, la réunification de toutes les forces vives tant à l'intérieur qu'à l'extérieur du Pays, sans aucune discrimination politique et sociale, est indispensable,

-Considérent que le **Conseil de Régence** est le symbole de cette Union Nationale,

-Considérants que nos maquis populaires et patriotiques du Nord au Sud du Pays, depuis la chute du Royaume, ont lutté dans le silence et l'oubli et ont souffert au plus profond de leur âme de l'isolement et du manque de direction politique pour faire connaitre le sens de leur combat,

-Conscients des difficultés de toutes natures auxquelles nous avons à faire face pour être crédibles, entendus et supportés et réalisant que notre Union Nationale, à ses débuts est une structure d'accueil des patriotes de bonne volonté tant à l'extérieur que sur le terrain national,

En attendant le ralliement des autres leaders de la génération montante qui réalise le bien fondé de l'union sacré pour la libération nationale, à la lumière des expériences passées de l'histoire des peuples opprimés pour recouvrer leur indépendance et leur liberté,

NOUS, SOUSSIGNES, FAISONS LE SERMENT SOLENNEL,

par le PRESENT PACTE dont dispositions suivent, de

CONDUIRE SOLIDAIREMENT LA LUTTE de LIBERATION NATIONALE

JUSQU'A LA VICTOIRE FINALE:

Article 1: NOUS, en souscrivant à ce pacte solennel, DECLARONS sur l'honneur que, dans notre lutte de libération nationale contre l'occupant étranger, nous nous engageons à faire des sacrifices suprêmes pour l'intérêt supérieur de la Nation, en dehors de toutes considérations d'intérêts et d'ambitions personnels.

Article 2: Nous formons une **DIRECTION POLITIQUE COLLEGIALE PROVISOIRE** dont les fonctions seront définies d'une manière définitive au CONGRES NATIONAL qui doit se tenir sur le territoire national.

Article 3: Ce pacte est fait en 3 exemplaires et tenu secret.

Fait à Paris le 18 JUIN 1981

Suivent les signatures des parties au Pacte:

SURYADHAY,   Chao Sisouk Na CHAMPASSAK,   Ngon SANANIKONE,   Khamphan PANYA

Kouprasith ABHAY   Houmphanh SAIGNASITH

Phoumi NOSAVAN   VANG PAO

Some former top Royal Lao Government officials and military personnel living in exile reconvened in Paris in June 1981 to form a national effort to fight and advocate for peace and freedom in their country of Laos.

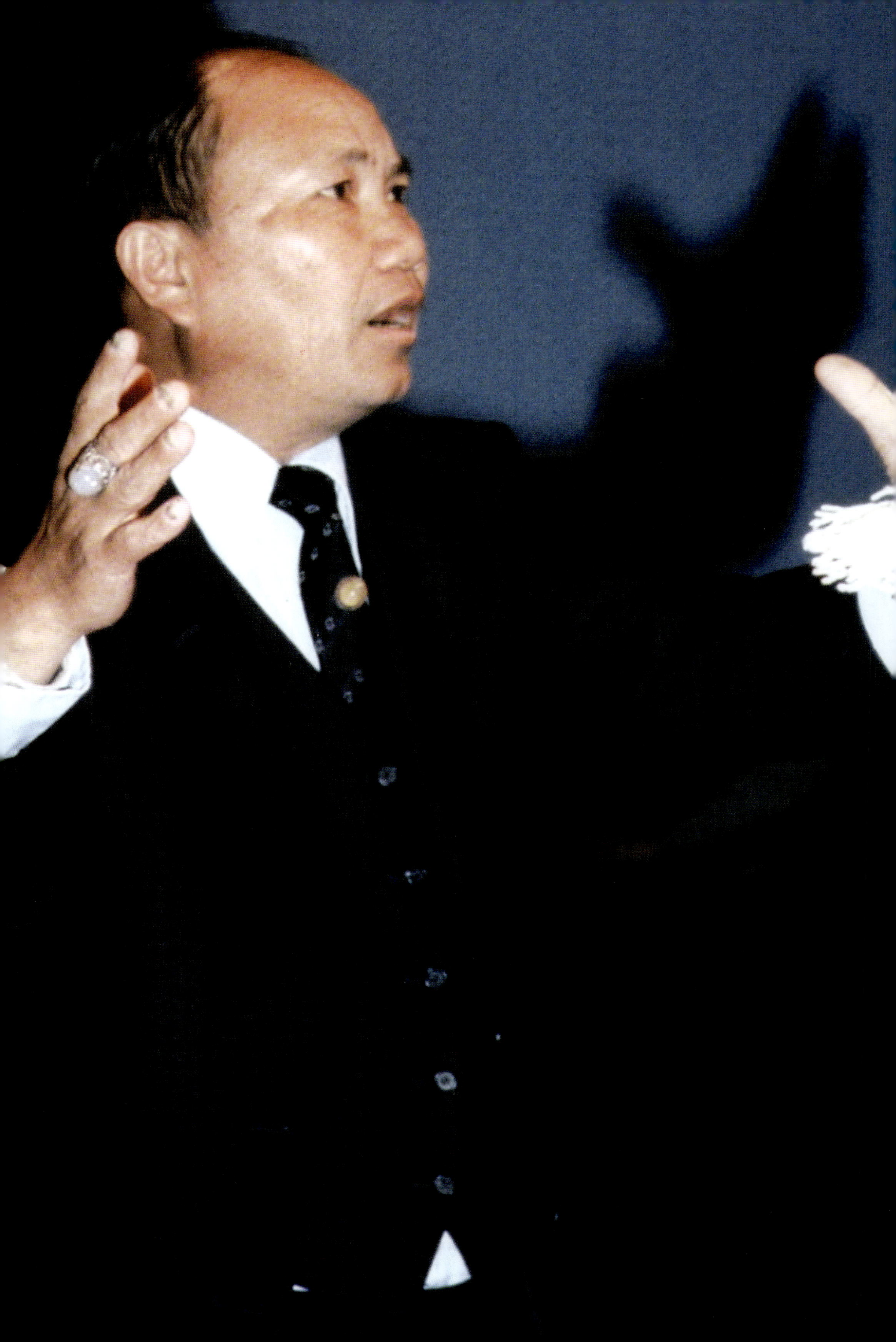

"To the American people we say this: help us learn to help ourselves so that we may no longer be any sort of burden on American society. Help us build our mutual assistance associations so that we can help ourselves more effectively…We do not seek handouts; instead, we seek only a helping hand up. It is in that spirit that I am today urging all Hmong leaders gathered here to take a message back to their people. That message is simply this: try to get jobs—any kind of job—so that we may demonstrate for all to see that the Hmong truly want to work."

* * *

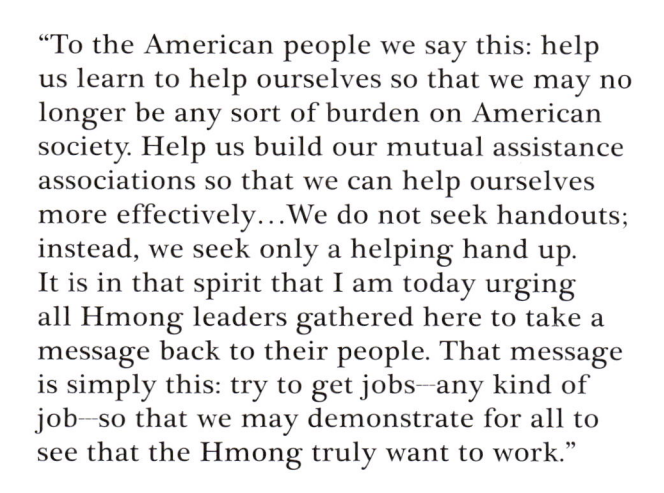

GENERAL VANG PAO
MINNESOTA HISTORICAL SOCIETY
ST. PAUL, MINNESOTA
JUNE 1981

Hais rau cov pej xeem Ameliskas tias, thov lawv pab qhia peb kom peb pab tau peb tus kheej, xwv peb thiaj tsis ua ib qho kev khuam siab rau lawv nyob rau Ameliskas teb. Kom lawv pab peb tsim tsa tej Koos Haum, kom peb muaj kev tshwj xeeb, thiab kom cuag ncua thiaj yuav ua kom peb pab tau peb tus kheej. Peb tsis thov kom lawv yug peb tab sis thov kom lawm pab peb kom peb sawv tau tso. Kuv xav thov hais rau cov thawj coj Hmoob uas tuaj ntawm no kom coj cov lus peb sib sab laj no mus hais rau cov pej xeem. Lub ntsiab lus mas yog li no, yuav tau mus nrhiav hauj lwm, txawm yog hauj lwm dab tsi los xij, peb yuav tsum ua tiag ua kom qhia tau rau pej xeem sawv daws tias peb Hmoob yeej txaus siab ua hauj lwm (tsis nyob tos leeg twg noj xwb).

(TRANSLATION - LUS TXHAIS)

left
General Vang Pao spoke at Lao Family Community of Minnesota in 1981.

VANG XANG COLLECTION

"Laos desperately needs a constitution that is representative of the wishes of the people. Therefore, future elections must allow for multi-parties, election laws must be firm and clear, outside observers should be invited to witness the election process, and there must be a mechanism to hold the elected officials accountable to the people who elected them."

* * *

GENERAL VANG PAO
"PEACE DOCTRINE ON LAOS"
WRITTEN ON NOVEMBER 26, 2003
RETRIEVED FROM XANG VANG
JANUARY 2012

Former Royal Lao Family members and high ranking military officers of the United Lao National Liberation Front, or Neo Hom Kou Xat, convened in California to discuss the future of Laos while living in exile at their first conference in 1981. *From left to right*: Lt. Colonel Vang Fong, Khamphan Panya's son, Chanthong Chantalasith, Hounphanh Saiyansith, Prince Sisouk Nachampassak, Phagna Prince Luang Outhong Savanouvong, Prince Sauryavong Savang, unknown (owner of the building), General Vang Pao, General Kouprasith Abhay, Khamphan Panya, and an assistant to Prince Savang. The political organization committee elected Chao Phagna Luang Muang Chanh Outhong Souvannavong as President and General Vang Pao as Vice President.

CAPTAIN VANG NENG COLLECTION

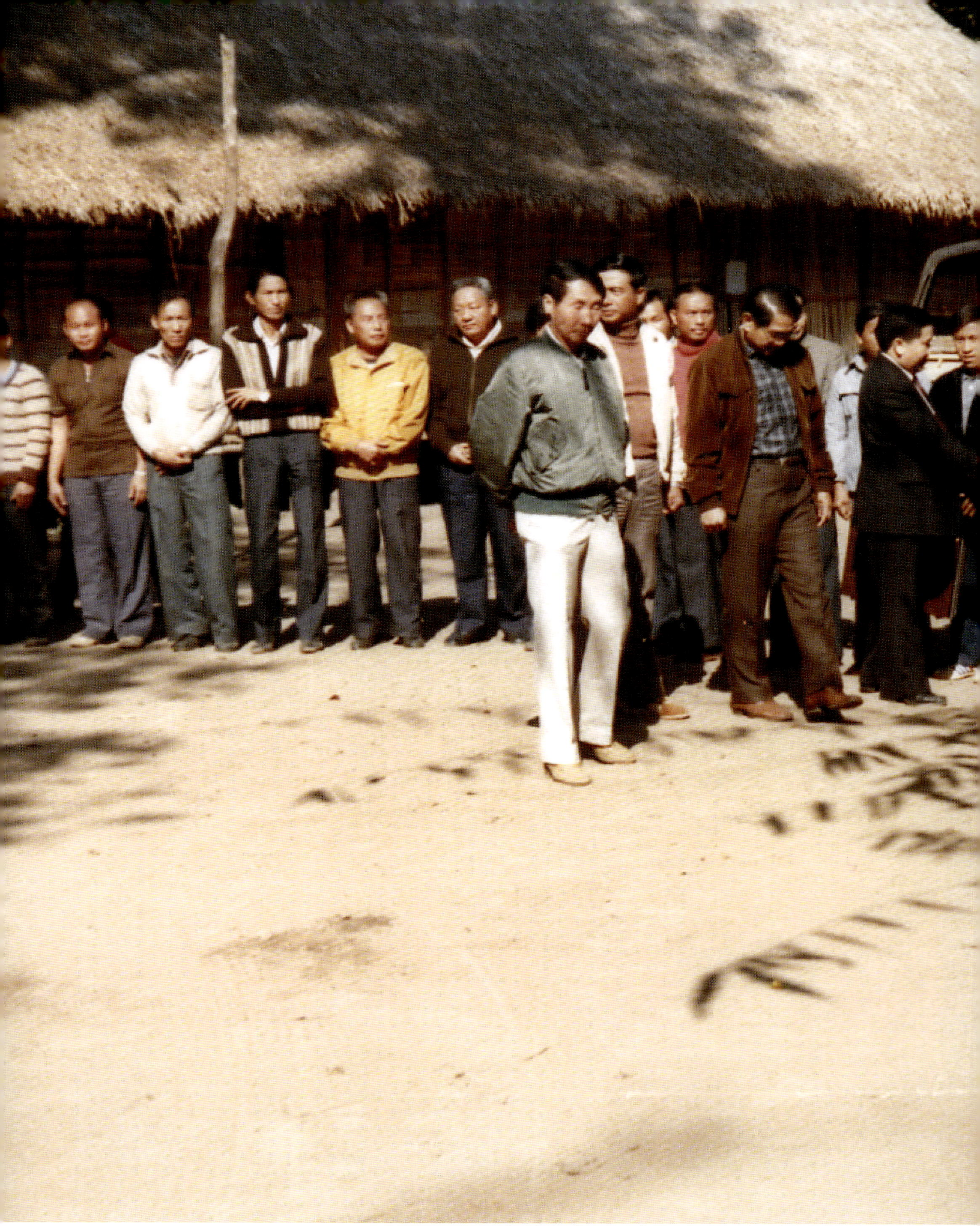

General Vang Pao visits some of his former friends in Thailand. Early 1980s.

CAPTAIN VANG NENG COLLECTION

"As future leaders, you must make the impossible possible. You must make the hopeless hopeful. You must make those unhappy happy. You must give courage to those who live in fear. You must care when no one else cares. And you must sacrifice when no one else is willing to sacrifice."

* * *

GENERAL VANG PAO
"A TIME OF CHANGE AND OPTIMISM" SPEECH
PROM CENTER, OAKDALE, MINNESOTA
JULY 2008
RETRIEVED FROM CHA VANG
NOVEMBER 2010

Yuav ua ib tug thawj coj, koj yuav tsum ua kom tau yam lwm tus xav tias ua tsis tau. Koj yuav tsum ua kom cov neeg tag kev cia siab lawm kom muaj kev cia siab. Koj yuav tsum ua kom cov neeg muaj kev ntxhov siab kom zoo siab. Koj yuav tsum txhawb cov muaj kev ntsai kom txhob txhawj. Koj yuav tsum nrog txhawj thaum nws muaj kev txhawj, thiab koj yuav tsum ua kam kom tau rau sawv daws.

(TRANSLATION - LUS TXHAIS)

right
General Vang Pao at Vang Xang's house in Frogtown in St. Paul, Minnesota, in 1982.

VANG XANG COLLECTION

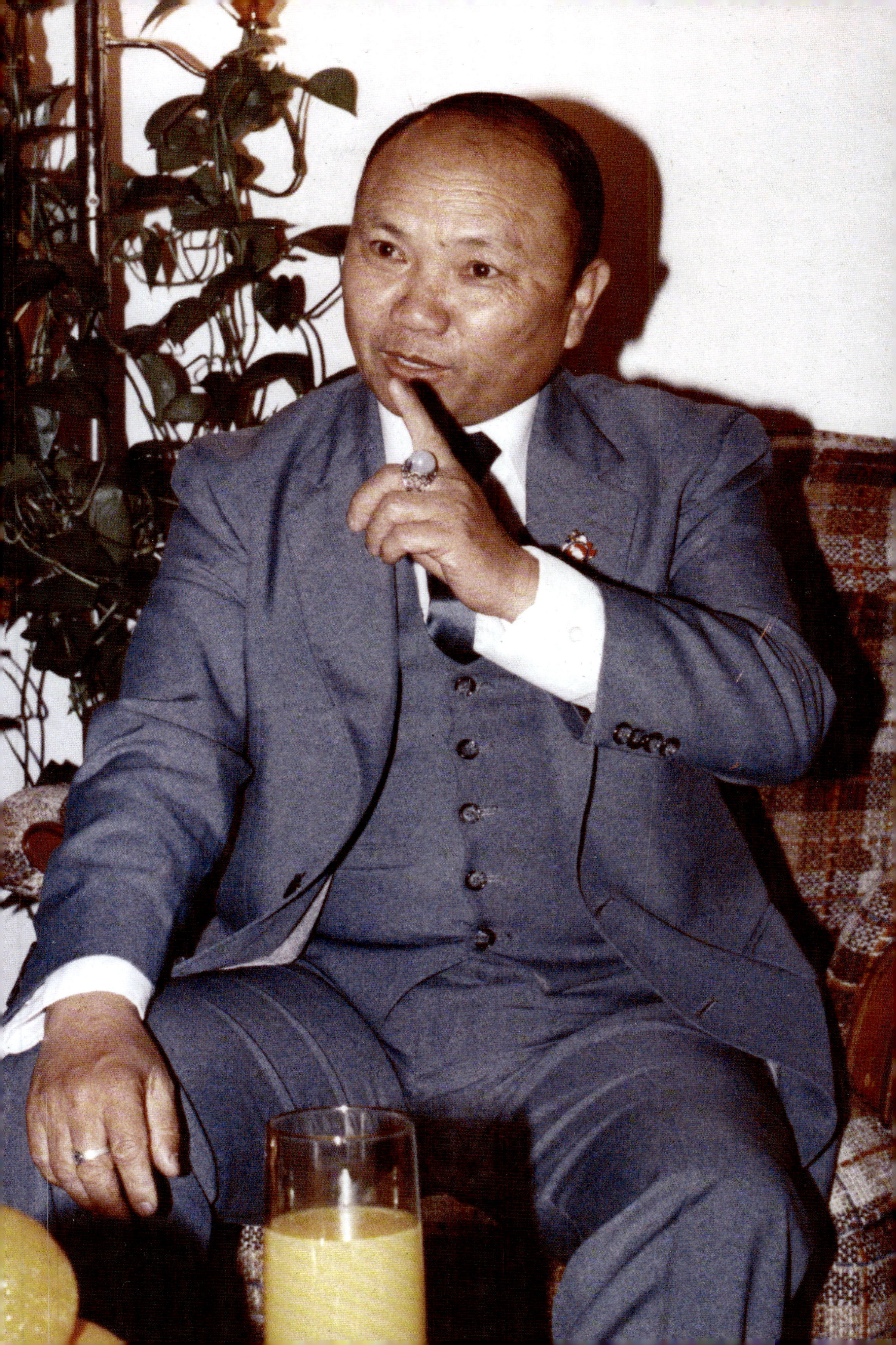

1.

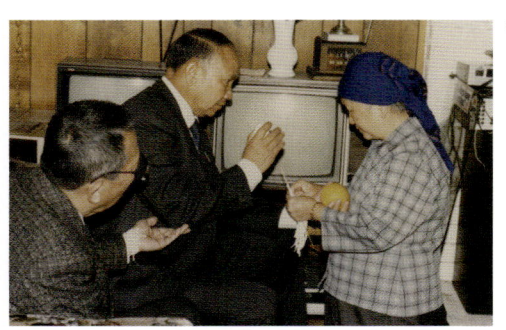

2.

3.

4.

5.

6.

7.

8.

9.

"As a leader, I love my Hmong people—even the oldest and poorest ones—because I am Hmong."

* * *
GENERAL VANG PAO
AUTHOR'S INTERVIEW
SEPTEMBER 2005

Ua ib tug thawj coj, kuv hlub kuv haiv neeg Hmoob—tsis hais tus laus los tus txom nyem—vim tias kuv yog Hmoob.

(TRANSLATION - LUS TXHAIS)

1. ZONG LIA VANG COLLECTION
2. CAPTAIN VANG NENG COLLECTION
3. THE GVP FAMILY COLLECTION
4. LIA VANG COLLECTION
5. DR. KOU VANG COLLECTION
6. MOUA SUE COLLECTION
7. KOU YANG COLLECTION
8. NICOLAS PHA COLLECTION
9. LANG VANG COLLECTION

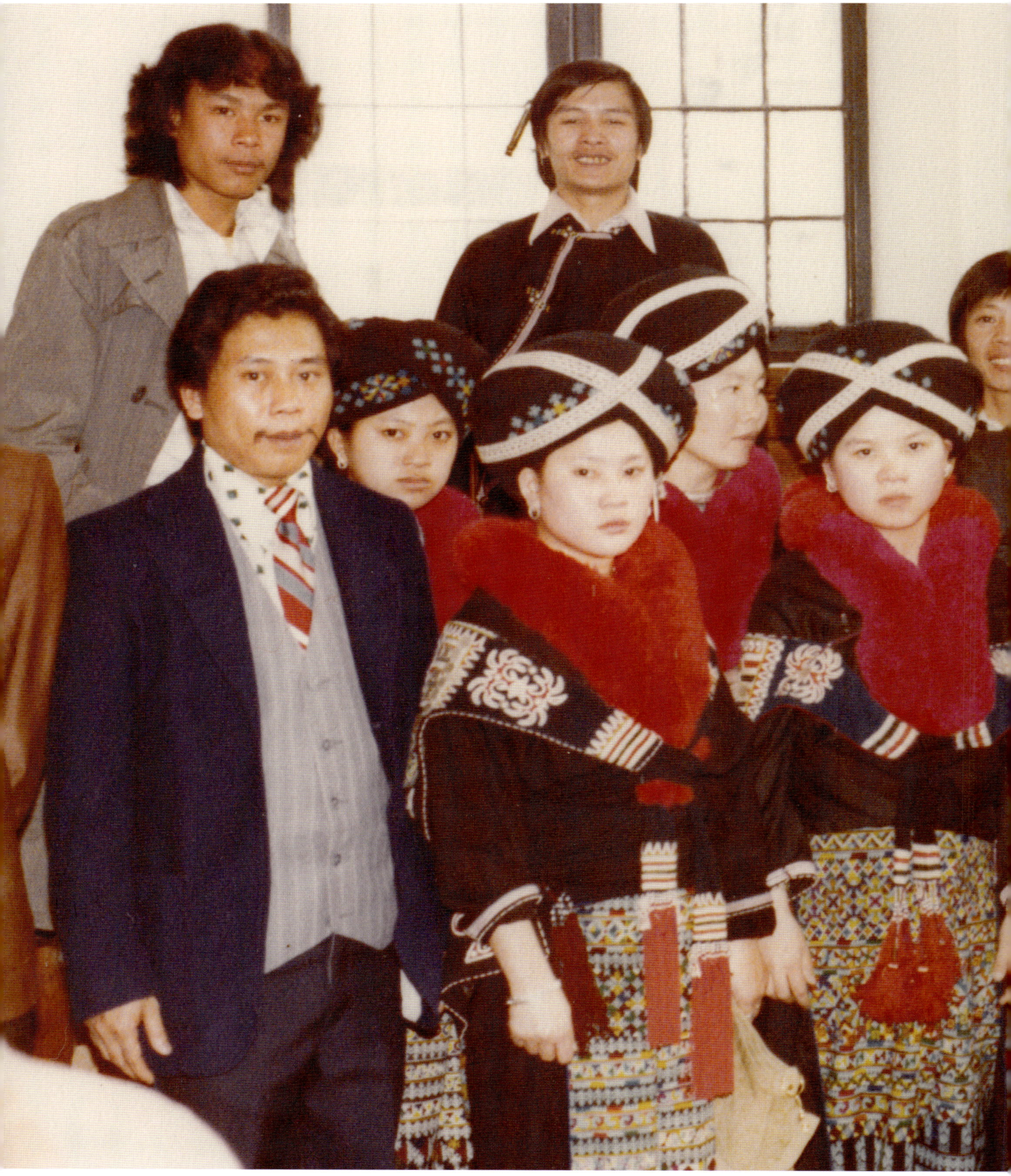

left
General Vang Pao poses with the Mien (Yao) ethnic group, who were among the many refugees from Laos resettling in California in the early 1980s.

WA CHONG VANG COLLECTION

"If the majority of the Laotian generals had the same leadership stamina and visions as General Vang Pao, the outcome of the war may had been different. They were quite the opposite. They only wanted titles and fame. For General Vang Pao, he was very clear about the military mission that was presented to him by the United States and the King in Military Region II. Despite the many life threatening injuries he endured during combat, he still had not given up the fight against enemy forces.

"Although General Vang Pao only received a third grade education, he was very skillful and knowledgeable at everything. He could lead a battle. He would never leave his soldiers behind. He was charismatic and could win the people's trust. He played his politics well. You could not underestimate his ability. He spoke fluent in Vietnamese, Lao, Hmong, Thai, and French and understood English completely. He was one of only a few who had that kind of talent."

* * *
CAPTAIN VANG NENG
GENERAL VANG PAO'S BODYGUARD
AUTHOR'S INTERVIEW
DECEMBER 4, 2010

Captain Vang Neng was one of General Vang Pao's bodyguards in Long Cheng prior to 1975. In the United States, he continued to work closely with General Vang Pao in helping the Hmong and Lao in Thailand with their refugee resettlement processes. Captain Vang Neng also served as President of the non-profit organization Lao Family Community of Minnesota in 1983-84.

CAPTAIN VANG NENG COLLECTION

At a meeting while on a trip to Thailand in 1982, General Vang Pao discussed the difference between non-profit and for-profit organizations and their roles in assisting recent immigrants or refugees who resettled in the U.S.

WA CHONG VANG COLLECTION

General Vang Pao along with his personal aide, Moua Song, met with former U.S. President Richard Nixon in Washington, D.C., in January 1984. Besides catching up with each other's daily lives, according to the General's personal assistants, Moua Song and Xang Vang, General Vang Pao also asked Nixon to help bring the Hmong refugees in Thailand to the United States. According to Moua Song, Nixon said, "he could not help the General because he no longer had power." He suggested the General meet with the Carter Administration. Before leaving, "President Nixon signed two of his books for us," remembered Song. "One for me. One for VP. VP did not want his so he also gave me his."

TOP, FROM KONG MOUA COLLECTION
NEXT PAGE, NICOLAS PHA COLLECTION

An Illustration of His Remarkable Life 310

"When I first arrived [to the United States] I never thought of working to get rich for myself...

"My duty was to find ways to help my people to be economically independent and be educated so they could have a good life..."

* * *
GENERAL VANG PAO
EXTRACTED FROM YANG ENG
BROOKLYN CENTER, MINNESOTA
JULY 2009

Thaum kuv tuaj poob rau tebchaws Ameliskas kuv tsis tau xav tias kuv yuav khwv kom kuv nplua nuj...

Kuv txoj hauj lwm yog nrhiav kev thiab txhawb kuv haiv neeg Hmoob kom lawv khwv tau noj tau haus, kawm txawj kawm ntse es thiaj tau lub neej zoo...

(TRANSLATION - LUS TXHAIS)

General Vang Pao with Hmong community leaders and members in California on April 19, 1986.

MAJOR VANG YING COLLECTION

bottom right
General Vang Pao with Hmong leaders and members in Wisconsin, early 2000s.

XAI DOUA VANG COLLECTION

An Illustration of His Remarkable Life   312

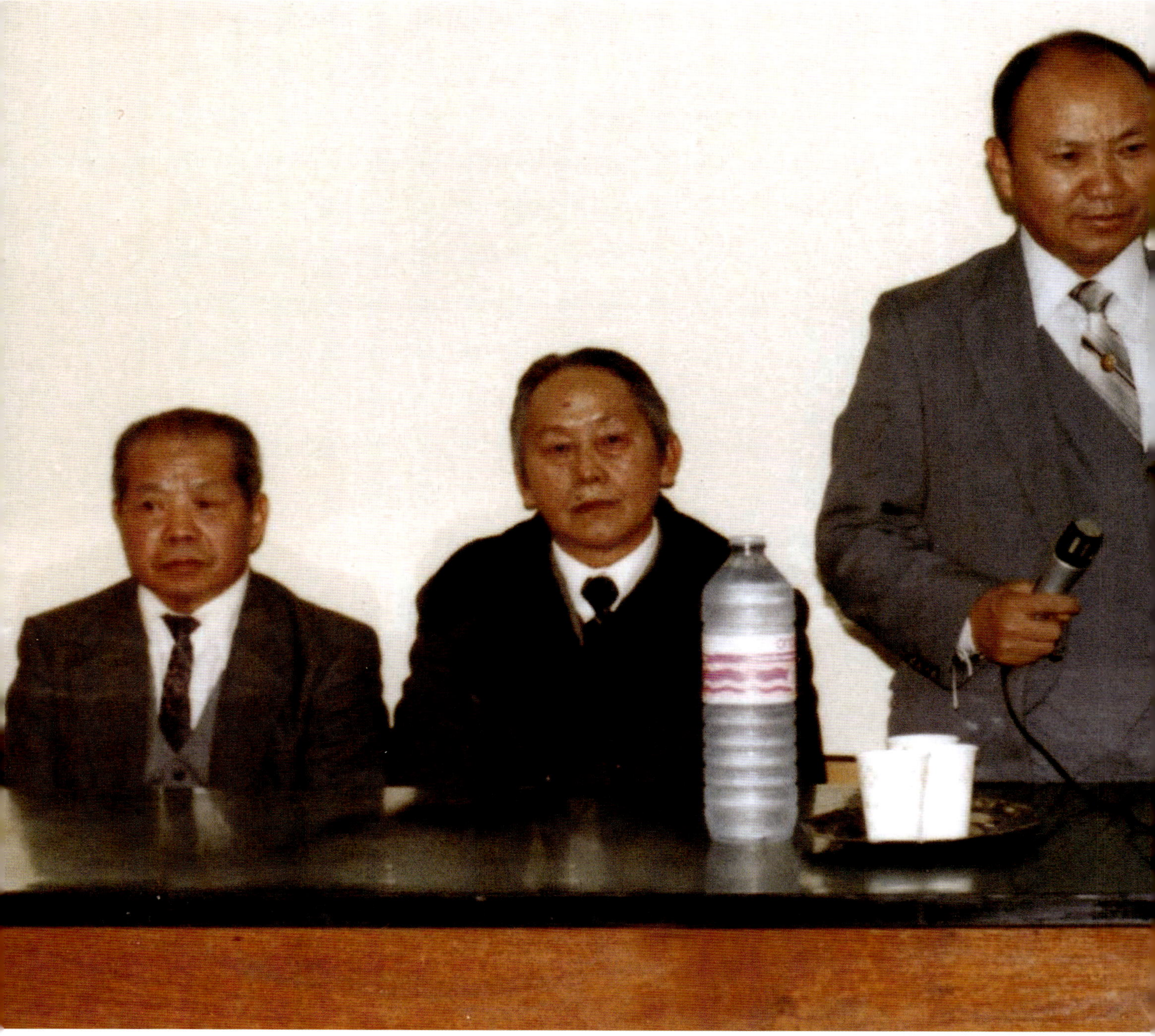

In 1988, General Vang Pao was invited to visit the Hmong of France. Among his guests at a meeting were former Hmong leaders: *left to right*, Deputy Governor of Xieng Khouang Youa Pao Yang, Nai Kong Nao Tou Lor, General Vang Pao, Former Justice Director Tougeu Lyfoung, Chaomouang Neng Thong Lee, and Nai Kong Youa Yao Hang.

CAPTAIN VANG NENG COLLECTION

NOTICE OF APPEAL TO THE BOARD OF IMMIGRATION APPEALS

SUBMIT IN TRIPLICATE TO:

IMMIGRATION AND NATURALIZATION SERVICE

In the Matter of:

YANG, Xay

File No. A26 750 545 (HEL)

1. I hereby appeal to the Board of Immigration Appeals from the decision, dated __25 July 1986__, in the above entitled case.

2. Briefly, state reasons for this appeal. (French Indochina)

The Petitioner, Xia Thao, and the Beneficiary, Vang Xay, are members of Hmong people, a self-autonomous tribe residing in what is present day Laos since the 18th century. The Hmong people are recognized as an autonomous tribe subject to their own self-governing rules, laws and customs. This autonomy is recognized by the Laotian Government, by granting the Hmong their own Hmong Mayor who has the power to govern the Hmong people pursuant to its own law, customs and traditions. The adoption of Beneficiary by Petitioner occurred in 1959 pursuant to Hmong law, custom and tradition, that dictated a man adopt the children and grandchildren of a deceased brother. Upon the death of Nao Tou Vang, Petitioner and her husband, Vang Pao, adopted the Beneficiary pursuant to Hmong custom, law and tradition in 1959. The Law relied upon by the RAC Director in denying the Petition was effective only after August 12, 1965, and does not apply to the adoption in question which occurred in 1959. Hmong law, custom and tradition was applicable and the adoption in 1959 constituted a legal adoption as recognized by the Laotian Government.

3. I __do__ (do) (do not) desire oral argument before the Board of Immigration Appeals in Washington, D.C.

4. I __am__ (am) (am not) filing a separate written brief or statement.

Signature of Applicant (or attorney or representative)

XIA THAO VANG
(Print or type name)

3316 W Central - Missoula, MT 59801
Address (Number, Street, City, State, Zip Code)

Date: August 8, 1986

August 4, 1986

Ref: File No
A 26 750 545 (

Board of Immigration Appeals
United States Department of Justice
301 South Park, Room 512
Federal Office Building, Drawer 10036
Helena, Montana 59501

Dear Sir:

I am writing to appeal the denied of my petition for granting visa to my daughter, Xay Vang and family in order for them to reunite with my family in the United States. My request for your re-consideration is based upon my firmed belief that I, indeed, am the legal mother and guardian of Xay Vang, and she is my adopted daughter. My family is Hmong, and I have lived and ... Hmong cultures and customs which has been in existance for .... Therefore, my adoption of Xay Vang was culturally legal under the Laotian constitution.

Eventhough the Hmong were living in Laos, they have unique distinguished set of cultures and customs of themselves. These cultural heritages are different from those of the Laotians (Low Land Lao). As a highland tribe, they were granted permission by the Lao King to rule and govern so, their legal structure was much different from that of the general Laotian population. Furthermore, because of the prolonged U.S. secret war in Laos, geographical separation, and the government's poor management system, the Hmong were never being educated and/or made aware of the new laws passed in Laos or its agreement with any foreign country. Therefore, Hmong rarely used Laotian Laws. Rather, they used their own discreeded traditions and customs as Laws governing themselves. According to Hmong marriage culture, it is required that the gloom pays certain amount of money, as fee to the bride's parents before the actual marriage ceremony takes place. After the marriage ceremony is completed, the bride will then be part of her husband's family and belong to his family clan. If, however, her husband is deceased, her children and she will belong to the husband's family because the family have already paid the required fee of her at the time of marriage. If she/the widow decides to re-marry, she must marry to a relative of her husband inorder to retain her children and material possession. If she married to someone out side of the family, then she will loss everything including her children to her deceased husband's family. Besides the custom, my husband, major general Vang, ... region in Laos in which my brother .. , Nao Tou Vang (... Vang's father) worked. After Mr. Nao Tou Vang's death, my husband and I had cared for his remained family member because there was no one to care for them. A year later, Xay's mother decided to re-marry and left Xay for us. I had no choice but to take her as my child. I have had Xay since she was four years old. Since I was not aware of the Laotian legal system and its requirement, my adoption was completed in accordance to the Hmong tradition and custom. It was done by the Major of Vang Xay, Youatong Yang, at Phakhet, Laos, on September 10, 1969.

It is my firmed belief that the provision on adoption in Laos are contained in chapter V, Section 2, of the Civil and Commercial Code of Laos, as amended on August 12, 1965, by discree Law N: 237 does not apply to my case. It denied an orphan - a victim of war - the right to have a place for survival and belonging. As you will note, my adoption of Xay Vang was not a choice of childless and without any other legitimate or illegitimate descendants. Rather, it was a choice between providing her with a place to live and foster her right as a human being - or dumping her the street and denying her the right to exist. I believe that my choice was right and it was done to fullfil my society's moral response and responsibility toward victims of war such as Xay Vang. Therefore, my adoption of Xay Vang was exceptional and her family, should be granted permission to reunite with me in this land of opportunity and freedom.

Below are some of the people who witnessed my adoption, they are:

1. Xay Cha Vue   N. 2407 Myrtle, Spokane, WA 99207
2. Bme Lng Vang   1900 S. 3rd West - Missoula, MT 59801
3. Ka Lao Yang   421 North Surrey - Missoula, MT 59801
4. A letter of verification from the President of Lao Family Community Inc. branch of Missoula

Thank you very much for your prompt consideration. If you need additional information, please don't hesitate to contact me.

Respectfully,

Xia Thao

January 18, 1991

Editors
New York Review of Books
250 West 57th Street
New York, N.Y. 10107

Sirs:

This is in reference to your issue of November 22, 1990, and the exchange of letters - and charges - between Jonathan Mirsky and William E. Colby.

I am sure you neither need nor want more polemics on those unresolvable issues, and I hesitate to offer anything further. I would be remiss, however, if I failed to make a few points for the record, referring specifically to the last three paragraphs of Jonathan Mirsky's letter.

I was the CIA's senior representative in Laos from September, 1970, to May, 1973. When Mirsky states that "CIA's involvement in this (opium) traffic was widely known in the Sixties and Seventies, and was amply documented in Alfred McCoy's book <u>The Politics of Heroin</u>", my hackles rise. While I cannot speak with any authority on the Sixties, I can say plenty about the Seventies.

Briefly, the U.S. mission in Vientiane under Ambassador G. McMurtrie Godley did everything humanly possible to put the kibosh on narcotics traffic. The CIA station as part of that mission was fully committed and involved in the effort under Godley's direction. Sustained hell-raising with top levels of the Royal Lao Government led to passage of a law proscribing all forms of narcotics traffic. Pressures were applied down-echelon to see that the law was enforced. Air America and other contractors were fully integrated in the process, and inspection of all aircraft was conducted rigorously and consistently. There were no exemptions, and this included Lao officials (generals) active in military operations.

The McCoy book on which Mirsky relies for evidence to the contrary is questionable on several grounds, only one of which I will address here. I urge any interested reader to look hard at McCoy's sourcing, reflected in his voluminous footnotes which do not always support the "facts" cited in the text. One of his most important sources on narcotics trafficking in Laos is General Ouane Rattikone, former commander-in-chief of the Royal Lao Army. Allegations of Ouane's involvement had been current for several years, and were a subject of great concern to the mission. I knew Ouane, and I confronted hard him on the issue more than once. He denied his involvement, not only to me but to the ambassador and to other U.S. officials. I might add that our independent investigative resources were applied to Ouane, with no concrete results, only more generalized allegations. Two staffers from the Senate Foreign Affairs Committee later visited Laos, approached Ouane independently, and met with similar denials.

Now we learn that during the same timeframe (August, 1971), Alfred McCoy, an unknown academic, visited Laos, made a cold approach to the general, and was given the full story in exquisite detail, enough to flesh out a chapter of his book. Bearing in mind that Ouane's English was negligible, one can only wonder if McCoy debriefed him in French, Lao or Lahu. Perhaps Ouane gave it to him in writing, replete with all the facts and figures McCoy needed to build up his story. In a pig's eye he did! Frankly, I don't believe that Ouane gave McCoy the time of day.

Out of this fiction, McCoy goes on to develop the theme of General Vang Pao's involvement in the opium trade, which Mirsky argues that he has confirmed independently. I cannot vouch for what did or did not take place back in the early Sixties as alleged by Mirsky's unnamed source. But I can guarantee that during the Seventies Vang Pao was <u>not</u> involved in the opium business. He did <u>not</u> have a heroin refinery at Long Tieng, or anywhere else. If he were involved, or if he had a refinery, we would have run it to ground.

One last point. I have before me the Wall Street Journal article of August 28, 1990, and I have just read it for the fourth time in search of the statements <u>quoted</u> by Mirsky in the third paragraph of his letter. The statements do <u>not</u> appear! Did Peter Kann and Phillip Jennings write two versions of the same story? I am beginning to wonder where canard ends and calumny begins.

Very truly yours,

B. Hugh Tovar

Washington, DC 20016

left
A controversy surrounding General Vang Pao during the Secret War in Laos was the issue of drug (opium) trafficking. In the mid-1960s General Vang Pao terminated the growing and production of opium among his people. Plus, the Hmong rarely used the drug except for curing illnesses. However, author Alfred McCoy alleged that some top Laotian military personnel, including General Vang Pao, and the CIA were drug trafficking in his book "The Politics of Heroin." This allegation had a ripple effect, which triggered a response from the former CIA Chief of Station in Laos, B. Hugh Tovar. He replied that he was not aware of General Vang Pao having a refinery for the drug, and that the allegation was falsely made against the General.

A LETTER FROM HUGH TOVAR TO EDITORS OF THE NEW YORK REVIEW OF BOOKS, 18 JANUARY 1991, FOLDER 38, BOX 06, WILLIAM COLBY COLLECTION, THE VIETNAM CENTER AND ARCHIVE, TEXAS TECH UNIVERSITY. ACCESSED 15 JUN. 2012. <HTTP://WWW.VIETNAM.TTU.EDU/VIRTUALARCHIVE/ITEMS.PHP?ITEM=0440638048>.

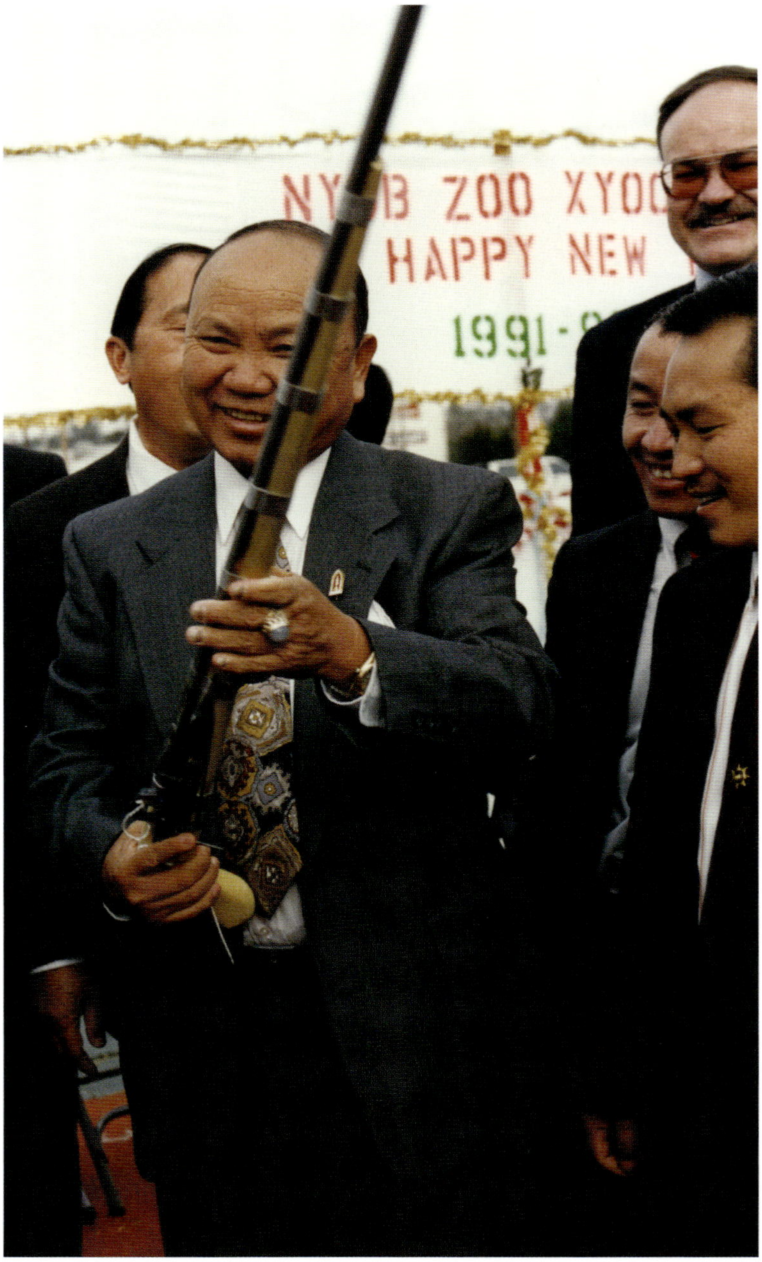
NYOB ZOO XYOO
HAPPY NEW
1991-9

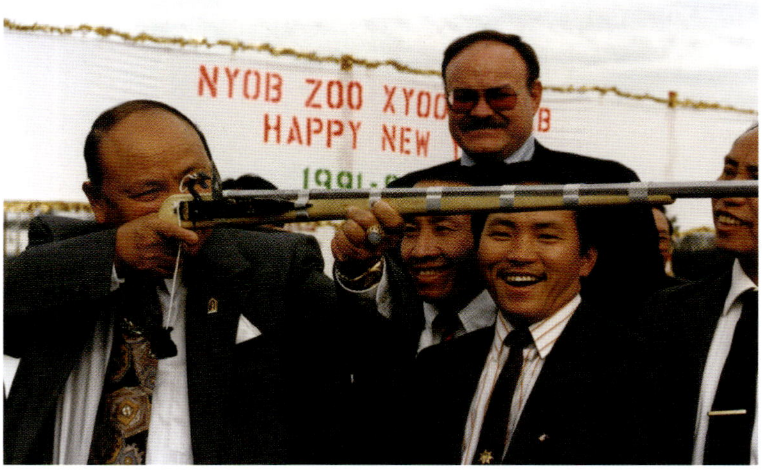
NYOB ZOO XYOO
HAPPY NEW

top left
Hmong community leaders and members in California organized a veterans event for General Vang Pao at the Fresno National Guard Armory. More than 500 people came to celebrate and participate with General Vang Pao and his veterans. The boy in the light-blue suit is Chi Neng Vang, General Vang Pao's youngest son. *Above*, GVP observes a well-equipped aircraft and a model of an old T-28.

CAPTAIN VANG NENG COLLECTION

far left
During the 1991-1992 Hmong International New Year Celebration in Fresno, General Vang Pao receives a Hmong flintlock gun as a gift from a long-time friend.

CAPTAIN VANG NENG COLLECTION

An Illustration of His Remarkable Life 320

1.

2.

3.

1. General Vang Pao with American friends, late 1980s. THE GVP FAMILY COLLECTION

2. General Vang Pao with Major Vang Thai and Nao Thai Vang (back) in Fresno, California, in 2008.
CAPTAIN VANG NENG COLLECTION

3. General Vang Pao in Fresno, 1992.
CAPTAIN VANG NENG COLLECTION

4. Former Mayor Youa Tong Yang, General Vang Pao, and Colonel Waseng Vang, in Fresno, 1992.
CAPTAIN VANG NENG COLLECTION

5. General Vang Pao with his political advisor Stephen Young in St. Paul, early 2000s.
CAPTAIN VANG NENG COLLECTION

"General Vang Pao always believed that education is very important to all people. This was one of his key components that he constantly pushed for in Laos and now in the United States: for our children to study hard and be educated so they could become economically independent and be productive American citizens."

* * *

VANG XANG
EXECUTIVE DIRECTOR
HMONG AMERICAN MUTUAL ASSISTANCE ASSOCIATION
AUTHOR'S INTERVIEW
MAY 2009

On April 9, 1993, the Hmong Stout Student Organization at the University of Wisconsin-Stout invited General Vang Pao as one of the renowned keynote speakers to their Sixth Annual Educational Conference. His speech focused on the "Unity of Hmong in Higher Education." About 600 people attended the conference. Their purpose was "to bring the best speakers to present information which would help promote and motivate Hmong parents, high school, and college students to value higher education… We believe that this meaningful … information will serve people as a key to success in their future." In the picture, General Vang Pao with his advisors and members of the Hmong Stout Student Organization at the university's Memorial Student Center.

JEMING C. VANG COLLECTION

right
General Vang Pao with Hmong leaders and community organizers at the Hmong Intellectual Conference in St. Paul, Minnesota, in 1999.

CHENG LENG VANG XIONG COLLECTION

An Illustration of His Remarkable Life 324

HON. ROBERT K. DORNAN
OF CALIFORNIA
IN THE HOUSE OF REPRESENTATIVES
Thursday, May 11, 1995

Mr. DORNAN. Mr. Speaker, on Sunday, April 30, I was at the Vietnam Memorial here in Washington. I met personally with many Vietnam veterans and their families at the Wall there to remember the sacrifices of our soldiers and the 20th anniversary of the tragic fall of South Vietnam to communism.

One of the important ceremonies that I attended at the Wall was held by the Counterparts organization where thousands of Montagnards, Hmong, Laotians and Vietnamese attended to mark the 20th anniversary of the tragic and bloody Communist takeover of their homelands. Some of those in attendance at this somber and important event were Grant McClure, Commanding Officer of Counterparts and former advisor to the Montagnards in the Central Highlands of South Vietnam, Ambassador Bill Colby former director of the Central Intelligence Agency; Maj. Gen. Homer Smith head of the Defense Attaché Office during the fateful last hours in Saigon; Brig. Gen. Kor Ksor, a Montagnard leader; Maj. Gen. Vang Pao, Commander of Military Region II for the Royal Lao Army and head of Hmong Special Forces; General Thonglit Chokbenbun, Royal Lao Army Commander; Dr. Jane Hamilton-Merritt the distinguished Lao/Hmong scholar, author and photojounalist; and Philip Smith, Senior Legislative Assistant to former U.S. Congressman Don Ritter and current Director of the Center for Public Policy Analysis.

Mr. Speaker, I believe it is crucial for the United States and Thailand not to forget the tremendous sacrifices of our former Vietnamese, Montagnard, Hmong and Laotian allies during the Vietnam War. I call upon all Vietnam veterans and Americans to oppose the current U.S. State Department and Thai policy of forcibly repatriating many of these former Hmong and Vietnamese Special Forces Commandos and combat veterans from refugee camps back to the repressive Communist regimes that they fled.

Mr. Speaker, it is important to make a part of the public record the speech that Maj. Gen. Vang Pao gave at the 20th Anniversary Ceremony which describes so well the major contribution made by many of our former allies and so many American soldiers during the Vietnam war.

left
U.S. Rep. Robert K. Dornan spoke on the record in recognizing the contribution American allies made during the Vietnam conflict on May 11, 1995.

"REMARKS BY MAJ. GEN. VANG PAO AT THE VIETNAM WAR MEMORIAL CEREMONY IN REMEMBRANCE OF THE 20TH ANNIVERSARY OF THE FALL OF SAIGON – HON. ROBERT K. DORNAN (EXTENSION OF REMARKS - MAY 11 1995)." THOMAS.LOC.GOV COLLECTION

REMARKS BY MAJ. GEN. VANG PAO AT THE VIETNAM WAR MEMORIAL CEREMONY IN REMEMBRANCE OF THE 20TH ANNIVERSARY OF THE FALL OF SAIGON

STATEMENT OF MAJOR GENERAL VANG PAO

Dear Honorable Guests, Fellow Veterans, Ladies and Gentlemen: We are gathered here today at this ceremony to mark the 20th Anniversary of the tragic fall of South Vietnam, Laos and Cambodia to invading Communist forces. But, we are also gathered here to recognize and honor those men and women who sacrificed and lost their lives in the Vietnam War—the Second Indochina War—fighting for freedom, democracy, and for the peace and security of Southeast Asia and the United States.

Tens of thousands of Lao and Hmong soldiers and their families who fought against the invading Soviet-backed North Vietnamese Army during the war are buried in unmarked graves in Laos and Vietnam. They fought to defend their country and to help the United States against the expansion of Soviet Communism through its proxy regime in Hanoi. But, their names are not on the Vietnam Memorial Wall here in Washington. So, we must be vigilant to keep alive their memory in our hearts and tell the story of their brave sacrifices to our children and our children's children so that their memory and the important cause that they fought for is not forgotten by future generations.

In Laos, from 1969 to 1970, the Lao and Hmong Special Forces under my command captured and occupied the strategic site of the Plain of Jars (Thong Haihin) which was crucial to the overall course of the war effort. The Plain of Jars is near the border of North Vietnam and was controlled by three North Vietnamese divisions. During heavy fighting the Lao and Hmong Special Forces under my command defeated the North Vietnamese troops and captured many Soviet-supplied tanks, artillery pieces, anti-aircraft guns, trucks and many hundreds of tons of small arms and other equipment which cost Moscow an enormous amount of money. The Superpowers—the Soviet Union and the United States—were surprised that such a small number of Hmong and Lao soldiers could defeat such a large force of the North Vietnamese Army and then occupy and defend the Plain of Jars. This battlefield victory saved many Americans from having to fight against these North Vietnamese troops and their weapons as well as greatly slowing the advance of Communism in Southeast Asia for many additional years.

It is also important to note the major contribution made by the Lao and Hmong soldiers of the Royal Lao Army in locating and destroying many of the North Vietnamese Army's supply lines along the Ho Chi Minh Trail. The Lao/Hmong Special Forces caused heavy losses to the North Vietnamese troops and rescued many hundreds of downed American pilots.

The United States did not lose the Vietnam War on the battlefield. The United States withdrew from the Indochina War in 1975 because of world politics, U.S.-Soviet detente, American-Chinese relations and U.S. domestic opposition to the War. However, the United States eventually won the war in world politics in the struggle between Communism and Capitalism. Communism in the Soviet Union and Eastern Europe collapsed with the help of freedom fighters like the Hmong and Lao combat veterans who assisted the United States in resisting the expansion of international Communism. Many Communist countries changed to become free countries because of the sacrifices of the Laotian and American men and women who defended freedom and democracy during the Cold War. Therefore, we must recognize and honor those men and women-in-arms who fought and died in the Vietnam War and remember that freedom, democracy and peace will once again return to Laos, Vietnam and Cambodia in the near future.

Thank you for joining me here today to mark this important occasion. God bless you all.

---

left

In the U.S., General Vang Pao spent his time advocating for Congress to officially recognize his soldiers and their sacrifices for the U.S. during the war. He spoke for proper recognition and the veterans benefits that they deserved, such as this remark he made to Congress in 1995.

"REMARKS BY MAJ. GEN. VANG PAO AT THE VIETNAM WAR MEMORIAL CEREMONY IN REMEMBRANCE OF THE 20TH ANNIVERSARY OF THE FALL OF SAIGON – HON. ROBERT K. DORNAN (EXTENSION OF REMARKS - MAY 11, 1995)." THOMAS.LOC.GOV COLLECTION

祝贺国际苗族文化研讨会暨
TO INTERNATIONAL MIAO(HMONG) CULTURE SYMPOSIUM &

The International Symposium on the Hmong (Miao) People in Jishou, China, in 1994. Then General Vang Pao had a vision in connecting the Hmong worldwide together. This must be done by organizing an event that would enable them to exchange their shared arts and musics, business and trade, culture, education, and history. The General appointed Mr. Xang Vang to co-chair the symposium with Mr. Houa Lao Hue, of China. There were 82 Hmong-Americans that attended the symposium. The second symposium was held in St. Paul, Minnesota, in 1995. The sypmposium drew many Hmong scholars and business leaders from around the world except from Burma.

XANG VANG COLLECTION

"I have been leading and observing the Hmong people for more than 30 years. I see the Hmong as a peaceful suburb group of people. We are one of the most disadvantage group of the minorities in the world. We, the Hmong, have to use every means to learn from and to catch up with civilized group on today's technology life.

"It is my understanding that the Symposium will be held to promote Hmong Culture, Education, and Business. I can see that these three topics are fundamental foundations to bring Hmong people to the best integration and to the various societies that Hmong happen to live in."

* * *

GENERAL VANG PAO
LETTER TO BUSINESS AND CORPORATE SPONSORS
APRIL 12, 1995
RETRIEVED FROM CAPTAIN VANG NENG
NOVEMBER 2010

Kuv coj Hmoob thiab pom Hmoob lub neej los tau tshaj 30 xyoo. Kuv pom hais tias Hmoob yog ib haiv neeg nyob ywj siab thiab tsis nyiam plaub ntuj. Peb Hmoob yog haiv neeg uas tseem tsis tau pom txoj kev vam meej piv rau lwm pawg neeg tsawg (other minority group) nyob rau hauv qab ntuj khwb. Peb cov Hmoob yuav tau sim txhua yam, txhua txoj hau kev kawm kom peb caum tau cov neeg vam meej nyob rau lub tebchaws no.

Kuv ntseeg tau tias ua lub Symposium los txhawb txog Hmoob tej kab lis kev cai, kev kawm ntawv, kev ua lag luam. Kuv xam pom tau hais tias peb yam no yog peb yam yuav txhawb tau peb lub neej Hmoob kom los nyob tau koom zej koom zos nrog lwm haiv neeg uas Hmoob nrog nyob.

(TRANSLATION - LUS TXHAIS)

top
Organizers of the Second International Symposium on Hmong People held in St. Paul, Minnesota, in 1995. The first symposium was hosted by the Hmong Chinese in Jishou, Hunan Province, China, in 1994.

YANG LONG COLLECTION

right
A support statement by Minnesota Governor Arne H. Carlson to welcome the Hmong people to the symposium.

CAPTAIN VANG NENG COLLECTION

far left
At the symposium were former Director of Justice in the Royal Lao Government Phagna Tougeu Lyfoung, Xia Sher Moua, and General Vang Pao. The symposium was also attended by Hmong from all over the world, including a Hmong Chinese scholar, who was greeted by the General, *left*.

YANG LONG COLLECTION

August 26, 1995

Warm greetings to those attending the second annual International Symposium on Hmong People. Welcome to Minnesota!

I am pleased to learn of the sponsorship of the Hmong Youth Association of Minnesota. Your good example will make a great difference to your friends and communities. I know your leadership will be important to our future.

A visit to our North Star state, with its more than 10,000 beautiful lakes is a rewarding experience and I hope that you will take time to enjoy the cultural and entertainment opportunities in the Twin Cities during your stay.

Best wishes for a productive and memorable symposium.

Warmest regards,

ARNE H. CARLSON
Governor

"The Hmong community in America has been very fortunate in that we get to share in all the American holidays that we have inherited as new citizens of this great country. In addition, we still get to retain our own special celebrations throughout the year. One of these special Hmong celebrations is the Hmong New Year that will take place during the Thanksgiving weekend. The Hmong New Year gives us a great opportunity to share our history, our culture, our customs, our music, our food, and our visions for the future with the broader American community."

* * *

GENERAL VANG PAO
LAO FAMILY DINNER SPEECH
NOVEMBER 2006
RETRIEVED FROM CHA VANG
NOVEMBER 2010

Tsoom Hmoob uas tuaj nyob tebchaws Ameliskas muaj hmoo heev vim tias peb tseem tau koom nrog cov pej xeem nyob tebchaws vam meej no los so hauj lwm tib yam li lawm. Tsis tag li xwb, peb tseem tau los so noj peb lub tshiab peb caug nyob rau lub caij Thanksgiving thiab. Hmoob lub tshiab peb caug (New Year) yog lub caij zoo rau peb Hmoob tau ntuav txuj ci, tej kab li kev cai, tsoos tsho, suab paj nruag, zaub mov, thiab peb lub neej yuav ua mus tom ntej rau tej pej xeem Ameliskas uas nyob ib puag ncig hauv peb lub zej zog tau paub tau pom.

(TRANSLATION - LUS TXHAIS)

right
General Vang Pao plays the famous Hmong instrument *qeej* at the Hmong International New Year Celebration in Fresno, California, in 1997.

COLONEL LY TENG COLLECTION

next page
In 1996, Lao Veterans of America organized a veterans ceremony to honor those who served during the Secret War in Fresno, California. About 5,000 veterans attended the event.

CAPTAIN VANG NENG COLLECTION

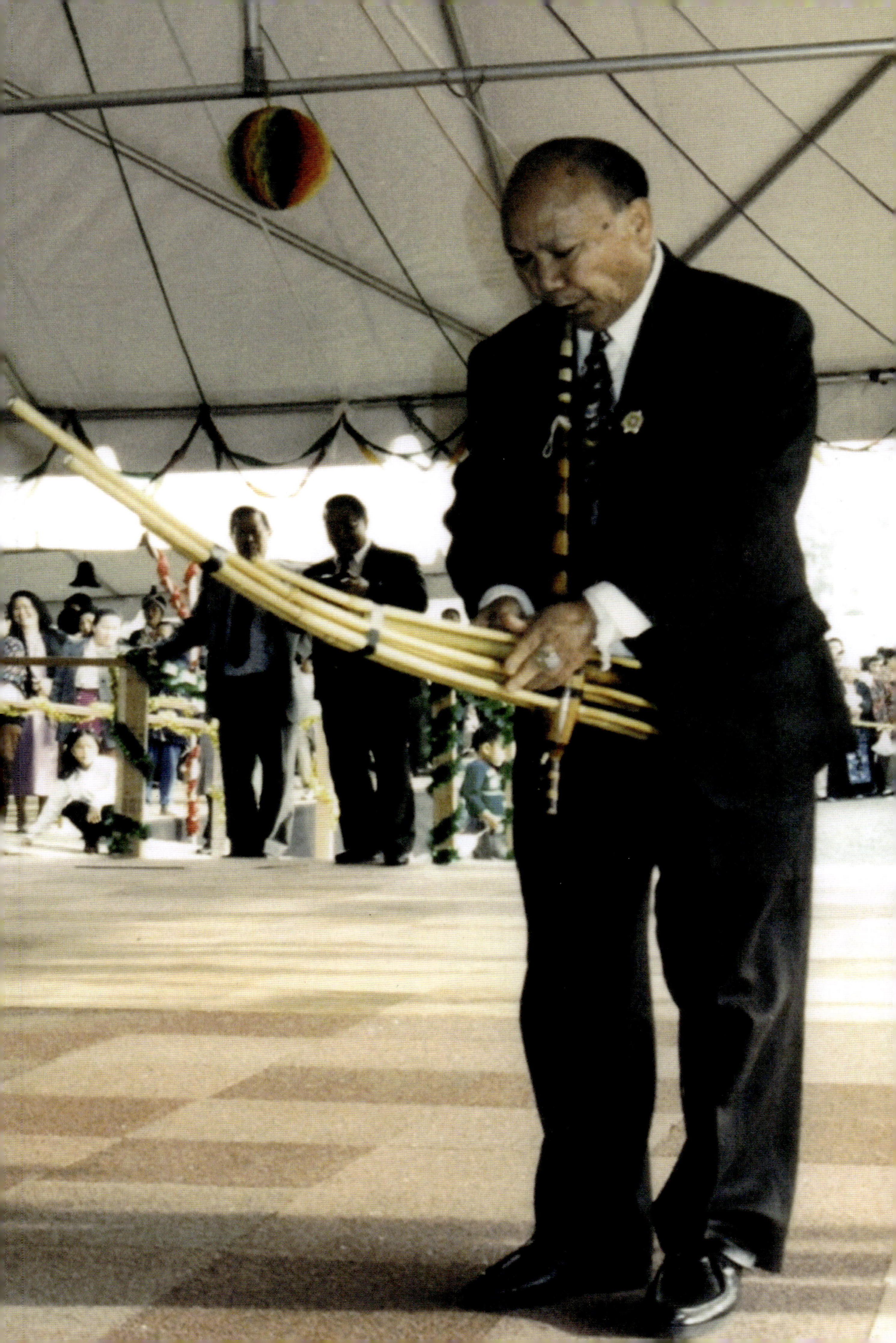

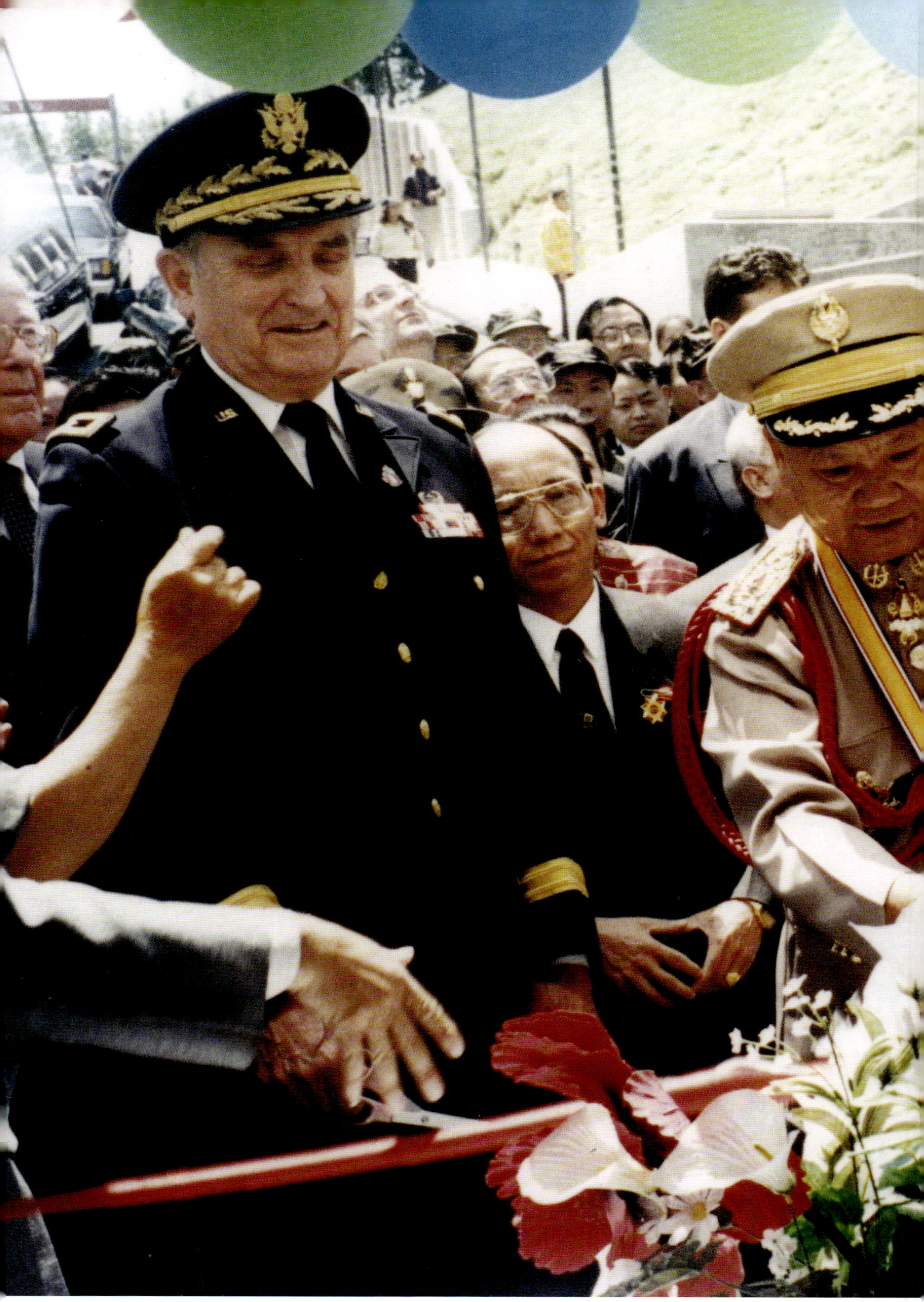

An Illustration of His Remarkable Life   334

"For 15 years, our military casualties were numbered at approximately 35,000, with many more civilians killed. On the other hand, the enemy received enormous losses, including far higher casualties—both killed and wounded—as well as the destruction of heavy military artillery tanks, trucks, and other weapons amounting to billions of dollars. The US lost some 58,000 troops in Southeast Asia and we are saddened and sympathetic to this major loss. However, we believe that without our defensive military efforts, the number of US casualties would be higher."

**

GENERAL VANG PAO
STATEMENT AT THE UNITED STATES CONGRESSIONAL FORUM
WASHINGTON, D.C.
OCTOBER 14, 1999
RETRIEVED FROM CAPTAIN VANG NENG
DECEMBER 4, 2010

Ua rog tau 15 xyoos, kev ploj tuag ntawm cov tub rog muaj txog li 35,000 leej neeg. Ntxiv ntawd, kuj muaj coob tus pej xeem raug tua tuag tib yam nkaus. Yog muab tig los saib, cov yeeb ncuab raug kev puas tsuaj lawm ntau tshaj peb lawm ntau heev. Yog muab ntaus ua nyiaj mam keb puas tshuaj ntawm phom loj, tsheb hlau sib tua, tsheb thauj koom thiab tas nrho tej riam phom raug nyiaj dollar ntau heev (billions of dollars). Tsoom fwv tub rog Ameliskas muaj li 58,000 tus tub rog tau tag sim neej nyob rau tebchaws Southeast Asia, peb kuj hlub thiab pab lawm tu siab kawg. Txawm li cas los peb ntseeg hais tias yog tsis muaj peb Hmoob cov tub rog nrog pab tiv thaiv, kev puas tsuaj ntawm tub rog Ameliskas yuav coob tshaj li ntawm lawv tau hais cia.

(TRANSLATION - LUS TXHAIS)

The Vietnam Veterans Memorial Wall in Washington, D.C. The memorial, also known as *The Wall*, was built to honor the American soldiers who served and died in the Vietnam War. This memorial was designed by 21-year-old Yale University student Maya Lin, completed in 1982, and accepted by the U.S. President two years later. When the memorial was finished there were 57,159 names. According to The Vietnam Veterans Memorial website as of 2010, the number of American casualties listed on the granite wall was 58, 267. *Above*, General Vang Pao lays a wreath honoring the fallen soldiers at the Wall.

TOP, NOAH VANG COLLECTION
ABOVE, TONG HLAO VUE COLLECTION

right
A widely known national Hmong and Laotian veterans memorial plaque at the Arlington National Cemetery in Washington, D.C.

KONG VANG COLLECTION

**DEDICATED TO
THE U.S. SECRET ARMY
IN THE KINGDOM OF LAOS
1961 - 1973**

IN MEMORY OF THE HMONG AND LAO COMBAT VETERANS AND THEIR AMERICAN ADVISORS WHO SERVED FREEDOM'S CAUSE IN SOUTHEAST ASIA. THEIR PATRIOTIC VALOR AND LOYALTY IN THE DEFENSE OF LIBERTY AND DEMOCRACY WILL NEVER BE FORGOTTEN.

ຈະຈາລຶກໄວ້ຕຫລອດໄປ

YUAV TSHUA TXOG NEJ MUS IB TXHIS

LAO VETERANS OF AMERICA
MAY 15, 1997

An Illustration of His Remarkable Life 336

"General Vang Pao was the biggest hero of the Vietnam War. For 10 years, Vang Pao's soldiers held the growing North Vietnamese forces to approximately the same battlelines they held in 1962. And significantly for Americans, the 70,000 North Vietnamese engaged in Laos were not available to add to the forces fighting Americans and South Vietnamese in South Vietnam."

* * *

WILLIAM E. COLBY
CIA DIRECTOR, 1973-1976
ARLINGTON NATIONAL CEMETERY
RETRIEVED FROM THE WWW.ARLINGTONCEMETERY.NET
NOVEMBER 2010

General Vang Pao with Hmong and Laotian veterans gathering at the Arlington National Cemetery to erect the plaque DEDICATED TO THE U.S. SECRET ARMY IN THE KINGDOM OF LAOS 1961-1975 in Washington, D.C., in May 1997. See previous page for plaque.

CAPTAIN VANG NENG COLLECTION
LEFT PHOTO FROM MRS. XAI KOUA VANG COLLECTION
FAR LEFT FROM CAPTAIN CHERZONG VANG COLLECTION

An Illustration of His Remarkable Life 338

"I have met many leaders during my professional career. However, General Vang Pao stood out among many of them. I find that he possessed several strong leadership qualities. They are: (a) a passion for those he represented; (b) a commitment to the causes that he believed in; and (c) an utmost loyalty to the people he worked with."

* * *
LEE PAO XIONG
DIRECTOR OF THE CENTER FOR HMONG STUDIES
PROFESSOR OF HMONG STUDIES & AMERICAN GOVERNMENT
CONCORDIA UNIVERSITY, ST. PAUL
AUTHOR'S EMAIL INTERVIEW
OCTOBER 2012

General Vang Pao gives Hmong stitched storycloths, or *pajntaub*, as gifts to politicians and friends during the erecting of the plaque.

ALL PHOTOS FROM KANG YEE VANG COLLECTION

An Illustration of His Remarkable Life 340

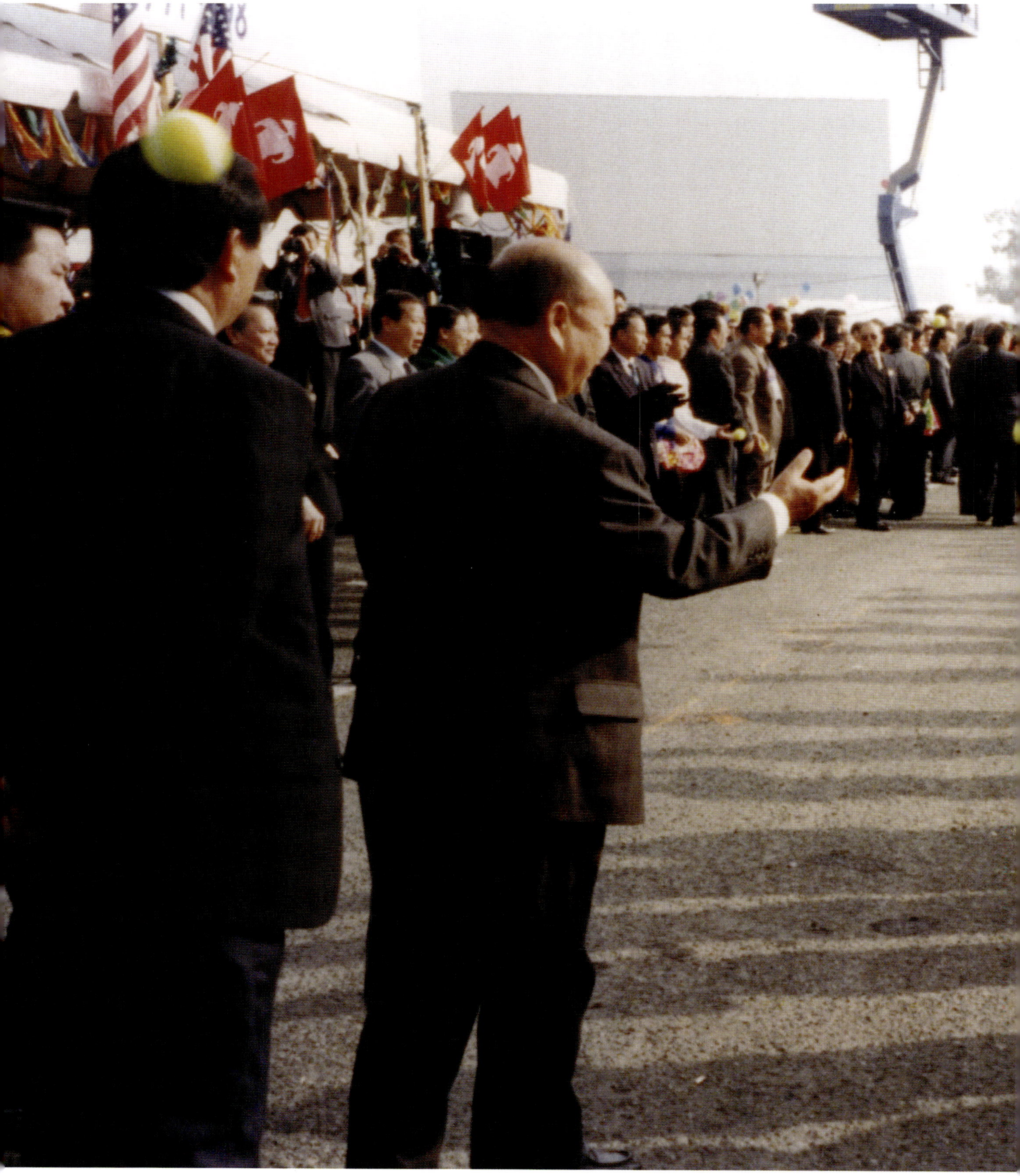

An Illustration of His Remarkable Life 344

top left
The late Congressman Bruce Vento of Minnesota, spoke at the Minnesota Hmong New Year in St. Paul in the late 1990s. He and General Vang Pao had worked on several issues concerning the Hmong and Lao veterans and the community. Vento was well respected by the leaders and members of the Hmong community.

MRS. XAI KOUA VANG COLLECTION

above
General Vang Pao worked tirelessly to advocate with federal and state governments to fully recognize the Hmong and Lao veterans. In 1999, General Vang Pao and Hmong community members and veterans met with Governor Tommy Thompson, of Wisconsin, and his staff, *top right*, to discuss state legislations to recognize Hmong and Lao veterans. Following the meeting, they both receive bigger than life-sized license plates etched in honor of their public services from members and friends of the non-profit organization Lao Veterans of America—Wisconsin Chapter.

CAPTAIN VANG NENG COLLECTION

General Vang Pao along with his delegation in Washington, D.C., on March 1999. During the visit, he addresses members of U.S. Congress on the human rights violations against the Hmong and Laotian people in Laos.

DR. STEPHEN VANG COLLECTION

An Illustration of His Remarkable Life 346

"To all of us, as his children, he was a wonderful father. He was our hero. He was a great hero and leader to his people."

* * *

SISOUK VANG
ONE OF GENERAL VANG PAO'S SONS
INTERVIEW WITH AUTHOR
NOVEMBER 2010

General Vang Pao's family at his 70th birthday celebration in Orange County, California, in 1999. The people in these two pictures are his wives, sons, daughters, nephews, nieces, sons-and-daughters-in-law, and grandchildren.

General Vang Pao's sons are: Francois C. Vang, Wa Chong Vang, Neng Chu Vang, Jang Cheng Vang, Somsanouk Vang, Sisouk Vang, Chai Vang, Somwang Vang, Chaleunsouk Vang, Chee Vang, Zong Lu Vang, Ge Vang, Cha Vang, Sue Vang, Meng Vang, Chu Long Vang, Chu Leng Vang, and Chi Neng Vang. His daughters are: Mai Ker Vang, May Ko Vang, May Kao Vang, Maikia Vang, Mai Kou Vang, Ying Vang, and Mai Nhia Vang.

PHOTOS FROM CAPTAIN VANG NENG COLLECTION

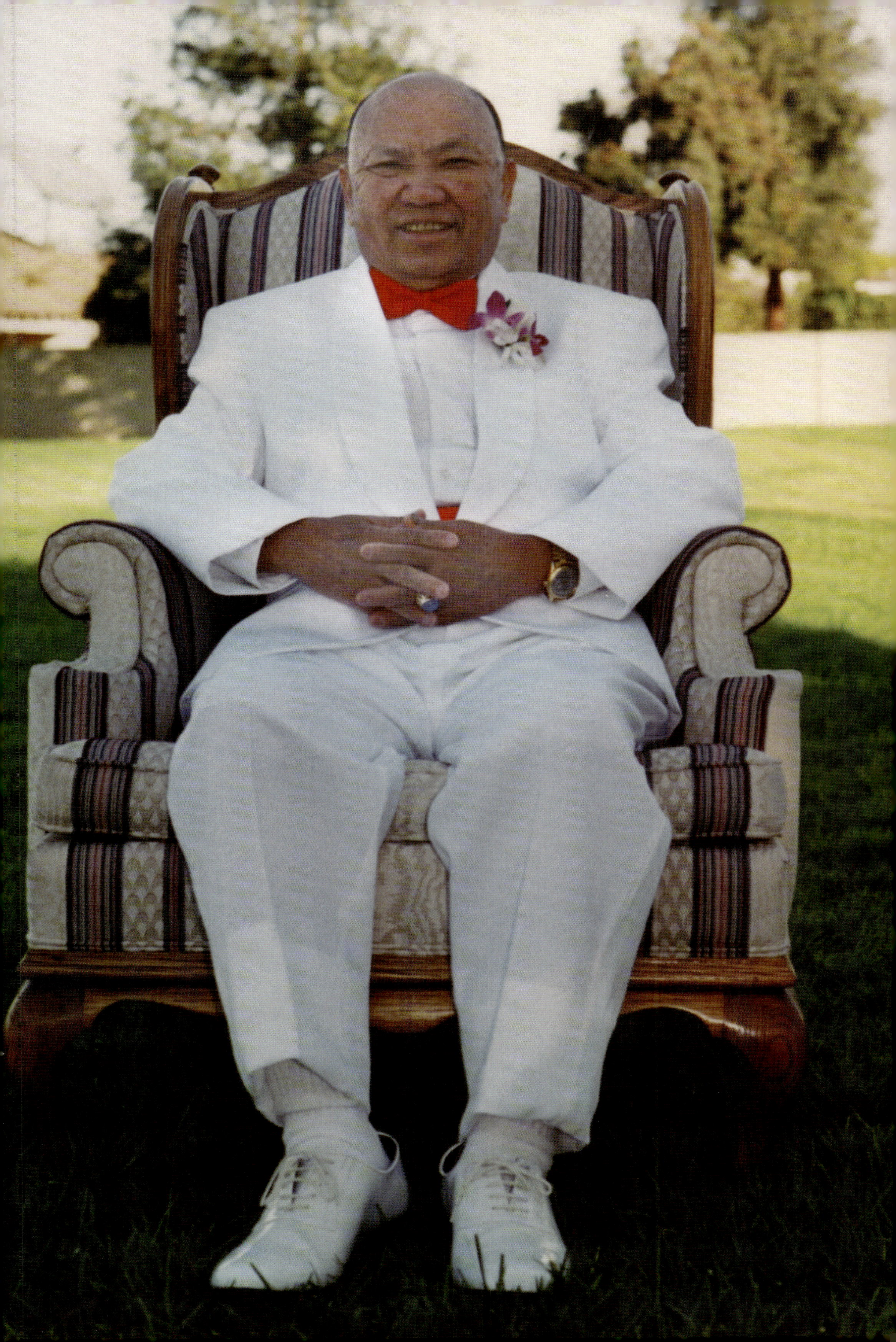

"For Hmong man and woman to become leaders, he or she has to learn to lead [their] family first. We are in a civilized country; we must make room for women to take leadership roles. This is respect. Therefore, the husband has to know how to respect the wife as he respects himself. And the wife has to be a good role model so that [she] can be a good example for her family and children and the community."

* * *

GENERAL VANG PAO
HMONG COMMUNITY CONFERENCE IN 2009
WAUSAU, WISCONSIN
RETRIEVED FROM HMONG TODAY
FEBRUARY 3, 2011

General Vang Pao always supported Hmong women's issues. The General poses with Hmong women community leaders and members in the early 2000s. In 2009, General Vang Pao was invited to a Hmong community women's forum in Wausau, Wisconsin, where he addressed some of the core concerns facing Hmong household families, such as rising divorce rates, domestic violence, wedding dowry, etc.

CAPTAIN VANG NENG COLLECTION

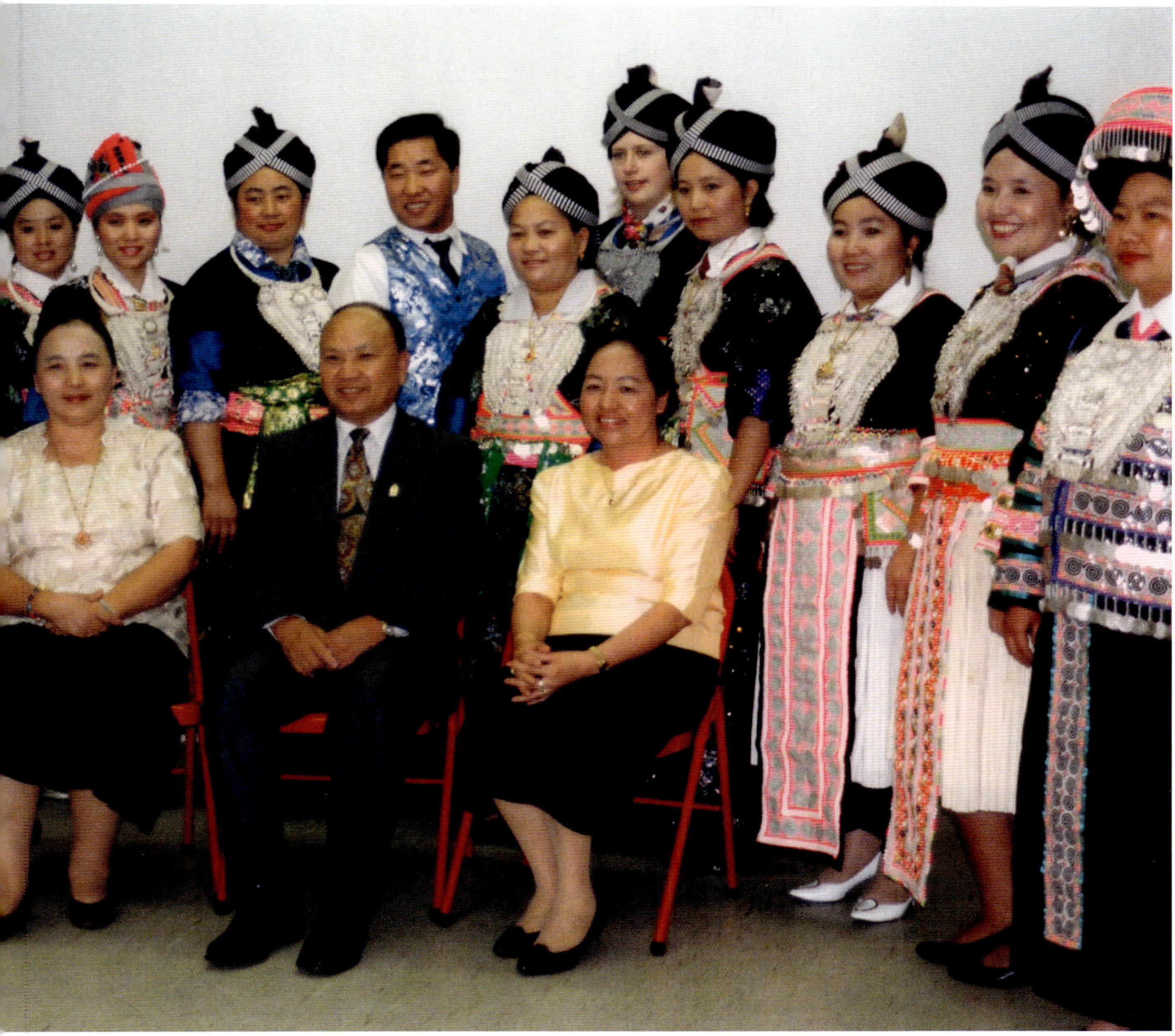

Lao and Hmong soldiers who fought courageously
can soldiers in Laos during the Vietnam War.
of profound bravery, loyalty, and commitment
during the Vietnam conflict is an inspiration
people of both countries.
generations of our enduring appreciation
sacrifice that must never be forgotten.
through the efforts of the City of
Lao Hmong-American War Memorial
contributions of members
community.
California

In 2005, General Vang Pao and Fresno Mayor Alan Autry unveiled this 6-foot bronze memorial honoring the sacrifices the Hmong and Lao soldiers made during the CIA-sponsored Secret War in Laos. This 29-ton statue depicts an injured American pilot being rescued by two Hmong soldiers, and is located at the Fresno County Courthouse Park in Fresno, California.

LEFT PHOTO FROM THE GVP FAMILY COLLECTION VIA LANG VANG.
TOP PHOTOS FROM NOAH VANG COLLECTION

An Illustration of His Remarkable Life 352

"In light of the current economic, political and humanitarian emergency in Laos—which has reached crisis proportions for so many people ..., I strongly urge the 12 Signatories to the Paris Peace Accord (1973) and others in the international community to take full responsibility and assume a leadership role in helping to bring peace, democracy, human rights and economic stability to Laos."

* * *

GENERAL VANG PAO
STATEMENT TO U.S. HOUSE OF REPRESENTATIVES
OCTOBER 14, 1999
RETRIEVED FROM CAPTAIN VANG NENG
DECEMBER 2010

Co-founders of the United Lao Council for Peace, Freedom, and Reconstruction at a meeting in St. Paul, Minnesota, in 2005. *Left to right:* Former Lao Ministry of Foreign Affairs Dr. Bounsang Khamkeo, former Military Region V commander General Thonglith Chokbengboune, former Military Region II Commander General Vang Pao, former Lao Secretary of State for Public Health Dr. Khamphai Abhay, Prince Ophat Nachampassak, and former Royal Lao Army General Khamkhong.

ZONG LU VANG COLLECTION

"We cannot live forever. We must prepare and build a future for our children. So after our generation, there will not be a gap in our leadership to lead the Hmong forward."

* * *
GENERAL VANG PAO
FRESNO, CALIFORNIA
DECEMBER 2010

Peb yuav tsis nyob tag mus sim neej. Peb yuav tsum npaj lub neej zoo rau peb tej menyuam. Xwv tom qab peb phaum no dhau lawd thiaj tsis muaj kev tu ncua ntawm peb kev coj Hmoob mus rau lub neej tom ntej.

(TRANSLATION - LUS TXHAIS)

General Vang Pao's great grandchildren surprise him with a Happy Birthday cake at one of his sons' homes in Minnesota in 2005. Since he was always occupied with community events, such occasions as this were special because he hardly had any time with his children and grandchildren.

VANG XANG COLLECTION

right
General Vang Pao with his great granddaughter in Lino Lakes, Minnesota, in 2005.

VANG XANG COLLECTION

An Illustration of His Remarkable Life 356

For those of us Hmong who can call America home, we are fortunate indeed. We live in the most generous and prosperous nation on earth. We have opportunities that other fellow Hmong throughout the world cannot even dream of because they have never known it.

    Yes, we are fortunate indeed! We have worked very hard and are now witnessing the fruits of our labor. Our children are becoming valedictorians of their schools; we now have lawyers, doctors, engineers, commercial airline pilots, and even politicians!

* * *
GENERAL VANG PAO
SPEECH AT THE CENTER FOR HMONG STUDIES
CONCORDIA UNIVERSITY
JUNE 28, 2005
RETRIEVED FROM LEE PAO XIONG
OCTOBER 2010

Hais rau peb cov Hmoob uas muab lub tebchaws no hu ua peb lub tsev los yog peb lub tebchaws, peb muaj hmoo kawg li. Peb tau tuaj nyob rau lub tebchaws uas zoo tshaj thiab muaj ntau txoj hau kev pab rau peb tshaj nyob rau hauv ntiaj teb. Peb muaj ntau txoj ncauj kev uas lwm tus Hmoob nyob rau ntau lub tebchaws twb tsis ua npau suav pom txog li vim tias lawv yeej tsis tau pom dua.

    Yog lawm, peb yeej muaj hmoo kawg li. Yog vim peb yeej tau ua hauj lwm hnyav heev yav dhau los, li ntawd niaj hnub no peb thiaj tau txais txoj kev vam meej. Xws li peb cov me nyuam muaj feem mob siab hlo mus kawm tau ntawv zoo heev ua tus thawj ntawm lawm lub tsev qhia ntawv, niaj hnub no peb kuj muaj kws hais plaub ntug, kws kho mob, kws txuaj cuab yeej, kws tsav dav hlau, thiab cov khiav haujlwm tebchaws.

(TRANSLATION - LUS TXHAIS)

General Vang Pao with his wives Chia Vang and May Song Vang at a congratulatory party for the Hmong boys and girls dance teams at Arlington Senior High School in St. Paul, Minnesota, on January 15, 2005.

ZONG LU VANG COLLECTION

top left
Minnesota State Senator Mee Moua and General Vang Pao at the Hmong Freedom Week Celebration at the McMurray Field—Como Park, St. Paul, Minnesota, in July 2006. In 2002, Moua was elected as a state senator, which was the highest political office held by a Hmong-American, in a special election in St. Paul. She served two terms in the Minnesota Senate from 2002 to 2010 and represented Senate District 67. During her term, Moua chaired the Judiciary Committee.

NOAH VANG COLLECTION

An Illustration of His Remarkable Life 358

"I have led the Hmong to a land of better opportunity, a place of hope for our children in America. Today we have Hmong with bachelor's degrees, master's degrees, and doctoral degrees whereas 30 years ago we had none. Our Hmong are amazing people."

* * *
GENERAL VANG PAO
HMONG INTERNATIONAL NEW YEAR
FRESNO, CALIFORNIA
NOVEMBER 2004

Kuv tau coj haiv neeg Hmoob tuaj nyob rau thaj av uas muaj ntau ntau txoj ncauj kev, qhov chaw uas muaj kev cia siab rau tej me nyuam. Niaj hnub no peb muaj Hmoob coob leej tau: bachelor's degrees, master's degrees, thiab doctoral degrees, uas 30 xyoo dhau los lawm peb yeej tsis tau muaj dua ib zaug li. Peb haiv Hmoob yog ib haiv neeg tshajlij tshaj plaws.

(TRANSLATION - LUS TXHAIS)

right
General Vang Pao in 2006.
MONG VANG COLLECTION

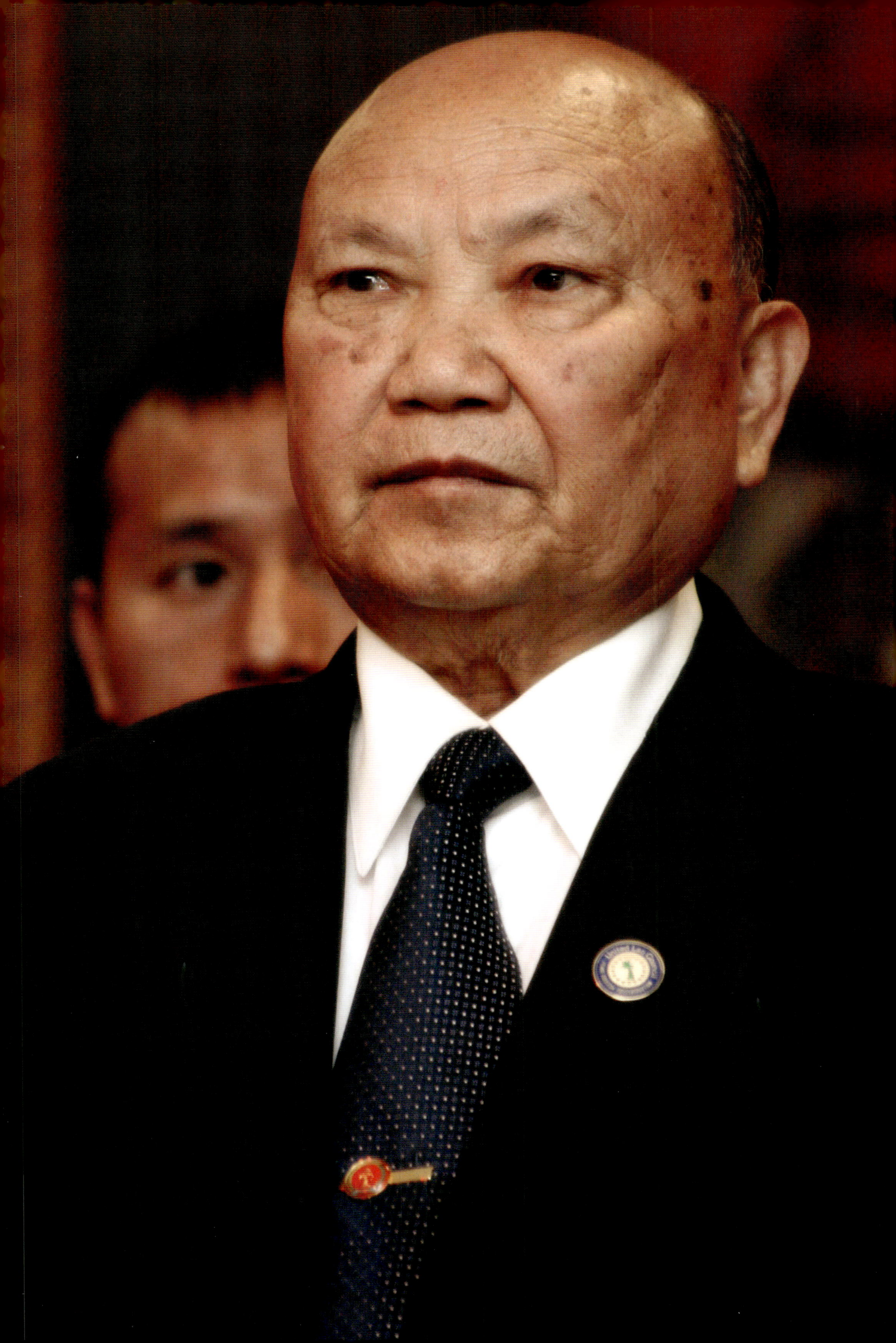

Proclamation

SGU SERVICE IN DEFENSE OF FREEDOM
Laos 1961 - 1975

Whereas, Laos was declared to be a neutral country by the Geneva Accords and Agreements of 1954 and 1962 so that no foreign troops should fight on Lao Territory; and

Whereas, the North Vietnamese Communists and their allies in China and the Soviet Union did not respect the neutrality of Laos and the freedoms of all the Lao peoples so that the Free World was forced to stand behind the legitimate government of Laos and the Lao peoples to prevent the military conquest of Laos by Communist forces, and

Whereas, United States efforts needed support from local ground forces to confront Communist aggression in Laos by opposing Communist forces in close combat, to provide timely and accurate intelligence on the movement of Communist forces, and rescue its flyers whenever their aircraft crashed in Laos; and

Whereas, North Vietnam contrary to international law used Lao territory for its war of aggression against South Vietnam by building the Ho Chi Minh supply trail from North Vietnam to South Vietnam through Laos, forcing the United States to interdict such illegal use of Laotian territory; and

Whereas, the United States needed to have reliable ground forces guard its Navigation Radar stations in northern Laos which were used to guide its bomber aircraft accurately to their targets in North Vietnam;

Therefore, in January 1961 Colonel James W. Lair and General Vang Pao agreed that Major Vang Pao would recruit Hmong and other Laotians to serve in Special Guerilla Units to accomplish the above strategic purposes in defense of Lao freedom and independence and in opposition to Communist aggression and tyranny. Soldiers in the Special Guerilla force were trained and paid directly by the United States as part of the Vietnam War. We, James W. Lair and Vang Pao, the officers initially responsible for establishing the Special Guerilla Units, hereby proclaim that the Special Guerilla Units provided faithful, dedicated, and excellent service to the just cause of democracy and freedom in Laos, the ideals of the entire Free World during the Cold War, and the highest strategic interests of the United States of America and her allies in self determination.

Affirmed this 20th day of November 2006

Colonel James W. Lair   General Vang Pao

General Vang Pao and Colonel James W. Lair signed the SGU SERVICE IN DEFENSE OF FREEDOM Proclamation, *left*, to implement the non-profit organization Special Guerrilla Units (SGU) Veterans and Families of USA, Inc., based in St. Paul, Minnesota, in 2006.

PROCLAMATION AND PHOTO FROM XANG VANG COLLECTION

"As a Hmong in this lifetime, I am thankful to all of you for organizing this Happy Birthday party for me. Your love, your compassion, and your respect mean everything to me."

* * *

GENERAL VANG PAO
BIRTHDAY CELEBRATION SPEECH
OAKDALE, MINNESOTA
NOVEMBER 20, 2005

Ua ib tug neeg Hmoob rau tiam no, kuv thov ua tsaug rau txhua tus uas nej tau sib pab npaj lub koob tsheej cawv xeeb rau kuv (Birthday Party). Nej txoj kev hlub, kev txhawb qa, thiab fwm kuv, muaj txiaj ntsig ntau rau kuv heev.

(TRANSLATION - LUS TXHAIS)

Noah Vang presents a poster of General Vang Pao's short history timeline at his 76th birthday celebration at the Prom Center in Oakdale, Minnesota, in 2006. *From left to right:* Noah Vang, former Hmong 18 Councils President Shong Leng Xiong, General Vang Pao, Vang Ge, and former Captain Vang Neng.

NOAH VANG COLLECTION

right
General Vang Pao at his 76th birthday celebration.

NOAH VANG COLLECTION

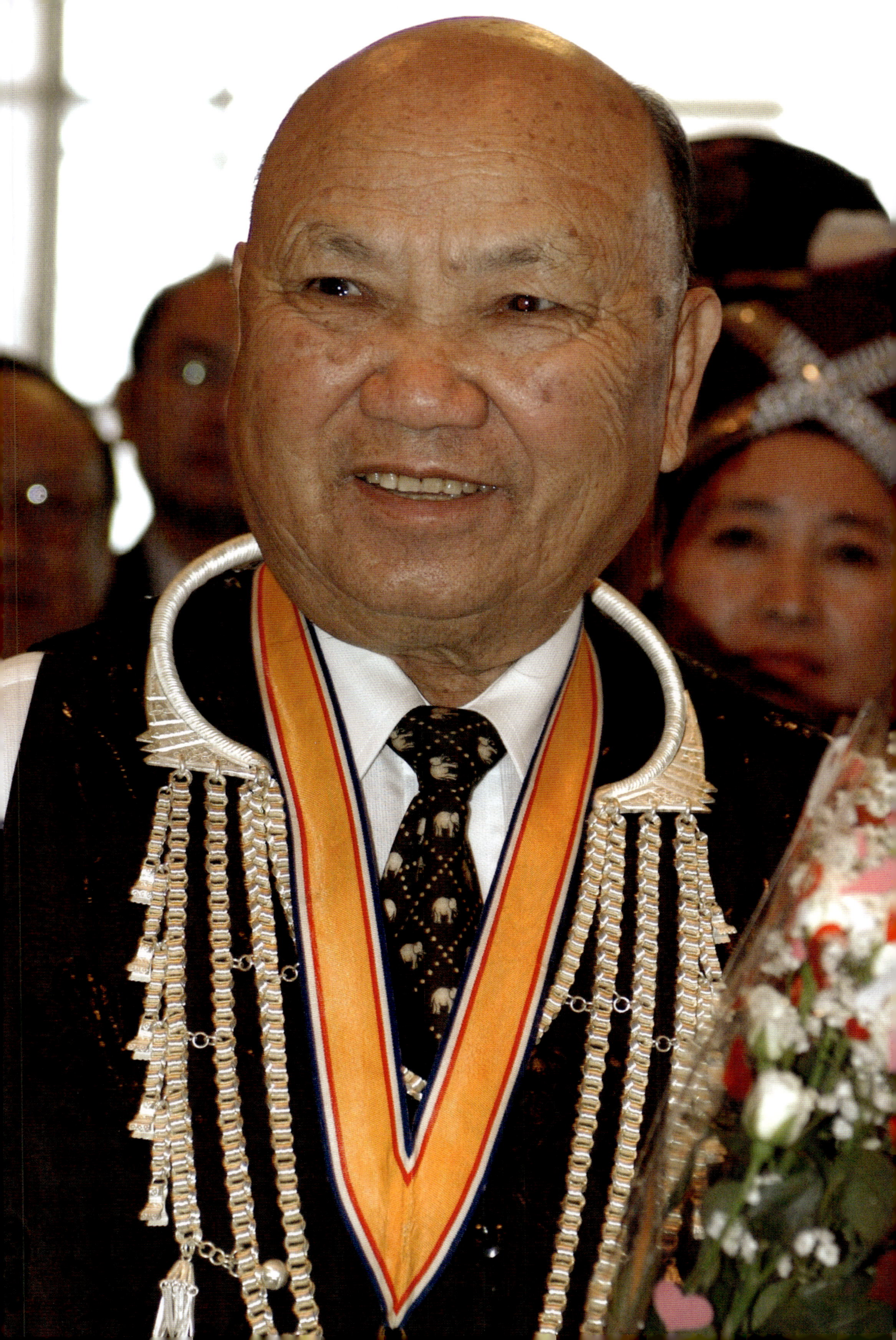

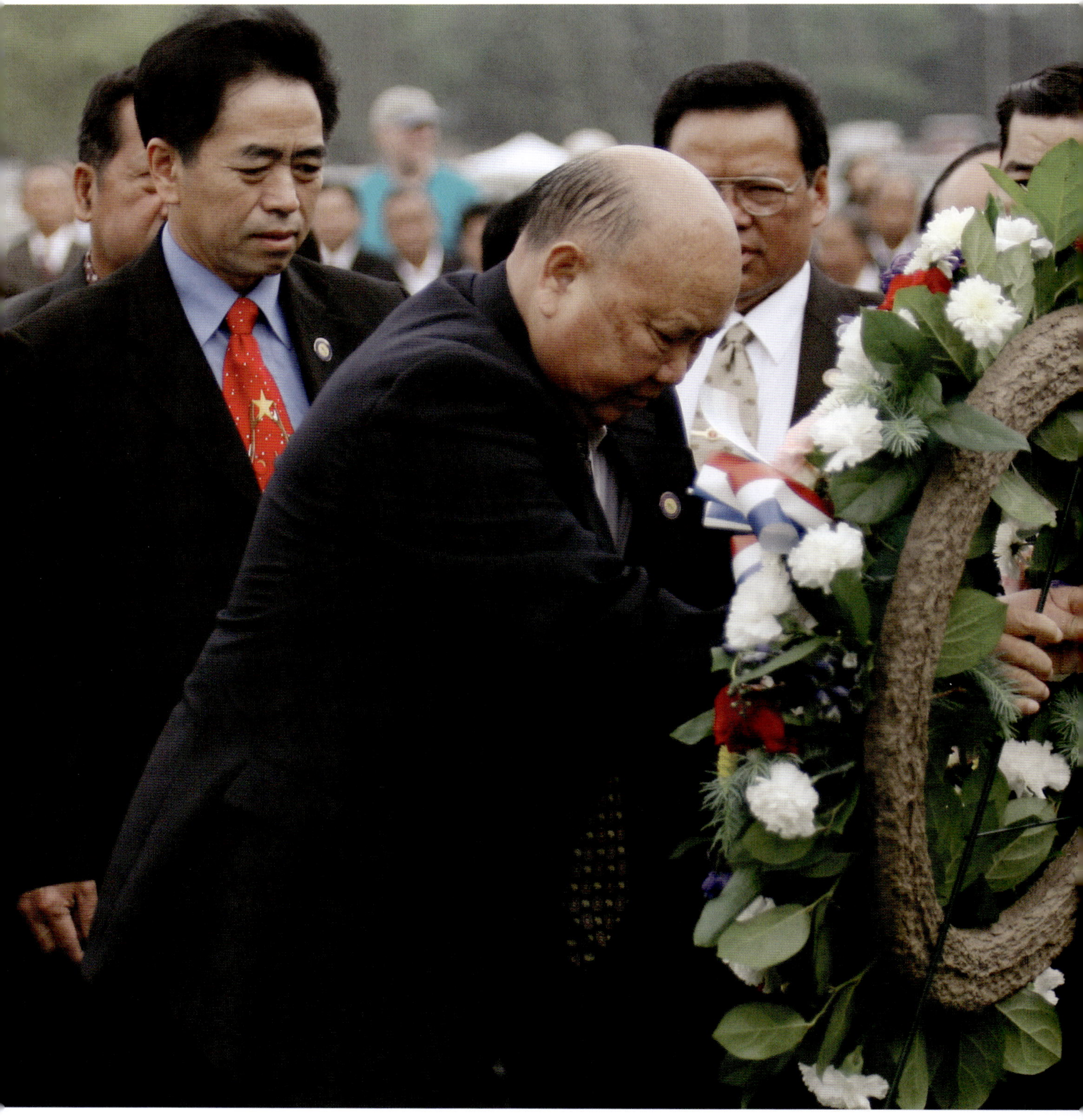

"For most people, they only get to read about and see great leaders, who make history, from afar. For me, it is different, because I was fortunate to be fathered by one of these special people. So, every day, I get to witness the commitment, sacrifice, service, and love that my father gives to his people. And I have been blessed to be able to learn about what it takes to truly lead and to make history. In watching my father for over 30 years now, I have come to appreciate the fact that many great people who leave their mark on history are born with greatness in their destiny. It is in their destiny and they serve at a level that normal people cannot because throughout their whole life they burn with a passion as hot as the volcanic lava that spills over when a volcano erupts! They are always focused and passionate during their entire lifetime, even during dark and difficult times. Unlike us common people, we can get excited—but usually our excitement, focus and passion last far shorter. The only thing that has value and gives purpose for my father, in his life, is the Hmong people. That is what makes him great and separates him from us normal people! I just wish there were more people like him in this world."

* * *

CHA VANG
GENERAL VANG PAO'S SON
EMAIL INTERVIEW WITH AUTHOR
DECEMBER 8, 2010

left
General Vang Pao lays a wreath honoring the fallen soldiers of the Secret War hosted by the Lao Veterans of America at the Dakota County Fairgrounds, Farmington, Minnesota, in May 2007. *Standing left to right:* Tong Ger Vang, Tong Hlao Vue, and Former Colonel Yang Chao.

SHIA YANG COLLECTION

An Illustration of His Remarkable Life 366

"We're thrilled that the government has finally realized that General Vang Pao is innocent and dropped the unjust charges against him. We're disappointed, however, that this deeply flawed prosecution and unfair sting operation is continuing against the other defendants."

∗ ∗ ∗

JOHN KEKER
"GOVERNMENT DROPS CHARGES AGAINST GENERAL VANG PAO"
BY KEKER & VAN NEST LLP
SEPTEMBER 18, 2009

Supporters of all ages rally in demand for the release of General Vang Pao and 11 others who allegedly were trying to overthrow the Lao Government. This rally was held at the state Capitol building in St. Paul, Minnesota, in July 2007, one of many demonstrations across the U.S. seeking for the U.S. to drop the charges. The case was completely dismissed soon after his death in January 2011.

NOAH VANG COLLECTION

top right
General Vang Pao with his lawyer John Keker and his associates at the appreciation luncheon in San Francisco, California, in October 2009.

XIA YANG VANG COLLECTION

middle right
General Vang Pao is being escorted out of the U.S. federal court house in Sacramento, California, by family members and supporters in 2007.

WAMENG MOUA OF HMONG TODAY COLLECTION

below right
GVP and his family members who attended the appreciation luncheon with Keker and his associates in San Francisco, California, in October 2009.

XIA YANG VANG COLLECTION

An Illustration of His Remarkable Life 368

General Vang Pao speaks to Hmong community leaders and members at the *Pe Tsiab*. To the *right* of the General is former Major Nengsho Xiong, of Warren, Michigan. At the late General Vang Pao's funeral service in Fresno, California, in February 2011, Xiong was the *Txiv Xaiv* or Spiritual Master of the Ceremony on the final evening of the service. The *Pe Tsiab* event was well attended by community members and veterans, including former T-28 Pilot Vang Teng, *middle right*.

SHIA YANG COLLECTION

top right
Zong Xeng Vang, of Vietnam, is a special guest visiting General Vang Pao in St. Paul, Minnesota, in November 2007. He is a former Vietnamese government official who specialized in minority issues throughout the country of Vietnam.

XANG VANG COLLECTION

right
Special guests visit General Vang Pao and his family in California on March 9, 2008.

YEU TONG HLAO VU COLLECTION

Although his federal court case was still pending in Sacramento, California, General Vang Pao was granted permission to travel out of state. He and his family came to the Hmong New Year Celebration in Minnesota during the Thanksgiving Weekend in 2007. General Vang Pao gave his blessing to the Hmong community leaders and members at the *Pe Tsiab* at Lao Family Community Center. *Pe Tsiab* is a special Hmong cultural ceremony that happens before the official start of the New Year festivities. "All of you have been very supportive of my family and me as we are going through a tough time at this moment," said the General at the *Pe Tsiab*. "I missed all of you, and let us continue to strengthen our support and love for one another for the many years to come."

SHIA YANG COLLECTION

"It is my destiny to continue to help the Hmong community until the good Lord takes me, but there will be a time when there must be a transition of leadership to a new generation of Hmong leaders. A generation that I hope will be compassionate, that can love, that can sacrifice, that can protect, and that can lead the Hmong people worldwide to meet a better and brighter future. There must be a new leadership that can put the people before themselves."

* * *

GENERAL VANG PAO
"A TIME OF CHANGE AND OPTIMISM"
PROM CENTER SPEECH
JULY 3, 2008
RETRIEVED FROM CHA VANG
NOVEMBER 2010

Nyob ntawm lub ntuj tso kom kuv pab haiv Hmoob mus txog hnub Yawm Saub coj kuv mus, tab sis yuav muaj ib hnub uas nws yuav tsum muaj cov thawj coj tshiab. Kuv cia siab tias cov thawj coj tshiab ntawd yuav muaj kev txhawj xeeb, hlub txaus, ua tam tau, pab thaiv tau, thiab coj tau peb haiv Hmoob thoob ntiaj teb mus rau lub neej kaj lug rau yav tom ntej. Yuav tsum muaj tus thawj coj tshiab uas muab pej xeem ua ntej nws tus kheej.

(TRANSLATION - LUS TXHAIS)

In 2007, under the provisions of the U.S. Patriot Act and the Real ID Act, some Hmong were defined as terrorists (during the Bush Administration). This triggered a national response from the community. Many wrote and rallied their congressional leaders to have the Hmong name removed from such labelling. General Vang Pao also personally communicated with U.S. Senator Norm Coleman (R-Minn.) to have the Hmong name be taken off the Patriot Act as a terrorist organization. In December, President Bush signed the H.R. 2764, which excluded the Hmong from being considered as terrorists. "Hmong refugees, who dedicated their service to America during the Vietnam War, have looked to the U.S. as a place of hope and a sanctuary from persecution," Coleman expressed in a statement.

VANG XANG COLLECTION

right
General Vang Pao presents his long-time friend U.S. Senator Norm Coleman with the poster *A Generation of Hmong Leaders* in 2008. Coleman, a Republican, was seeking General Vang Pao's support for his re-election to the U.S. Senate seat against DFL-endorsed Al Franken.

VANG XANG COLLECTION

An Illustration of His Remarkable Life 372

373

General Vang Pao, Mrs. May Song Vang, and Mrs. Chia Moua (in blue) with the Hmong community leaders and members in San Diego, California on May 4, 2008.

THE GVP FAMILY COLLECTION

top left
General Vang Pao and Mrs. May Song Vang posing with the pageant contestants at the Hmong New Year Celebration in South Carolina in 2009. *Below left*, General Vang Pao with the Hmong community leaders and members in the Tulsa, Oklahoma on May 16, 2009.

THE GVP FAMILY COLLECTION

"General Vang Pao has been quoted to be a soldier's soldier, a man amongst men, a leader amongst leaders. To the Hmong people, General Vang Pao represents hope and freedom.

"General Vang Pao's ability to inspire is one of his greatest gifts to the Hmong people. His ability to transcend and touch people of all generations is a testament to the unconditional love he has for his people, and the Hmong peoples' love for him. General Vang Pao, through courage, bravery, and leadership, once inspired a nation of Hmong and Lao people with a sense of patriotism to fight for their country and freedom.

"Today, his vision and speeches motivate the Hmong people towards education and instilling family values into our lives. General Vang Pao has made it possible for all of us to be proud that we are Hmong."

***

KOU VANG
GENERAL VANG PAO'S GRANDSON
EMAIL INTERVIEW WITH AUTHOR
DECEMBER 6, 2010

"My friends, it is not just a coincidence that we gather every summer over July 4th to celebrate, to play sports, to reminisce, and to peer into the future. The American July 4th celebration has great meaning and great significance. It is so much more than just fireworks, good food, and parades. If we could go back in time to July 4, 1776, we would be able to witness the signing of the Declaration of Independence in Philadelphia. My friends, July 4, 1776 is the birth date of this great nation!

"There is great similarity between the American July 4th celebration and our Hmong-American Soccer Festival celebration. The American July 4th is an annual celebration to commemorate the courage and faith of the founding fathers in their pursuit of liberty.

"The Hmong-American July 4th Soccer Festival celebration too is an annual celebration to commemorate the courage and faith of the Hmong people and their pursuit of liberty.

"And so, it is only appropriate that we, the Hmong-American people, celebrate our re-birth during the Fourth of July! In 1975, we were a people without a country, a people without a home. We were all refugees, a people who had to leave our mother land or risk death. So we left not knowing where we all would end up or how it all would even end."

* * *

GENERAL VANG PAO
SPEECH ON JULY 4, 2006
RETRIEVED FROM CHA VANG
NOVEMBER 2010

Athletes compete in the game of volleyball, one of a handful of sports that are played at the Hmong Freedom Celebration Week. Each year approximately 15,000 to 25,000 Hmong people throughout the U.S. attend the event, making it one of the largest public gatherings in Minnesota.

NOAH VANG COLLECTION

right
General Vang Pao at the Hmong Freedom Week Celebration at McMurray Field—Como Park, St. Paul, Minnesota, July 2009.

YEU TONG HLAO VU COLLECTION

An Illustration of His Remarkable Life 376

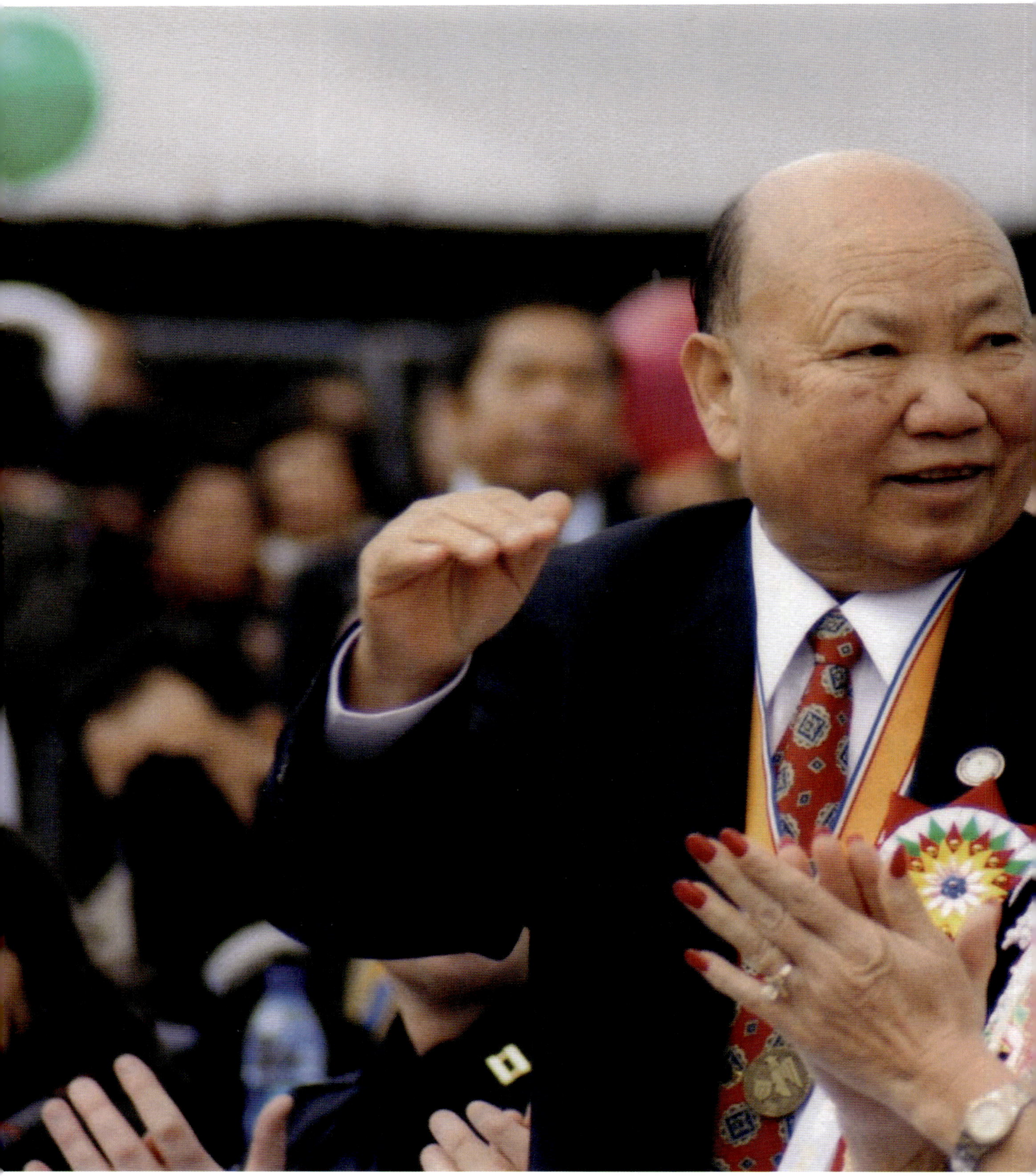

General Vang Pao and Mrs. May Song Vang at the 2008-2009 Hmong International New Year Celebration in Fresno, California.

YEU TONG HLAO VU COLLECTION

"Education is the key to the future..."

***

GENERAL VANG PAO
"PEACE DOCTRINE ON LAOS"
WRITTEN ON NOVEMBER 26, 2003
RETRIEVED FROM XANG VANG
JANUARY 2012

Kev kawm ntawv yog tus yawm sij rau lub neej yav pem suab...

(TRANSLATION - LUS TXHAIS)

right
General Vang Pao was featured in the Hennepin County Library's 'NYEEM NTAWV' or 'READ,' which was an educational campaign to encourage students to read.

HENNEPIN COUNTY LIBRARY COLLECTION VIA CHALENG N. LEE

NYEEM NTAWV

READ

NAIS PHOOS VAJ POV
General Vang Pao

Ntsuag Nos
Ib Tug Cinderella Hmoob
Cov hloov kho
Jewell Reinhart Coburn nrog Tzexa Cherta Lee
Tus kos duab Anne Sibley O'Brien

Hennepin County Library

Copyright 2010 Hennepin County Library   Poster funded by the Library Foundation of Hennepin County, Minnesota

SACRAMENTO HMONG
KALIA VAJ
KATHY VANG
AMY VANG
3RD MISS HMONG

General Vang Pao delivers a speech to a crowd at the Sacramento Hmong New Year Celebration in 2009-2010.

"My grandfather's leadership is extraordinary. General Vang Pao has strengthened the Hmong community since Laos and continues to this day to empower the Hmong community here in the United States and all over the world. General Vang Pao's continuous dedication and service to the Hmong society has been without boundaries. His support and push for higher education and culture preservation of our youths today, has relentlessly been his first priority. General Vang Pao has established numerous community centers in various states and programs to help assist diverse age groups, to promote self growth, to become successful individuals. The sacrifices General Vang Pao has made have given the Hmong community the opportunity to grow and blend alongside American society. Our roots are embedded with each other, whether we like it or not. Who we are today, and who we become in the future, is tied to this man one way or another. With his continual vision of prosperity for his people, General Vang Pao will persist to maintain and build a stronger united society for the Hmong."

* * *
XENG VANG
GENERAL VANG PAO'S GRANDSON
EMAIL INTERVIEW WITH AUTHOR
DECEMBER 9, 2010

General Vang Pao at the Lao/Hmong National Festival in Oshkosh, Wisconsin, during Labor Day Weekend, 2010.

YE VUE COLLECTION

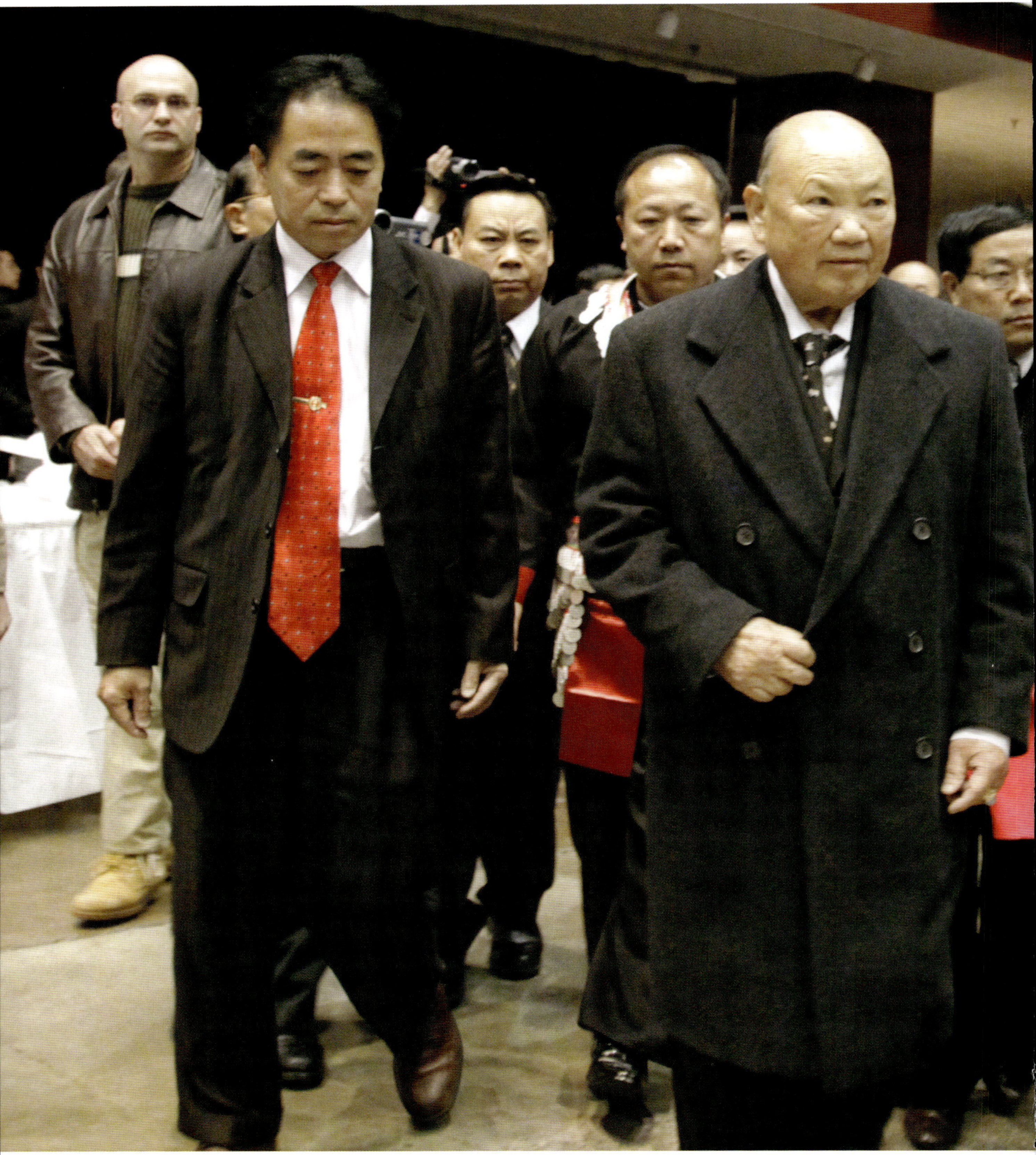

Hmong New Year attendees warmly greet General Vang Pao, U.S. Senator Amy Klobuchar, and Governor-elect Mark Dayton (behind), who were among the special guests at the Hmong New Year Celebration in St. Paul, Minnesota, on November 25, 2010.

NOAH VANG COLLECTION

An Illustration of His Remarkable Life 388

"Our Hmong life today is not the life we once lived 100 years ago. We are not the same anymore. We are far more advanced and more prosperous. In order for us to go forward, we must change our attitudes. We must be willing to lend our hands to help one another and not tear each other down as we have in the past and not be jealous of each other's successes. We must maintain our values and principles and not let the worst get in our way or practice the wrong things that will lead us into ruin."

* * *

GENERAL VANG PAO
SPEECH AT THE HMONG NEW YEAR
ST. PAUL, MINNESOTA
NOVEMBER 26, 2010

Peb Hmoob lub neej hnub no tsis zoo li lub neej 100 xyoo dhau los lawm. Peb tsis yog cov neeg zoo li qub lawm. Peb paub tab thiab txawj ntse, thiab muaj noj muaj haus. Yuav kom peb Hmoob lub neej nce ib qib ntxiv mas peb yuav tsum tau hloov peb tus cwj pwm. Peb yuav tsum sib txhawb thiab sib pab tsis yog sib lauj thiab sib rhuav raws li peb tus cwj pwm qub, thiab tsis txhob xam khib rau lwm tus txoj kev vam meej. Peb yuav tsum khaws peb txoj kev ua neej thiab peb txoj kev ntseeg cia, tsis txhob pub kom txoj kev phem los cuam tshuam thiab txhob xyaum qhov tsis yog kom coj peb mus rau txoj kev puas tsuaj.

(TRANSLATION - LUS TXHAIS)

General Vang Pao at the Hmong New Year Celebration in St. Paul, Minnesota, on November 25, 2010.

NOAH VANG COLLECTION

General Vang Pao's Beliefs & Visions

* * *

[GENERAL VANG PAO] believes that although the Hmong have no country of their own, they are blessed by God to be living in many different countries throughout the world where they share citizenships with others; and

[GENERAL VANG PAO] believes that, though they have lost their own written language, the Hmong have excelled in retaining their heritage, culture, and traditions that were passed down from many generations in proud oral histories and teachings; and

[GENERAL VANG PAO] believes that all Hmong have the responsibility, each of them, of living in peace and harmony with their fellow citizens in whichever country they live—be it Laos, China, France, Germany, The United States, Thailand, Vietnam or elsewhere; and

[GENERAL VANG PAO] believes that all Hmong prefer to be economically independent and to enrich the well-being and quality of life for all wherever they reside; and

[GENERAL VANG PAO] believes that the Hmong are dedicated to continually promote and seek better and higher education so that they can adapt to their surroundings and improve their lives in the new millennium;

Therefore, [GENERAL VANG PAO] recommends that:

The Hmong shall recognize the country in which they live as their own beloved country. Each Hmong should exercise his or her civic rights and perform his or her civic duties and be protected by the laws of the country that they are citizens of;

Each Hmong shall be free to worship the religion of his or her choice, and also to preserve the Hmong heritage, culture, and traditions so that the Hmong people can remain in the world with identity, dignity, pride, and autonomy;

The Hmong should assist one another to enhance their unity and should help each other build successful and prosperous businesses to compete in the global markets;

The Hmong must take the opportunity to accept and learn the Hmong Romanized Popular Alphabet (RPA) as their own written script as it is closest to writing in English, which is becoming the global language for writing, speaking, and communications, and to diligently use the schools provided by local and federal governments for their advancement; and

Each Hmong—young and old—should sacrifice and volunteer his or her time and contribute financial support to foundations and non-profit organizations that would help and strengthen the Hmong people worldwide.

* * *

Throughout General Vang Pao's distinguished career, he shared many of his beliefs and visions with his advisers, politicians, leaders, and the Hmong community as a whole wherever he went. As a child, he was influenced by unparalleled causes that shaped his views and deepened his personal convictions to help his people and the country of Laos.

During The New Millennium Hmong-American Convention in Fresno, Ca., on December 24, 2010 ,General Vang Pao outlined some of his visions that would unify and strengthen the Hmong communities worldwide. His beliefs and visions are what he had attempted to accomplish. He also left behind a message that whoever wants to lead the Hmong people, he hoped that these passages may be a moral or principle guide for him or her to achieve and succeed in taking the people forward. Although General Vang Pao never saw the final draft, he verbally authorized some of his senior advisors to draft the language in this document and make it available to the public. The passages on this page summarize General Vang Pao's beliefs and visions for his people and country. **

———————————————————

***Retrieved from Wa Chong Vang and Xang Vang. The version in this book has been modified from the original one to fit our readers. Photo of General Vang Pao taken on December 24, 2010, in Fresno. Courtesy of Ye Vue.*

An Illustration of His Remarkable Life   392

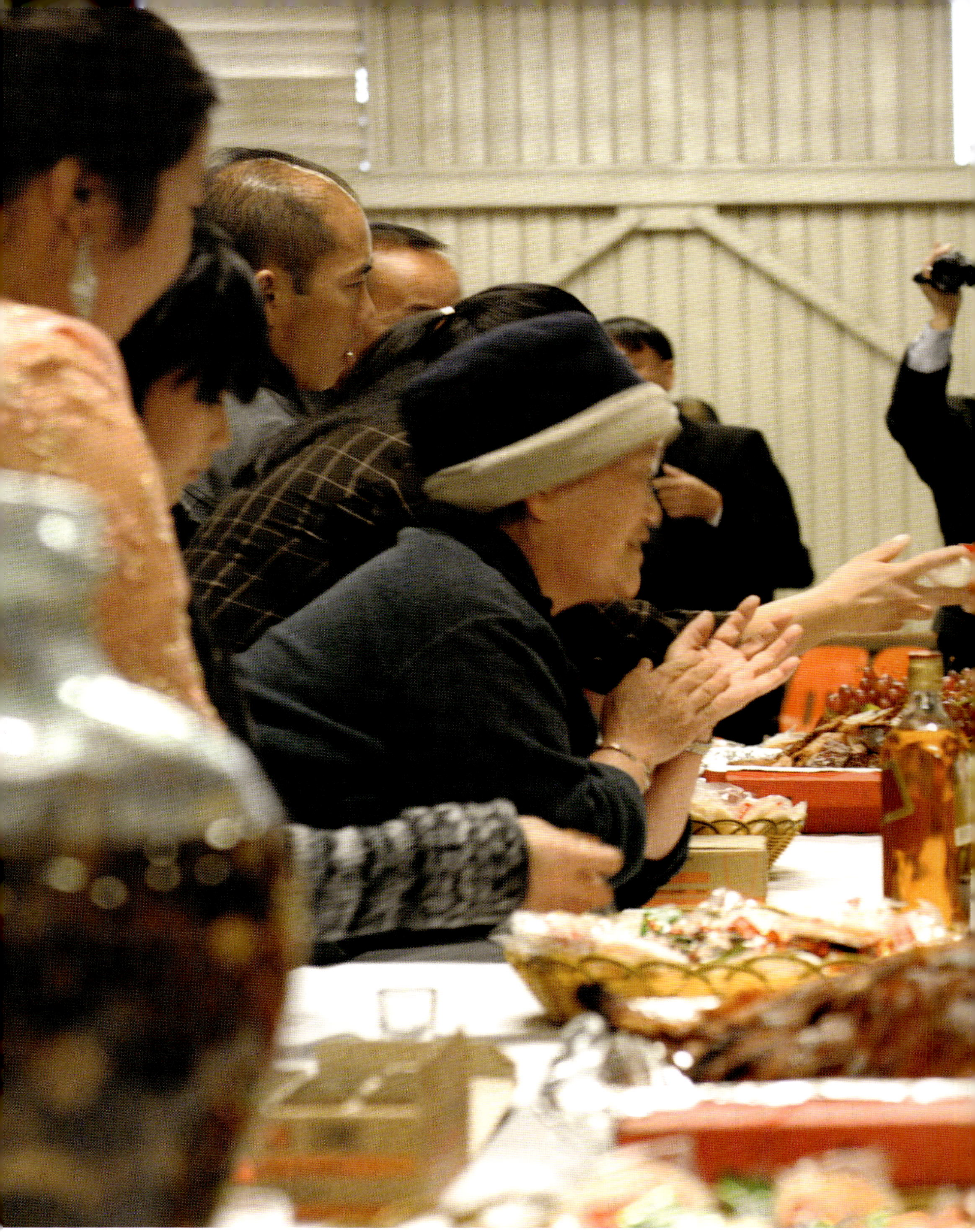

General Vang Pao and Mrs. May Song Vang at the pre-Hmong New Year ceremony, or *Pe Tsiab*, prior to the start of the International Hmong New Year Celebration 2010-2011 in Fresno, California.

YE VUE COLLECTION

General Vang Pao and Mrs. May Song Vang at the Hmong International New Year Celebration in Fresno, California on December 26, 2010.

NOAH VANG COLLECTION

top right
General Vang Pao blesses everyone with good health and prosperity for the incoming New Year. *Left to right:* Prince Ophat Nachampassak, Lao Thai Vang, General Vang Pao, and his son-in-law Kong Xiong, at the ribbon-cutting ceremony during the Hmong International New Year Celebration on December 26, 2010. This is what I remember about General Vang Pao during this very moment.

"On this day, I will always remember how General Vang Pao fought through every difficult second of his life to make sure that those who are left behind received the best of his words of wisdom.

"On this day, I was witness to how he truly had shown the people what unconditional love and the devotion to public service meant.

"On this day, I saw that his ailing health was never the obstacle that prevented him to be with the people he had devoted his entire life and career for.

"On this day, in me, his spirit will always live on."

NOAH VANG COLLECTION

"Hnub no zoo hnub, peb kwv tij neej tsa thoob plaws ntiajteb no, tau tuaj sib koom nyob ntawm Fresno no xa lub xyoo laus txais lub xyoo tshiab. Lub xyoo 2010 ntawd, yam twg plig tsis zoo kom poob nrog dej tshoob poob nrog rau hluav taws kub mus.

"Yam nej ho xav yuav xav tau kom tau raws lub siab xav. Dej tshiab kom tau haus, qav tshiab kom tau noj, tu tub tu kiv kom puv vaj puv tsev, khwv nyiaj khwv txiaj kom puv nas, ua qoob ua luam txhab xeeb, tu tsiaj tu txhuv kom puv nkuaj, ua laj ua kaj kom suab nom ciaj tswv, yim ua mas kom yim zoo, yim ua mas kom yim nce. Es kom kuv qhib lub Tsiab Pebcaug Xyoo 2011 no tawm tuaj txij hnub no mus."

* * *

NAI PHOO VAJ POV
COV LUS KAWG NWS TAU HAIS RAU TSIAB PEBCAUG
HMONG INTERNATIONAL NEW YEAR CELEBRATION
FRESNO, CALIFORNIA
DECEMBER 26, 2010
RETRIEVED FROM HMONG TODAY

An Illustration of His Remarkable Life

Kom sawv daws txais kev noj qab nyob zoo.
Xav tau dab tsi los kom tau.

GENERAL VANG PAO

"To my fellow Hmong, born as a Hmong in this lifetime, I love everyone very, very much. I uplifted everyone's life from a very poor living condition where salt was not affordable to most. I led everyone with the opportunity to be educated so we can prosper.

"We've been to this country [United States] for 35 years and we've maintained our unity and prosperity. We've come a long way, with my leadership, taken a very big step forward. I want to remind my fellow Hmong that we must remain united, one cannot escape being Hmong. Everyone must love one another so we can carry on our Hmong heritage…"

* * *

GENERAL VANG PAO
HIS FAREWELL WORDS
FRESNO, CALIFORNIA
FEBRUARY 2011
(TRANSLATION BY THUA VANG)

Hais rau tsoom Hmoob sawv daws, yug los ua Hmoob tiam no kuv yeej hlub hlub sawv daws. Rub sawv daws lub neej ntawm qhov txom txom nyem, pluag pluag twb tsis muaj ntsev noj. Coj los kom txawj ntaub txawj ntawv, kom muaj noj muaj haus.

Peb tuaj txog tebchaws [Ameliskas] no 35 xyoos, peb sawv daws yeej tuaj noj sib pab haus sib ce. Yeej coj cov Hmoob ua neej zoo los lawm ib theem es hais rau cov kwv tij neej tsa Hmoob hais tias kawg nkaus sawv daws sib hlub xwb. Khiav tawm lub npe Hmoob tsis tau. Sawv daws yuav tsum sib hlub es sawv daws thiaj li muaj neej ua…

(TRANSLATION - LUS TXHAIS)

left
On Christmas Eve, December 25, 2010, General Vang Pao personally distributed 1,000 copies of this 11x17 poster to the people at his party at the Fresno Fair Grounds in Fresno, California. In the text, he wished for everyone's good health and prosperity. The sword General Vang Pao is holding was a gift given by King Sisavang Vong for his leadership in saving the King while he was under house arrest by the Pathet Lao in Luang Prabang, Laos, in 1946.

CHAI VANG COLLECTION

City of Saint Paul
Proclamation

Whereas; for over a decade, General Vang Pao served to protect his people and nation, in the Kingdom of Laos from foreign aggression, having attained the rank of Major General and commissioned in the Royal Army of Laos by King Savang Vatthana; and

Whereas; in partnership with the United States government and military, General Vang Pao committed to help fight foreign aggression in Laos in 1960, and would lead the Hmong and Lao in the Vietnam War for the next two decades; and

Whereas; General Vang Pao paved the way for resettling his fellow Hmong across the United States after the war, to include founding the first non-profit social service organization for Hmong and other Southeast Asian refugees, Lao Family Community Center; and

Whereas; the City of Saint Paul specifically, and the Twin Cities in general, are home to one of the largest concentrations of Hmong in the United States and General Vang Pao was a great servant to the Hmong people, a revered leader in the Hmong community, and served honorably and courageously in defense of liberty during the Vietnam War;

Now, Therefore, I, Christopher B. Coleman, Mayor of the City of Saint Paul, do hereby proclaim Friday, February 04, 2011, to be:

General Vang Pao Day

in the City of Saint Paul

In Witness Whereof I have hereunto set my hand and caused the Seal of the City of Saint Paul to be affixed this Fourth Day of February in the Year Two Thousand Eleven.

Christopher B. Coleman, Mayor

City of St. Paul Proclamation and City of Fresno Resolution, *right*, acknowledging the late General Vang Pao's contribution to public service.

City of FRESNO
RESOLUTION

WHEREAS, **GENERAL VANG PAO'S** exemplary military career during the Vietnam War has been well documented. He served as the military chief of Xiengkhuang Province, and in 1961 he was recruited by Bill Lair of the CIA to form a secret army to provide strong opposition to the Vietminh and Pathet Lao, communist forces seeking to invade South Vietnam and overtake Laos. **GENERAL VANG PAO'S** remarkable military prowess earned him the title of Phagna Norapramok, Lord Protector of the Land, from His Majesty, the King of Laos, King Savang Vatthana;

WHEREAS, His subsequent tireless efforts in gaining congressional approval to resettle Hmong refugees in the United States were just the beginning of his new life. In 1977, he founded the first Hmong-Lao non-profit organization in Orange County, California, starting a new era of community service and leadership to achieve community building and the creation of strong and prosperous Hmong communities in the United States. At the same time, **GENERAL VANG PAO** continued to advocate for the return to freedom and democracy in Laos, by founding several pro-democracy and international human rights organizations; and

WHEREAS, Fresno has always been dear to **GENERAL VANG PAO'S** heart, as it is the home of the largest Hmong community in the nation. He was as often visiting and celebrating in Fresno as he was living in Orange County. This truly was his second home, where he could be found throughout the New Year celebrations, at various community functions or just staying with local families who welcomed him as a Father. He worked closely with the City of Fresno to facilitate the development of a thriving Hmong community and knew several City of Fresno Department Directors by name; and

WHEREAS, **GENERAL VANG PAO** delighted in witnessing the entrepreneurial activities and civic engagement of his people here who boldly started businesses or engaged in public service, such as City Councilman Blong Xiong, and actively participated in local veterans' events and parades. Like a true soldier and devoted leader, **GENERAL VANG PAO** worked for his Hmong people until his last breath and his last step, and on January 6, 2011, the Hmong people lost their hero, their leader, and their Father.

NOW, THEREFORE, BE IT RESOLVED, that while **GENERAL VANG PAO** has gone on to a better world, the memory of his great deeds will continue to inspire future generations of Hmong people and the wisdom of his words will continue to guide them toward a bright future. **GENERAL VANG PAO** may be gone from this earth, but his spirit remains forever in the hearts and minds of the Hmong people.

DATED this 13th day of January, 2011.

ASHLEY SWEARENGIN, Honorable Mayor

LEE BRAND, Council President

CLINTON J. OLIVIER, Acting Council President

BLONG XIONG, Councilmember

ANDREAS BORGEAS, Councilmember

OLIVER L. BAINS III, Councilmember

LARRY WESTERLUND, Councilmember

SAL QUINTERO, Councilmember

Congresswoman Betty McCollum
Serving Minnesota's 4th Congressional District
1714 Longworth HOB ♦ Washington, DC 20515
www.mccollum.house.gov

For Immediate Release: January 7, 2011
Contact: Maria Reppas, (202) 225-6631 / (202) 527-0149 maria.reppas@mail.house.gov

Congresswoman McCollum Honors Passing of General Vang Pao

Washington, DC – Congresswoman Betty McCollum (MN-04) entered the following statement into the Congressional Record, recognizing the death of Hmong military leader General Vang Pao.

"I rise today to honor the life, service and sacrifice of General Vang Pao, who passed away yesterday evening in Clovis, California. General Vang Pao was a historic Hmong military leader who led his people against communist forces during a turbulent time in Laos from 1961 to 1975. In this country, General Vang Pao served as a civilian leader who continued to lead the Hmong-American community for nearly four decades.

"My heart-felt sympathy goes out to General Vang Pao's family and to all the Hmong-American families in Minnesota and across the U.S. Over the years, I had the honor of joining General Vang Pao at many events such as: the Hmong American New Year celebrations and the July Soccer Festival celebrations in St. Paul, as he had always come to the Twin Cities to join the Hmong community for those events. Most recently, I had the great honor of joining him for the grand opening celebrations of the Hmong Village Center on the Eastside of St. Paul on October 30, 2010. Although frail from his failing health and sitting in his chair, the General was in good spirit and spoke eloquently to a large gathering crowd at the celebrations. Sadly, this was the last time I saw him.

"General Vang Pao's influence has touched the Hmong-American community deeply, and I know the community will continue to share and cherish the memories of his legacy for future generations to come. In honor of Gen. Vang Pao's lifetime of service to his people and loyalty to the U.S., I am pleased to submit this statement for the Congressional Record."

Congresswoman Betty McCollum serves on the House Appropriations and Budget Committees.

Minnesota Congresswoman Betty McCollum spoke on the record in Congress honoring the death of General Vang Pao. 19th District of California Rep. Jeff Denham also gave his acknowledgment of the late General in a floor speech. *Right,* Minnesota State Senate Resolution authored by Senator John Harrington honoring the late General Vang Pao. In the House, Rep. Rena Moran also introduced a resolution for the General.

CONGRESSIONAL RECORD FROM CHAO LEE
MINNESOTA SENATE RESOLUTION FROM JAMES CHANG

MINNESOTA LEGISLATURE

A Senate resolution

honoring the life and work of General Vang Pao.

WHEREAS, General Vang Pao was born on December 8, 1929, in Nong Het, Xiangkhuang Province, Laos; and

WHEREAS, Vang Pao fought as a teenager against the Japanese in Laos during World War II, first as an interpreter and then as a Sergeant in the French colonial army; and

WHEREAS, in 1954, Vang Pao became an officer in the Royal Lao Army of the newly independent Laos; and

WHEREAS, as an officer in the Royal Lao Army, Vang Pao was the only ethnic Hmong to attain the rank of Major General in the Royal Lao Army; and

WHEREAS, as Major General in the Royal Lao Army, Vang Pao was the Commanding Officer of Military Region II of Laos, the region which saw the heaviest fighting during the Indochina War; and

WHEREAS, as a military leader, Vang Pao led many successful battles, often against overwhelming odds; and

WHEREAS, through the efforts of General Vang Pao and his Hmong forces during the Vietnam War, countless American lives were saved; and

WHEREAS, General Vang Pao was an important friend and ally to America; and

WHEREAS, for over 50 years, General Vang Pao was a preeminent leader of the Hmong people and a major factor in the success of Hmong-Americans as they continued to become vital contributing members of American society; and

NOW, THEREFORE, BE IT RESOLVED by the Senate of the State of Minnesota that it honors the life and work of General Vang Pao, and extends condolences to his family, friends, and the entire Hmong-American community upon his passing.

BE IT FURTHER RESOLVED that the Secretary of the Senate is directed to prepare an enrolled copy of this resolution, to be authenticated by the Secretary's signature and that of the Chair of the Senate Rules and Administration Committee, and transmit it to the family of General Vang Pao.

Cal R. Ludeman
Secretary of the Senate

Amy T. Koch
Chair, Senate Committee on
Rules and Administration

John M. Harrington
State Senator, District 67

LETTER OF CONDOLENCE

January 9, 2011

To: The General Vang Pao Family and
General Vang Pao Memorial Services
c/o Prof. Lee Pao Xiong

We were deeply saddened to hear the news of General Vang Pao's passing away, and we would like to express our sincere condolence to you and the General Vang Pao family on behalf of ourselves and many other Hmong folks around us in China. Words really cannot express how sad we feel, for we are all in a state of shock. However, our thoughts are with the General Vang Pao family and the rest of American Hmong community during this difficult time.

This is a time to mourn for the Hmong people in both America and the rest of the world. We have just lost a true leader of the Hmong people, and we cannot imagine how hard this is for the Hmong community in America, but please remember that there are millions of Hmong here in China who care about you and share your loss. The loss is not only yours in America and Laos; in fact, it is a great loss for the entire Hmong people all over the world.

We were truly fortunate to have a man such as General Vang Pao in the history of Hmong people. General Vang Pao was the greatest leader ever in Hmong modern history, who made remarkable contributions to the Hmong and thus to the multiethnic world. With his incomparable heroic courage and insight, he led the Hmong in Laos to fight for a new life of freedom and dignity under the extremely hard and complex conditions of his time. Moreover, though we were separated by mountains and seas and national boundaries, the globalized communications made us well aware of his great concern and compassion towards the life of Hmong people all over the world. It was due to General Vang Pao's leadership that the Hmong were transformed from unknown remote mountain dwellers into a globally renowned peoplehood. Remember that "Those who live in the hearts of others never die," and the General left behind an immortal example to all posterity. His merits and bounties shall be enshrined in each heart of Hmong people from now to future generations.

In the way as conveyed in the ancient traditional Hmong prayers and rituals, it is our belief that our great King Chiyou shall send his millions of numina to welcome home the heroic spirit of his greatest heir soldier, though it is a long and arduous journey crossing numerous mountains and rivers for the Hmong hero soul to return to our Hmong ancestors' wonderland.

With the deepest condolence,

麻勇斌(MA Yongbin), 杨培德(YANG Peide), 张晓（ZHANG Xiao）, 龙宇晓（Jason Yu-Xiao LONG）, 杨忠(YANG Zhong), and 李一如（LI Yiru） from the Guizhou Hmong Community；杨永华（YANG Yonghua），王元丰(WANG Yuanfeng), 李国文（LI Guowen), 陶小平(TAO Xiaoping), 艾卫民(AI Weimin), and 王友林(WANG Youlin) from the Sichuan Hmong Community, China.

State of Wisconsin
2011 - 2012 LEGISLATURE

LRB-0969/1
SRM:kjf:md

2011 ASSEMBLY JOINT RESOLUTION 6

January 27, 2011 – Introduced by Representatives SHILLING, BARCA, BERNARD SCHABER, E. COGGS, FIELDS, GRIGSBY, HINTZ, MOLEPSKE JR, PASCH, PETROWSKI, SEIDEL, SPANBAUER, TURNER, ZEPNICK and ZIEGELBAUER, cosponsored by Senators KAPANKE, COWLES, ERPENBACH, GROTHMAN, SCHULTZ, TAYLOR and VINEHOUT. Referred to Committee on Rules.

Relating to: the life and service of General Vang Pao.

Whereas, Vang Pao was born on December 8, 1929, and died on January 6, 2011; and

Whereas, Vang Pao participated in the resistance efforts after the Japanese invaded and occupied French Indochina in World War II; and

Whereas, after World War II, Vang Pao was recruited by the French to combat the Viet Minh; and

Whereas, Vang Pao was the only ethnic Hmong to attain the rank of general in the Royal Lao Army; and

Whereas, Vang Pao commanded the Secret Army during the 1960's and 1970's with support and training from the U.S. Central Intelligence Agency; and

Whereas, Vang Pao immigrated to the United States after the communist group Pathet Lao seized control of Laos in 1975; and

Whereas, thousands of Hmong refugees followed in Vang Pao's footsteps and bravely escaped persecution and repression in Laos and resettled in the United States; and

Whereas, Vang Pao is revered by many in the Hmong community for his leadership and many accomplishments; now, therefore, be it

Resolved by the assembly, the senate concurring, That the Wisconsin legislature commemorates the life and service of General Vang Pao, and mourns his passing.

(END)

The State of Wisconsin passed a resolution honoring the late General Vang Pao during the 2011-2012 sesson.

DOCUMENT FROM HTTP://DOCS.LEGIS.WISCONSIN.GOV/2011/RELATED/PROPOSALS/AJR6.PDF

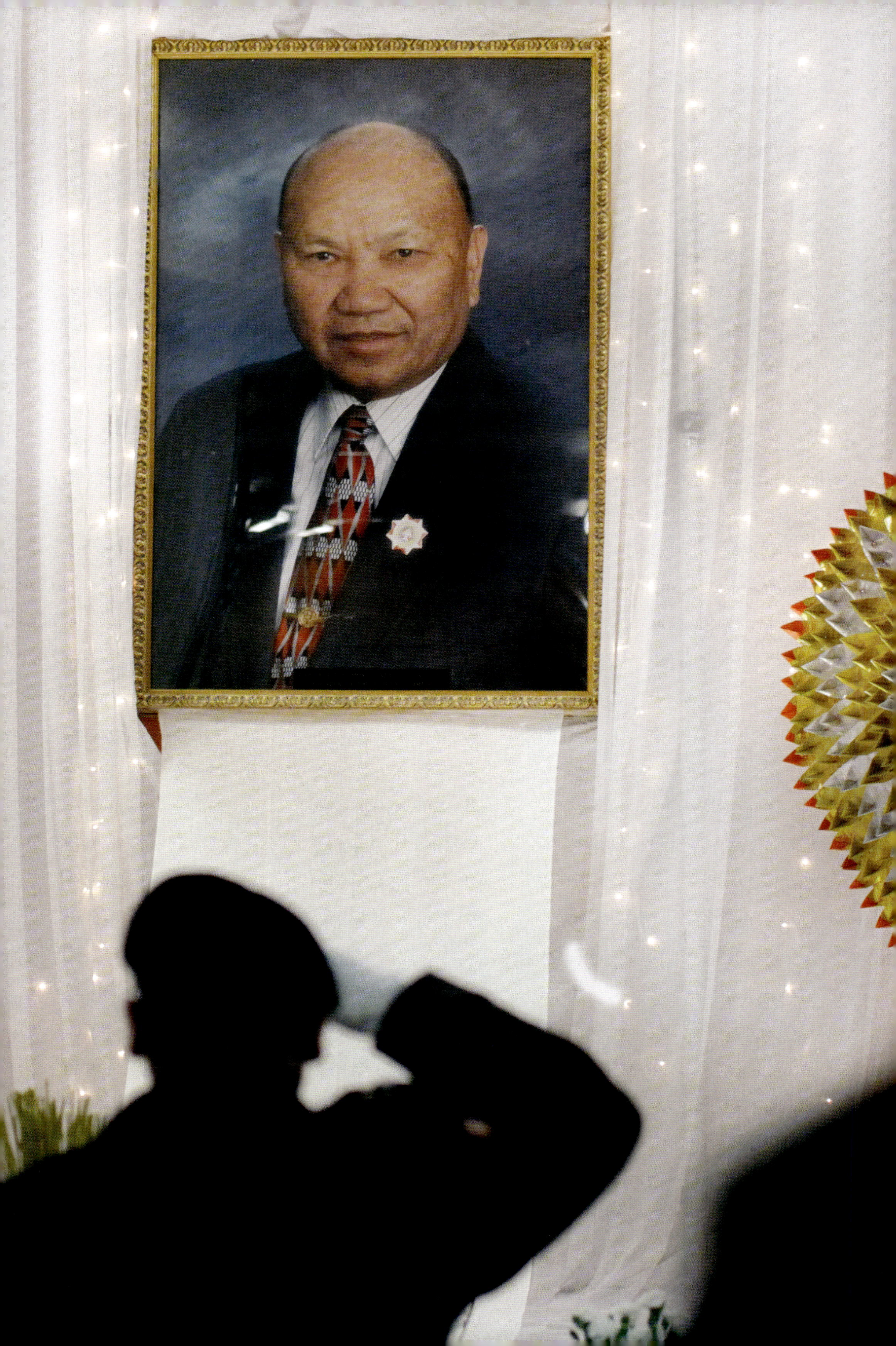

A TRIBUTE TO MAJOR GENERAL VANG PAO

HON. JIM COSTA
OF CALIFORNIA
IN THE HOUSE OF REPRESENTATIVES
Wednesday, January 26, 2011

Mr. COSTA. Mr. Speaker, I rise today with my colleagues Mr. CARDOZA, Ms. BORDALLO and Mr. KISSEL to honor the memory of Major General Vang Pao of Fresno, California, who passed away Thursday January 6th after a battle with pneumonia.

Major General Vang Pao led the Royal Lao Army during the Secret War in Laos, fighting against the People's Army of Vietnam in cooperation with the Central Intelligence Agency and United States military forces. Bravely leading thousands of soldiers in a guerilla war against communism, Vang Pao became a hero, due to his leadership and dedication.

Growing up in the Xiengkhuang province, Vang Pao became interested in military service early in life. He left his family farm as a teenager to join the French Military in defense of his fellow Hmong as the Japanese invaded, and began a historic military career. At the end of World War II, and the departure of the Japanese, Vang Pao was recruited as an officer in the First Indochina War to fight the Viet Minh.

As he rose within the Royal Lao Army, Vang Pao was heralded for his valor and dedication and was the only ethnic Hmong to attain the rank of General in the Royal Lao Army. In the early 1960's, when the CIA recruited Hmong men in Laos to join a guerrilla unit during the Vietnam War, Vang Pao was chosen to be the commander. As his Hmong soldiers rescued downed American pilots from enemy territories and defended American outposts in Laos, he gained a reputation for being a disciplined, honorable leader.

The Hmong soldiers also attacked many North Vietnamese convoys that were using the Ho Chi Minh trail from North Vietnam into South Vietnam. By attacking these supply routes, thousands of U.S. soldiers' lives were saved in South Vietnam. Vang Pao and the Royal Lao Army valiantly fought for their cause throughout the entire Secret War.

Immigrating to the United States in May of 1975, Major General Vang Pao was instrumental in negotiating the resettlement of thousands of his fellow Hmong. Vang Pao continued his leadership after his exit from military service. He was active in fostering U.S.-Lao relations, and combating human rights abuses abroad, as well as serving as an icon and mentor to the Hmong-American community. A widely respected figure, General Vang Pao was a constant feature at Hmong-American events and celebrations nationwide.

Major General Vang Pao is survived by his widow, Mrs. May Song Vang, 25 children, 68 grandchildren, 17 great grandchildren and numerous friends and community members.

Mr. Speaker, I ask my colleagues to join Mr. CARDOZA, Ms. BORDALLO, Mr. KISSEL and myself in honoring the life of Major General Vang Pao as we offer our condolences to his family and celebrate his memory and service to our country.

HONORING THE LIFE AND ACCOMPLISHMENTS OF GENERAL VANG PAO

(Mr. DENHAM asked and was given permission to address the House for 1 minute.)

Mr. DENHAM. Madam Speaker, I rise today to honor the life and accomplishments of General Vang Pao. General Pao passed away on Thursday, January 6, 2011, and today marks the sixth and final day of the Hmong spiritual practices which are traditionally conducted by the Hmong community after the passing of an individual. I stand here today to support the internment of General Vang Pao in Arlington National Cemetery.

The accomplishments and service that General Vang Pao has given to the United States are not only numerous, but are everlasting. Not only was General Vang Pao determined to protect his country, but he served to protect the lives of American soldiers. He fought to cut off the Ho Chi Minh Trail so that supplies could not be utilized to fuel the enemy's war efforts. He provided aid and support to downed American pilots, in addition to defending American outposts.

The leadership of General Vang Pao helped save thousands of U.S. servicemembers' lives and was an influential force during the Vietnam War. The dedication and service of the general not only earned him the title of Lord Protector of the country, but has also made him a hero in both the Hmong community and the United States of America.

HON. WALLY HERGER
OF CALIFORNIA
IN THE HOUSE OF REPRESENTATIVES
Wednesday, January 26, 2011

Mr. HERGER. Mr. Speaker, I rise today to honor and pay tribute to General Vang Pao, the revered leader of the Hmong community residing in my Northern California congressional district and throughout the United States. I join that community in mourning his loss.

It is fitting for all Americans to pause and reflect on General Vang Pao's steadfast alliance with the United States during the Vietnam War. General Vang Pao commanded the Secret Army, a highly effective CIA-trained and supported force that fought against the Pathet Lao and People's Army of Vietnam. His tremendous courage and leadership aided American soldiers against aggression from the North Vietnamese. By fighting valiantly at our nation's side, he helped preserve and protect our way of life.

Our nation should not forget General Vang Pao's contributions to the American cause. We must also remember the Hmong who lost their lives or who were forced out of their homeland as they fought against the evils of communism. They sacrificed tremendously and deserve our enduring gratitude.

---

left
A Hmong-American veteran salutes a portrait of the late General Vang Pao at the Lao Family Community Center in St. Paul on January 7, 2011.

NOAH VANG COLLECTION

right
All three documents were retrieved from the Congressional Record and the collections of the respective members, who are in the House of Representatives.

> "Father, you will always be known and remembered as the greatest man in Hmong history."
>
> * * *
> FRANCOIS CHAO VANG
> ONE OF GENERAL VANG PAO'S SONS
> FAMILY HANDBOOK
> FRESNO, CALIFORNIA
> FEBRUARY 2011

> "Father, we will wait for you to come and lead us again."
>
> * * *
> NENG CHU VANG
> ONE OF GENERAL VANG PAO'S SONS
> FRESNO, CALIFORNIA
> FEBRUARY 2011

left
A bronze state of the late General Vang Pao was exhibited to the public during his Soul Release 'Tso-Plig' Ceremony in St. Paul, Minnesota, from May 27-29, 2011.

NOAH VANG COLLECTION

right
The late General Vang Pao's body at the mortuary before being escorted to the six-day funeral service at the Fresno Convention Center in Fresno, California, on February 4, 2011. His body is buried at Forest Lawn Cemetery in Glendale, California, which is about 45 minutes from his hometown, Westminster.

NOAH VANG COLLECTION

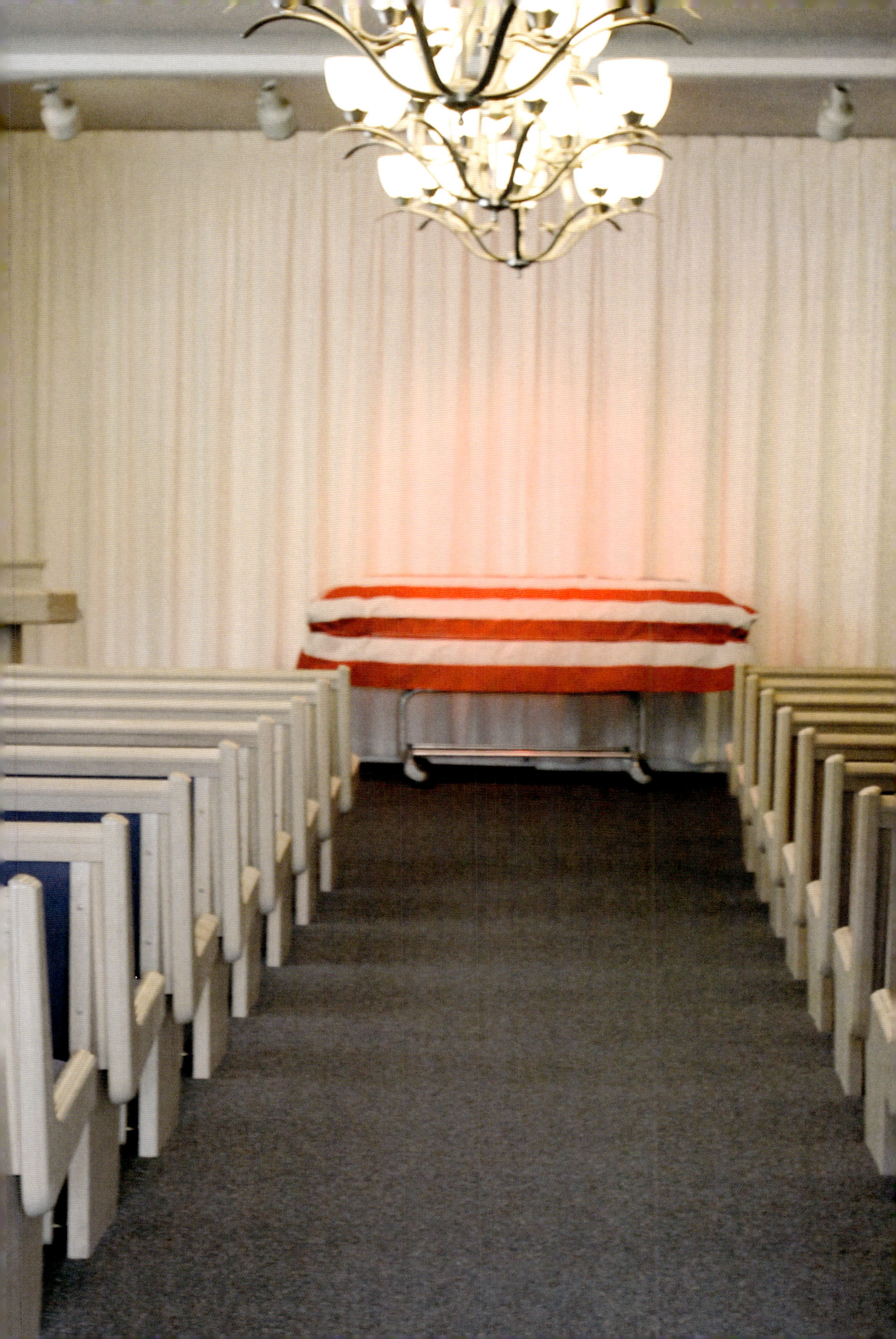

"What a legacy General Vang Pao has left for all of us."

—BOB NOBLE
PRESIDENT OF AIR AMERICA ASSOCIATION

"Thank you to the Vang family, relatives, the SGU and Lao Hmong Coalition for allowing me to express condolences from my Air America colleagues. It is an honor to be here with you and to talk about a great man, General Vang Pao. I would like to acknowledge the SKY [CIA] personnel, Ravens, and Air Commandoes- all who were a part of the Laos experience.

"As a young man, it was my privilege to know General Vang Pao and participate in his fight for the right of the Hmong people to live in peace as well as becoming our allies in the Vietnam War. I can still see this energetic, charismatic man running to my helicopter to catch a ride to Lima Site 32 [Bouam Long], Ba Na, Phou Bia, Muang Cha, Sala Phou Khoun, and other villages that were threatened by enemy attack. He would sit next to me and ask about my life. Thus began our conversations. His compassion in a time of great turmoil left me aware of this man's love for family and his people which governed his life and was a force that made him a great leader. Taking Vang Pao to the Plaine des Jarres and other hot spots was an amazing experience, just watching his presence change the tide of war. He would jump out of my helicopter and I would observe his actions of leadership as he gathered his troops and led them into battle.

"My Air America comrades and I have fought, bled, and died with you [Hmong]. I have personally comforted, tended to your wounded and returned your honored dead to their families and villages. This is the sorrowful part of war. One of our pilots, Captain Jack Knotts brought

General Vang Pao and Jerry Daniels out of Long Cheng. In the aftermath, VP still led his people. He brought them to the United States.

"It was my privilege to address two thousand Hmong at your New Year celebration in Seattle, Washington at the Seattle Center a few years ago. Seeing your young people full of life performing the traditional ball toss ritual took me back to Long Cheng where I first experienced it. I had a speech prepared but reading about your fathers' and grandfathers' escape from Laos, which were mounted on large boards at the Center by SGU veterans, changed my direction entirely. In the end all I could say is, 'I am sorry for leaving you when you needed my comrades and myself the most. It was heartbreaking for all of us when our government ordered us out.'

"It is enlightening to look around this room and experience how you have adapted to a new country and have flourished with the guidance of your beloved leader, General Vang Pao. I have met doctors, lawyers, educators, and leaders who have obtained this status by the educational and life freedoms that our country has offered you. I can truly see how the Hmong people have excelled and will continue to play an important part as America forges forward. How lucky we are as Americans to have the Hmong people among us. What a legacy General Vang Pao has left for all of us. It will be a privilege for me, my Air America colleagues, and others to meet with you during this great Celebration of Life for General Vang Pao."

* * *

BOB NOBLE
PRESIDENT OF AIR AMERICA ASSOCIATION
"VANG PAO'S CELEBRATION OF LIFE - EULOGY FEBRUARY 4, 2011"
FRESNO, CALIFORNIA

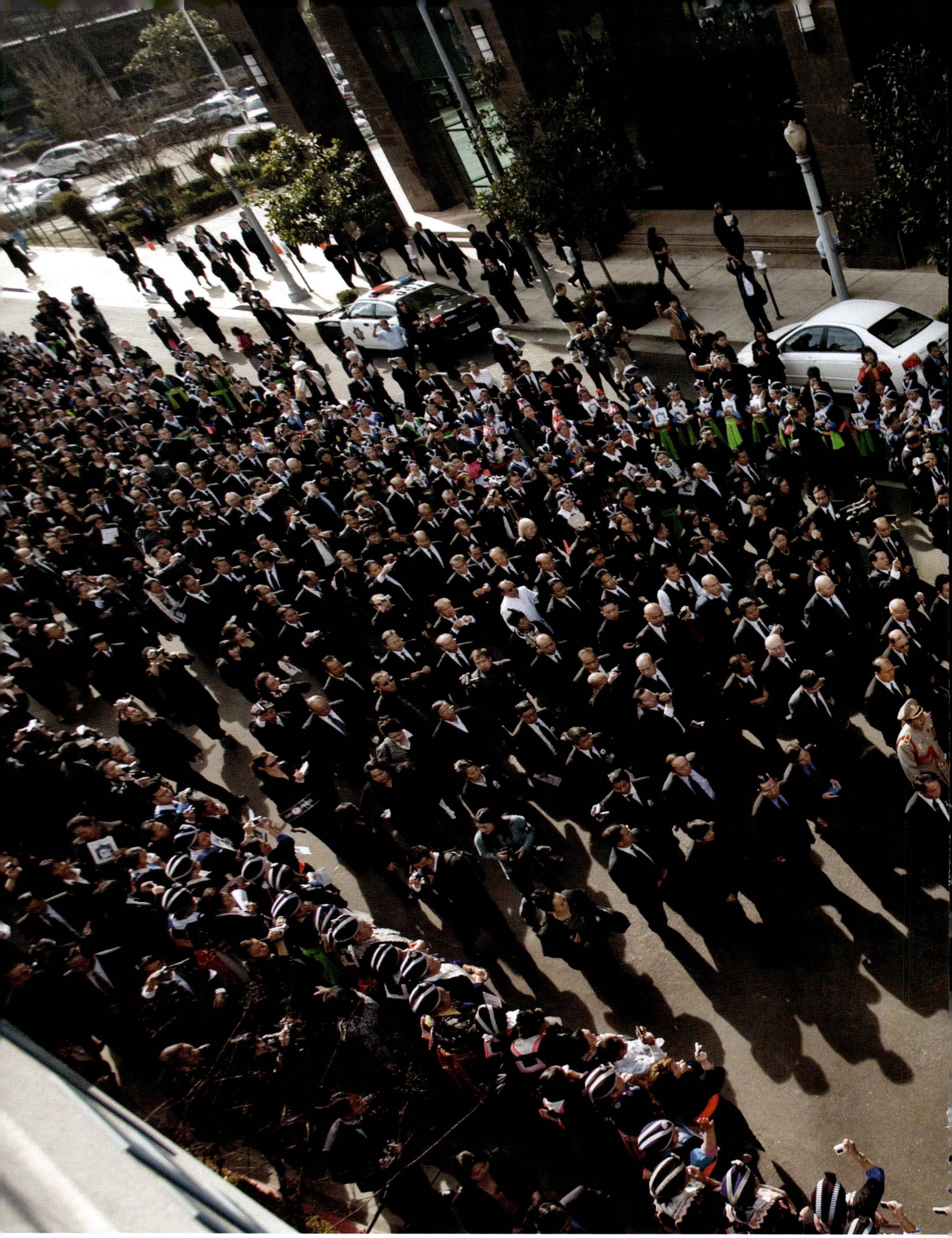

Funeral procession for General Vang Pao at the Fresno Convention Center in Fresno, California, on February 4, 2011. More than 30,000 people attended the service.

MANNY CRISOSTOMO/SACRAMENTO BEE/ZUMAPRESS.COM
COLLECTION

An Illustration of His Remarkable Life   412

"The General Vang Pao Family wishes to remind the Hmong People and the Friends of the Hmong People that General Vang Pao loved them in his life time and will watch over them from beyond this life. He would want the Hmong People to remain strong, to love each other, to work together, to continue to work hard and prosper, to raise future generations who will carry on the proud heritage of the Hmong People, so that the Hmong People may continue to advance to a bright future."

* * *

EXCERPT FROM "GENERAL VANG PAO'S FAMILY STATEMENT"
WRITTEN BY CHAO VANG
ONE OF GENERAL VANG PAO'S SONS
JANUARY 9, 2011
RETRIEVED FROM CHAI VANG

Nai Phoo Vaj Pov tsev neeg thov tshaj rau peb haiv neeg Hmoob thiab Hmoob cov phooj ywg hais tias Nai Phoo Vaj Pov hlub lawv heev nyob hauv nws lub neej thiab txawm nws tag sim neej lawm los nws yuav saib xyuas thiab pov hwm sawv daws. Nws yeej xav kom Hmoob sib hlub, sib puag xwbpwg, sib pab, ua ib pab ib pawg, koom tes thiab txhawb cov neeg phaum tom ntej uas yuav coj lub neej Hmoob kom vam meej kaj lug mus rau yam peb suab (future).

(TRANSLATION - LUS TXHAIS)

On February 5, 2011, the second night of the late General Vang Pao's funeral service, each of his children gave his or her tribute to their father. Speaking first was the General's oldest son, Francois Chao Vang. One by one, they shared a brief story of how they remembered their father. They also thanked everyone, including more than 300 organizations and public officials, for contributing the financial resources the family needed to conduct their father's funeral.

NOAH VANG COLLECTION

General Vang Pao's Lifetime Conviction

"

All my life, I have devoted everything to my Hmong people. I consistently sought out the best for them. I always encouraged every child to reach his or her full potential because they are our future.

Everything that I did, I did it with three things in mind: first, I wanted to make sure my Hmong people were globally recognized; second, I asked that we preserve our distinguished and unique culture because it gives us an identity and symbolizes who we are in the world; and third, I never wanted anyone to look down upon us as a people, but for us to utilize every given opportunity to strive for the better so that we can be the ideal role model in every community that we live in.

"

* * *
GENERAL VANG PAO
RETRIEVED FROM ZONG LIA VANG
CEDAR HILL, TEXAS
JUNE 2011
(HMONG TRANSLATION BY XAO CHOR VANG)

Nai Phoo Vaj Pov Txoj Kev Ua Neej

"

Tag nrho kuv lub neej, kuv muab tso phluav rau kuv haiv neeg Hmoob, thiab ib txwm nrhiav yam zoo rau kuv cov Hmoob xwb. Hais rau cov me tub me nyuam kom sawv daws yuav tsum rau siab thiab muab lawv txhais tes ncav kom deb li deb tau vim lawv yog peb Hmoob lub neej yav tom ntej.

Txhua tsav txhua yam kuv ua los kuv muaj peb (3) yam nyob rau nruab siab: Ib (1): Kuv yuav tsum ua kom thoob ntiaj teb no paub txog peb haiv neeg Hmoob. Ob (2): Peb yuav tsum khaws peb tej kab li kev cai teej tug, vim nws thiaj qhia tau tias peb yog leej twg thiab los qhov twg los. Peb (3): Tsis xav kom leej twg saib tsis taus peb haiv neeg Hmoob, peb yuav tsum siv txhua txoj hauv kev kom peb xwb pwg sib txig nrog luag lwm haiv neeg, peb thiaj ua tau ib tug qauv zoo pub rau tej pej xeem thiab lub zej zog peb nyob.

"